San Diego Christian College
2100 Greenfield Drive
El Cajon, CA 92019

PSYCHOLOGICAL SENSE OF COMMUNITY

RESEARCH, APPLICATIONS, AND IMPLICATIONS

THE PLENUM SERIES IN SOCIAL/CLINICAL PSYCHOLOGY

Series Editor: C. R. Snyder

University of Kansas
Lawrence, Kansas

PSYCHOLOGICAL SENSE OF COMMUNITY

RESEARCH, APPLICATIONS, AND IMPLICATIONS

EDITED BY

ADRIAN T. FISHER

Victoria University
Melbourne, Australia

CHRISTOPHER C. SONN

Edith Cowan University
Perth, Australia

AND

BRIAN J. BISHOP

Curtin University
Perth, Australia

KLUWER ACADEMIC / PLENUM PUBLISHERS
New York, Boston, Dordrecht, London, Moscow

ISBN: 0-306-47281-3

©2002 Kluwer Academic / Plenum Publishers, New York
233 Spring Street, New York, New York 10013

http://www.wkap.nl/

10 9 8 7 6 5 4 3 2 1

A C.I.P. record for this book is available from the Library of Congress

CONTRIBUTORS

Josefina Alvarez, Department of Psychology, DePaul University, 2219 North Kenmore Avenue, Chicago, IL 60614-3504, USA.

Helen Vrailas Bateman, Learning Technology Center, Box 45 Peabody College, Vanderbilt University, Nashville TN 32703, USA.

Kimberly D. Bess, Department of Human and Organizational Development, Box 90 Peabody College, Vanderbilt University, Nashville TN 37203, USA

Brian Bishop, School of Psychology, Curtin University, GPO Box U1987, Perth 6845, Australia.

Anne Brodsky, Department of Psychology, University of Maryland Baltimore County, 1000 Hilltop Circle, Baltimore MD 21250, USA.

Sheridan Coakes, Coakes Consulting, Level 5 Edgecliff Centre, 203-233 New South Head Road, Edgecliff, NSW 2027, Australia.

Margaret I. Davis, Department of Psychology, DePaul University, 2219 North Kenmore Avenue, Chicago, IL 60614-3504, USA.

Pam D'Rozario, Victoria Park Chiropractic Clinic, 165 Swansea Street, Victoria Park East WA 6101, Australia.

Pat Dudgeon, Centre for Aboriginal Studies, Curtin University, GPO Box U1987, Perth WA 6845, Australia.

Joseph R. Ferrari, Department of Psychology, DePaul University, 2219 North Kenmore Avenue, Chicago, IL 60614-3504, USA.

John Fielder, Centre for Aboriginal Studies, Curtin University, GPO Box U1987, Perth WA 6845, Australia.

Adrian T. Fisher, Department of Psychology, Victoria University -- Footscray Park, PO Box 14428, Melbourne City MC, Melbourne VIC 8001, Australia.

Wendy M. Garrard, 1104 18th Avenue South, Nashville, TN 37212, USA.

Jean Hillier, School of Architecture, Construction and Planning, Curtin University, GPO Box U1987, Perth WA 6845, Australia.

Joseph Hughey, Department of Psychology, University of Missouri -- Kansas City, 5100 Rockhill Road, Kansas City MO 64110, USA.

Leonard A. Jason, Department of Psychology, DePaul University, 2219 North Kenmore Avenue, Chicago, IL 60614-3504, USA.

Susan E. Lewis, 401 Chamberlin Park Lane, Franklin TN 37069, USA.

D. Adam Long, Department of Psychology, 301 Wilson Hall, Vanderbilt University, Nashville TN 37203, USA.

Colleen Loomis, Veterans Affairs Palo Alto Health Care System, Stanford University School of Medicine, Palo Alto CA, USA.

Beverly Mahan, Center for Mental Health Policy, Vanderbilt University, 1207 18th Avenue South, Nashville, TN 37212, USA.

John Mallard, Centre for Aboriginal Studies, Curtin University, GPO Box U1987, Perth WA 6845, Australia.

Christine M. Marx, Johns Hopkins Bloomberg Public Health, Baltimore MD USA.

Ron Miers, WCIG Employment Services, 151 Nicholson Street, Footscray Vic 3011, Australia.

John R. Newbrough, Department of Human and Organizational Development, Box 90 Peabody College, Vanderbilt University, Nashville TN 37203, USA.

Bradley D. Olson, Department of Psychology, DePaul University, 2219 North Kenmore Avenue, Chicago, IL 60614-3504, USA.

Darlene Oxenham, Centre for Aboriginal Studies, Curtin University, GPO Box U1987, Perth WA 6845, Australia.

Clare Pollock, School of Psychology, Curtin University, GPO Box U1987, Perth 6845, Australia.

Douglas D. Perkins, Department of Human and Organizational Development, Box 90 Peabody College, Vanderbilt University, Nashville TN 37203, USA

Grace M. H. Pretty, School of Psychology, University of Southern Queensland, Toowoomba QLD 4350, Australia.

Tomi Redman, TRANX, PO Box 186, Burwood Vic 3125, Australia.

Lynne D. Roberts, School of Psychology, Curtin University, GPO Box U1987, Perth WA 6845, Australia.

Sandra Sigmon, Department of Psychology, University of Maine, Orono ME 04469, USA.

Leigh M. Smith, School of Psychology, Curtin University, GPO Box U1987, Perth WA 6845, Australia.

C. Richard Snyder, Department of Psychology, University of Kansas, Lawrence KS 66045, USA.

Christopher C. Sonn, School of Psychology, Edith Cowan University, 100 Joondalup Drive, Joondalup WA 6127, Australia.

Paul W. Speer, Department of Human and Organizational Development, Box 90 Peabody College, Vanderbilt University, Nashville TN 37203, USA

Stacy R. Whitcomb, Department of Psychology, University of Maine, Orono ME 04469, USA.

PREFACE

Our work on psychological sense of community has been ongoing for more than a decade. As community psychologists, it has always been a part of our background knowledge, and a frame of reference for us. Despite the notable efforts by some community psychology researchers, it is a concept that has not had the impact on psychology that Seymour Sarason envisioned in 1986.

The major impetus for our involvement stems from the Biennial Conference of the Society for Community Research and Action held in Tempe, Arizona in 1991. It was at this meeting that Brian Bishop and Adrian Fisher first met Bob Newbrough and Paul Dokecki from Peabody. Newbrough and Dokecki, along with theologian Bob O'Gorman, presented their sense of community and community development work undertaken in a Catholic parish. It was work that had an immediate resonance in the utility of the theory in addressing a significant social problem.

In Australia, Brian and Adrian worked on their own projects and with their students to determine how well sense of community could be applied to a variety of problems, settings, and populations. Christopher Sonn used the theory as a part of his doctoral research on the settlement of an immigrant population. While we continued this work, the links with our colleagues at Peabody College were extended with a series of visits across the Pacific. Together we witnessed a growth in interest in sense of community theory in our discipline, and in related areas.

At the most positive level, we witnessed the growth of a new set of applications of a powerful theory, but one that required significant refinement in terms of its nature, impact, and measurement. At the most cynical level, we viewed the loss of meaning in the term as it was used as everything from a research theory to a slogan used by land developers in their advertising. At times, it seemed that to just invoke the term community was seen as a way of solving social problems -- a panacea without any real intervention or meaning. Indeed, even community itself is often not defined, we just assume that it is there and it is good -- whatever it is.

The genesis of this book was our interest in the many and varied ways in which community can be defined and measured. We chose researchers who have been undertaking work in sense of community that can provide some type of exemplars of the research, methods, or applications that can lead to a fuller understanding of sense of community, where it comes from, and what it actually can do for individuals and groups. It is anticipated that the authors have been able to provide a clearer conceptualization and understanding of the reality of sense of community -- what it can and cannot achieve.

We wish to express our thanks to quite a few people who have contributed to the development and realization of this book. Firstly, the authors who have taken the time and enthusiasm to their chapters, and the various editorial demands placed upon them. A large number of students, colleagues, and authors have contributed to the refereeing and reviewing of chapters so that we can provide authors with the necessary feedback. We also express our appreciation to Eliot Werner and Rick Snyder for accepting and encouraging the proposal, and to Sarah Williams for the final editorial assistance.

At Victoria University, we wish to thank the Faculty of Arts and the computing staff for access to printing facilities set up to use this peculiar US sized paper. The School of Psychology at Edith Cowan University provided Chris with time and travel costs to visit Melbourne for editorial work. Finally, special recognition is given to the Department of Psychology of Victoria University for making available a substantial amount of time to Adrian to work on this book.

CONTENTS

PART V: METHODOLOGICAL AND THEORETICAL DEVELOPMENTS

PSYCHOLOGICAL SENSE OF COMMUNITY

RESEARCH, APPLICATIONS, AND IMPLICATIONS

PART I

INTRODUCTION

Chapter 1

PSYCHOLOGICAL SENSE OF COMMUNITY:
Theory, Research, and Application

Kimberly D. Bess
Vanderbilt University

Adrian T. Fisher
Victoria University

Christopher C. Sonn
Edith Cowan University

Brian J. Bishop
Curtin University

INTRODUCTION

The idea that we belong to communities and that these communities provide benefits and responsibilities is one that has gained a growing appreciation in the last decade. As a reaction to the urbanization faced by many people, globalization, cross-national forms of media and their impact on cultures, physical and social isolation from family and friends, and a growing fear of change and the unknown, images of community, belonging and support have become paramount. However, what is actually meant by community, how a community functions, and what are the benefits and costs of community membership has not necessarily been well explored.

For many, the idea of community evokes images of the small town or close neighborhood. People know each other, often have been resident for some generations, and provide various types of instrumental or emotional support to other members of the community. It is an idealization in place and time of feeling a part of a place, with those around knowing us and caring about us. In many ways, it reflects the *Gemeinschaft* idea put forward by Tönnies (1955) of the village in which relationships are governed by kinship and centered on the parish church.

Some of the reification of community reflects a model often perpetuated through North American media and accepted into a broader world context, rightly or wrongly. The new urbanism movement in town planning attempts to capture and maximize much of this, for example, in Seaside in Florida and Ellenbrook in Australia. The new urbanist ideals are expressed in terms of memories of what neighborhood used to be like, images of front porches in small town mid-west, of people recognizing each other on the streets, looking out for each other, looking after each other, and keeping on eye on the young folk as well to make sure they are behaving. Indeed, the time is turned back, with the *walkability* being a key planning concept, in order to reduced the use of automobiles within the community and to promote the opportunities for interaction between residents. While these may be valued qualities for many people, and can reflect a way of life that is very desirable, one can question the extent to which such communities ever really existed, and the extent to which people are willing to give up individuality and privacy to meet the community good. The reality of community life is that there are many formulations of community, some far more positive than others.

What is actually meant by community is another of the issues to be considered. There is a long tradition of theorizing the nature and meaning of community in the social sciences, in particular sociology. Many theorists have been interested in defining community and understanding the impact of industrialization, urbanization, and other forces on society and community. In fact rural sociologist Hillery (1955) was able to catalogue 94 different definitions of community. Durkheim (cited by Worsley, 1987) argued that solid social ties are essential to one's wellbeing; the absence of ties with family, community and other networks increases the risk of anomie and other negative psychosocial outcomes. Others, like Tönnies, Weber, and Marx, have all presented perspectives on social systems and the changing nature of these systems (Worsley, 1987). Tönnies (1955, 1974), for example, depicted two forms of social organization in his concepts of *Gemeinschaft* and *Gesellschaft*, while Weber distinguished between *Vergeimenschaftung and Vergesellschaftung*. These notions were developed to reflect the changing nature of society and to clarify the foundations of community.

If the past, the ideal was the village with kinship links, or the small town in which people may have lived for generations, the ways in which a community may now form and operate are quite different. It has been argued that this Gemeinschaft concept was never true for the USA (Bernard, 1973) (and Australia) as the low densities of population did not allow the formation of such closely knit communities. *Locational* communities based in a specific area and reflect the older model, *relational* ones are those that have been formed because of some common interest, issue, or characteristic that the members share, showing a newer idea of community. Heller (1989) also indicated that there are forms of communities that come together to exert a shared power. Not surprisingly, we are all members of more than one community. The relative importance of these communities, and our allegiances to them, vary in importance across time and circumstances (Fisher & Sonn, 1999).

Newbrough (1992, 1995) argued for a third position. He linked Dewey and Bentley's (1946) concepts of causation (self-action, interaction and transaction), Toulmin's (1990) notions of the development of science (pre-modern, modern and post-modern) and Kirpatrick's (1986) views on community. Dokecki (1996) explored these linkages further, and a fuller notion of the approaches to community was developed. The pre-modern phase was associated with *Gemeinschaft* and with the dominant notion of causality that Dewey and Bentley (1946) referred to as "self action." Fraternity was a core concept with hierarchically structured communities. With the Battle of Westphalia came the emergence of the modern period and the rise of *Gesellschaft* communities. Interaction was seen as the dominant notion of causality objects behaved like billiard balls. The machine is the metaphor for this period and individual Liberty was the aim, although this is mixed with social order through the exercise of power and obedience to laws.

Thomas Kuhn's pronouncements on scientific paradigms (1970) heralded the beginning of the post modernist period. This is the period of the 'third position.' Newbrough saw this as a double shift, a shift from both *Gemeinschaft* and *Gesellschaft*. The form of post-modern science is still developing, but some of the essential characteristics have emerged. These include awareness of cultural and temporal differences in social phenomena, willingness to use multiple methodologies and an acceptance that the world is socially constructed. A post-modern approach recognizes the importance of process and does not necessarily accept the concept of universal truths. The intrusion of ideology, values and world views into science has been recognized and the need for a 'human science' based on the awareness of the centrality of the scientist as an active agent. For example, the concepts of emic and etic in anthropology and cross-cultural psychology can be seen to reflect western colonization and hegemony.

Newbrough (1995) sees the third position as being one in which liberty, fraternity, and equality are balanced. Friendship and love are seen as key ingredients with a balance of the demands of the 'one' and the 'many.' He also saw post-modernism as being the appropriate scientific model to understand community (and community psychology). He wrote: "A truth claim is a temporary statement of limited generalizability about what we think we know. It is open to debate and is expected to be superceded, but for now it is the best we have. **This is a liberating notion!**" (pp. 11-12, emphasis added). The challenge for those studying SOC is to come to terms with a more fluid concept of community and people's relation to it.

The loose use of the term *sense of community* (SOC), in both lay language and in our professional jargon hides another series of important issues that are to be explored in the chapters of this book. For many, sense of community is seen as some type of end state, a positive in and of itself. Others see it as a predictor of other positive, or negative, outcomes. That is, we need a sense of community in order to achieve a series of benefits. Still another way of understanding sense of community is as a process in which the members interact, draw identity, social support, and make their own contributions to the common good.

THEORIES OF SENSE OF COMMUNITY

In his 1974 ground breaking book, *The psychological sense of community: Prospects for a community psychology,* Seymour Sarason argued persuasively the need to focus on developing a discipline with the concept of *psychological sense of community* at its core. Sarason believed that SOC held the key to understanding one of society's most pressing problems, the dark side of individualism, which he saw manifested as alienation, selfishness, and despair (Dalton, Elias, & Wandersman, 2001). According to Sarason (1986), one of the goals of his book was to communicate three interrelated opinions that he had formed as a result of his work in community mental health: (a) the lack of sense of community was extraordinarily frequent; (b) it was a destructive force in living; and (c) dealing with its consequences and its prevention should be the overarching concern of community psychology.

Sarason's work on SOC originally served two purposes in the emerging field of community psychology. It provided a unifying metaphor or theme and reflected one of the core values of the field -- the belief that healthy communities exhibited an extra-individual quality of emotional interconnectedness of individuals played out in their collective lives (Dalton, et al, 2001). By 1986, Sarason's call had been answered. The *Journal of Community Psychology* issued two special editions devoted to research on SOC, and different research teams had developed scales measuring SOC (Davidson & Cotter, 1986; Doolittle & MacDonald, 1978; Glynn, 1981; Riger & Lavrakos 1981).

Perhaps the biggest impact in converting Sarason's theoretical call into some form of reality has been from McMillan and Chavis (1986). In order to understand the ways in which sense of community could actually operate, they proposed a model in which four components of sense of community could be seen and understood. The first level provides the component of *membership* -- a series of interacting factors of boundaries (who is in and who is out), shared history, common symbols, emotional safety, and personal investment. Membership confers upon people a set of rights and responsibilities that are always characterized by the belonging to a community. One draws identity by being a member of the community, has emotional support, and is reinforced for the behaviors that are beneficial to the functioning of the community itself.

The second level is that of *influence*. In the McMillan and Chavis (1986) model, influence is seen as an internal process that reflects the perceived influence that a person has over the decisions and actions of the community. It also has the counterpoint of the amount of influence that the group has over the individual memberships. In a positive sense, the influence component provides a balance that allows to the individual to make their contribution to the community, but also has a reasonable level of freedom for their own self-expression. At the negative end of the continuum, there are two possible outcomes. One is that the influence of the group is so strong that it demands high conformity, suppressing self-expression. The other potential negative is that the individual, or a small sub-group, can dominate the mores and behaviors of the community.

Another way in which influence can be considered is in line with Heller's (1989) idea that a community can form in order to exert some power that the members have. That is, for members a strong value of the community is that they are able to combine their skills, knowledge, etc., in order to exert an influence externally. In this way, the community may be able to influence policy, resource allocation, or other decision-making processes for the benefit of the members of the community, or to achieve an end that is valued.

Integration and fulfillment of needs reflects the benefits that people derive from their membership of a community -- McMillan and Chavis (1986) refer to the motivation of reinforcement that members receive by having their needs met through their membership. McMillan and Chavis indicate that some of the needs that can be fulfilled through community membership are the status achieved through group membership, demonstration of competence by members, and the shared values that are exhibited by the group. For them, strong communities can provide these opportunities for their members, thus reinforcing the value of membership of the community.

The final component of the model is *shared emotional connection*. This part of the model of sense of community refers to the sharing of significant events and the amount of contact that members have with each other. Because the community has had significant events, whether the members have actually taken part in them, there is a bond that can be developed between the members. The numbers of events, the salience of these events, and the importance of them in conferring merit or status to the community and its members all influence the development of a shared emotional connection between community members. Whether the events are positive or negative, they still have significant impacts on the development of emotional connections between members.

However, the story of SOC since 1986 shares many of the same characteristics as the allegorical tale relayed in John Godfrey Saxe's poem, *The Blind Men and the Elephant.* The blind men in this story venture out in search of knowledge about an elephant only to find themselves unable to agree on its nature. The task of defining sense of community seems doable at first glance. Like the elephant, its presence seems to fill the air; like the blind men, researchers of SOC have found the construct elusive and frustrating. Sarason (1974) recognized -- even as he argued for its centrality in community psychology -- that the concept SOC, although intuitively obvious, was not one that would lend itself to the traditional methods of psychology. He warned, "The concept *psychological sense of community* is not a familiar one in psychology... it does not sound precise, it obviously reflects a value judgment, and does not sound compatible with 'hard' science" (p. 156). It is within this context that researchers have taken up the challenge of trying to make PSC a theoretically and practically useful construct. Like the blind men who sought to describe the true nature of the elephant, researchers' attempts to define SOC have yielded little agreement (Hill, 1996).

One factor that complicates the picture is the lack of agreement that surrounds the definition of SOC. Chipuer and Pretty's (1999) review of the SOC literature suggests the scale of the debate over the definition. They point to the lack of consensus over whether SOC is a cognition, a behavior, an individual affective state, an environmental condition, a spiritual dimension. To compound the problem, the term community itself remains an unclear concept in the field.

Puddifoot (1996) points to two significant problems in the way researchers have defined community that have led to the conceptual muddle surrounding the term. First, he argues, community is defined too broadly as a *catchall* term and that it risks losing its specific meaning and its conceptual utility. For example, community has been used to refer to such diverse entities as neighborhoods, community groups, institutions, religious groups, work organizations, professional organizations, and it has been used at different levels of analysis ranging from small groups such as family units to nationalities (Dalton, et al., 2001). Secondly, he contends that the practice of referring to communities by type may lead to an artificial polarization. The primary example of this is the common practice of referring to two qualitatively distinct, yet often related, types of community, relational and locational.

At a more prosaic level, the definitional debate is also reflected in the abbreviations used for sense of community. Even within the chapters of this book, there are three different abbreviations used -- SOC, PSC, and PSOC. While for some these differences are matters of choice, there is an important differentiation that can be made. For some, SOC is the term when referring to an analysis at the group level of experience of community. In this way, PSC and, to a lesser extent, PSOC refer to the individual experience of sense of community. Of course, other disciplines use SOC as a concept, leaving the psychology to us.

The debate over the definition of community has necessarily spilled over into how researchers define SOC. For example, Dunham (1986) criticizes McMillan and Chavis' (1986) definition of SOC for reasons related to how they define community and specifically with the same concern that Puddifoot (1996) had about community being used as a catchall term. Dunham argues, "In their enthusiasm to formulate a definition that satisfactorily describes a sense of community, McMillan and Chavis actually have pointed to the characteristics that describe the solidarity of the social group" (p. 400). Chipuer and Pretty (1999) also observe the inconsistent usage of the term. They point out that terms such as neighboring, social cohesion, and community identity are sometimes used synonymously with SOC and sometimes as related terms. Again, how researchers define community would affect their usage and definition of SOC. The question of whether SOC manifests differently within these types of communities remains unclear. McMillan and Chavis claim that their theory applies to both, but others (Chipuer & Pretty, 1999; Hill, 1996) caution that such assumptions should not be made. When community is described as a geographical location, the salient features of sense of community are inextricably linked to a physical location in that the sameness or commonality shared is that landscape. In a relational community, the significance of the physical landscape is less -- or absent altogether.

Despite the complexities posed by the definitional problems with community and sense of community, there is a growing consensus in the field that SOC is best viewed as context specific (Hill, 1996; Puddifoot, 1996; Rapley & Pretty, 1999; Sonn, Bishop, & Drew, 1999; Wiesenfeld, 1996). However, the assumption of generalizability embedded in so much of social science, and in the policy making push ways in which lessons from one place or time can be applied to others, provide dilemmas for the research and interpretation of finding related to sense of community. How best should it be studied -- or are there differing methods to be used to understand the different types of questions being posed and outcomes and understandings being sought? While much of social science is built on logical positivist foundations and methods, the use of qualitative approaches, or combinations of methods, can provides deeper levels of understanding of process and impact.

Research on Sense of Community

Research into SOC, like other human phenomena, is bound by two sets of questions: the *what* questions and the *how* questions. The *what* questions refer to the specific types of questions researchers pose and the type of phenomena about which they inquire. The *how* questions refer to the methods used to answer the questions. The answers to these questions are to a large extent predetermined by how one responds to the epistemological question of what constitutes valid knowledge. Many researchers of SOC have, indirectly, found themselves caught up in the issues that drive this epistemological debate between logical-positivists and post-positivists.

Despite the general recognition of the need to seek out new methodological approaches that can capture the richness of everyday experience, community psychologists interested in SOC have largely employed traditional quantitative methods in their research (Chipuer & Pretty, 1999; Hill, 1996; Rapley & Pretty, 1999). The vast majority of research on PSC has focused on establishing SOC as a measurable construct (Chipuer & Pretty; 1999; Hill, 1996; McMillan & Chavis, 1986). Specifically, researchers have been interested in the extent to which SOC is correlated to, or predictive of, a variety of similar or related constructs (e.g., cohesion, neighborliness, loneliness, belongingness, satisfaction) and how these issues play out in different community contexts (e.g., workplaces, neighborhoods, schools).

McMillan and Chavis' (1986) work on SOC exemplifies this issue. Their theory represents one of the few formal theories of PSC (Hill, 1996) and has become the most widely used and accepted in the field (Chipuer & Pretty, 1999; Hill, 1996, Rapley & Pretty, 1999). The theory and accompanying measure, the *Sense of Community Index (SCI)* (Perkins, Florin, Rich, Wandersman, & Chavis, 1990) follow the classic hypothetical-deductive approach to theory building and rely on two basic assumptions of logical positivism: reductionism and generalizability. In this way, the methodological approaches provide for, mostly, statistical descriptions and comparisons, with the predictive power of regression and other models used to understand some of the ways in which the level of SOC has impacts on the groups being studied. While there have been many factor analytic studies attempting to establish the structure of SOC, there has been a paucity of studies utilizing statistical techniques which would allow for the modeling of the differential impacts of SOC within varying segments of a community.

SOC: An Organic Whole or the Sum of the Parts?

Implicit in McMillan and Chavis' (1986) theory is the assumption that the reduction of a phenomenon to its most elemental parts will yield the greatest truth or knowledge. Their theory draws on a large body of research findings from social psychology, including group dynamics, power, conformity, social competence, and group cohesion. In their model of SOC, they propose a definition based on four dimensions, these dimensions are then broken down further into subcategories. Together these elements constitute SOC.

Sonn et al. (1999) question McMillan and Chavis' approach raising the age-old theoretical question: Does the whole equal the sum of the parts? This question has implications on two levels. First, in the case of the SCI, does the aggregate score of the components capture an individual's SOC? If SOC is a feeling that one experiences, as McMillan and Chavis suggest, then by breaking that feeling into elemental parts, the essential quality of the experience is lost.

More broadly speaking, both from a theoretical and an empirical perspective, treating SOC as a multi-dimensional construct has problems. As Hill (1996) notes with the exception of Perkins, et al.'s (1990) SCI, measures of SOC have typically been developed without a theoretical framework. The majority of researchers (Buckner, 1988; Davidson & Cotter, 1986; Doolittle & MacDonald, 1978; Glynn, 1981; McMillan & Chavis, 1986; Riger & Lavrakos 1981) have used a factor-analytic approach to establish the components of SOC. This method while establishing the groups of factors does not indicate how they relate to SOC or establish validity of the construct. Moreover, factor analytic studies of the components of the SCI have not shown conclusive empirical evidence to support McMillan and Chavis' original vision of SOC as a multidimensional construct (Chipuer & Pretty, 1999). Chavis and Pretty (1999) report that the problem has been compounded in that "the inconsistent psychometric properties of the subscales have led many researchers to eliminate items that are included in the SCI in order to maximize their psychometric properties" (p. 637). This is problematic, considering that the SCI is reported to be the most validated measure of SOC.

Chipuer and Pretty (1999) have gone so far as to suggest that given the weak results of their study on the internal factor structure of the short form of the SCI, that researchers use the SCI as a uni-dimensional measure. Others (Buckner, 1988; Davidson & Cotter 1986) have reached the similar conclusions with other measures of PSOC identifying only one factor or dimension for SOC. Despite the mixed, if somewhat unpromising, findings presented in the literature, the underlying assumption that still operates with regard to PSOC is that it is multidimensional (reducible) and continued use of advanced statistical methods will ultimately allow researchers to identify the salient component parts the make up the construct.

A second aspect of the whole-part debate concerns whether SOC should be measured at the individual level or the community level. While some researchers have focused exclusively on the individual correlates of SOC (e.g., Royal & Rossi, 1996), others have tried to examine SOC at the community level (e.g., Hedges & Kelly, 1992). Hill (1996) concludes from her review of the literature that most researchers understand SOC as related to "variables beyond individual relationships and behaviors" (p. 433) suggesting further that SOC be considered in the aggregate. While some have used individual responses collectively to construct a community level variable, Sonn, et al. (1999) have called for an additional step urging researchers to go beyond the individual and examine the processes that lead to shared connections and group formation.

Finally, Sarason (1986) has cautioned researchers not to overlook how PSOC emerges out of the dynamic relationship between individual and community:

> The part (individual) and the whole (social context), figure/ground, the lesson from Gestalt psychology is that the figure we see is determined in large part by the ubiquitous background and that figure and ground are always changing. In studying sense of community we have to learn how to reverse figure and ground, how to go from data back to the palpable individual because we know that in that process both figure and ground will change and a new gestalt will emerge (p. 407).

Sarason's point illustrates the dialectical nature of the whole-part relationship of PSOC in which the community and the individual are both essential and necessary contributors to the ongoing process of building community health.

Some (Chipuer & Pretty, 1999; Puddifoot, 1996; Sonn, et al., 1999) have begun to question the heavy reliance on traditional positivistic methods in SOC research -- a criticism that has been leveled against the field more generally (Tolan, Chertok, Keys, & Jason, 1990). One can understand the caution with which researchers have approached qualitative methodologies (more in keeping with the phenomenological or hermeneutic traditions), given the dominant culture of research universities in which the value of research is often linked to the extent to which it produces predictive or quantifiable knowledge. In addition, practical concerns, such as lack of training in alternative methodologies (Tolan, et al., 1990) and professional advancement, have discouraged researchers from venturing into new territories. Yet, the costs have been high in terms of advancing the field's understanding of SOC in the area of theory development (Chipuer & Pretty; 1999; Sonn, et al., 1999) and as a dynamic and intersubjective phenomenon (Rapley & Pretty, 1999; Wiesenfeld, 1996).

The logical-positivist position holds that only *apodictic* or certain knowledge should be admissible in scientific inquiry. The post-positivist position suggests that researchers should strive for assertoric knowledge -- that is, knowledge based on evidentiary claims that compete among other claims for community acceptance (Polkinghorne, 1983). As Polkinghorne points out, the acceptance of assertoric knowledge opens up the possibility of employing a range of methodologies in social science research. The implication, then, is that the research question should drive the methodology rather than the methodology dictating the type of questions to be asked. This distinction becomes important when examining the type of research that has been done and the types of questions being addressed in relation to SOC.

Expanding SOC Methodology

The influence of post-modernism has meant that community psychology has been able to utilize (or rediscover) a greater range of methodologies than in recent times. The flexibility has allowed us to be less concerned with methodology and to concentrate on the substantive aspects of social issues and community and cultural phenomena. The increased methodological sophistication that ahas arisen though the acceptance of a multiplicity of epistemologies (e.g., Altman & Rogoff, 1984; Pepper, 1942) has allowed us to investigate questions that rigid positivism has difficulty with. The notion of 'experimental' can now be freed to apply to how we think about issues, and not simply to laboratory research.

For example, phenomenological and hermeneutic approaches offer alternatives consistent with the values and epistemological stance of community psychologists. These approaches are concerned with the psychology of everyday living and explicitly recognize that knowledge is contextually bound by: (1) the particular perspectives of time and place, (2) the perspectives of the stakeholders, and (3) cultural and historical influences (Polkinghorne, 1983). Both have in common the research goal of achieving intersubjective agreement. The general aim of the phenomenological approach is to identify and describe the structures of everyday experiences, whereas a hermeneutic approach focuses on the interpretation of the meaning of the phenomena of everyday living. Polkinghorne describes the complementary nature of the two approaches:

> Hermeneutics supplements the descriptive approach by seeking to understand human actions and expressions. Because the meanings of actions are not always immediately apparent, interpretive techniques are required to make the meanings clear. In doing the work of interpretation it is often necessary to call upon the information about the basic structures uncovered by descriptive methods. (p. 214)

Research that tries to describe the essence of SOC would exemplify a phenomenological approach. Research seeking to understand how individuals within communities construct their understanding of SOC might employ hermeneutic techniques. Brodsky and Marx's (2001) of study of SOC of the Caroline Center, a Catholic mission focusing on the job training and education of low-income women, exemplifies the possibility of this approach. They used an iterative technique in which the "qualitative study (focus group interviews) led to hypotheses that were tested quantitatively, which then were followed up with a refined analysis of the qualitative data" (p. 164).

With the increase in the use of qualitative approaches in psychology, newer sets of questions can be asked about SOC. We are now able to research the ways in which people report the experience of community to them, the stories that hold communities together, and how people develop identity and meaning from their community membership. Interviewing, open-ended questions, and narratives are now tools of research that facilitate the advance of knowledge.

Is There a Dark Side to PSOC?

Sarason's original conceptualization of SOC arose out of his experiences in community mental health and the problems he encountered in that context. His reference to SOC as a value has resonated with others in the field, and, by and large, community psychology has accepted the assumption that a healthy community is one in which there is a strong sense of community at both the individual and the collective levels. This has also been an underlying assumption of research conducted on SOC. Traditional research methodologies have reinforced this perspective treating SOC as a bi-polar construct, equating high scores on SOC with healthy communities and by implication interpreting low scores as an indication of low functioning. Some have cautioned against this unbridled (and by implication uncritical) enthusiasm for SOC. Dunham (1986) has called McMillan and Chavis' (1986) version of SOC *utopian* and points out that there is dark side of SOC with which we must reckon. According to McMillan and Chavis' definitional criteria, racist groups such as the Klu Klux Klan, would potentially meet the criteria for a strong healthy community. Brodsky's (1996) work with resilient single mothers in risky neighborhoods illustrates Dunham's point as well. Her findings suggest that this group's negative SOC contributed to their psychological well-being and adjustment.

The point is that one must not underestimate the importance of an individual who can think and act independently. Communities whose members do not possess a strong sense of self (e.g., self-efficacy, self-identity) run the risks of engaging in "group-think" behavior. Wiesenfeld (1996) has made a related argument with respect to the focus on *sameness* in SOC research. Conceptualizations of SOC, as Wiesenfeld argues, often fail to take into account the need to understand the role of dissent and diversity as another key component of community health. This again speaks to the need to look at the whole picture including the strengths of individuals within communities.

FOCUS OF THE BOOK

While there has been a considerable amount written about the nature of community, particularly in the popular press, the research base is not well articulated. Indeed, community seems to be a word that is assumed to have a shared meaning, and all actions that flow from the identification of community issues, concerns or problems work with that tacit understanding. However, there is far from consensus in the research and literature about either of these. There are those who believe that only locational communities should be considered, or that the nature of what community is and does for the members should be restricted. While these can be seen as limitations because of lack of theoretical and methodological consistency, they also provide opportunities to develop new and deeper understandings of the nature and operations of SOC.

In this book, we focus on research around the topic of sense of community. While some of us work with the model proposed by McMillan and Chavis in 1986, there are other ways and theoretical models of community that are also used in research. In this way, it is proposed that the readers will be exposed to the different models of community, different levels of analysis and different ways in which the research is undertaken and their implications.

A key organizing principle of the book is that authors have been set a series of themes to address in their chapters. In this way, the book provides a set of research-based exposes of enormously different communities, using very different research methods and approaches, but there is also an overall coherence in the writing structure that will enable readers to compare and contrast the work in the different chapters. The organizing themes are:

1. Theoretical basis of the research
2. Conceptualization of the community
3. Level of analysis for the research and why this is appropriate
4. Research methods used and why these were chosen in comparison to others findings
5. Theoretical implications of the findings
6. Practical/applied implications of the findings
7. Policy implications for the findings
8. Methodological implications of the findings

In developing this book, we chose authors who represent some quite different understandings and interpretations of community. The groups on whom they focus in their research, and the methods they use while exploring these groups covers a vast spectrum of social science methodologies. Importantly, the authors are drawn from Australia as well as the USA in order to provide understandings of community research across a wider geographical and cultural context, not related to one country or geographical area.

Organization of Chapters

Following this introductory chapter, the book is set into four major, but inter-related, sections reflecting the nature of the communities being addressed, or specific theoretical and methodological issues. The first set of chapters relate specifically to aspects of community in defined physical locations, the next set concern relational communities which develop within specific types of settings in which members interact. The third section is relational communities, with the nature of how community provides them with social support, identity, or other buffers. The final three chapters deal with issues of method and theoretical developments in order to understand the ways in which communities can operate differently for different people and groups.

Locational Chapters

While much of the research presented in this book, and the nature of community itself, deal with groups and their members, the first chapter deliberately focuses at the individual level. Sigmon, Whitcomb, and Snyder propose that the nature of the places in which we live and work is used to maintain one's identity and serves to provide barriers to outside challenges. The decorations we use are personalizing of the spaces, emphasizing our identity as well as imposing a sense of control over these spaces. Sigmon, et al., maintain that there are significant psychological benefits that may accrue through this personalization and cotrol.

While Sigmon, et al. have focused on the individual's ability to make a place their own -- to develop it as home -- Jean Hillier has a much more macro focus. In her chapter, Hillier explores a series of issues related to the ways in which urban planners supposed design community into the physical settings of land developments. Although she places a great emphasis on the need for community, she indicates that much of sense of community has to do with the interactions between people, not necessarily the physical settings in which they live. Indeed, her descriptions show that some of the least planned areas have the highest and most valued interactions and sense of belonging. In contrast, many planned, and expensive, areas are more characterized by exclusion.

Joe Hughey and Paul Speer also tackle the nature of poorer areas and the ways in which various networks are able to build the sense of control and belonging that people have in their area. Hughey and Speer bring to light the multiple levels at which community can operate, and the levels of power that are observed -- from informal power exerted by drug dealers, through to the formal power of police and other authorities. Their contribution allows us to understand how the local residents are able to bring their stories to the fore and make changes in institutional responses to activities in their areas to improve living conditions and the potential for their children.

Specific Settings

Sense of community is often associated with the neighborhood or town in which one lives. The model developed by McMillan and Chavis (1986) and measures of sense of community (e.g., Davdison & Cotter, 1986; Perkins, et al., 1990) exemplify this. However, the nature of community and the settings in which it may develop vary greatly from these simple conceptualizations. A series of chapters have been prepared to study the nature of sense of community in specific settings that deviate from the normal residential setting. These are settings in which people may spend much of their time, some are negative, some work related, and some more reflective of transcendent goals.

Custodial settings are considered to be very negative environments in which to live and work. As people have been locked up for various crimes, the image is of violent and uncaring places. However, Redman and Fisher, in their examination of young women in a custodial setting found a much more complex set of factors operating. For many of those interviewed, the custodial setting actually provided a place of greater safety and more positive connections than they experience in the external community. However, much of the connection was not with the other inmates, but with the staff of the facility -- providing some concern for rehabilitation and recidivism rates.

The ways in which sense of community develops, and the functions that it serves in a more voluntary residential setting is presented by Ferrari, Jason, Olson, Davis, and Alvarez, in their study of Oxford House substance abuse rehabilitation programs. Within the Oxford House community, members work on an abstinence model with substantial support from the other members. This research provides a model in which the influence of members over each other is not used to maintain simple conformity but to act to bring about a sense of balance and control in their lives to remain abstinent. By undertaking various roles within the House, members gain experience of responsibility for themselves and the others, providing a strong empowering process. Unlike, other communities, members of Oxford house can also be expelled for breaches of the rules, so the sanctions are also very real.

While the first two chapters in this section reflect settings in which there is a strong rehabilitative emphasis, and some degree of compulsion, Mahan, Garrard, Lewis, and Newbrough explore quite a different setting. Their study provides a deep analysis of the sense of community within an academic community -- a college of a university. The collegial image of tenured academics in the university is the stereotype often put forward, a stereotype that ignores many of the members of the community. In this chapter, Mahan and her colleagues examine the range of employees in order to understand how they differentially experience a sense of community. Not surprisingly, perhaps, the stereotyped male tenured academics seems to derive the strongest sense of community from their immediate academic work -- but with an important factor of trust coming into play. Female faculty in non-tenured positions experienced the lowest level of sense of community. The non-academic employees often drew their sense of community from other forms of relationships aligned to, but separate from, their immediate work.

The ways in which sense of community operates in a church parish is the topic of the chapter by Ron Miers and Adrian Fisher. Interestingly, Sarason (1974) drew on the place of religions as an example of sense of community. In this parish, the members have been faced with a series of organization setbacks, and a loss of direction for the future. A number of interesting finding emerge that reflect the members of the parish value their community and want it to prosper. However, there is uncertainty about direction and who will lead in these developments. It was also found that the members value their community so much that they placed barriers in the way of potential members -- perhaps fearing the change that newcomers would bring.

In the final chapter of this section, Helen Bateman reports on sense of community in several different middle schools. Two of the schools were designated as magnet schools for specific academic areas (although selection was by lottery), the third school was a community school (so designated because of the community classes for adults held after school hours. A number of issues were found in common across the schools in contributing to the students' sense of community, most notably the sense of safety that the children experienced. Strong differences emerged where the students in the magnet schools reported a higher sense of community, attributed to their opportunities to display their skills and learning in school-wide and community-based forums. In these ways, the students were able to what the school had done for them, as well as being able to demonstrate these to a broader, external community. Bateman demonstrates how these aspects of sense of community can be explained in an embedded ecological model of development.

Specific Groups

The previous two sections have chapters that have focused, more or less, and communities based around some type of shared location. It is from this shared location that the members are able to derive their community identity. In this section, the sense of community experienced by members of specific types of relationship groups is explored. That is, these are people who are members of their communities because of some shared characteristics in common, whether they share the same place or not.

Continuing and extending her work on adolescents, Grace Pretty has also made a major shift in her conceptualization of the role of sense of community in her chapter. Pretty takes the opportunity to examine the relationship between sense of community and sense of place, with a specific look at the ways in which these are able to contribute to adolescent identity development. She sees a nesting of person, place, and community, with the healthy development of the person's identity as a member of community dependent upon being able to make their identity, and be accepted at each level.

How members of immigrant communities are able to make positive adjustments and contribute to their new countries is an issue challenging policy makers and advocates in many countries. In his chapter, Chris Sonn explores settlement issues from a sense of community model in order to understand the supports that the home culture provides and how these translated to the new country. Sonn demonstrates that a strong membership in the home community from which the person comes assists in the adjustment to the new country. However, he also demonstrates the sense of community experienced is a form of process in which the newcomers negotiate their place and identity in relation to both the new countries to which they have come, as well as the home countries that they have left.

The contentious issue of sense of community on the internet is explored by Roberts, Smith, and Pollock. They examine how people interact and the forms of identity that they assume when using different types of virtual environments to interact with others. Although there are ways in which the participants adopt new identities, or mask their real ones, there are strong indications that they also experience a number of the elements associated with sense of community. Some are reflected in the clear membership boundaries imposed, forms of social support offered, private language and symbols used, and the sanctions used under the influence sphere to ensure members adhere to permitted forms of behavior. It appears that the anonymity offered by the virtual environments can actually facilitate the social interaction and openness that membership of communities is usually seen as encapsulating.

Dudgeon, Mallard, Oxenham, and Fielder explore whether the conceptualization of sense of community is specifically western or if it can be applied to other groups. They draw on the experiences of a number of the authors as indigenous Australian social scientists as well as other Indigenous people to articulate a number of key issues about community for Aboriginal Australians. They demonstrate some of the ways in which community has meaning for Aboriginal Australians -- particularly relationships to the areas from which they come and their family lines.

What Dudgeon et al. also reflect extremely well are ways in which external attribution of community can be very inaccurate. For the Aboriginal people, there is the problem of the use of community as an over-inclusive term for other peoples. In this way, they are all put together as one group, denying the vast diversity that occurs within the specific group -- but which actually means that they are many different groups. This can be extrapolated into the setting of government policies that do not provide differentiation between the needs and histories represented by the variety of the people themselves.

Theoretical and Methodological Issues

In the final section, the chapters deal with several issues of theoretical and methodological importance in understanding psychological sense of community and how it may operate at different levels and in different places. Much of the research and writing on sense of community has been representative of a single type of community, or a very static notion of community. However, even in his original writing, Sarason (1974) was explicit in stating that communities must change across time and place.

Bishop, Coakes, and D'Rozario present a mix of two issues in their chapter in rural community. One is the different types of methods that are employed and the types of questions that different approaches allow one to answer. This is crucial in the move away from simple measures of a logical-positive tradition to modeling and qualitative methods that allow demonstrations of different operations in different locational and relational communities.

The second major finding from Bishop, et al. is the ways in which the historical development of communities are reflected in the current operations – including the unstated rules of the communities, ideas of belonging and the place of newcomers, and ways in which social clubs and other groups can be seen as power bases for some of the longer standing residents. Using these factors, many of the older communities have effective barriers to the easy inclusion of newcomers and the maintenance of traditional approaches to social organization.

In an attempt to untangle the intrapsychic and behavioral components of SOC and social capital, as well as advancing the more sophisticated use of quantitative methods, Perkins and Long utilize hierarchical linear modeling. This tested the impacts at both the individual and group (block) level. In order to do so, they have been able to create a briefer and more focused SOC index, were able to examine SOC over time, and at the different levels.

Perkins and Long provide two key findings that help to advance the understanding of both the theoretical and operational aspects of SOC and social capital. They found that SOC operates substantially at both the community as well as the individual level, although this varies with time, and at both levels. Second, SOC was the strongest and most consistent predictor of collective efficacy, neighboring behavior, and participation in block associations. The SOC-efficacy link represents a major contribution to the literature, given the surprising lack of empirical data relating SOC with efficacy or empowerment, and the prominence of both in community psychology.

In the final chapter, Brodsky, Marx, and Loomis explore the theoretical nature of multiple communities and multiple senses of communities. Their work is crucial in understanding the ways in which we are all members of many communities, whether that membership is achieved or ascribed, and how we balance these memberships in order to draw identity, support, fulfillment, and direction in our lives. One of the key issues that Brodsky and her colleagues deal with is the impact of communities that we perceive as negative to ourselves, or to our children. They explore how certain groups are able to extricate themselves from the networks reflective of community membership in order to make a better life. This is an issue in sense of community that is often not addressed because the assumption of community is so often that such connections must be positive.

REFERENCES

Altman, I., & Rogoff, B. (1984). World views in Psychology: Trait, interactional, organismic, and transactional perspectives. In D. Stokals and I. Altman (Eds.), *Handbook of environmental psychology* (Vol. 1, pp 1-40). New York: Wiley.

Bernard, J. (1973). *The sociology of community*. Glenview, Ill.: Scott Foresman.

Brodsky, A. E. (1996). Resilient single mothers in risky neighborhoods: Negative psychological sense of community. *Journal of Community Psychology, 24,* 347-363.

Brodsky, A. E., & Marx, C. M. (2001). Layers of identity: Multiple psychological senses of community within a community setting. *Journal of Community Psychology, 29,* 161-178.

Buckner, J. C. (1988). The development of an instrument of measure neighborhood cohesion. *American Journal of Community Psychology, 16,* 771-791.

Chavis, D. M., & Pretty, G. M. H. (1999). Sense of community: Advances in measurement and application. *Journal of Community Psychology, 27,* 635-642.

Chipuer H. M., & Pretty, G. M. H. (1999). A review of the Sense of Community Index: Current uses, factor structure, reliability and further development. *Journal of Community Psychology. 27,* 643-658.

Dalton, J. H., Elias, M. J., & Wandersman, A. (2001). *Community Psychology: Linking individuals and communities.* Belmont, CA: Wadsworth.

Davidson W., & Cotter P. (1986). Measurement of sense of community within the sphere of city. *Journal of Applied Social Psychology, 16,* 608-619.

Dewey, J., & Bentley, J. (1946). *On knowing and the known.* Boston: beacon.

Dokecki, P. (1996). *The tragi-comic professional: Basic considerations for ethical reflective-generative practice.* Pittsburgh, PA: Duquesne University press.

Doolittle R., & MacDonald, D. (1978). Communication and a sense of community in a metropolitan neighborhood: A factor analytic examination. *Communication Quarterly, 26,* 2-7.

Dunham, H. W. (1986). The community today: Place or process. *Journal of Community Psychology, 14,* 399–404.

Fisher, A. T. & Sonn. C. C. (1999). Aspiration to community: Community responses to oppression. *Journal of Community Psychology, 27,* 715-725.

Glynn, T. (1981). Psychological sense of community: Measurement and application. *Human Relations, 34,* 789-818.

Hedges A., & Kelly, J. (1992). *Identification with local area: Report on qualitative study.* London, UK: H.M. Government.

Heller, K. J. (1989). The return to community. *American Journal of Community Psychology, 17,* 1-16.

Hill, J. L. (1996). Psychological sense of community: Suggestions for future research. *Journal of Community Psychology, 24*, 431-438.

Hillery, G. A. (1955). Definitions of community: areas of agreement. *Rural Sociological, 20*, 194-204.

Kirkpatrick, F. G. (1986). *Community: A trinity of models*. Washington, DC: Georgetown University Press.

Kuhn, T. (1970). *The structure of scientific revolutions*. Chicago, IL; University of Chicago Press.

McMillan, D.W., & Chavis, D.M. (1986). Sense of community: A definition and theory. *Journal of Community Psychology, 14*, 6-23.

Newbrough, J. R. (1992). Community psychology for a post-modern world. *Journal of Communuity Psychology, 20*, 10-25.

Newbrough, J. R. (1995). Toward community: A third position. *American Journal of Community Psychology, 23*, 9-31.

Pepper S. C. (1942). *World hypotheses*. Berkeley, CA: University of California Press.

Perkins, D. D., Florin, P., Rich, R. C., Wandersman, A. & Chavis, D. M. (1990). Participation and the social and physical environment of residential blocks: Crime and community context. *American Journal of Community Psychology, 18*, 83-115.

Polkinghorne, D. (1983). *Methodology for the human sciences: Systems of inquiry*. Albany, NY: State University of New York Press.

Puddifoot, J. (1996). Some initial considerations in the measurement of community identity. *Journal of Community Psychology, 24*, 327–337.

Rapley, M., & Pretty, G. M. H. (1999). Playing Procrustes: The interactional production of a "psychological sense of community." *Journal of Community Psychology, 27*, 695-713.

Riger S., & Lavrakos P. (1981). Community ties, patterns of attachment, and social interaction in urban neighborhoods. *American Journal of Community Psychology, 9*, 55-66.

Royal, M., & Rossi, R (1996). Individual-level correlates of sense of community: Findings from workplace and school. *Journal of Community Psychology, 24*, 395–416.

Sarason, S. B. (1974). *The psychological sense of community: Prospects for a community psychology*. San Francisco: Jossey-Bass.

Sarason, S. B. (1986). The emergence of a conceptual center. *Journal of Community Psychology, 14*, 405–407.

Saxe, G. S. *The Blind Men and the Elephant*. Retrieved 10/23/01. Http://wordfocus.com/word-act-blindman.html.

Sonn, C. C, Bishop, B. J, & Drew, N. M. (1999). Sense of community: Issues and considerations from a cross-cultural perspective. *Community, Work and Family, 2*, 205-218.

Tolan, P., Chertok, F., Keys, C., & Jason L. (1990). Conversing about theories, methods, and community research. In P. Tolan, C. Keys, F. Chertok, & L. Jason (Eds.) *Researching community psychology: Issues of theory and methods*. (pp. 3-8) Washington, DC: American Psychological Association.

Tönnies, F. (1955). *Community and association*. Norfolk, UK: Lowe & Brydone.

Tönnies, F. (1974). Gemeinschaft and Gesellschaft. In C. Bell and H. Newby (Eds.), *The sociology of community: A selection of readings* (pp.5-12). London, UK: Frank Cass and Company.

Toulmin, S. (1990). *Cosmopolis: The hidden agenda of modernity*. New York: Free Press.

Wiesenfeld, E. (1996). The concept of "we": A community social psychology myth? *Journal of Community Psychology, 24*, 337-345.

Worsley, P. (1987). *The new introducing sociology*. Ringwood, Australia: Penguin.

PART II

LOCATIONAL COMMUNITIES

Chapter 2

PSYCHOLOGICAL HOME

Sandra T. Sigmon and Stacy R. Whitcomb
University of Maine

C.R. Snyder
University of Kansas

> It takes a heap o' livin' in a house t' make it a home.
> (Edgar A. Guest, *Home*)

INTRODUCTION

What comes to mind when someone says the word "home?" The meanings for the term home are numerous. Everyone probably has a sense of what is meant by the phrase "going home" or what is meant by characterizing a place as "homey." For example, when looking through a new house, a prospective buyer may say that it "feels like home." In this chapter, we outline our scientific approach for understanding the concept of home. We provide empirical support for a brief measure that taps into the construct that we have labeled *psychological home*. In addition, we will summarize studies that have provided evidence for the reliability and validity of this measure (Sigmon, Boulard, & Snyder, 1998). Although research is in the early stages of development, we believe there are far-reaching implications for this construct.

We have approached the psychological home construct from an individual differences perspective. This differs from the group perspective in which individuals or communities come together to form meaningful units, or groups. Our approach is quite different from those perspectives represented in other chapters in this book. Whereas other researchers may focus on individuals drawing their identity from community life that is shared with others, we focus on how an individual reinforces his or her self-identity in a physical environment to represent that part of their identity that is not shared with others. Thus, our construct focuses on what an individual does to the environment to make it better and to reflect his or her own self-identity. Our purpose is to better understand how individuals make a physical structure or space their home or more home-like, why this is important to them, and what benefits are accrued from such efforts. We also will relate the psychological home concept to the literature on sense of community and sense of place. All of these constructs represent attempts to make sense of and explain our need to belong and identify with our surroundings. Within this context, psychological home describes the dynamic interaction between a psychological need and physical structures. This process is closely associated with an individual's sense of self and attachment to the physical surroundings.

Uses of the Term Home

First, let us look at how the term is defined in the nomenclature. Webster's Ninth New Collegiate Dictionary defines "home" as "(1) one's place of residence or (2) the focus of one's domestic attention." The adjective phrase "at home" is defined as "(1) relaxed and comfortable, (2) at ease, or (3) in harmony with the surroundings." The verb "home" is defined as "(1) to go or return home or (2) to proceed or direct attention toward an object." In all forms, there is mention of either a directed focus on, or an emotional experience of, one's surroundings. The second component of the definition of home, "the focus of one's domestic attention" is fundamental to the psychological home construct. "Focus" implies some action or energy directed at one's physical surroundings.

On the other hand, Webster's *Ninth New Collegiate Dictionary* defines a "house" as "a building that serves as living quarters for one or a few families." Historically, writers have differentiated the terms house and home. For example, Shakespeare in *Henry IV* lamented, "He hath eaten me out of house and home." Thus, house and home have been differentiated with respect to the purely physical aspects and emotional aspects of one's surroundings. As the chapter heading suggests, it takes a lot of work to make a house a home. These observations suggest that effort and resources must be directed toward the transformation from a house into a home. Along these lines, researchers have differentiated between the uses of physical spaces (Barker & Schoggen, 1973) and the meaning that is attached to those physical spaces (O'Donnell, Tharp, & Wilson, 1993).

Throughout history, home has had both spiritual and emotional connotations. For example, "Swing low, sweet chariot, Coming for to carry me home" from the old, anonymous, Southern spiritual, connotes a celestial or spiritual home. Disillusioned with the world, Ralph Waldo Emerson penned "Goodbye, proud world! I'm going home; Thou art not my friend and I'm not thine" in *Poems* (1847). Many authors have written about the emotional aspects of the term. For example, Pandects (533 AD) wrote, "One's home is the safest refuge to everyone." Similarly, Oliver Wendell Holmes in *Homesick in Heaven* wrote, "Where we love is home, Home that our feet may leave, but not our hearts." Although the colloquial expression "Home is where the heart is" captures the emotional component of home, it fails to address the dynamic interaction between a physical space and our need to have our surroundings reflect who we are.

Interestingly, home also has been used in nationalistic and patriotic senses. For example, Irving Berlin (1938) inspired Americans with the lyrics from *God Bless America* with, "From the mountains to the prairies, To the oceans white with foam, God bless America, My home sweet home!" Moreover, home appears to have little to do with furnishings or wealthy trappings. For example, John Howard Payne in his opera *Clari, the Maid of Milan* (1823) wrote "Mid pleasures and palaces though we may roam, Be it ever so humble, there's no place like home." Similarly, Saki wrote "Poverty keeps together more homes than it breaks up," in the *Chronicles of Clovis* (1911). Perhaps the epitome of home has been symbolized by Frank L. Baum's character Dorothy in the classic book, *Wizard of Oz*, clicking her heels together and proclaiming, "There's no place like home, there's no place like home." Clearly, literature and the media have conceptualized the term home in diverse ways. In this chapter, we will present our definition, conceptualization, and research on the construct of psychological home.

Empirical Beginnings

We posed several questions in our efforts to study psychological home empirically? Does psychological home have any significance for psychological well-being? Given that so much has been written about the meaning of the term home, how does making a physical surrounding "home-like" benefit someone? How do we make a house a home? Most individuals might argue that it does not necessarily take a "heap of living," yet there is some sense that we have to "do" something to make an abode a home. We have to imprint it in some way, make it ours. Why do we spend so much time and energy making a house our home? Our conclusion was that time and energy are invested into transforming a house into a home because they experience positive consequences from doing so. This concept of action and benefit represented the basis for further development of the psychological home construct.

In addition to a primary physical location (i.e., a person's house), many individuals will often make an aspect of their office homier. Office workers may place a personal photograph or memorabilia in their cubicle to make that space their own. What drives us to do this? Could it be that we are afraid of being swallowed up and losing our individuality in a sea of cubicles (Snyder & Franklin, 1980)? We desire to belong to groups and community, yet we also want to keep a place in our hearts and surroundings that is separate from others. We need to impact our surroundings (e.g., house, dorm, office space, car) in such a way that it reflects our personality, our sense of self, and in so doing, derive benefits. We contend that modifying physical space to have it better reflect our self-identity reflects the core of psychological home.

Are there cultural issues related to psychological home? From the extant literature, it appears that this concept applies across all cultures. Consider the nomads on the steppes of Asia who move their homes daily to follow their herds of horses. They arrange and decorate their huts to reflect their identity. Each day they disassemble their homes, move with the herd and then rebuild their homes in the middle of the dusty, dull, arid plains. This rebuilding includes decorating the inside of their felt-walled homes with bright, colorful ancestral belongings -- displayed so that the look of the home is consistent across time despite the daily dismantling and reassembling.

In the recent movie *Castaway*, Tom Hanks plays a character marooned on a deserted island. In addition to his need for companionship (e.g., his treating of a volleyball as a person), he makes his imprint on this island. For example, in the cave that represents his only shelter, he decorates the walls with paintings of people who give his life meaning and purpose, "his beloved." He saves and protects a FedEx package that symbolizes his work identity. On his return to his former life, he decorates the sails of his raft (his new home) with figures from the package. In his new island home 'décor,' we see that his identity is tied to the island by necessity. But, it should be emphasized that he has stronger links to another place, and the pictures illustrate his intent to return to that former home.

This movie character's behavior epitomizes the need to change an environment in order to have it better reflect who he is as a person. In this particular instance, it could be argued that the character's need to establish psychological home on the island enabled him to survive the ordeal. The pictures he kept and drew in his cave home reminded him of the place where he felt a sense of 'belonging.' Psychological home refers to this process of making a space home, regardless of the physical structure of the 'house.'

How early did this psychological need develop in our evolution as a species? The psychological home need applies to more than just gathering skins to keep warm or building a fire to survive; it goes beyond the basic survival needs. Although initial attempts to make an environment more home-like may have been to mark and identify territories, psychological home has evolved to represent our need to have our environment reflect an aspect of our identity. Although early socialization practices may have focused on developing community relations and the accrual of community benefits for doing so, an individual's need to have his or her environment mirror back self-identity continued to evolve. In relation to the physical environment, needs for community and individuality have continued to evolve with both producing positive benefits for the individual.

Although much has been written about the subject of home in the literature, the construct of home has not been consistently approached from a scientific or empirical framework. Although earlier researchers from social geography (e.g., Seamon, 1979) to environmental psychology (e.g., Horowitz & Tognoli, 1982; Sixsmith, 1986) wrote about or investigated the meaning of home to individuals, researchers have not addressed the issue of why individuals differ with regard to the amount of time and energy they invest into making a place their own, what they might gain from these actions, and how this might relate to their self-theory. Early attempts to better understand the meaning of home focused on what the environment imparted to the individual rather than what an individual might do to the environment out of a psychological need or motive. Our research on psychological home represents initial attempts to address these issues.

Relationship Between Psychological Home and Sense of Community

At this point, we step back and look at broader, related concepts in the literature. Historically, a sense of community referred to identification with, or sense of belonging, to a group of individuals. In addition, sense of community could be applied to those individuals tied to a specific geographic location. Although researchers have struggled to agree on a precise definition for sense of community (e.g., Hill, 1996), most would probably agree that sense of community transcends individual relationships and behaviors. Other areas of agreement may include the notion that individuals might share an emotional connection irrespective of geographic location, the opinion that context is crucial in gaining a better understanding of community, and the position that diverse ways of assessing community at the individual and aggregate level need to be pursued. Areas of contention still surround whether sense of community refers to individual or group experience and how to best measure this construct (e.g., Chavis & Pretty, 1999).

Some posit that observations made 15 years ago (Hillery, 1984, as cited in Puddifoot, 1996) still hold true for reviews of today's literature; there remains a territorial-based camp and a social networks based camp within the field of sense of community study. Others maintain that recently the sense of community literature has seen a shift from the focus on geographical settings as a means of defining psychological sense of community (PSC) "to include notions such as members' sense of significance, solidarity, and security" (Sonn & Fisher, 1996, p. 417). In this respect, many people attain identities and experience feelings of belonging from relational communities. In other words, the consideration of territorial aspects has become less important than the consideration of the social relationships aspects (Royal & Rossi, 1996).

Wiesenfeld (1996) notes that the literature reflects "community" as defined by "we" suggesting a homogeneous group of people who think, feel and behave in similar ways. She argues that this is an idealized version of community and suggests that community is a dialectic and dynamic process affording diversity within the group. Both of these definitions focus on the importance of social network relationships, as does McMillan and Chavis' (1986) model used to investigate psychological sense of community (PSC) among communities. Their model (which McMillan, 1996 has since revisited) encompasses membership, influence, integration, fulfillment of needs, and shared emotional connection (Sonn & Fisher, 1996), but does indirectly recognize that physical place may be related to or influenced by these variables.

Sonn and Fisher (1996) applied this social model to the study of people labeled "Coloured" in South Africa during Apartheid. They noted that shared history and identity are central to development of psychological relatedness and contribute positively to the development of individuals and groups. These researchers found that high levels of in-group (i.e., ethnic origin group) interaction can provide an individual with support as well as provide a context for reconstructing group identity and conception of community.

PSC has been investigated in many varied populations. For example, Lounsbury and DeNeui (1996) developed a scale for measuring PSC in college populations. They found that higher PSC scores were related to smaller schools, membership in Greek (fraternity/sorority) life, and extroverted personality type. From a developmental perspective, researchers (Pretty, et al., 1996) found that older adolescents had a lower PSC rating than younger adolescents and predicted loneliness scores in teens. In Italy, PSC and life satisfaction were compared across a small town, a small city and a neighborhood in a large city (Prezza & Constantini, 1998). Researchers there found levels of both constructs were higher in the town than the larger municipalities.

Other investigators point out, however, that there is little theoretical agreement about the nature of community identity (Puddifoot, 1996). Researchers appear to treat PSC as different types of variables. Some studies treat PSC as a trait, others suggest it is "an extra-individual, aggregate variable" (Hill, 1996). Across the different camps, however, methodologies for studying PSC have been fairly consistent, generally measuring the perceptions of individual community residents (Puddifoot, 1996). Despite disagreeing on character, origin, and dimensions of community identity, researchers have come to similar conclusions on the nature of community identity (Puddifoot, 1996).

It can be said that PSC "is a principle organizer of the affective aspects of the members of a community for a community" (Garcia, Giuliani, & Wiensenfeld, 1999, p. 730). Research on PSC consistently finds an "important and complicated relationship between the neighborhood (as a residential community) and [PSC], contrary to the proliferation of communities that are not based on place" (Chavis & Pretty, 1999). A recent study, describing PSC through McMillan and Chavis' (1986) model as it evolved in an urban barrio in Venezuela, illustrated the "psychological significance of physically creating one's home to meet basic shelter and safety needs within the community" (Chavis & Pretty, 1999, p. 638).

In examining the sense of community literature, it appears that there are some similarities and differences relative to psychological home. The level of analysis for most of the sense of community studies have focused on belonging and attachment needs of an individual to groups or geographic locales. This construct of PSC would seem to relate to a psychological need to be a part of a larger group or social context. Conversely, psychological home relates to how an individual expresses self-identity in relation to a physical environment. Psychological home also demonstrates an individual's need to develop an identity independent from the social community, as well as to establish a safe refuge from the group or to lay claim to a portion of the geographic location. Struggling to balance the dialectic relationship within an individual may involve more energy and time, but ultimately may provide a balance in an individual's life that would beneficially help to reduce stress and enhance psychological well-being.

Relation Between Psychological Home and Sense of Place

Although investigators studying PSC generally operationalize terms in one camp or the other, it seems difficult to separate the *group* under study from *place* in many investigations. Philosophers of place suggest that our sense of community and home is tied to our sense of place as "where we are [is] an inextricable part of who we are" (Smith, Light, & Roberts, 1998, p. 17). Although place can be defined as location, position or duties within society (Hay, 1998), or even where people view themselves in relation to others (i.e., context), creating a "collective sense of place amongst themselves" (Shotter, 1996, p. 210), these definitions are not very applicable to this discussion. Deciding on a common definition of sense of place is not straightforward either, but generally definitions include aspects of an emotional response to a space or object. Alternatively, giving meaning to a location is also a definition of place (Low & Altman, 1992).

Place is not necessarily a specified, tangible spot on a map. In addition to specific places such as Central Park, the Great Barrier Reef, or Cape Cod, categories that share common characteristics (e.g., schools, neighborhoods) have been conceptualized as places. Even non-physicalities, such as cyberspace, can be operationalized as "place," although it may be more accurate to term web sites as symbolic places. Place can also be defined as a product of human interaction with the physical features of an environment, an interaction that endowed those features with a singularity and emotional significance that geography does not capture (Pred, 1983; Wasserman, Womersley, & Gottleib, 1998).

This type of intimacy with the land can be stated as identifying themselves and their communities with natural landmarks; it is subjective, relating to personal identity and meaning in life (Howard, 1998). Some authors have postulated that "an individual's sense of self is partially represented by beliefs associating the self with the environment" (Cantrill, 1998, p. 303). In addition, finding place can be "a matter of finding ourselves" (Malpas, 1998, p. 39), because "insofar as any individual or group succeeds in making a place, it will be a place that enables the individual to be himself or herself, or the group to be itself" (Smith, et al., 1998, p.5). Making places is a process of carving or claiming space by first marking the space, usually followed by naming the place, thereby allowing it to collect a history (Smith, et al., 1998).

Alternatively, sense of place can be viewed as being related to autonomy, in that, acting on the environment, making space have more meaning, creates a place, and gives one a sense of autonomy (Pastalan & Polakow, 1987). Privacy protects autonomy and physical context can promote privacy, thereby promoting a sense of autonomy (e.g., assisted living in apartment vs. cottages; Pastalan & Polakow, 1987). The sense of place literature has been characterized as being eclectic with regard to methodology (e.g., Pred, 1983) and inconsistent in its empirical approach to better understanding the attachment of individuals to a particular location.

Psychological home relates to how individuals impart their self-identity to a particular physical locale. Thus, our construct can be viewed as a specific type or sub-type of sense of place. Although the sense of place literature appears to be more related to geographic locations, there are some aspects in newer writings that may have implications for psychological home. For example, attachment of individuals to specific geographic locations may be correlated with psychological home. Attachment to a geographic location as well as to a person's home could be assessed (i.e., homeland or hometown vs. dwelling). Although it may be difficult to construct a specific measure to assess sense of place, rootedness in place is probably highly correlated with psychological home. Sense of place seems to imply a passive process by which identification occurs, meaning is imparted by events associated with locale, whereas psychological home represents a dynamic process by which an individual manipulates the environment to reflect his or her self-identity.

CONCEPTUAL BASIS OF PSYCHOLOGICAL HOME

In our model, psychological home is defined as a sense of belonging in which self-identity is tied to a particular place. This construct reflects an underlying motive that is driven by an individual's need to identify a sense of self with a physical locale. It is assumed that this motive transcends time and place in that it is: (1) a dynamic process that continues throughout the life-span, and (2) it is not just specific to home of origin. Therefore, once psychological home is established, this motive is relatively stable and resilient. However, some situations may influence the level of psychological home at any particular time (e.g., getting married, house-hunting, house fires). For example, an individual who is rebuilding a house after a fire may be required to put more energy and work into establishing the new home. The need for psychological home may stay constant but at certain points, more work and energy output may be required.

What comprises psychological home? We contend that psychological home consists of cognitive, affective, and behavioral components (see Figure 1). The cognitive component consists of attributions about our selves in relation to the environment. For example, what does the term home come to mean for an individual? What types of beliefs does an individual hold about home? Is establishing a home-like environment a priority in an individual's life? What does an individual think are the benefits of psychological home? How much is an individual's self-theory tied to a physical location? The affective component reflects the emotions and feelings that surround the establishment and maintenance of psychological home. For most individuals, feelings of security, warmth, attachment, consistency, resiliency, identity, and familiarity may be associated with one's home. The behavioral component represents the actions that individuals take to make a physical location more home-like. Individuals may manipulate, construct, move, and structure their physical environment so that it better reflects their self-identity. Thus, all aspects of our experience impact psychological home.

How does this motive develop? As children, we are exposed to individuals and environments that differ in their manifestation of psychological home. Early memories may be linked to strong affect. For example, smells, sights, and sounds of our home of origin or our grandmother's home have particularly strong links in our memory. Psychological home develops from our interactions with our early environments and early interactions with family of origin, peers, and extended family. Although it would not be expected that psychological home would have genetic links, it would certainly have strong familial and environmental contributions to its development.

How does psychological home function? What is the purpose? As individuals manifest psychological home, they experience the positive benefits of this connection to the physical environment. As individuals structure their environment to reflect their self-identity, they project onto the environment who they are, who they would like to be. They make seek refuge from life's complexity, and surround themselves with things that reinforce who they are -- the good qualities.

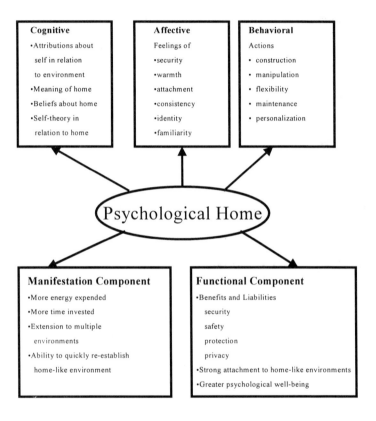

Figure 1. Components of Psychological Home

Creating a psychological home offers a psychological refuge that provides security, safety, protection, and assurance. An individual's home can come to represent a haven from the stresses of the external world. Such a home can reduce anxiety and help us cope with change. Constructing a home reinforces our ability to be separate from others and yet be a part of others. This motive may provide us with consistency, familiarity, stability, but also provides us with flexibility.

The psychological home construct includes manifestation and functional components. The manifestation component consists of the manipulation, construction, and maintenance of a home-like environment. Individuals high in psychological home will expend more effort in constructing and manipulating their environment to make it more personally salient. In addition, these individuals will extend this motive to environments other than their domicile. These individuals may decorate their office or car with items that are reflective of their self-identity. Some individuals may display photographs of loved ones or sports items to reflect their favorite pastimes. In this respect, there may be some overlap between identification with a group (e.g., others who support a sports team) and the need to manipulate a space to reflect self-identification (i.e., I am a fan of this team). Regardless of the types of items they choose, individuals high in psychological home will expend time and energy in the manipulation and personalization of their environments.

Although individuals high in psychological home will demonstrate an affinity for stability, they will be flexible in constructing a home-like environment. Although it might be expected that these individuals would actually suffer more when their handiwork is destroyed (e.g., house fire), individuals high in psychological home have an adaptive flexibility in re-establishing home bonds. This flexibility may increase their resiliency in the face of a traumatic event that could result in the loss of physical home. Individuals high in psychological home would be able to reconstruct a home environment more efficiently than those low in psychological home resulting in a more rapid return to normalcy after the trauma. Because of their resiliency, these individuals would demonstrate greater psychological well-being in the long-term.

The functional component of psychological home consists of the benefits or liabilities obtained from a relationship with a physical place -- security, safety, protection, privacy, positive or negative feelings, etc. It is assumed that individuals high in psychological home will demonstrate stronger (positive) attachment to their home and other home-like environments (e.g., office space, dorm room). In addition, it is assumed that individuals will differ in the intensity of emotions and reinforcement value associated with those environments. In particular, it would be expected that high psychological home individuals would score higher on positive affect, psychological well-being, goal-directed behavior, and need for affiliation than low psychological home individuals.

Development of the Psychological Home Scale

In order to test the above assumptions, a scale was developed to measure psychological home and a series of validation studies were conducted (Sigmon, et al., 1998). The initial validation studies were carried out with undergraduate samples, later studies with community populations have produced similar results.

For the first validation study, 40 items were generated that were thought to reflect the manifestation and functional components of psychological home. The majority of the described studies were conducted with undergraduate samples at two universities, one in the Midwest and one in the Northeast (approximately 90-95% Caucasian) of the USA. In the first study, a sample of 242 participants (males = 111, females = 131) completed a 40-item scale using a 1 to 7 anchor (1 = strongly disagree, 7 = strongly agree). Choosing the items with the highest inter-item correlations (ranging from .29 to .64) resulted in 8 items (see Appendix A) with a Cronbach's alpha of .85 (M = 47.93, SD = 7.21). Examples of items include "I add personal touches to the place where I live," "I work at making a place my own," and "I get a sense of security from having a place of my own." Across four subsequent studies, Cronbach's alphas ranged from .84 to .90. Eight week test-retest reliability was r = .72.

In terms of concurrent validation, the Psychological Home Scale correlates positively and significantly (p < .01) with the Mental Health Index (MHI; r = .14 to .43), Psychological Well-Being subscale of the MHI (r = .17 to .46), Affiliation (r = .30 to .36), Hope (r = .15 to .26) and Desirability of Control (r = .24 to .62). Significant negative correlations were found with the Psychological Distress subscale of the MHI (r = -.17 to -.36), State-Trait Anxiety Inventory-Trait (r = -.18 to -.36), and Negative Affect (r = -.14 to -.35.) In terms of discriminant validity, no significant correlations were found with Social Desirability (r = -.03 to .04) or Locus of Control (r = -.06 to -.12). On measures of Psychological Well-being, Social Well-being, and femininity, participants in the high Psychological Home group scored significantly higher than participants classified in the low Psychological Home group. Significant main effects were found for gender across all studies, with females consistently scoring higher than males.

To examine the construct validity of the measure, participants (n = 89) were selected who scored in the top 20%, middle 20%, and lower 20% on the Psychological Home Scale. Participants were asked to arrange an experimental room to make it "look like their own." They were provided with various materials (e.g., posters, blankets, prints, plants, books) and were given unlimited time to arrange the space. After finishing arranging the room, participants were asked to indicate how typical this room would be for them. The majority of participants indicated that their arrangement of items was indicative of how their living space would be. Trend analyses indicated that participants high in Psychological Home spent more time arranging the room than individuals in the other two groups and placed more items in the room when compared to the other groups.

Videotapes were made of the rooms prior to and immediately after participants had arranged the room. Two independent raters viewed the tapes of the room for each participant and rated the rooms on a 1 (not very) to 7 (very) rating scale using the following dimensions: coziness, simplicity, and tranquility. Participants in the high Psychological Home group received significantly higher ratings on coziness and tranquility dimensions, and lower ratings on the simplicity dimension compared to medium and low Psychological Home group members. This initial study validates that individuals high in psychological home spend more time making a surrounding their own and objective observers can note the difference.

The results of these studies indicate that the Psychological Home Scale is a psychometrically sound questionnaire with acceptable reliability and validity. Participants who score high on this scale tend to report more positive psychological functioning and, in an experimental situation, spend more time and effort in attempting to make a place their own. Individuals high in psychological home may experience greater feelings of hope resulting in the belief that they can adapt to a changing environment while maintaining a sense of stability. Although females tend to score higher on the measure, there were no significant gender differences in the amount of time spent arranging the room or number of items placed in an experimental room. Even though these initial studies provide support for the measure, further research needs to be conducted with diverse populations to explore the extent to which psychological home applies to other measures of sense of place as well as sense of community.

Implications of Psychological Home

Psychological home represents an attempt to better understand how an individual's sense of self is associated with the physical surroundings. The drive to manipulate and personalize one's environment so that it better reflects self-identity appears to have positive emotional consequences. Individuals who are high in psychological home score higher on measures of psychological well-being and score lower on measures of negative affect than individuals who are low in psychological home.

It is also expected that individuals high in psychological home will be more resilient after trauma. Researchers have investigated the effects of disruptions in place attachment (see Brown & Perkins, 1992) and found that overall, place disruptions have negative effects on individuals' attachment to a locale and sense of identity. However, it is possible that reactions to natural disasters and crimes that violate the sanctity of the home are experienced or coped with differentially in individuals who vary in the degree of psychological home. For example, those high in psychological home may be able to rebound more quickly to losses or destruction of homes by being able to more quickly develop a sense of home in a new place. These individuals have constructive ways of approaching stressors and are flexible in their interactions with the environment. Although initial assaults on their physical homes may be devastating, they will rebound much quicker in reaction to such stressors.

Recognizing that individuals vary in psychological home has implications for many social policies. For example, allowing individuals to personalize temporary environments (e.g., hospital rooms, birthing rooms) and more permanent environments (e.g., for the elderly moving to retirement or nursing homes) may be more important to some than others. Indeed, it may be essential to psychological well-being for some people. Allowing people to "remodel" their environs could promote faster adjustment for individuals and perhaps result in even more adaptive outcomes in hospital environments. For example, Langer and Rodin (1976) found that allowing nursing home residents the choice of simply caring for a plant resulted in a greater sense of well-being and alertness than residents who were not given this responsibility. Allowing nursing home residents to individualize their settings may lead to more adaptive coping in response to illness or distress. In addition, psychological home may be considered when developing housing policies and evaluating the needs of the homeless. Some homeless individuals go to great lengths to personalize their surroundings and become very distressed when their belongings are disturbed. It may be that some of these individuals have stronger need for psychological homes than others. A greater flexibility in institutional policies regarding personalizing physical space may have immediate and long-lasting benefits for their consumers.

FUTURE RESEARCH

More research is needed on diverse populations. There may be cultural differences that need to be identified. In particular, research needs to be done to address areas of similarity and difference with sense of place and sense of community. Research should also address the gender differences and factors related to gender and psychological home. Although some researchers have begun to investigate the relationship between women and home (e.g., Ahrentzen, 1992), that relationship may be altered as more and more women work outside of the home. It is unclear how these social and economic changes might affect psychological sense of home in each gender. More research is needed on belongingness and assessing how this relates to psychological home. In general, these literatures need to address the advantages and disadvantages of these constructs. Future research should focus on identifying antecedents, concomitants, and consequences associated with psychological home.

SUMMARY

In this chapter, we have presented the background and initial research on a new construct called psychological home. Psychological home refers to an individual's need to identify sense of self with a physical locale. This construct refers to a dynamic process by which an individual manipulates, structures, and maintains an environment to make it reflect one's sense of self. The benefits of this time and energy output include positive, emotional consequences that contribute to overall psychological well-being. Initial studies have produced a reliable and valid instrument to assess the construct, but future research needs to address the generalizability of the measure to more diverse populations and assess its relation to sense of place and community.

REFERENCES

Ahrentzen, S. B. (1992). Home as a workplace in the lives of women. In I. Altman & S. M. Low (Eds.), *Place attachment*, (pp. 113-138). New York: Plenum Press.

Barker, R.G. & Schoggen, P. (1973). *Qualities of community life*. San Francisco: Jossey-Bass Publishers.

Brown, B.B. & Perkins, D.D. (1992). Disruptions in place attachment. In: I. Altman & S. M. Low (Eds.) *Place attachment*, (pp. 279-304). New York: Plenum Press.

Cantrill, J. (1998). The environmental self and a sense of place: Communication foundations for regional ecosystem management. *Journal of Applied Communication Research, 26*, 301-318.

Chavis, D. & Pretty, G. M. H. (1999). Sense of community: Advances in measurement and application. *Journal of Community Psychology, 27*, 635-642.

Garcia, I., Giuliani, F., & Wiesenfeld, E. (1999). Community and sense of community: The case of an urban barrio in Caracas. *Journal of Community Psychology, 27*, 727-740.

Hay, R. (1998). Sense of place in developmental context. *Journal of Environmental Psychology, 18*, 5-29.

Hill, J. (1996). Psychological sense of community: Suggestions for future research. *Journal of Community Psychology, 24*, 431-438.

Horowitz, J., & Tognoli, J. (1982). Role of home in adult development: Women and men living alone describe their residential histories. *Journal of Applied Family & Child Studies, 31*, 335-341.

Howard, I. (1998). From the inside out: The farm as place. In A. Light & J.M. Smith (Eds.), *Philosophy and geography III: Philosophies of place* (pp. 147-167). Lanham, MD: Rowman & Littlefield Publishers, Inc.

Langer, E. J., & Rodin, J. (1976). The effects of choice and enhanced personal responsibility for the aged: A field experiment in an institutional setting. *Journal of Personality and Social Psychology, 34*, 191-198.

Lounsbury, J., & DuNeui, D. (1996). Collegiate psychological sense of community in relation to size of college/university and extroversion. *Journal of Community Psychology, 24*, 381-394.

Low, S. M., & Altman, I. (1992). Place attachment: A conceptual inquiry. In I. Altman & S. M. Low (Eds.), *Place attachment* (pp. 1-12). New York: Plenum Press.

Malpas, F. (1998). Finding place: Spatiality, locality, and subjectivity. In A. Light & J.M. Smith (Eds.), *Philosophy and geography III: Philosophies of place* (pp. 21-43). Lanham, MD: Rowman & Littlefield Publishers, Inc.

McMillan, D. (1996). Sense of community. *Journal of Community Psychology, 24*, 315-325.

McMillan, D. W. & Chavis, D. M. (1986). Sense of community: A definition and theory [Special Issue]. *Journal of Community Psychology, 14*, 6-23.

O'Donnell, C.R., Tharp, R.G. & Wilson, K. (1993). Activity settings as the unit of analysis: A theoretical basis for community intervention and development. *American Journal of Community Psychology, 21,* 501-520.

Pastalan, L. & Polakow, V. (1987). Life space over the life span. *Journal of Housing for the Elderly, 4,* 73-85.

Pred, A. (1983). Structuration and place: On the becoming of sense of place and structure of feeling. *Journal of the Theory of Social Behaviour, 13,* 45-68.

Pretty, G., Conroy, C., Dugay, J., Fowler, K., & Williams, D. (1996). Sense of community and its relevance to adolescents of all ages. *Journal of Community Psychology, 24,* 365-379.

Prezza, M. & Constantini, S. (1998). Sense of community and life satisfaction: Investigation in three different territorial contexts. *Journal of Community and Applied Social Psychology, 8,* 181-194.

Puddifoot, J. (1996). Some initial considerations in the measurement of community identity. *Journal of Community Psychology, 24,* 327-336.

Royal, M., & Rossi, R. (1996). Individual-level correlates of sense of community: Findings from workplace and school. *Journal of Community Psychology, 24,* 395-416.

Seamon, D. (1979). *A geography of the lifeworld: Movement, rest, and encounter.* New York: St. Martin's Press.

Sigmon, S.T., Boulard, N.E., & Snyder, C.R. (1998, August). *Psychological home.* Paper presented at the annual meeting of the American Psychological Association, San Francisco, CA.

Sixsmith, J. (1986). The meaning of home: An exploratory study of environmental experience. *Journal of Environmental Psychology, 6,* 281-298.

Shotter, J. (1996). A sense of place, Vico and the social production of social identities. *British Journal of Social Psychology, 25,* 199-211.

Smith, J., Light, A., & Roberts, D. (1998). Introduction: Philosophies and geographies of place. In A. Light & J.M. Smith (Eds.), *Philosophy and geography III: Philosophies of place* (pp. 1-19). Lanham, MD: Rowman & Littlefield Publishers, Inc.

Snyder, C. R., & Franklin, H. (1980). *Uniqueness: The human pursuit of difference.* New York: Plenum.

Sonn, C. C., & Fisher, A. T. (1996). Psychological sense of community in a politically constructed group. *Journal of Community Psychology, 24,* 417-430.

Wasserman, D., Womersley, M., & Gottlieb, S. (1998). Can a sense of place be preserved? In A. Light & J.M. Smith (Eds.), *Philosophy and geography III: Philosophies of place* (pp. 191-213). Lanham, MD: Rowman & Littlefield Publishers, Inc.

Wiesenfeld, E. (1996). The concept of "we": A community social psychology myth? *Journal of Community Psychology, 24,* 337-345.

APPENDIX A

PSYCHOLOGICAL HOME SCALE

Directions: Read each item carefully. Using the scale below, please select the number that best describes <u>YOU</u> and put that number in the blank space provided. Remember there are no right or wrong answers.

1	2	3	4	5	6	7
strongly disagree	slightly disagree	somewhat disagree	not sure	somewhat agree	slightly agree	strongly agree

_____ 1. I have grown attached to many of the places I have lived.
_____ 2. I put a lot of time and effort into making a place my own.
_____ 3. I feel more relaxed when I'm at home.
_____ 4. I surround myself with things that highlight my personality.
_____ 5. I get a sense of security from having a place of my own.
_____ 6. I add personal touches to the place where I live.
_____ 7. I take pride in the place where I live.
_____ 8. I work at making a place my own.

Chapter 3

PRESUMPTIVE PLANNING
From Urban Design To Community Creation In One Move?

Jean Hillier[i]
Curtin University

INTRODUCTION

In this chapter, I explore the issue of whether planners can "create community," as one of the current catchphrases in Western Australia (WA) suggests. In doing so, I subject to reasoned critique several of the main themes evident in Western Australian: community-development processes; their physical, neighborhood-based location, a presumption that social relations follow urban form, their inclusivity or aspect of 'togetherness,' and the diversity of their inhabitants. As Talen (2000, p. 172) pointedly writes: "the problem, for planners, is that the notion of community is easily misinterpreted and misapplied, and planners have not exhibited any particular sign that their use of the term is well thought out."

I examine conceptual issues of whether community is a social or a physical construct and indicate how planners and urban designers have attempted to plan communities from Ebenezer Howard onwards, through the British new towns movement to the present fascination with New Urbanism and urban villages. I ask whether communities are fundamentally inclusive or exclusive and the implications of this. Do communities tend to exhibit diversity or homogeneity with respect to resident demographics?

I discuss the topic of how a sense of place, or place attachment, relates to a sense of community. I question the extent to which place is instrumental in creating a sense of identity [ii] which in turn leads to creation to community.

I examine current Western Australian planning guidelines for "community design" (WAPC, 1997a and b; 2000) and cite examples of planned urban village and urban regeneration schemes in the Perth metropolitan region. In concluding, while I endorse several of the design elements currently favored in Western Australia, I warn against a potential reification of community through urban design and the unwitting 'creation' of ersatz communities which have no real meaning for their inhabitants.

Community As Social Or Physical Construction?

Rationale for the concept of 'community' is hotly debated between those who regard community as having a physical, territorial basis and those who regard community as a social process. Territory has been at the center of ecological and ethnological ideas of community derived from an extension of the study of so-called 'community' behavior in primate animals to that of human behavior (Parsons, 1966; Thorns, 1976). The emphasis is on the interrelationship between territory and human 'community,' as manifest in activities such as the erection of physical boundaries, including walls, which are biologically interpreted as a reflection of humans' need for security and the occupation of a defined territory. Indeed, as Bauman (2000, p. 80) writes: "the designing of 'spaces to bar access to spaces' seems to be the hottest preoccupation of American urban planners and the most profitable branch of the building industry."

Alternatively, there is a recognition that "identities, loyalties and economic dependencies" (Morris, 1996, p. 132) cannot be adequately understood through a local, geographically delimited lens. Community may be a social phenomenon, based on psychological, social, and cultural processes and interactions that occur between people (see, for example, Chavis & Newborough, 1986; McMillan & Chavis, 1986). Regardless of individual characteristics, there exist motives, interests, and needs which lead people to come together and "establish socioemotional ties that make them feel (at least in terms of the dimension which unites them) as part of a single whole" (Wiesenfeld, 1996, p. 339): a community. The question should be asked, however, whether need fulfillment and shared emotional connections are appropriate goals for planning.

Research examining people's psychological attachments to place and the role of place in creating attachment and identity links both physical and social aspects of community. If, as Rivlin (1987) suggests, in the United States, on average people move every five years and homeownership changes every seven years, neither house nor neighborhood is a permanent feature of a person's life. Moreover, if place attachments are developed through a person's everyday experiences of the tangible surroundings of their home locale (Feldman, 1996), to what extent can place attachments form and be relatively enduring?

Feldman (1990) proposes that it is through ongoing, satisfying involvement in a particular locale that people may develop generalized ideas, feelings, values, and behavioral dispositions that relate their identity to that place.[ii] Attachment to place, therefore, would appear to involve the temporal development of 'roots,' emotional and/or symbolic connections which create personal feelings of comfort.

There appears little agreement on the role of place in community formation. Authors such as Baum and Valins (1979) suggest that crowded, high density living conditions may be linked to social withdrawal, whilst Festinger, Schacter, and Back (1950) and Ebbesen, Kjos, and Koneeni (1976) offer evidence that neighbors are more likely to form social ties with each other if they use the same (semi-) public spaces and make face-to-face contact. More recently, Kuo, Sullivan, Coley, and Brunson (1998) emphasize the aesthetic importance of common spaces in generating neighborhood social ties.

Salvation by Bricks Alone?

Probably harking back to the work of Tönnies in the 1880s, there is a feel-good aspect to community that town planners have long attempted to artificially induce. From Ebenezer Howard, Frank Lloyd Wright, and Le Corbusier to the present day, there has been a belief that reforming the physical environment can revolutionize the total life of a society. Urban design is regarded as an active force, "directing the community onto the paths of social harmony" (Fishman, 1982, p. 4). Yet, as Fishman points out, the three practitioners above never subscribed to the doctrine of 'salvation by bricks alone,' the idea that physical facilities could by themselves create community, into which trap later followers have tumbled. Howard, Wright, and Le Corbusier clearly understood that well-intentioned urban design would be worse than useless if its "benevolent humanitarianism" (Fishman, 1982, p. 5) simply ignored fundamental social inequalities. They recognized that successful urban reconstruction needs to be allied with political and social reconstruction and proposed detailed programs for radical changes in the distribution of societal wealth and power. However, all too often, the co-operative socialist (Howard), Jeffersonian democratic (Wright) and revolutionary syndicalist (Le Corbusier) aspects of their work have been omitted by their followers who have extracted the physical concepts from their socio-political contexts. Hence, ideas of collective public ownership (Howard), brotherhood (Wright), and freedom through large-scale communal organization (Le Corbusier) have disappeared from view.

A philosophy of (re)building communities in the wake of the physical and social destruction of World War 2 underpinned the construction of the British new towns (Thorns, 1976). The new towns were to comprise small neighborhood units of approximately 5,000 homes, built in 'traditional design' and which would "seek to reconstruct through the design and layout employed, the social organisation of the village with its characteristic of 'communal solidarity'" (Thorns, 1976, p. 31). The neighborhood unit was conceived as a 'balanced' unit with regard to socio-economic and other demographics of its residents. It was anticipated that social relationships would form between neighbors of different ages, socio-economic status and so on, thereby creating a true 'community.'[iii] The neighborhood unit, in this manner, embodied a utopian image of a desirable community life to which people should aspire.

Much of the rationale for the new 'turn to community' may be found in Putnam's (1993) argument that social capital is the key element in processes by which communities are formed and strengthened over time. Putnam defines social capital as the set of relationships and structures in civil society that provide resources for people to act as citizens in their community (1993, p. v). It is noteworthy that Putnam's emphasis is on social structures rather than the physical structures of planners and urban designers.

Putnam's work has been developed in Australia by Cox who defines social capital as referring to "the processes between people which establish networks, norms and social trust and facilitate co-ordination and co-operation for mutual benefit" (1995, p. 15). Social capital is, therefore, the sum of relationships and networks that provide the basis for a general sense of well-being and promote integration between people (Hugman & Sotiri, 2000).

Key indicators or manifestations of social capital include aspects of trust, reciprocity (Cox, 1995; Winter, 2000), voluntarism and membership of networks (Cox, 1995, Hugman, & Sotiri, 2000), co-operation, time, community, and democracy (Cox, 1995). Community and social capital are dependent variables; community defined in this instance as the "immediate society within which people live and work," implying that communities of place are important in building social capital.

Putnam's original ideas on social capital were superseded, however, by his later work (1994, 1996, 2000) that graphically depicts the decline of social capital in all its manifestations. Putnam blames pressures of time on families of employees who work increasingly long hours, financial pressure and problems of accessibility due to urban sprawl, but his main 'culprit' is the rise of private TV sets. Watching TV (and one could also include video, DVD and the internet) alone or in family groups has replaced active membership of clubs and associations. Electronic networks have replaced physical face-to-face networks.

As households interact less with their neighbors and know fewer residents in their neighborhoods, desire for privacy and security has overtaken a desire for communitarianism in local geographical areas. Contact with 'real' people is shunned in favor of a closed world whose inhabitants can be both chosen and manipulated and which can be entered with ones self-identity obscured (e.g., chat rooms) (Bauman, 2001; Lieven, 1999). (See Roberts, Smith, and Pollock, this volume for a discussion of the internet and sense of community.)

IMAGES OF PLACE OR PLACES OF IMAGE?

Some 40 years after the British new town movement, and in response to media-led perceptions of declining social capital and the city as hostile, competitive, individualistic, socially and environmentally unsustainable, planners in the USA, Britain and Australia are again turning to urban design as a means of 'creating community,' believing community to be the cornerstone of social capital, and the panacea we all need in our lives. Image-makers (planners, marketing gurus, etc.), re-enchanted with (often sanitized) concepts of place, culture, and tradition are revalorizing locality and community, even to the extent of creating new images of place (e.g., The Rocks in Sydney), and attempting to orchestrate a sense of belonging on residential estates (via entry statements, etc.) (see Hastings & Dean, 2000).

The New Urbanists, influenced by the work of Andreas Duany and Elizabeth Plater-Zyberk (1992; 1994), Peter Calthorpe (1993; 2001), and Peter Katz (1994) in the United States, denigrate social 'communities' of interest ("everywhere communities") as "the 'gated communities' of the mind" (Calthorpe & Fulton, 2001, p. 3). They champion the urban values that they believe created 'community' in the past; a nostalgic community of small-town life in which neighbors lent each other cups of sugar and sat chatting on front stoops/porches. The Congress for the New Urbanism's Charter explicitly advocates several principles of 'community design' at all spatial scales -- from the building, the block and the street, through the neighborhood to the region, including: "neighborhoods should be diverse in use and population; *communities should be designed* for the pedestrian and transit as well as the car; cities and towns should be shaped by physically defined and universally accessible public spaces and community institutions; urban places should be framed by architecture and landscape design that celebrate local history, climate, ecology, and building practice" (Congress for the New Urbanism, 1998, emphasis added).

Through explicit design and through spectacle (e.g., new revivals of 'traditional' local Festivals such as the Fremantle Sardine Festival, Spring in the Valley, etc) and image, it may be possible to create a spurious sense of togetherness and participation in urban life. "In a world in which communal emotions are in short supply ... there is a steady consumer demand for *community substitutes*" (Bauman, 2000, p. 79). Events such as the above readily meet such a demand. They display the trappings of community, but, like most other consumption objects, they are predominantly image-related, ephemeral, and essentially disposable.

Planners are heavily involved in such image-making. There seems to be a new consensual belief in the role of urban design as a fundamental element of community-building. There is an explicit connection made between spatial form and social process through a relation between architectural design and an ideological 'community' lifestyle. As the US

Foundation for Traditional Neighborhoods states: "Bonds of an *authentic* community are formed" (cited in Audirac & Shermyen, 1994, p. 163; emphasis added).

Public space is seen as a communal vessel for shared activity. As such, the piazza/town square and the galleria/shopping street or mall, are seen as physical containers for this new spirit of public urban community. That is, provided that the public are consuming, not loitering and are not in a group of people, especially young males, and particularly, young black males, a point to which I return later.

Designed Togetherness

What, then, are the tangible ingredients of this designed community of togetherness? In WA, commercial streetscapes sprout pavement cafes and coffee shops rather like a spreading multicolored fungus of awnings and street umbrellas. But whose idea of community is this? Who sits in the cafes, sipping macchiatos, caffe lattes, and cappuccinos? A glance around the cafes in Fremantle, Subiaco, or Leederville (the accepted 'benchmarks' in WA) reveals patrons to be mainly white professionals. Is this real pluralism, something which has meaning for all groups in Australia, or is it rather that the higher income consumers' ideas and definitions have become the influential ones for planners who themselves identify with this lifestyle?

With regard to residential areas, the WA State Planning Strategy Discussion Paper on *The Community* (WAPC, 1995) lists various physical design elements which may lead to a "sense of community to be engendered into our urban environment" (WAPC, 1995, p. 24). Such design elements include:

- an identifiable suburb name. To this end, new residential developments in the Perth metropolitan area tend to have their own logo or symbol, which is highlighted on an entry statement and repeated on street signs and even lampposts;
- the creation of small sub-divisional precincts;
- safe design which discourages crime;
- a diversity of living and working environments; and
- provision of infrastructure "to assist the development of community spirit and focus" (WAPC, 1995, p. 26).

Principles which are regarded as key "aspects to create community" (Day, 1999) have been enshrined in the planning manual *Liveable Neighbourhoods: Community Design Codes* (WAPC, 1997a) and its second edition *Liveable Neighbourhoods* (WAPC, 2001). Based on urban design texts popular in Britain in the 1970s and 1980s, and revived by the New Urbanists, (e.g., Bentley, et al., 1985; Lynch, 1960, 1981; Newman, 1972), thus heightening the image of nostalgia, the Codes (1997)/Requirements (2001) represent a state planning ministry's recommendation for designing urban form in ways which, theoretically, will promote people's interaction and social integration. The principles reflect those of the Congress for the New Urbanism depicted above in what is essentially a highly functional concept of community.

The Community Design Codes/Requirements suggest increased *diversity* through use of mixed land use zoning, encouraging, for instance, office and retail developments within residential subdivisions. Mixed uses, theoretically, will decrease car usage and increase pedestrian use of the area throughout the day, thus increasing opportunities for people to encounter one another, interact and 'create community.'[iv] Diversity is also expressed through a desire for a return to the notion of socio-cultural and economic 'social mix' espoused in the British new towns. "The interaction of people with people from other walks of life is achievable through urban design elements" (Day, 1999, p. 35).

The concept of *walkability* is fundamental to the Codes/ Requirements, linked as it is to the potential for increasing human interaction. The suggested 400 meter radius, theoretically equating to five minutes walking time, has become something of a mantra, with circles overlain on plans everywhere. However, as several authors recognize, an 800 meter return journey may be easily accomplished by an able-bodied young person with little luggage, walking on flat land on a spring day in coastal Perth, while the trip may be virtually impossible for the elderly, those carrying heavy shopping, negotiating hills in 40°C (105°F) in summer. (See, for example, MacCallum's (1999) study of Karratha in north-west WA.)

A further key aspect is that of *"increased residential density"* (WAPC, 1997a, p. 8; 2001, p. 15). Whilst increased densities may facilitate higher levels of public transit provision and potential viability of neighborhood shops, Altman (1975), Merry (1987), and Lewis (1999) demonstrate that residents deal with perceived neighbor proximity 'problems' in reality by leading private lives with minimal contact and by trying to insulate their neighborhoods from change by carrying out their NIMBY campaigns in political and public forums.

Planning guidelines have been, and are in the process of being, modified to permit a variety of lot sizes and types (to facilitate housing diversity[v]), housing frontages to streets and lower front fencelines (to facilitate street surveillance, safety of passers-by and from burglary, by creating more 'eyes-on-the-street,' and a more attractive streetscape), minimum setbacks and maximum building heights (WAPC, 1997a). All these features should invite 'interest' in an attractive environment at street level.

In some New Urbanist-inspired developments, such as Ellenbrook, some 35km by road from the CBD, in the north-east of the Perth metropolitan area, "a return to the more traditional values of community living" (Ellenbrook Community Brochure, 1994) is "facilitated" by 'guidelines' which are a condition on sale of a property. Housing must comply with the guidelines that cover: no street fencing, the color of buildings, structure of mailboxes, and landscaping of front yards. The philosophy is, apparently, that development needs to be controlled tightly if it is to achieve the desired result of creating a community akin to that found in an unplanned traditional English village, or 1930s American small-town.

Ellenbrook is an illustration, par excellence, of the tendency of planners and developers to pick up on the "pro forma application of community as artifact" (Talen, 2000, p. 179) and apply it in a superficial manner. 'Community' is the rhetorical buzzword. In the Autumn 2001 edition of the management company's newsletter, *Ellenbrook Community,* the word 'community' appears on no less than 35 occasions.[vi] Kunstler's comments on New Urbanist-inspired attempts to 'create community' in the USA also seem to apply in WA: "the half-baked knockoffs and rip-offs that are proliferating … using the rhetoric about *community* as a sales gimmick without delivering any real civic amenity … [Australians] are so lost when it comes to the real issues of community and place that they can be gulled by just about any lame come-ons. The comers-on themselves seem equally confused" (1996, pp. 194-195, emphasis in original). The creation of 'community' in Ellenbrook has become an artifact of a particular suburban master-planning formula.

Property development manuals widely in use in WA also embrace the idea of physically 'creating community' in a "community-development process" (Reynolds & Solomon, 1998, p. 17). Following the *Community Builders Handbook* (1968), the authors state that "local communities are represented by neighborhoods" (1998, p. 127), and indicate, in their Property Development Process Model, that community clearly follows construction.

While I agree with many of the design elements that the WA Community Design Codes encourage, I nevertheless question whether the nostalgic sense of community that planners seek is not simply an illusion. The socio-economic conditions in which their rose-tinted communities appear to have flourished in the 1920s and 1930s were very different from those at the beginning of the Twenty-first Century. Friends, family and neighbors congregated round the piano at a time of economic depression and high unemployment in a lifestyle without TV, video, or internet to bring globalized, individualized entertainment. Few women were in the waged workforce, there were no household refrigerators or freezers, no supermarkets, and very few family cars, so women shopped daily, on foot, for perishable goods. Local networks and forms of mutual assistance evolved around shopping, housework, and childcare. With the expansion of the service sector since the 1960s, and the repeal of discriminatory legislation preventing married women from working in the public sector, more women have joined the waged labourforce. Their incomes facilitated an increase in car and freezer ownership, all of which have resulted in a fundamental alteration in shopping patterns as the 'family shop' is undertaken weekly or even monthly by car, with purchases stored in a freezer until required. The recent growth of Home Replacement Meals (HRMs) has further exacerbated a lack of demand for daily shopping.

In other words, the circumstances in which local 'communities' of place developed in the 1920s and 1930s do not exist today. Neither would we wish to recreate those social circumstances. Now that society has been "liberated" (Chavis & Wandersman, 1990, p. 61) from the traditional proxemic residential concept of community, and people tend to develop their multiple communities around interests, are planners effectively wasting their breath in attempts to "design for communities" (WAPC, 1997a, p. 19) and "encourage friendly neighborhoods that people take pride in" (WAPC, 1997b, p. 4)?

Such an approach tends to conflate the several concepts of community, outlined earlier, into a geographical community of place. I contend that it is only in the rare circumstances when people's interests and location overlap that localized community organizations establish and flourish. For example, the various "Friends of X" groups that tend to self-generate in response to a perceived threat to X, or the Resident Action Groups (RAGs) established to protest against Y. Many planners' main experiences of local 'communities' will occur through an encounter with their 'turf wars' or politics of place.

If local communities of place would appear to self-generate in response to a perceived planning threat to residents' lifestyles or property values (Chavis & Wandersman, 1990), I wonder, somewhat cynically, whether selective rumor-mongering in a local area by planners could more effectively "foster community" for far less financial outlay than expenditure on entry-statements, bricks, and mortar!

IS COMMUNITY TANGIBLE?

What might a 'sense of community' imply in a tangible manner? Chavis and Wandersman (1990) suggest that it entails 'knowing' one's neighbors sufficiently to borrow tools, visit informally and ask for help. The authors' 1979 survey of respondents in a Nashville neighborhood in the United States revealed their variable 'neighboring relations' (measured by level of social contact) to be highly correlated with people feeling a sense of community. However, it also correlated with 'block problems' (1990, p. 56). There appears to have been no analysis of responses by length of residence. It is, therefore, difficult to ascertain whether the Chavis and Wandersman study concurs with the 'phase hypothesis' reported by Thorns (1976, pp. 146-147) in which the degree of communal solidarity is found to decline over time, and to give way to an individualistic pattern of living. Results from several studies undertaken in the 1970s and 1980s (e.g., Doolittle & MacDonald, 1978) demonstrate a clear inverse relationship between variables measuring a sense of community (neighboring) and pro-urbanization (privacy, etc.). Privacy issues, fence disputes and those of 'overlooking' by neighbors represent what are probably the most common complaints and objections received by local planning officers in the late 1990s and early 2000 (personal communication).

Windass's (2000) work offers a valuable update on Chavis and Wandersman's concepts of neighboring relations and sense of community. Windass adapted Chavis and Wandersman's (1990) questionnaire for use in Livingston, an outer suburban residential estate of c250 households some 25km from the center of Perth, Western Australia.[vii] Livingston had been specifically designed and marketed towards a 'community lifestyle' since development commenced in 1990. It was one of the first residential estates in Western Australia to incorporate lavish entry statements and estate badging.

Windass's research compared survey results from a control group of 10 Residents' Committee (RC) members (on the premise that RC members would be more likely to be active contributors to their community) with a random sample of 25 non-RC member residents, one per household. The survey was conducted by doorstep interview.

Livingston represents typically middle class suburbia. All respondents were owner-occupiers aged between 30 and 45. Most were employed in semi-professional occupations. The only differences between RC members and non-members are that members tend to be longer-term estate residents (averaging 6.1 years) compared with 4 years for non-members, and that more RC member respondents were women (80% compared with 56% of non-members).

The Livingston results provide an important insight into 'community relations' and 'neighboring.' When asked to value the *importance of the estate* to themselves, on an ascending scale of 1 to 5, all 10 RC members responded with a score of 5. The average score for non-members was 3.6.

Women also tended to place a greater level of importance on the estate than did men. This may be linked to the higher proportion of women respondents who were not in waged labor, and who could be assumed to spend more time in and around their homes.

More importantly, however, is the outcome that respondents from professional occupations significantly regarded the estate as being less important to them (average score 2.7) than do semi-professionals (average score 4.1) and non-professionals (average score 4.75). Professionally occupied respondents may well have substituted workplace relationships and communities of interest for a geographical community of place. The estate may be regarded as a place 'to come home to' after work to relax. Thus, it becomes a place to live rather than a place to socialize and interact with neighbors.

Similar results were found in response to questions investigating whether residents regarded a *sense of community* on their estate as important (again on an ascending scale of 1 to 5). Members of the RC (average score 4.9) rated an estate sense of community significantly higher than did non-RC member residents (average score 3.3). Such results may be attributed to RC members' commitment and social networks gained through joining the association. It could also indicate that those residents who feel that a sense of community is important to them join the RC.

Women (average score 4) placed a higher degree of importance on a sense of community than did men (average score 2.8), while professionals' (average score 2.6) desire for a local sense of community was much lower than that of semi-professionals (3.7) and non-professionals (3.75). This may relate to the proportion of daily time spent on the estate.

In response to questions inquiring about *resident interaction* with neighbors, RC members were found to have a significantly higher number of neighboring relations than their non-RC member counterparts. For example, RC members appear to know more people by given name (a total of 207 people's names known) than do non-RC members (10 names known) and interact with more people socially within Livingston (49 people) than do non-RC members (4 people). Similarly, professionals living in Livingston tend to know far fewer people's given names (a total of 13) than do either semi-professionals (67) or non-professionals (122) and interact with far fewer local people socially (3 in total) compared with 19 for semi-professionals and 18 for non-professionals.

In summary, whereas Chavis and Wandersman's (1990) research omitted reporting analysis of independent variables, such as gender, occupation and length of residence, Windass's Livingston survey enables further insight. The Livingston findings identify strong relationships between residents' profile and sense of community. Residents are more likely to have a greater sense of community if they are female, a long-term resident, are employed in a non-professional occupation or are unwaged and belong to the Residents' Committee. In contrast, professionally occupied males are less likely to join the Residents' Committee, and give substantially less importance to belonging to a community of place.

Non-RC members painted a picture of individualism (privacy) and a sense of community explicitly *not* tied to place (their estate). Despite its design as a 'community lifestyle' estate, Livingston is not a geographical community of place for most residents. For some, 'community' and social capital have evolved, mainly through belonging to the Residents' Committee. Others are clearly not interested in belonging actively to a local community of place, presumably interacting more widely in various communities of interest.

In contrast, a study by Hillier, Tonts, Jones, Fisher, and Hugman (2001) of the low socio-economic residents of Midland/Midvale demonstrates strong evidence of a series of cohesive local communities. Midland/Midvale is located in the eastern suburbs of Perth. It is an area that formerly housed workers in the now defunct railway workshops and sale yards/abattoir complex. Many of the current residents are the families of workers retrenched from these industries who still live in the original housing constructed post-World War II for the industries.

The population structure is skewed towards a mature age profile with a high proportion of old seniors. The area has twice the proportion of seniors found in the Perth metropolitan area as a whole. Almost one third of households contain only one person, relating partly to the high proportion of seniors. Approximately 60% of one person households contain people aged 55 years and over, and 44% contain people aged 65 years and over.

Couples with children are the next most common household type, accounting for one quarter of households. Couples are less common than in other areas, while one parent families are much more common. The percentage of one-parent families in the area is almost twice that for the metropolitan area as a whole. Approximately one fifth of households contain one-parent families. Two thirds of the 3986 residents in the area are Australian born, of whom 345 (9% of the total) are Indigenous Australians.

The area has a majority of persons resident who are not in the labor force. This is partly, but not wholly, attributable to the high proportion of seniors. Unemployment is also higher than for the Perth metropolitan area. In 1996 unemployment was 17.3%, compared with 8.3% for the Perth metropolitan area. Unsurprisingly, household incomes are low. In 1996, over half of households had incomes under $500 per week.

Hillier, et al.'s (2001) research indicates the presence of strong community feelings in Midvale; both between the Indigenous population, and also between the non-Indigenous population across public/private tenures. The research suggests that social capital does exist in Midvale, although predominantly on an informal basis. There may not be overt official membership of clubs and associations, but there are certainly networks of collaboration and local volunteering to help friends and neighbors. Volunteering activities mentioned include: watching a neighbor's house or car while they are away, feeding neighbors' pets or watering indoor plants while they are away, giving people lifts to facilities and services, running errands/messages for less mobile people, acting as an emergency telephone service for people without access to phones as well as the odd emergency repair, and so on.

A sense of community appears to be strong on a block basis rather than an estate basis as a whole or a Midland/Midvale basis. It is within these block communities that virtually everyone knows everyone else on first name terms and is involved more or less with some sort of volunteering. As stated above, these communities of feeling cross tenure patterns. They tend to relate to length of time of neighboring, regardless of tenure.

The Perth findings related above resonate with those reported by Merry (1987) and Ross and Jang (2000) in which residents of working class neighborhoods tend to rely on informal social networks of personal relationships. In such communities, residents visit, help each other out, lend materials and so on and form mutually supportive social bonds which appear to be much stronger than those of the residents of a deliberately planned 'community' such as Livingston.

Community as Inclusion or Exclusion?

The WA concept of *Liveable Neighbourhoods* is based on the idea that a sense of community is associated with the symbolic interaction that occurs through people's use of the physical environment. As McMillan and Chavis (1986) suggest, common symbols (such as estate logos) may contribute to the membership component of a sense of community. Such 'territorial markers' and the creation of 'defensible space' (Newman, 1972), through potential street surveillance, may deter neighborhood blue-collar crime and/or enhance perceptions of safety. Chavis and Wandersman (1990, p. 58) wrote that "as residents feel safer and more secure ... they are likely to interact more with their neighbors, (and) feel a greater sense of community."

While community may be defined as a feeling of membership (McMillan & Chavis, 1986, p. 9), of inclusion, an 'us', there is always a 'them,' the excluded and alienated other (Suttles, 1972). In the political economy of uncertainty in which we now live (Harvey, 1989; Bauman, 1998), when "trend-setters in lifestyle are notable by their mobility ... seemingly free from the need to be anywhere in particular" (Healey, 2000, p. 55), when people's livelihoods "That rock on which all life projects and aspirations must rest to be feasible" have become "wobbly, erratic and unreliable" (Bauman, 1998, p. 51), an ambient fear steals in. For many, uncertainty does not foster a sense of community, but rather the opposite. Those with choice tend to move to places where "there are more 'people like us', not in the search for community, but in the search for security (of their house investment)" (Healey, 2000, p. 56; Lewis, 1999).

The City of Gosnells' safer community campaign made residents feel less safe than previously. By highlighting apparent problem areas in which crimes could be committed, local residents had a heightened perception of threats to their safety, some now seemingly living in fear and paranoia (Curtin University student survey, 2000). Respondents surveyed about a proposed public space in the area (Ellis Brook Green Link), replied that they would probably not use the space as they were concerned about its level of safety. Residents whose properties backed onto the space also expressed concerns about the potential for criminals to access their homes. (Similar side-effects were found by Hay (1995) in his work in Adelaide.) Far from fostering a sense of community and interactions, the program heightened the us and them feelings.

In Perth, groups of Aboriginal people who enjoy 'outdoor living' (but not the type of outdoor living as depicted by urban designers) have been progressively 'cleansed' from public parks near the city center -- from Russell Square, Wellington Square, and East Perth -- as these areas have been regenerated and gentrified into upper class residential areas of 'people like us'. Aboriginal people, the Other, them, not 'us,' are forced to locate well away from these "purified communities" (Morgan, 1994, p. 84), out of sight of the incoming residents. Bauman writes, ironically in the case of Perth, that agencies of governance and developers "cannot honestly promise their citizens a secure existence and a certain future, but they may for a time unload at least part of the accumulated anxiety, and even profit from it ... by demonstrating their energy and determination in the war against ... alien gate-crashers who have intruded into once clean and quiet, orderly and familiar, native backyards" (1998, pp. 63-64). The irony in Perth is that it is we, Western Australians, planners, and developers, who have intruded into the 'native backyards' of Aboriginal people, rather than the other way round.

Perth is residentially segregated by lifestyle. It is a "multiplex city" (Healey, 2000) where neighbors often have very different life patterns and little desire for contact with each other. As such, community affirms itself by exclusion, defining itself by what it refuses to admit rather than by a conscious knowledge of what it includes (Bourke, 1998). The more overwhelming a sense of insecurity (a mixture of social and economic uncertainty), the more intense grows a 'parochial spirit' (Bauman, 1998, p. 64). This parochial spirit seeks reassurance by demanding the 'taming' of the other, to secure certitude of something. Focus on creation of a sense of community can thus "breed the worst kind of social exclusion and cultural elitism" (Talen, 2000, p. 178).

Boundaries are important (McMillan, 1996; McMillan & Chavis, 1986). People need boundaries to protect against perceived threat, to make emotional safety possible and to set up the barriers between 'us' and 'them.' The sight of the abject 'other' (e.g., the poor, people of color, gays and lesbians) 'too close for comfort' (Young, 1990, p. 144), via the TV screen, local newspaper, and so on, leads the more wealthy to erect exclusionary boundaries around themselves and their loved ones (family and property).

Boundaries may be legislative, such as law and order mechanisms, covenants, etc, or physical, such as walls, gates, electronic surveillance, etc, aimed at excluding or excising the other from the community (Davis, 1992, 1998; Hillier & McManus, 1994). As Zygmunt Bauman writes, concern is "not about making the plight of the poor easier, but about getting rid of the poor" (1998, p. 56).

Community as Diversity or Homogeneity?

One of the key elements of community in WA is regarded as being diversity: "a variety of lot sizes and housing types to cater for the diverse need of the community" (WAPC, 1997a, p. 2). Recommendations are made to "create a cross-section of society through different apartment sizes, house sizes and units" (Day, 1999, pp. 33-34). Day suggests that residential "segregation" by lifestyle and socio-economic demographics is undesirable and "can be addressed by urban design principles, and help foster a more diverse community." He continues: "the interaction of people with people from other walks of life is achievable through urban design elements" (1999, p. 35). As Calthorpe and Fulton (2001) point out, social mix involves not simply integrating middle class residents into working class neighborhoods, but also including more low-income housing in the rich suburbs.

These are worthy sentiments, reminiscent of the social balance objectives of the British new town planners. Although Calthorpe and Fulton recognize that social mix is "very frightening to many communities" (2001, p. 281) and that people with the ability to choose tend to live among others of, perceived, similar lifestyle and socio-economic status, the authors blame a lack of social mix not on resident preference, but on an absence of political will.

Evidence from residential surveys in the British new towns reveals that people preferred to live in homogeneous neighborhoods among 'people who live in houses like ours' and 'people like us' for a variety of reasons, ranging from emotional comfort to maintenance of property values. Even with a mix of housing types there still tended to be a distillation of residents along lines of socio-economic status (surveys reported in Thorns, 1976, pp. 86-87). As Thorns concludes, "the planners have not succeeded in fulfilling their declared objectives principally because the individuals who migrated to the new towns have not shared their conception of what the new community should look like and be" (1976, p. 89).

Young also critiques objectives of designed social balance or mix. She suggests that "all too often ... the socially dominant group sets the terms of integration to which the formerly segregated groups must conform" (1999, p. 244) and questions whether people should feel pressured to mix with strangers who are likely to be distant if not disrespectful.

Even McMillan admits that his earlier theorizing was mistaken when he "insisted that theory had to support the creation of a diverse community" (1996, p. 320). He now "appreciate(s) the search for similarities" (1996, p. 320), citing several other empirical studies which confirm that perceived homogeneity rather than diversity stimulates group interaction. Examples from Perth would appear to corroborate the above. The recent wave of development of New Urbanist inspired 'urban villages' in the Perth metropolitan area which purport to sell a 'lifestyle' appears to have attracted population homogeneity rather than diversity.

East Perth and Eastern Horizons -- Impossible Triangles?

In East Perth (an inner urban, brownfield regeneration development), a "model dynamic community" (EPRA, 1992) of ultimately 3,900 people, the residential population is comprised of largely white, middle-class, young professionals looking to live in a prestigious suburb close to the CBD. The predominant uses of the site, apart from residential, will be art galleries, cafes, an hotel, high-technology offices, and retail facilities. Although some 1,000 units of 'affordable housing' were proposed in the original, Federal government-funded Building Better Cities scheme, a change of government and a redesign of the project, together with the deliberate excision of the State public housing agency, Homeswest (now the Ministry of Housing), has drastically reduced the affordable housing component. Prices currently ranging from c$200,000 to over $1 million are unaffordable for the majority of society.

East Perth has proved attractive to the relatively wealthy and footloose housing class of singles and DINKS (double income, not kids). It is an exclusive suburb, "where you are as welcome as your money" (Byrne, 2000, p. 18). Byrne's analysis of the imagery utilized in marketing East Perth is revealing. The EPRA brochure represents the new Belvidere development as being "truly one of Perth's finest addresses. Superb, multi-level homes nestle amongst beautiful, long-established trees and a true sense of community is already flourishing amongst the locals on the hill" (undated). Are the rich, 'nestled' in their evocative Vanguard or Victory Terrace apartments, really choosing 'community' or the marketed image of community? Does the beautiful and conforming necessarily engender the good?

Only some five or so years ago, however, Belvidere was an old industrial area, described by Byrne as "characterised by stained, red-brick buildings, triangular-shaped grey, asbestos roofs, wild oats, cracked bitumen paving and discarded paint cans. The 'locals on the hill' were not retired empty nesters or affluent yuppies, but were instead an eclectic mix of the elderly, truant school-children, the unemployed, youth, Aboriginal people, migrants, low-income earners and long-dead pioneers" (2000, p. 18). What is really telling though, is not what the newly created Belvidere community includes, but what it excludes. Where are the Aboriginals now? They are safely relegated to the domain of public art adorning the sewage works. Where are the unemployed, the low-income earners and so on? The only 'locals' who remain from this list are the pioneers in their cemetery homes.

The transformation of Belvidere into an "exclusionary totalising vision" (al-Hindi & Staddon, 1997, p. 350) is underwritten by an explicit marketing text that has defined a commodity laden with mythical content. The advertizing messages and architectural form represent cultural signs offering the initiated a "pure vision of sophistication and opulence" symbolized by "gourmet granite kitchens" (advertizement hoarding, 2000), a far cry from the granite kitchens of the original Indigenous inhabitants of the area.

East Perth has become the archetypal "private neighborhood" (Merry, 1987) characterized by residents' alikeness rather than cohesion and a sense of belonging which comes from a stable social identity rather than stable social relationships; where residents help each other by staying away from each other; where peace and quiet are achieved through privacy and avoidance rather than intimacy. Walking through East Perth streets of a weekend, it would appear that nobody lives there. Few or no residents are visible on their balconies or 'passing the time' with neighbors.

Giving identity to East Perth is a new 'landmark' sculpture installed at a major traffic junction within the project area. The sculpture is called "The Impossible Triangle" (see Figure 1). Reproduced on the cover of the EPRA newsletter, *The Easterly*, the caption beneath the photograph reads: "The Impossible Triangle forms the illusion of a perfect triangle only from the privileged viewpoint" (EPRA, 1999, cover). As Byrne (2000, p. 17) suggests, the impossible triangle is a good metaphor for the East Perth project; "it requires a privileged viewpoint to bring together the illusion of something that actually exists rather than it being just a trick -- an illusion. If one is outside that privileged viewpoint, the illusion quickly deteriorates into a crazy jumble of odd constructs and empty promises."

Who speaks for the poor in such 'communities' (see, Hillier & van Looij, 1997)? This is a moot point. On viewing the original New Urbanist development at Seaside in Florida, Scully remarked: "so the rich, who can choose, choose community, or at least its image. How much more must the poor ... want community? If Seaside and the others cannot in the end offer viable models for that, they will remain entirely beautiful but rather sad" (1994, p. 230).

Frug (1997, p. 56) comments that New Urbanist planners are in a bind: "they are reluctant to insist on building communities with a genuinely diverse population because they fear that to do so would threaten their market. Yet they are reluctant not to insist on diversity because failure to do so would undermine the value of what they are doing." What transpires is little more than a "repackaged version of the Garden City" priced effectively for the high-end residential market as Audirac, Shermyen, and Smith (1990, p. 473) and Audirac (1992) predicted.

Figure 1. East Perth's Impossible Triangle, Open and Closed Views

Towards the other end of the residential spectrum, the WA Department of Housing and Works' (DHW) New Living program seeks to regenerate its large public housing estates such as at Midland/Midvale; its Eastern Horizons project. One of the program objectives is to reduce the proportion of DHW tenants from almost 70% of the total resident population in some instances, to a figure generally around 12%[viii]. Existing residents are offered opportunities to purchase their homes (which few can afford), move to a new DHW property elsewhere or to remain on the estate.

Research findings from focus groups conducted with residents of Midland/Midvale (Hillier, et al., 2001) reveal anecdotes about public sector tenants who had chosen to move from Midvale, ending up in either Ellenbrook (some 15km to the north-east), in Neerabup (some 30km to the northwest), or in Northam (some 100km to the east). Other stories emerged of elderly widows in public housing accommodation being requested to move to a single bedroom unit, and being unable to take all of their "treasures" with them due to lack of space in their new home. As these residents are elderly, have no car and do not drive, their tales of isolation and depression are probably symptomatic of a larger problem.

Indigenous families appear to bear the brunt of relocation. Some public tenants are being relocated to Northam, 100km distant. Many are unhappy in their relocated homes and return to the Midland area, to a future of homelessness, overcrowding, and continuing relocation. Indigenous social capital is on the verge of collapsing.

Research from both Australia and overseas (see, for example, Taylor, 1995; Hastings, et al., 1996) has indicated that whilst perhaps not overtly expressed in resident associations, there is, nevertheless, a strong sense of community on public housing estates. Informal or 'background' community networks provide support for shopping, child- and elderly dependant-minding activities, and so on. It may in fact be that planners are actually destroying stronger communities than their regeneration attempts will 'create' on these regenerated estates. Much research remains to be done around this issue.

From the brief examples described above, albeit not an exhaustive list of either new suburban developments or public estate regeneration schemes, it would appear that the planners have been strongly committed to certain views as regards the nature of urban society of 'community' that should be produced. In the new urban villages, such as East Perth, residents appear not to share ideals of social balance and intermixing with those 'from other walks of life.' The urban villages are, thus, in danger of becoming essentially a collection of individuals, more carefully planned for than in other developments, but by no means an interactive 'community;' beautiful, but rather sad.

CONCLUSIONS

Recent empirical research demonstrates a distinct class-based difference with regard to both a sense of community and social capital. In what could be described in Australian terms as 'battler' neighborhoods, where residents of low socio-economic status struggle against the poverty trap, often on public housing estates, or where there is a tenure mix of long-term private and public renting and owner-occupation of old housing stock, there is evidence of a strong sense of community. This community could be primarily one of interest (survival or 'getting by') or one of place, or coincidentally of both. Social capital is also strong. Whilst residents may have little money to spare for club or association membership payments, social capital is characterized by informal structures of voluntarism, reciprocity and trust.

In more middle-class neighborhoods, typically owner-occupied residential estates and suburbs, people living adjacent may have very little contact with each other and often have very different life patterns (Healey, 2000; Windass, 2000). Those with an ability to choose do so to be in a local area where the other residents are perceived as being 'like us.' People belong to multiple communities, primarily of interest, rather than of geographical location. Such communities are exclusionary; a "war declared on strangers" (Bauman, 1995, p. 128), where, entry statements, gates, high walls and surveillance cameras say "Keep Out" as much as "Welcome Home." In such a world we find *The West Australian*'s depiction of 'Neighbour of the Year' (see Figure 2).

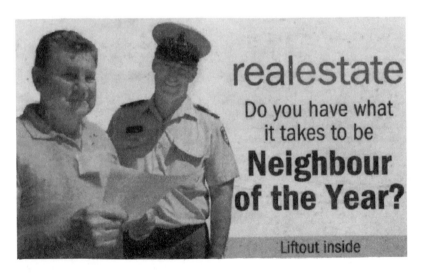

Figure 2. Neighbour of the Year (Photograph Courtesy of Western Australian Newspapers)

Ephemeral communities of place may establish in response to perceived threats to residential 'amenity', mainly property values. Is community, then, primarily an economic phenomenon? Local community movements tend to be reactive, defensive and conservative -- the classic NIMBY, seeking to export or exclude the perceived 'bads' of urban life while fencing in the 'goods.' These communities are tenuous, based on emotion, and the key emotion is fear. Such a community will tend to remain endemically precarious and, hence, bellicose and intolerant, neurotic about security, and paranoid about the hostility and ill-intentions of 'others.'

I believe that planners in WA need to be on guard against a potential reification of community as an entity independent of its components; an impersonal object of urban design rather than of people. The current planning philosophy appears spatially deterministic: to hold that the application of the *Liveable Neighbourhoods* Initiative in WA will produce a desired social product. It encourages the idea of a model solution, but as Nicholson (1992, p. 226) points out, "it is an unfortunate fact that once new ideas have been adopted and established, planners and architects often proceed to apply them rigidly, whether to a greenfield site or to a city centre" -- and model solutions beget model problems.

Are we in the process of manufacturing and selling ersatz communities; the construction of a believable symbol of community where no community exists? Are we "trading the humanity and richness of a living city for a conceptual simplicity which benefits only the designers, planners, administrators and developers" (Thorns, 1976, p. 89)? Are attempts to 'create community' a return to spatial environmental determinism, some 50 or so years after it was discredited and discarded? As MacCannell (1992, p. 89) has warned, "the complexity of this feat of social engineering ... should not be underestimated, nor should the drive to accomplish this feat be underestimated."

Community is effectively not a product that can be 'created' through urban design and architecture alone. It is a process that is, effectively, intangible -- a network of social relations and understandings. It is a connectedness between people who have more in common than a fear of the other translated into electronic surveillance, burglar alarms, and security patrols. Communities are social rather than physical constructs and "social networks which may exist in any particular locality are not amenable to 'creation' through public policy action" (Evans, 1994, p. 108).

This chapter has shown that planners and local residents often dwell in different realms; they speak past rather than with each other. For planners, 'community' stands for a geographical congregation of diverse, yet solitary residents; for neighbors' helping hands; for friendly pedestrian passers-by. For many property-owning residents of inner and middle suburbia, however, increased densities and social mix threaten their amenity, their property values and everything they have grown to love and cherish (Lewis, 1999; Bauman, 2000).

It is probably more useful for urban planners to understand the choices which people make to sustain or challenge specific patterns of relationships than to argue about the semantics of what are effectively multiple languages of 'community' (Morris, 1996). The relations between space, place, culture and identity are complex and multidirectional. One person's sense of neighborly community may well be another's invasion of privacy depending on their interpretation of the situation. Planners should not simply presume socio-environmental determinism between urban form and social behavior. Nor should they seek to "educate" (Calthorpe & Fulton, 2001) ignorant citizens in what is deemed to be good for them by all-knowing experts. Individuals are not passive recipients of community structures; they are active agents in their own lives.

NOTES

[i] My thanks to Glen Windass for allowing me to use the fruits of his unpublished research efforts in Livingston, to Jason Byrne for access to his research data from East Perth, and to an anonymous referee for their generous and valuable comments and guidance.

[ii] See also Proshansky Fabian, & Kaminoff (1983) for detailed discussion of place-identity.

[iii] In the USA, however, neighbourhood units did not traditionally aim at social integration. The 'sense of community' referred to in Clarence Perry's (1929) conception was based on a homogeneous social class, as were the neighbourhoods of the American New Towns. It was only after the 1970 Urban Growth and New Community Development Act that new towns were explicitly expected to achieve socioeconomic integration (Audirac & Shermyen, 1994).

[iv] It should be noted that there is a fundamental difference between resident interaction and a sense of community (see Talen, 2000).

[v] I am grateful to an anonymous referee who confirmed my personal view of Ellenbrook as "touted as an example of New Urbanism. It isn't. Those guidelines might apply to any planned suburban sprawl subdivision".

[vi] E.g., by substituting 'estate' for 'block' as in Chavis and Wandersman's original instrument.

[vii] Parry and Strommen (200, p. 21) indicate a range of target reductions in public housing presence from 68% to 20% (Karawara), 53% to 12% (Lockridge), 32% to 12% (Coolbellup) and 10.3% to 5.7% (Midland-Midvale).

REFERENCES

Al-Hindi, K. F., & Staddon, C. (1997). The hidden histories and geographies of neotraditional town planning: The case of Seaside, Florida. *Environment & Planning D, Society and Space, 15,* 349-372.

Altman I. (1975). *The environment & social behaviour: Privacy, personal space, territory, and crowding.* Monterey, CA: Brooks/Cole.

Audirac, I., Shermyen, A., & Smith, M. (1990). Ideal urban form and visions of the good life. *Journal of the American Planning Association, 56,* 470-482.

Audirac, I. (1992). Is the development debate of the 1990s to resonate as a fanfare for community? *Journal of the American Planning Association, 58,* 514-516.

Audirac, I., & Shermyen, A. (1994). An evaluation of neotraditional design's social prescription: Postmodern placebo or remedy for suburban malaise? *Journal of Planning Education and Research, 13,* 161-173.

Baum, A., & Valins, S. (1979). Architectural mediation of residential density and control: Crowding and the regulation of social contact. In Berkowitz L. (Ed.), *Advances in Experimental Social Psychology*, Vol. 12, (pp. 131-175). New York: Academic Press.

Bauman Z. 1995 *Life in fragments.*, Oxford, UK: Blackwell.

Bauman, Z. (1998). The poor – and the rest of us. *Arena Journal*, no. 12, 43-66.

Bauman, Z. (2000). What it means 'to be excluded': Living to stay apart – or together? In Askonas, P., and Stewart, A. (Eds), *Social inclusion,*(pp. 73 –88). Basingstoke, UK: Macmillan.

Bauman, Z. (2001). *Community.* Cambridge, UK: Polity Press.

Bentley, I., Alcock A., Murrain P., McGlynn S., & Smith G. 1985 *Responsive environments.* Oxford, UK: Butterworth.

Bourke, S. (1998). George Eliot: Community ends. *Australasian Victorian Studies Journal*, 4.

Byrne, J. (2000). *Green around the gills: Environmental justice and the inner city.* Baltimore, MD: Institute for Policy Studies, Johns Hopkins University.

Calthorpe, P. (1993). *The next American metropolis.* New York: Princeton University Press.

Calthorpe, P., & Fulton, W. (2001). *The regional city: Planning for the end of sprawl.* Washington, DC: Island Press.

Chavis, D., & Wandersman, A. (1990). Sense of community in the urban environment: A catalyst for participation and community development. *American Journal of Community Psychology, 18,* 55-67.

Chavis, D., & Newbrough, J. (1986). The meaning of 'community' in community psychology. *Journal of Community Psychology, 14,* 335-340.

Congress for the New Urbanism. (1998) *Charter of the New Urbanism.* Website [http://www.cnu.org].

Cox, E. (1995). *A truly civil society.* Sydney, Australia: ABC Books.

Davis, M. (1992). *City of quartz.* New York: Vintage Books.

Davis, M. (1998). *Ecology of fear.* New York: Metropolitan Books.

Day, S. (1999). *Creation of community through urban design.* Unpublished Planning Report, Department of Urban & Regional Planning, Curtin University, Perth, Australia.

Dean, J., & Hastings, A. (2000). *Challenging images: Housing estates, stigma and regeneration.* Bristol, UK: Policy Press.

Doolittle, R., & MacDonald, D. (1978). Communication and a sense of community in a metropolitan neighborhood: A factor analytic examination. *Communication Quarterly, 26,* 2-7.

Duany, A., & Plater-Zyberk, E. (1992). The second coming of the American small town. *Wilson Quarterly, 16,* 19-50.

Duany, A., & Plater-Zyberk, E. (1994). The neighborhood, the district and the corridor. In Katz, P. (Ed.), *The New Urbanism: toward an architecture of community* (pp. xvii-xx). New York: McGraw Hill.

East Perth Redevelopment Authority. (1992). *East Perth.* Perth, Western Australia: EPRA.

East Perth Redevelopment Authority. (1999). *The Easterly,* December.

Ebbesen, E., Kjos, F., & Sullivan, W. (1976) Spatial ecology: Its effects on the choice of friends and enemies. *Journal of Experimental Social Psychology, 12,* 505-518.

Ellenbrook Joint Venture. (1994). *Ellenbrook Community Bulletin,* Autumn.

Ellenbrook Management Propriety Ltd. (2001). *Morgan Fields Covenants and Building Conditions.* Perth, Western Australia: EMPL.

Ellenbrook Management Propriety Ltd. (2001). *Ellenbrook Community,* Autumn. Perth, Western Australia: EMPL.

Evans, B. (1994). Planning sustainability and the chimera of community. *Town & Country Planning, 63(4),* 108.

Feldman, R. (1990). Settlement-identity: Psychological bonds with home places in a mobile society. *Environment & Behaviour, 2,* 183-229.

Feldman, R. (1996). Constancy and change in attachments to types of settlements. *Environment & Behaviour, 28*, 419-445.

Festinger, L., Schacter, S., & Back, K. (1950). *Social pressure informal group.* New York: Holt, Rinehart & Winston.

Fishman, R. (1982). *Urban Utopias in the Twentieth Century.* Cambridge, MA: MIT Press,.

Frug, G. (1997). New urbanism or new suburbanism? *Harvard Design Magazine,* Winter/Spring, 56.

Harvey, D. (1989). *The condition of postmodernity.* Oxford, UK: Blackwell.

Hastings, A., McArthur, A., & McGregor, A. (1996). *Less than equal? Community organisations and estate regeneration partnerships.* Bristol, UK: The Policy Press.

Hay, I. (1995). The strange case of Dr Jekyll in Hyde Park. Fear, media and the conduct of an emancipatory geography. *Australian Geographical Studies, 33*, 257-271.

Healey, P. (2000). Connected cities. *Town & Country Planning,* February: 55-57.

Hillier, J., & McManus, P. (1994). Pull up the drawbridge: Fortress mentality in the suburbs. In Gibson, K., & Watson, S. (Eds), *Metropolis now* (pp. 91-101). Sydney, Australia: Pluto Press.

Hillier, J., & van Looij, T. (1997) Who speaks for the poor? *International Planning Studies, 2(1),* 7-26.

Hillier, J., Tonts M., Jones R., Fisher C., & Hugman, R. (2001) *Strengthening communities: The contribution of housing policy and planning.* Work in Progress Paper, AHURI, Melbourne.

Hugman, R., & Sotiri, M. (2000). *Housing, social capital & stronger communities* AHURI Positioning Paper, Curtin University, Perth.

Katz, P. (ed). (1994). *The New Urbanism: Toward an architecture of community.* New York: McGraw Hill.

Kunstler, J. (1996). *Home from nowhere.* New York: Simon and Schuster.

Kuo, F., Sullivan, W., Coley, R., & Brunson, L. (1998). Fertile ground for community: Inner-city neighbourhood common spaces. *American Journal of Community Psychology, 26*, 823-851.

Lewis, M. (1999). *Suburban backlash.* Melbourne, Australia: Bloomings Books.

Lieven, A. (1999). Tale of two cities. *American Prospect,* August/September, 30-34.

Lynch, K. (1960). *The image of the city.* Cambridge, MA: MIT Press.

Lynch, K. (1981). *A theory of good city form.* Cambridge, MA: MIT Press.

MacCallum, D. (1999) *Sense of place in a modern town centre: Community perceptions in Karratha.* Report for Postgraduate Diploma in Urban & Regional Planning, Department of Urban & Regional Planning, Curtin University, Perth. (unpubd)

MacCannell, D. (1992). *Empty meeting grounds.* London, UK: Routledge.

McMillan, D., & Chavis, D. (1986). Sense of community: A definition and theory. *Journal of Community Psychology, 14*, 6-23.

McMillan, D. (1996). Sense of community. *Journal of Community Psychology, 24*, 315-325.

Meppem, T. (1999). *Strategic policy development for public sector organisations: A communicative framework for sustainable regional development planning* Unpublished PhD thesis, University of New England, Armidale, Australia.

Merry, S. (1987). Crowding, conflict, and neighborhood regulation. In Altman, I., and Wandersman, A. (Eds), *Neighborhood and community environments,* (pp. 35-68). New York: Plenum Press.

Morgan, G. (1994). Acts of enclosure: Crime and defensible space in contemporary cities. In Gibson, K., and Watson, S. (Eds), *Metropolis now,* (pp. 78 –90). Sydney, Australia: Pluto Press.

Morris, E. (1996). Community in theory and practice: A framework for intellectual renewal. *Journal of Planning Literature, 11*, 127-149.

Newman, O. (1972). *Defensible space.* New York: Macmillan.

Nicholson, G. (1992). The rebirth of community planning. In Thornley, A. (Ed.), *The crisis of London.* London, UK: Routledge.

Parry, L., & Strommen, S. (2001). *New living report: An assessment of impacts on tenants and the community in the urban renewal of Lockridge and Langford, Western Australia.* Unpublished report, Swinburne University, Melbourne, Australia.

Parsons, T. (1966). The principal structures of community. In Warren, R. (ed.), *Perspectives on the American community.* New York: Rand McNally.

Proshansky, H., Fabian, A., & Kaminoff, R. (1983). Place-identity: Physical world socialization of the self. *Journal of Environmental Psychology, 3,* 57-83.

Putnam, D. (1993). *Making democracy work.* Princeton, NJ: Princeton University Press.

Putnam, D. (1994). Bowling alone: America's declining social capital. *Journal of Democracy, 6(1),* 65-78.

Putnam, D. (1996). The strange disappearance of civic America. *American Prospect,* Winter, 34-48.

Putnam, D. (2000) *Bowling Alone: The collapse and revival of American community.* New York: Simon & Schuster.

Reynolds, H., & Solomon, P. (1998). *The property development process: Western Australia.* Perth, Western Australia: Victor Press.

Rivlin, L. (1987). The neighborhood, personal identity, and group affiliations. In Altman, I., and Wandersman, A. (Eds.), *Neighborhood and community environment,* (pp. 1–34). New York: Plenum Press.

Ross, C., & Jang, S. J. (2000). Neighborhood disorder, fear and mistrust: The buffering role of social ties with neighbours. *American Journal of Community Psychology, 28,* 401-420.

Scully, V. (1994). The architecture of community. In Katz, P. (Ed.), *The New Urbanism: Toward an architecture of community,* (pp. 221-230). New York: McGraw Hill.

Suttles, G. (1972). *The social construction of communities.* Chicago: University of Chicago Press.

Talen, E. (2000). The problem with community in planning. *Journal of Planning Literature, 15,* 171-183.

Taylor, M. (1995). *Unleashing the potential: Bringing residents to the centre of estate regeneration.* York, UK: Joseph Rowntree Foundation.

Thorns, D. (1976). *The quest for community.* London, UK: Allen & Unwin.

Tönnies, F. (1955). *Community & society.* New York: Harper.

Urban Land Institute. (1968). *The community builders handbook.* Washington, DC: Urban Land Institute.

Western Australian Planning Commission. (1995). *State planning strategy, discussion paper, The community.* Perth, Western Australia: WAPC.

Western Australian Planning Commission. (1997a). *Liveable neighbourhoods: Community design code,* summary booklet. Perth, Western Australia: WAPC.

Western Australian Planning Commission. (1997b). *Liveable neighbourhoods: Community design code.* Perth, Western Australia: WAPC.

Western Australian Planning Commission. (2000). *Liveable neighbourhoods, (2nd Edition).* Perth, Western Australia: WAPC.

Wiesenfeld, E. (1996). The concept of 'we': A community social psychology myth? *Journal of Community Psychology, 24,* 337-345.

Windass, G. (2000). *Planning for community: Can we create community?* Unpublished Honours thesis, Department of Urban & Regional Planning, Curtin University, Perth.

Winter, I. (Ed.) (2000). *Social Capital.* Melbourne, Australia: Institute of Family Studies.

Young, I. M. (1990). *Justice and the politics of difference.* Princeton, NJ: Princeton University Press.

Young, I. M. (1999). Residential segregation and differentiated citizenship. *Citizenship Studies, 3,* 237-252.

Chapter 4

COMMUNITY, SENSE OF COMMUNITY, AND NETWORKS

Joseph Hughey
University of Missouri – Kansas City

Paul W. Speer
Vanderbilt University

INTRODUCTION

In one of the earliest and most often referenced writings on sense of community, Seymour Sarason noted the inherent difficulty of linking the concepts of community and psychology (Sarason, 1974). The community concept brought with it a focus on extra-individual phenomena, such as geographic place, institutional dynamics, and power. The psychological orientation was believed to narrow focus to individual experience. In the 25 plus years following Sarason's observations, psychologists have developed a number of models of sense of community, and we have devised various instruments for the measurement of psychological sense of community. This work has deepened understanding of the psychology of community phenomena such as belonging and mutual commitment. However, this focus on psychological experience has been achieved at the cost of largely ignoring the role of community and social phenomena that strongly influence individual and group experience of community. This observation is not new. It was made by Dunham in a 1986 critique of research on psychological sense of community, concluding that we had "shot wide of the mark" by not incorporating aspects of community theory into our analyses (Dunham, 1986, p. 400). Similarly, Wiesenfeld (1996, p. 339) noted that the "homogeneous quality of community" had been overemphasized.

Our premise is that the embrace of interpersonal bonding and individualistic conceptions of community has come at the expense of adopting the prescribed ecological orientation to community (Trickett, 1984), one that directs our view to gaps and boundaries between groups and systems. A sharper focus on bridging gaps and spanning extra-individual boundaries can enhance the sense of community concept.

In this chapter, we examine concepts from community theory and social network analysis that can inform and enrich sense of community. Specifically, we explore a conceptualization of community, drawn from outside psychology, which can anchor sense of community in community theory. Next, concepts from social network analysis are examined as conceptual tools for bridging gaps and spanning boundaries. We close with an illustration of how relationships between community systems and boundary spanning were used, in one community in the USA, to address an unjust configuration of institutional relations.

CONCEPTUALIZATION OF COMMUNITY

The individual experience of community takes root in contexts of higher-level social phenomena (Sarason, 1974). Sarason anticipated the difficulty of understanding these phenomena: "these make a set of related issues no less difficult to study and comprehend than the nature of the atom or the working of the human body" (p. 131). Our view is that conceptualization of community must begin by acknowledging the challenging reality of conflict in communities. Importantly, conflict, which arises in part due to competing interests between extra-individual units, is endemic to community phenomena. Sociologists also struggle with the concept of community, often focusing on social level processes involving discordant interests. Integration of sociological and psychological perspectives holds the potential to improve our understanding of sense of community. Our concern with the potential value of interdisciplinary integration stems in part from a growing preoccupation with integration in the so-called natural sciences (e.g., Lewin & Regine, 2000) and partly from a commitment to change beyond the individual level of analysis. More than a few community psychologists have made the argument to utilize concepts from other disciplines (Maton, 2000; Rappaport, 1977; Sarason, 1976). Toward that end, we summarize a sociological framework for understanding community life.

In a chapter in Suttles's book, *The Social Construction of Communities*, Hunter and Suttles (1972), describe a four level framework of community differentiation. Three levels are germane to sense of community. The first level, "Face Block" is similar in geographic scope to the street blocks studied in environmental psychology (Taylor, 1997). Face blocks represent units that have meaning for residents based on face-to-face encounters, protection of children, and the potential of blocks to enter debates beyond their physical boundaries. A second level, "Defended

Neighborhood," is geographically larger than face blocks and contains some breadth of institutional presence, that is, commercial, religious, service institutions. Hunter and Suttles imply that sense of community in the defended neighborhood arises as much from conflict between defended neighborhoods as from a sense of belongingness within, "It exists, then, within a structure of parallel solidarities which stand in mutual opposition" (p. 58). This conceptualization of community highlights the often contentious nature of community life.

A third level, the "Community of Limited Liability" has the potential to be a rich source for understanding extra-individual community dynamics within which sense of community can unfold. Communities of limited liability are distinguished by three features. First, they are circumscribed in name and geographic boundaries by external entities such as commercial enterprises or governments. Hunter and Suttles (1972) assert, and we concur, the regular practice is for 'communities' to be delineated, if not wholly, then in large measure by outside institutional interests, for example, by governments, administrative units, foundations, and corporations. These entities subsequently constrain the flow of resources to communities with enormous implications for well-being. In one example we will explore later, the assignment of police protection and recreation opportunities for youth are largely constrained by these institutions. Resource control may be obscured, and manifestation of control nuanced, but external control is nevertheless real. As a result, issues of control and resource availability become essential features of how community life unfolds for individuals and groups. A second applicable characteristic of communities of limited liability is that individuals simultaneously and voluntarily "belong" to more than one such community, which strongly implies fragmentation of allegiance. This means the instrumental and emotional interests of individuals and groups are not wholly satisfied within one community. Necessity and choice propel us to navigate multiple communities, thereby establishing bonds that present conflicting demands -- a point also made by Trickett (1984). Community change, then, depends on patterns of regular and episodic transaction within and between communities of limited liability that entail conflict and temporary alliances. Hunter and Suttles's framework implies that sense of community must grapple with issues such as cohesion versus conflict, relationship development, and conflicting allegiances between groups.

Predominant approaches to sense of community emphasize social attachment and solidarity (Hill, 1996; McMillan & Chavis, 1986). Clearly, emotional connection, membership, use of shared symbols, and a common identity can be used to characterize and promote productive relationships in some community contexts. The value of this form of community experience is great. Nevertheless, the incomplete image of community conveyed by this approach is apparent when viewed from Hunter and Suttles's (1972) framework. The reality of conflicting interests in community cannot be ignored; they naturally manifest within communities, and interests routinely clash between communities, too. Take, for instance, the example cited by Heller (1989). He described the replacement of public transportation by the automobile thusly, "The trolley lines were bought by companies established by the giant oil companies and automobile corporations who then proceeded to dismantle their major sources of competition" (p. 5). The disruption of community and cementing of disadvantage these events unleashed, in at least the USA, have had far reaching negative consequences for generations.

Accommodating the cohesive elements of sense of community to the reality of boundaries and tension between groups can strengthen the sense of community concept. Regardless of whether a given community is defined geographically or relationally (Heller, 1989), we contend that sense of community can be strengthened by focusing on processes that deal with diverse internal differences in a way that has genuine potential to move external forces. In her important article, Wiesenfeld (1996) reinforces this point:

> How then can the redemption of minorities vis-à-vis the majority be reconciled with the fact that, just as there is diversity within the majority, diversity is also present within the minorities, and consensus or equilibrium is not necessarily the basis for growth, transformation, empowerment, and consciousness raising? The aim of this aspect of community psychology should be to acknowledge differences and polarities and put them to good use within the community. The alternative is to ignore them and thereby recreate the pattern in which holders of power have always ignored the voices of the powerless (p 343).

This agenda is deeply challenging. Part of what Wiesenfeld is saying is that we cannot expect individuals, or communities for that matter, to abandon their self-interest. Moreover, processes that promote homogeneity should not be preferred at the expense of the often more difficult path of intentionally developing solidarity that leads to collective action, a path more likely to lead to structural change and deeper sense of community. There is some literature suggesting that an over-reliance on cohesion that demands conformity and stifles dissent can have negative consequences (Frantz & Collins, 1999; Ross, 2000.) By collective action we do not mean conflict for conflict's sake but conflict in the service of agendas that stimulate community change to benefit the common good. This is a difficult route to follow; there is no point-by-point roadmap. But the direction appears correct and necessary. Newbrough (1992, p. 19) insightfully described the challenge as trying to be "psychology and community at the same time."

Community theory such as Hunter and Suttles (1972) provides a foundation for understanding the community context, but important questions remain. How can this expanded sense of community be formed, and what tools can be employed to help communities navigate shifting allegiances? Recent work on social networks provides direction. Although the backdrop of some recent work on social networks is the construct of social capital, the lessons are equally applicable to sense of community. Our purpose is not to sort out the relationship between social capital (Coleman, 1988; Putnam, Leonardi, & Nanetti, 1993) and sense of community; others have begun that task (e.g., Perkins, Fisher, Butterworth, & Hughey, 2000). Rather, we explore the value of network concepts to sense of community, and we apply social network concepts.

SENSE OF COMMUNITY AND SOCIAL NETWORKS

In a thorough and insightful review of social capital and networks, Burt (2000) advises researchers to turn their sights to social network processes responsible for formation of social capital. The community psychology concept closest to social capital is sense of community, and there was some early reasoning about the role of networks in sense of community. Burt's study of network processes is reminiscent of the way Sarason described the value of networks to sense of community. In an article most often noted for its call for divorce from clinical psychology, Sarason argued for a focus on the place of individuals in social networks, and he linked the network concept to sense of community (Sarason, 1976). He noted the potential value of networks lay more in "connections potentially available to us" (p. 322) than in our current connections. Importantly, this recommends expansion of an individual's base of relationships and strongly implies that heterogeneity in relationships is at least as important as cohesion. While strong interpersonal connections are surely important resources, the breadth of an individual's relational base enables one to tap a greater variety of resources for adaptation. Viewed from this perspective the sense of community concept refers to relationships we *might* have as much as those we already have and rely on. In endorsing the ecological orientation to community, Sarason highlighted the importance of networks,

> More correctly, the number of networks you can tap into is a criterion of the scope of your concept of a community. If you play with this way of thinking, you may find, as I did from experience, that the numbers you come up with are surprisingly large and that you are thinking about parts of the community ordinarily outside of your interests and ken (1976, p. 324).

Network expansion is emphasized here to assert the relevance of networks, especially distal networks, to sense of community. By focusing on concepts useful to cultivation of *potential* as well as current networks, sense of community can be extended beyond the interpersonal level; and, in so doing, make it a more useful tool for social change. Although there are some important differences between their analyses, generally speaking Sarason, Burt, and Hunter and Suttles imply the same thing. *To succeed in a diversity of environments, to build viable community settings that can stimulate community change and expand sense of community, individuals and groups need to develop and exercise features of social networks that function to position them at the boundaries of networks.* The features, described below, are those that propel individuals and groups across boundaries and into relationships that involve negotiation of fragmented interests.

Network Concepts

Central to Burt's analysis is the concept of "Structural Holes." In essence, structural gaps in social networks emerge at the boundaries between groups. (Burt's work is similar to Granovetter's important work on the adaptive value of "weak" social ties (Granovetter, 1973).) Both Burt and Granovetter argue that weaker connections usually found between groups present a number of meaningful advantages to those holding them. Gaps in network structures are looked upon as boundary spanning opportunities. These include access to new resources, such as information and control of resources, both directly through new contacts and indirectly through the contact's relationships. Access to new information arises because links are established to different varieties and amounts of information, or at a critical time to the interests of the individual or group. Control accrues to those individuals and groups with ties across gaps because they are better positioned to act on their self-interest and that of their group. Paradoxically, one crucial conclusion from their analyses is that denser and more cohesive networks can actually be a disadvantage, cutting off people and groups from important resources. This is the opposite of what might be expected from a sense of community orientation that emphasizes closeness.

Burt and Granovetter describe a pretty impressive array of evidence to support the claim of advantage for those who bridge "structural holes" or to those who take advantage of "weak ties" (Granovetter, 1973). Burt (1999, 2000) cites evidence that individuals obtain better employment and more quickly, show improved performance, receive better pay, promotions, and bonuses. Moreover networks lacking structural holes were consistently related to poorer outcomes. Burt employs two characteristics of networks that are crucial to his structural hole argument and that are applicable to sense of community -- "network constraint" and "network density."

"Network constraint" is the extent to which one network has fewer links other networks. Fewer links between groups in a constellation of networks reduces the number of structural holes and the opportunities structural holes represent. Applying network constraint to work settings, Burt

(2000) predicts a negative relationship between job performance and network constraint. Applied by community psychologists to, say, a community organization, the implication is that fewer links to other groups, especially those that control resources, would reduce the effectiveness of the organization to secure resources needed for the organization and its participants. Thus, creating settings that intentionally and strategically establish links across "structural holes" to other groups, especially those that control resources, could expand sense of community. It should be possible to set in place internal organizational processes to reduce network constraint thereby increasing sense of community. For instance, develop group regularities that bring rank and file members of the group into instrumental contact with other groups. We say rank and file to distinguish these from experts. It would also be important not to vest the bridging of structural holes in one or another person but to rotate those who make contacts.

"Network density" refers to interconnections between other networks to which a particular network is linked. The logic is that bridges to networks that are themselves deeply intertwined or insular reduces the diversity of available resources -- greater network density in those networks to which we are linked reduces our own reach. The implication of this for sense of community lies in the selection of groups or organizations to which a given community might seek to establish ties. This requires a strategic analysis about which groups to select for a possible relationship, and selecting other like-minded or similarly connected groups may not be the best route. For community organizations whose missions extend beyond internal social support, the implication is clear. Building bridges to networks that themselves have a diversity of relationships should better develop and sustain sense of community.

Clearly, there are many circumstances in which real value accrues to those who are embedded in networks of cohesive relationships (e.g., Perkins, & Taylor, 1996), but cohesive relationships may not be enough to sustain well-being or change a community reality that is oppressive. Securing external resources or fundamentally changing policy may well be limited by restricting relationships to dense or constrained networks, and, by extension, sense of community to cohesion. In discussing network concepts and child well-being, Burt (2000) addresses the importance to children of being embedded in dense family networks, but he emphasizes the added value of parent(s) who span structural holes to improve the family's economic circumstances. Similarly, for sense of community, Brodsky (1996), Brodsky, O'Campo, and Aronson (1999), and Speer, Hughey, Gensheimer, and Adams-Leavitt (1995) highlight the pitfalls of investing individual or group resources in processes that yield cohesion, but have little likelihood of wresting resources from environments that are unresponsive, or worse, hostile to their interests.

It seems to us that navigating the tension between internal cohesion and external relationships that have the ability to yield tangible resources is the crucial dynamic. We do not see this as an either-or proposition, nor do we see it as a simple matter. In a sense, it is the central challenge of community psychology. It has been articulated in our literature time and again (e.g., Lehman, 1971; Newbrough, 1992). In this regard, we see real value to incorporating the network analysis approach as a way to add diversity to sense of community. Specifically, Burt's structural hole mechanism can be used as a tool to extend the meaning of sense of community in a way that is compatible with our ecological orientation (Trickett, 1984). It has already been established that the structure of sense of community can vary according to context (Hill, 1996); so it makes sense that the kind of network mechanisms employed to promote sense of community should also vary by context. When internal cohesion or social support is the fundamental purpose, sense of community can be developed by interpersonal strategies that highlight common purpose and emotional attachment. When the purpose of a group is securing external resources or altering established social practices (Seidman, 1988), sense of community might better be developed by pursuing a dual strategy. First, develop internal cohesion by engaging members in practices that intentionally seek to bridge internal boundaries, and simultaneously embed the group in a context fundamentally oriented to spanning the "structural holes" of the group. Pursuing a strategy of cohesion coupled to, and propelled by, boundary spanning practices will allow participants to access the potential relationships necessary for developing an expanded sense of their community, securing resources, and generating social change. Below we offer an illustration of how spanning boundaries to access new networks of relationships stimulated change and yielded tangible resources for one disadvantaged population.

THE KENTUCKY STORY

As an example of how network concepts can be put to use, we describe the efforts of a community coalition that was initially developed to target substance abuse prevention and later shifted to a more nuanced route that entailed confrontation of deeper community and network issues. The story illustrates the interplay of institutional forces in communities of limited liability (Suttles, 1972) and the value of network concepts (Burt, 2000) to sense of community. By intentionally spanning several structural holes, the group was eventually able to access a broader array of networks that, in turn, generated resources necessary for structural change. The route to change was circuitous and marked by initial failure and repeated confrontation of network restrictions. First steps for the coalition were based on reliance on one dense network of service providers that failed to acknowledge diverse community interests and enact processes to span boundaries.

Background

This project was brought by a large U.S. foundation to a small community, population about 50,000, in the southern U.S. Five-year pilot funding was available to develop "ecological models" of intervention to prevent substance abuse. The funding targeted one disadvantaged minority neighborhood, and the effort centered on child social service agencies that were to develop nurturing environmental contexts for children. The program took the form of a coalition developed to target substance abuse, and also aimed to extend delivery of traditional services to the community's families.

Issue Versus Network Focus Strategy

Based on elevated rates of substance abuse and crime, the lead agency selected one neighborhood on which to focus. By posting flyers in the community, use of media, and the promise of free food, the agency attempted to enlist participation of the neighborhood in public meetings. Participants in initial meetings were apprehensive about addressing substance abuse problems, expressing fear of retribution from drug dealers, and they were uncertain as to how to effectively proceed. Although residents cared about substance abuse, they did not ask for the substance abuse program. Rather, the local agency applied for the national foundation grant on behalf of residents -- residents with whom it had little relationship. This underlying dynamic was manifested in agency personnel "pushing" residents to talk about substance abuse and residents believing they were being told what to address. From a community psychology perspective, this agency-community dynamic mirrored a common social regularity (Seidman, 1988) that enforced focus on one issue, substance abuse, rather than bridging structural holes to overcome network constraint and density.

Throughout this initial stage, community attendance was sporadic, and those who did attend usually did not return. In contrast interest and participation was high among service agency stakeholders. These professionals were embedded in dense service delivery networks that were constrained from links to the community. Their early predominance served to suppress participation of local residents who harbored feelings of intimidation and inferiority in a community setting largely staffed by professionals. To the credit of these professional-class personnel, they understood the unintended negative effects their overwhelming participation represented; and after the suppressive effects of their attendance were pointed to, a large number willingly left the group.

Even after departure of most service professionals, development of resident participation remained difficult. The effort to mobilize residents continued to be a struggle because relationships among those who did attend were thin, and most failed to return to future meetings. Despite the obstacles, a few residents did attend on a regular basis. However, some of these were involved in illicit drug trade. Two individuals had well-established reputations as key players in the local drug trade. One ran a pool hall that was notorious for drug involvement, and the proprietor (a coalition attendee) presented her attendance as an expression of commitment to youth. The two individuals participated in the coalition by derailing any serious discussion of prevention strategies the group considered. The presence of these reputed drug dealers further suppressed community attendance, and organization staff were struggling with how to respond because they wanted coalition building to be an "open process that yielded a sense of community and a shared approach to substance abuse."

This situation illustrates an attempt to develop a sense of community absent an appreciation of social networks. Agency personnel were attempting to build a community organization based on a predetermined issue, flyers, and food, and not an intentional strategy to connect a constellation of disparate community networks that could influence resources for solutions to deeper issues. The group was attempting to foster a sense of membership and shared image of a community problem without putting in place an explicit process to span network boundaries. Recognizing the effort was in a precarious position, the group initiated a series of planning events that set a different course for the project. First, the reputation of the drug dealers was scrutinized closely through conversations with community leaders, knowledgeable youth, and law enforcement. The assessment confirmed the reputation, and the two individuals were asked to leave the coalition. Second, a new project coordinator was appointed who had an appreciation of the need to develop relationships within the coalition itself. Most important, the process shifted from random recruitment through publicity to an explicit relational recruitment strategy based on networks within the community and between key segments of the community.

Overcoming Network Constraint

With a new staffing pattern and a shift in emphasis, the group focused on building relationships with a broader array of citizens, thus working to reduce the constraint of its network connections. The process began by explicit examination of existing networks of relationships among and between coalition staff and residents. Then, participants engaged in an eight-month process of home visits to carefully listen to neighbors and other residents of the community. Listening began with staff or residents explaining that each visit was part of a coalition-building process targeting substance abuse, but substance abuse was not to be the exclusive focus. With each home visited, the conversation ended by asking whom else in the community should next be visited. Importantly, visits focused on problems families faced about a range of issues -- housing, employment, public safety, and substance abuse. Key to listening was identifying "stories" of important problem-related events that happened to people in their neighborhoods. Stories were valuable because they communicated the genuine and immediate concerns of residents about "real world" events in their community, and they provided insight into the community institutions and social networks impinging on the issues.

Listening produced a variety of stories that reflected the experience of a growing number of potential participants for coalition activities. Coalition meetings were now devoted to reviewing the stories heard and individual concerns of those visited, and attendance increased and became more diverse. Together, staff and residents analyzed the issues brought to the meetings, and their analyses now involved identification of community institutions involved in issues, for example, the police, courts, and drug treatment systems. Analyses also included planned discussion about relationships between members of the coalition and individuals located in various community institutions. Institutions and individuals identified through this process were also visited and invited to participate in the coalition. By developing relationships across a wider spectrum of community networks, the coalition began to overcome its initial high level of network constraint with the concomitant effects of increasing participation and reshaping its issue agenda.

A Different Issue Emerges

One often repeated story was that residents of the neighborhood resented the police and their approach to policing. The residents' reality was that the police department had set up a unit called "community policing," but practices of the unit were antithetical to neighborhood understanding of what community policing should be. One representative illustration was that of a mother and her young son, aged 11. Her son, along with many other children, was playing basketball on an outside court at their public housing complex. Seeing a number of children gathered, a police patrol car drove *onto* the basketball court itself, and the officer used the car's loudspeaker to order the children to "disperse." Frightened, the young children ran into their apartments, and the officer drove away. During a coalition meeting, mothers complained that, although their children were the targets of frequent drug dealing within their housing complex and that they and had repeatedly called the police, the police refused to get out of their cars to investigate. Reflecting on this and similar stories, residents and coalition staff jointly selected the wide gap between residents and the police as the issue on which the coalition would focus its efforts. Though focused indirectly on substance abuse, participants saw a clear link between the police-community gulf and the ability to effectively support substance abuse prevention activities. As it stood, the relationship of residents to the police was confined to that of sporadic targets for enforcement in which the only choice for residents was retreat to their homes, and the only choice for police was the isolation of their automobile.

To develop an institution level relationship with the police department and to learn more about community policing, a "research meeting" between the coalition and the police department was set. The coalition developed a list of questions to ask the police about the department's policing approach and its "community policing" unit. This event was not intended to resolve the issue. Instead, the encounter revealed a broad relational gap between police and the neighborhood. Coalition participants believed that, although community policing nominally existed, the approach of this community-policing unit was contrary to common understanding of community policing. Rather than building relationships with residents, patrolling the same neighborhood, and working with communities to solve problems as defined by the community, the community policing unit patrolled in cars, rarely spoke with citizens, and shifted from one locale to another. Despite different views of the issue and the apparent impasse this represented, the relationship established through the research meetings yielded results. Spanning the "structural hole" between residents and police produced an unexpected benefit; the conversation uncovered a network within the police department that agreed with the residents.

After the research meeting, one officer in the department contacted the coalition staff and indicated that the perspective of the coalition was correct. The police department was not, in fact, practicing community policing. A second research meeting between the coalition and the police was conducted; but this time, the relationship was with a different network in the department. Eventually, this second police network joined with the coalition to examine how to communicate what the coalition was interested in having from the police and with whom it should develop a relationship. The latter information about whom to target for a relationship proved valuable. From a network perspective the coalition was able to establish links to different police networks, thereby reducing constraint, but the network density of both the police and the coalition obscured links to necessary resources.

Overcoming Network Density

Recognizing that the relational base of the coalition and its police contacts remained somewhat insular, coalition staff and residents engaged in another round of home visits, this time to test the idea of community policing. This issue struck a chord with residents who expressed both anger at the police and concern about local crime. Armed with a stronger base and a deeper understanding of the police department, the coalition again contacted the second police network that, in turn, connected the coalition to the "right" person in the department. As a result, the police were willing to do a pilot community-policing program, but its scope was narrow. The coalition pushed an expanded effort that would include at least half the neighborhood; but the police balked, claiming that resources were too limited to accommodate this request.

Despite progress in spanning network constraints and increasing coalition participation, the coalition faced a barrier that seemed insurmountable. The resource barrier to enacting community change desired by the coalition, and some police allies, needed to be overcome, so the coalition shifted its effort to networks potentially linked to community resources. Through another round of home visits and one-to-one conversations conducted by coalition participants, the key gateway to resources was identified as the mayor of the town, but network density within coalition and police networks obscured possible links to the mayor. In essence, the mayor controlled policing resources, and there was no link to the mayor. Over the next three months, a cascade of coalition led events overcame the network density of the coalition and police and led to expanded funding for a new form of community policing that was characterized by a mutual respect between residents and police. Some landmarks in the process included:

- Coalition participants, staff, and residents reengaged the professional-class staff who earlier left the coalition.
- Relationships with the reengaged agency staff, together with their less dense boards of directors networks and police networks, revealed a key bridge to the mayor -- a retired newspaper executive turned philanthropist.
- To identify specific funding, the second group of police exercised their networks within the police department and city government.
- The coalition, which now included a more diverse mix of institutions, initiated conversations with the philanthropist in which the full range of community concerns was addressed.
- The philanthropist, confronted with a diverse array of institutional networks, arranged a series of conversations between the coalition, the police, and the mayor that eventually led to sustained funding for the more genuine form of community policing.

By intentionally establishing links with more and less dense networks, a wider range of relationships became available to the coalition. These relationships yielded resources for the desired community change. Had the coalition followed the path of cohesion without the additional leverage that network boundary spanning provided, the effort would have remained stalled.

CONCLUSION

Now, this truncated description overlooks a multitude of events. What can be said is the path was not without conflict, and progress was not linear. For instance, a process that eliminated settings for drug dealing and chronic violence stretched some newly established relationships almost to the breaking point. Other outcomes, such as new playgrounds for children, were less divisive. The instructive point of the story is that the coalition served as a vehicle to overcome the density of individual networks by intentionally spanning structural holes to establish relationships to distal networks that controlled resources. Although no quantitative assessment of sense of community was conducted, it is our conclusion that attachment of participants to the coalition and cohesion among residents and the police increased. The process of home visits, the sharing of stories and experience of success on issues over a meaningful period of time no doubt built a sense of belonging and closeness for participants. What distinguished this process was its explicit use of boundary spanning between disparate segments of the community in a way that yielded tangible community change.

The central conclusion to be drawn from applying community theory and network concepts to the story is their value for deepening understanding of sense of community. Consistent with Hunter and Suttles's (1972) notion of communities of limited liability, the story highlights the importance of external institutions, that is, foundations, service agencies, and police to a community organization process intended to develop sense of community. Rather than detracting from the coalition effort, the fragmented interests uncovered by participants proved critical to eventual success. The upshot is that the conflict apparent in the story appeared to strengthen the effort to build a sense of community, a conclusion consistent with community theory and some sense of community literature (Wiesenfeld, 1996).

The story also reinforces the potential importance of paying explicit attention to networks in efforts to strengthen sense of community. Over 25 years ago, Sarason (1976) pointed to the value of incorporating social networks into community analyses. The concepts of network constraint and network density provide some practical tools to put Sarason's prescription into practice. By expanding links to a greater number and variety of networks the coalition was able to tap key community level resources. These network concepts can also be used to extend sense of community beyond the individual level, a step that we see as crucial to maintaining the vitality of the sense of community concept.

With respect to empowerment and power, a similar argument was made by Smail (2001). In questioning the worth of "senses of this and that" (Smail, 2001; p. 165), he asserts that over psychologizing, "diverts the investigator's (as well as the practitioner's) attention from a noxious environment to a kind of luxuriant jungle of 'cognitive' and moral concepts" (p.164). We believe his point is relevant to sense of community as well. Over-reliance on a sense of community that emphasizes cohesion absent the background of conflicting extra-individual interests and social network dynamics may ultimately marginalize a precious concept.

REFERENCES

Bosky, A. E. (1996). Resilient single mothers in risky neighborhoods: Negative psychological sense of community. *Journal of Community Psychology, 24*, 347-363.

Brodsky, A. E., O'Campo, P. J., & Aronson, R. E. (1999). PSOC in community context: Multi-level correlates of a measure of psychological sense of community in low-income, urban neighborhoods. *Journal of Community Psychology, 27*, 659-679.

Burt, R. S. (2000). The network structure of social capital. In R. Sutton & B. Staw (Eds.), *Research in organizational behavior*, (pp. 345-423). Greenwich, CT: JAI Press.

Burt, R. S. (1999). The social capital of opinion leaders. *Annals of the American Academy of Political and Social Sciences, 566*, 37-64.

Coleman, J. S. (1988). Social capital in the creation of human capital. *American Journal of Sociology, 94*, S95-S120.

Dunham, H. W. (1986). The community today: Place or process. *Journal of Community Psychology, 14*, 399-404.

Frantz, D, & Collins, C. (1999). *Celebration, USA: Living in Disney's brave new town*. New York: Holt.

Granovetter, M. S. (1973). The strength of weak ties. *American Journal of Sociology, 78*, 1360-1380.

Hill, J. L. (1996). Psychological sense of community: Suggestions for future research. *Journal of Community Psychology, 24*, 431-438.

Hughey, J., Speer, P. W., & Peterson, N. A. (1999). Sense of community in community organizations: Structure and evidence of validity. *Journal of Community Psychology, 27*, 97-113.

Hunter, A., & Suttles, G. (1972). The expanding community of limited liability. In G. Suttles (Ed.), *The social construction of communities*, (pp. 44-81). Chicago: University of Chicago Press.

Lehmann, S. (1971). Community and psychology and community psychology. *American Psychologist, 26*, 554-560.

Lewin, R., & Regine, B. (2000). *The soul at work*. New York: Simon & Schuster.

Maton, K. I. (2000). Making a difference: The social ecology of social transformation. *American Journal of Community Psychology, 28*, 25-59.

McMillan, D. W., & Chavis, D. M. (1986). Sense of community: A definition and theory. *Journal of Community Psychology, 14*, 6-23.

Newbrough, J. R. (1992). Community Psychology in the postmodern world. *Journal of Community Psychology, 20*, 10-25.

Perkins, D. D., Fisher, A., Butterworth, I., & Hughey, J. (July, 2000). *Community psychology perspectives on social capital theory, research, and applications*. Paper presented to the 32nd Annual International Meeting of the Community Development Society, St. John, New Brunswick, Canada.

Perkins, D. D. & Taylor, R. B. (1996). Ecological assessments of community disorder: Their relationship to fear of crime and theoretical implications. *American Journal of Community Psychology, 24*, 63-107.

Putnam, R. D., Leonardi, R., & Nanetti, R. Y. (1993). *Making democracy work: Civic traditions in modern Italy*. Princeton, NJ: Princeton University Press.

Rappaport, J. (1977). *Community Psychology: Values, research, and action.* New York: Holt, Rinehart & Winston.

Ross, A. (2000). *The celebration chronicles: Life, liberty and the pursuit of property value in Disney's new town.* New York: Verso.

Sarason, S. B. (1974). *The psychological sense of community: Prospects for a community psychology.* San Francisco: Jossey-Bass.

Sarason, S. B. (1976). Community psychology, networks, and Mr. Everyman. *American Psychologist, 31,* 317-328.

Seidman, E. (1988). Back to the future, community psychology: Unfolding a theory of social intervention. *American Journal of Community Psychology, 16,* 3-24.

Smail, D. (2001). De-psychologizing Community Psychology. *Journal of Community & Applied Social Psychology, 11,* 159-165.

Speer, P., Hughey, J., Gensheimer, L. K., & Adams-Leavitt, W. (1995). Organizing for power: A comparative case study. *Journal of Community Psychology, 23,* 57-73.

Suttles, G. (1972). *The social construction of communities.* Chicago: University of Chicago Press.

Taylor, R. B. (1997). Social order and disorder of street blocks and neighborhoods: Ecology, microecology, and the systemic model of social disorganization. *Journal of Research in Crime and Delinquency, 34,* 113-155.

Trickett, E. J. (1984). Toward a distinctive community psychology: An ecological metaphor for the conduct of community research and the nature of training. *American Journal of Community Psychology, 12,* 261-280.

Wiesenfeld, E. (1996). The concept of "we": A community social psychology myth? *Journal of Community Psychology, 24,* 337-346.

PART III

SPECIFIC SETTINGS

Chapter 5

SENSE OF COMMUNITY OF YOUNG WOMEN IN CUSTODY

Tomi Redman and Adrian T. Fisher
Victoria University

INTRODUCTION

Young women in custody are among the most marginalized, disempowered groups in our society (Alder & Hunter, 1999). The lack of attention afforded them by the general population is reflected in the lack of psychological research regarding their experiences and beliefs. While there is much anecdotal evidence related to women in custody and their experience of support and community in the custodial setting, there has been a paucity of systematic research. Anecdotal evidence and observations in Harris Correctional Facility[i] demonstrate that strong attachments that many young women appeared to develop while at Harris. These observations suggested that there might be a relationship between the residents' sense of community while in Harris, their ability to successfully reintegrate into the general community, and their rates of recidivism. These factors appeared to be further complicated by a lack of sense of community in the external environment, loneliness, and histories of abuse, trauma and instability.

This research reported here aims to explore these observations and investigate the relationship between sense of community in Harris, and external sense of community, loneliness, recidivism and reintegration on release. In this chapter, we explore the idea that young women in custody develop a sense of community with other residents, as well as with the staff. The chapter examines how these factors relate to the women's adjustment in the custodial setting, their rehabilitation and likely recidivism, and sources of community and support external to the prison.

FEMALES IN CUSTODY

In Australia, as in most Western countries, there are far fewer women in custody than men. For example, the UK and Canada have approximately one in five young offenders who are female (Jasper, Smith, & Bailey, 1998; Kowalski & Caputo, 1999), a similar rate to the state in which Harris is located. In this state, there are approximately 30 young women in juvenile detention at any given time, compared to about 150 young men in the same age group (10-21 years) in custody in juvenile facilities.[ii] Perhaps as a result of this disparity, there is a marked lack of research worldwide into women and incarceration, and almost no research on younger women in custody (Jasper, et al., 1998). It cannot be assumed, however, that the research on young men can be directly related to young women, who have clearly different issues.

Women differ from men in relation to their experiences of offending, criminalization, and punishment (Davies & Cook, 1998; Hancock, 1986; Kowalski & Caputo, 1999; Morris & Wilkinson, 1995; Sarri, 1983; Singer, Bussey, Song, & Lunghofer, 1995). Females commit different crimes from males, receive different punishments, and offend for different reasons. Drug abuse is the primary reason women enter prison (Henderson, 1998), with at least 90% of young women in Harris incarcerated for crimes related to their substance use.[iii] Women entering prison are more likely to come from backgrounds of socioeconomic disadvantage (Davies & Cook, 1998). The Department of Justice found that women in custody tend to come from backgrounds of extreme poverty (Department of Justice, 1996).

Maden, Swinton, and Gunn (1994) found that British, adult, female offenders had higher rates of psychiatric illness, personality disorder and substance abuse than did male offenders. Women prisoners in Texas were found to have higher anxiety than male prisoners and were more bothered by the stressors of prison life (Paulus & Dzindolet, 1993). In Australia, there is a high incidence of self-harm amongst women prisoners, and relatively high rates of suicide and suicide attempts (Davies & Cook, 1998; Leibling, 1994). A 1990 study of suicide and suicide attempts found that while women made up only 6% of the adult prison population, they accounted for almost 50% of self-harm or suicidal incidents, an unusually high proportion even in comparison to other female prison populations (Harding, 1990). The mortality rate for adult women on parole in Victoria is three times higher than for men (Davies & Cook, 1998).

The findings for adults reflect research on adolescent offenders. Adolescent offenders have been found to have high rates of affective disorders, including clinical depression, as well as high rates of trauma and anxiety disorders and relatively high presentations of borderline and schizoid personality disorders (Grisso, 1999). Grisso reported on a number of studies undertaken in the United States in recent years, which were remarkably consistent in finding a much higher prevalence of mental illness for adolescent offenders, compared to adolescents in the general population. In particular, female juvenile offenders have at least as great, or greater, a prevalence of mental disorders as do male juvenile offenders (Grisso, 1999). Although there are no statistics available on the incidence of suicide attempts and self-harm within the adolescent female prison population, it seems likely it will be similar to the high rates among adult female prisoners, given that the suicide rate for young people in Australia in general is increasing (Ford, 1999).

While many studies have highlighted the increased rates of mental illness with those in custody (Hokanson, Megargee, O'Hagan & Perry, 1976; Porporino & Zamble, 1984), this increase is generally explained by their incarceration rather than examining external factors such as lack of community, family breakdown, or histories of trauma or abuse. For example, while research recognizes the role of substance abuse in offending, no research was found specifically addressing the role of substance use for offenders, and the impact of forced withdrawal on their mental health. Some people may use substance abuse as a device to effectively block negative memories or emotions, possibly for years. However, one side effect of incarceration for many prisoners is that they are forced to become drug free, thus removing that device. It is possible that this contributes to mental health issues presenting after incarceration.

The connection between mental well-being and sense of community in custody may be highlighted by inmates' experiences of anxiety. Increased pre-release anxiety was demonstrated Bukstel and Kilmann (1980). Studies generally have attributed such anxiety to fears about reintegration with family and the external community, and adjustments to living without the structure and control inherent in a prison system (Bukstel & Kilmann, 1980; Davies & Cook, 1998; Paulus & Dzindolet, 1993). However, such research does not take into account any attachment and sense of belonging or community that may have developed during time in custody. Perhaps this pre-release anxiety may be at least partly explained by worries about losing the sense of community that individuals have developed while in custody. Many inmates do re-offend, which may be at least partly a result of wanting to return to custody and the connections made there.

American research show young female offenders have experienced more sexual abuse, and more often, than young males (Jasper, et al., 1998). Although no Australian literature on this has been found, the research on sexual abuse with young women in general has found that 79% of registered victims of childhood sexual abuse in 1990-91 were female (Community Services Victoria, 1992). "...[M]ost women prisoners have experienced some form of sexual assault or family violence prior to their imprisonment" (Department of Justice, 1996, p 48). One study at Harris found that a high proportion of the young women been involved with child protection services

(Stewart & Tattersall, 2000), suggesting high levels of child abuse. An unpublished study by a former Health Team leader at Harris[iv] found that of a sample of 67 custodial residents at Harris, 85% were survivors of physical violence from their parents or step parents, 62% came from families where a member of the immediate family was either presently incarcerated or had been incarcerated in the previous five years, and 45% came from families where a parent or other

Not surprisingly, child abuse has been linked with adolescent delinquency (Smith & Thornberry, 1995). A review of the literature on the consequences of child abuse (Knutson, 1995) shows a relationship between child abuse and neglect, and an increased likelihood of antisocial behavior and aggression in adolescence and adulthood. This link has been extended to offending (Bailey, Smith, & Dolan, 2001). For example, McCord's (1983) 40-year follow up of former male adolescent offenders indicated a relationship between their offending and childhood abuse. This relationship has also been demonstrated with female offenders (Rosenbaum, 1989). Victims of childhood abuse also have increased rates of substance abuse compared to those not abused as children (Bank & Burraston, 2001), and the link between substance abuse and offending is clear.

It is difficult to ascertain what proportion of abuse is related directly to families and what is related to the community in which the child is raised. Harsh and abusive discipline from parents is associated with lack of parenting skills, social and economic disadvantage, and parental substance abuse (Bank & Burraston, 2001). The lack of parenting skills and parental substance abuse could be attributed to the family, but social and economic disadvantage seems more generally related to the larger community. Of course, it is also possible to examine the role the community plays in parental problems. For example, the strength of a community has been linked to child abuse and the quality of parenting (Chavis & Newbrough, 1986), with higher rates of abuse in weaker communities.

To make the picture even more complex, it is also known that children exposed to violent communities are likely to suffer deleterious effects (Bell & Jenkins, 1993; Osofsky, Wewers, Hann, & Fick, 1993; Sheidow, Gorman-Smith, Tolan, & Henry, 2001), regardless of their family situation. These may include aggression, depression, and anxiety disorders (Sheidow, et al., 2001). It is difficult to determine how much of a young person's offending is related to their experience of childhood abuse, community violence, or social and economic disadvantage. The current study does not seek to answer these questions, but merely to raise this issue in order to highlight the histories of abuse that many young women in custody have experienced, and the complexities of that violence, particularly in relation to their sense of community.

Sense of Community and Custody

The concept of psychological sense of community embodies a belief in the importance of community to human well-being (Davidson & Cotter, 1991). According to McMillan and Chavis (1986) psychological sense of community comprises four parts: a) membership; b) influence; c) integration and fulfillment of individual needs; and d) shared emotional connection. By being a member of a community, one derives a series of benefits such as a shared identity, relationships with other members, ability to express their emotions, and the support received from other members in times of need. For the residents of Harris, and others in custodial settings, there is a significant issue of whether they have a community outside with which to connect on release, and the nature of the community that may develop inside the facility and whether this will enhance rehabilitation and eventual release.

The relationships and connections formed in custody can be seen as contributing to a sense of community as, in many respects, a custodial center takes the place of a neighborhood for prisoners during their time there. In custody, prisoners are constantly surrounded by other people -- including staff, clients, or external workers. Rokach (1997) has suggested relationships may be formed with these people for fear of social alienation. She suggests that such relationships may be formed particularly with other prisoners, because they feel something in common, if only a history of crime and being on the outside of the law-abiding community. Rokach also acknowledged that "jail may offer a warm and supportive community, unlike the community the criminal often comes from" (p. 268). Perhaps the relationships formed in jail serve to provide support, while also alleviating the fear of being in custody or fear of social isolation. However, observations and anecdotal evidence indicates that there are also strong relationships potentially developed with various types of staff, especially in facilities for younger offenders.

Baumeister and Leary (1995) have suggested that the need individuals have to belong with others motivates them to seek relationships that provide such a sense of belonging. Once people have found such relationships they are motivated to maintain those relationships. Some research has indicated that social bonds are more important for females (Morris, 1964; Thoits, 1991) than for males. However, to form such relationships, clients must feel safe. Whether these are the most positive or adaptive types of communities is open to question.

The concept of a competent community has been discussed in Community Psychology literature since the 1970's (Cottrell, 1976; Iscoe, 1974). A competent community "is one that can develop effective ways of coping with the challenges of living (and) ... have the capacity and resources to cope positively with adversity" (Sonn & Fisher, 1998, p. 459). This issue is important because the strength of a community has a positive relationship with quality of life for those within the community, as discussed above in relation to parenting (Chavis & Newbrough, 1986). Non-competent communities may not have the characteristics to facilitate integration and assist individuals to access the resources that are available (Pretty, Conroy, Dugay, Fowler, & Williams, 1996). They often comprise the lower end of the spectrum of advantage (including economic, educational and social advantage) and provide little support for their members, either in the form of resources or in the ability to facilitate access to existing resources.

It is possible that prisoners may form a non-competent community, consisting of individuals from marginalized and non-dominant groups who may be unwilling or unable to assist others to integrate and to cope with adversity. Often the general community portrays jails, both adult and juvenile, as negative environments. There is a widespread belief that they are violent, frightening places, which may actually make criminals worse rather than provide rehabilitative opportunities. Similar to the urban, low-income neighborhoods from which many prisoners come, they are "often perceived as uniformly unhealthy for, and unprotective of their residents" (Brodsky, O'Campo, & Aronson, 1999, p. 660), places in which residents feel alienation and lack of community. However, as Sonn and Fisher (1998) suggest, this may be too simplistic a view, and prisoners may actually "find ways to resist oppression and experience a sense of community" (p. 457) despite their difficult backgrounds.

In a study of inmate well-being, Wooldredge (1999) found that social interaction and the development of a sense of belonging are made more difficult when inmates feel less safe. Similar findings have been demonstrated in the non-custodial environment. Chipuer and Pretty (1997) found that young people who feel left out and isolated from those who live nearby, and who feel surrounded by strangers who do not care for them or want to know them, see their neighborhoods as unsafe, places to be feared. It is difficult to determine which direction this relationship takes: is the perception of an unsafe neighborhood the cause of the sense of isolation and lack of relationships; or is the lack of relationships the cause of the lack of sense of safety? Either way, the implications are relevant for those in custody, if young people do not feel safe in the custodial facility, they will be less likely to form relationships in the center. Alternatively, if they do not form significant connections with others, they may feel less safe during their time in custody. Regardless, their sense of belonging will be minimal in such environments.

It has been suggested that "…the ability of women to cope post-release may well be undermined by a profound sense of alienation and by the persistence and severity of problems which pre-dated their incarceration" (Davies & Cook, 1998, p. 20). In addition to pre-existing problems, release from incarceration raises many new problems, possibly including loneliness. Loneliness is an emotional response to the lack of a social network that provides support, caring and a sense of belonging (Weiss, 1973, cited in Rokach & Koledin, 1997). Rokach (1997) found that for the incarcerated men in her study, loneliness increased during their episode of custody. However this may not always be the case. If prisoners do form significant relationships while in custody, they may experience intense loneliness on release. Such loneliness may then contribute to a relapse into the drug-abusing communities to which they had previously belonged. As a reduction in reincarceration is associated with reduction in drug use (Wexler, DeLeon, Thomas, Kressel, & Peters, 1999), it may be that loneliness, either directly or indirectly, contributes to recidivism and criminality (Rokach & Koledin, 1997). Supporting this view is a study by Page (1991) indicating that when loneliness is prolonged it can result in adolescent delinquent behaviors and hopelessness.

Pretty and her colleagues have found that neighborhood sense of community significantly relates to adolescent loneliness, with the primary predictor of such a sense of community being the number of people from whom the adolescents receive support (Pretty, Andrewes, & Collett, 1994; Pretty, Conroy, Dugay, Fowler, & Williams, 1996). There have been no studies specifically addressing this issue with adolescents in custody. However, it seems possible that the number of people from whom incarcerated young women receive support may be related to their degree of loneliness, both during their sentence and post-release.

Unfortunately, on leaving custody many people return to the community from which they came, communities that provided little support or incentive to turn from crime and substance abuse. It is critical then that this is recognized, and that individuals are able to learn skills to enable them to deal with the problems associated with living in such an environment (Hartmann, Wolk, Johnston, & Colyer, 1997). Hartmann and colleagues illustrated this issue in their study of residents in a therapeutic community. About half of the residents interviewed indicated that they did not believe they could stay drug free if living in their old neighborhood.

Negative Sense of Community

In general, it is assumed that a sense of community provides positive benefits. However, Brodsky (1996) challenges this assumption, discussing the concept of a negative sense of community, whereby individuals make efforts to maintain a negative (or unconnected) relationship with a community as a way to moderate the potentially negative effects of a damaging or non-beneficial community. Brodsky reported that such a negative psychological sense of community could be adaptive for those who perceive their community to be a burden rather than a resource. This negative perception of their communities may exist for some young people in custody, who tend to come from communities with high rates of substance abuse, criminal offending, and violence, with an immediate family member had been a regular user of heroin or amphetamines.

One of the main reasons women in Brodsky's (1996) study did not participate in their 'risky neighborhoods' was a perceived lack of physical and emotional safety. Adolescents' neighborhood safety as one of their primary needs in relation to their sense of community in Queensland, Australia, and in Canada have identified (Chipuer & Pretty, 1997). This may be relevant for Harris clients, given the prevalence of substance abuse, violence and criminality in their backgrounds.

There is also some disparity in the literature on the impact of prison adjustment on recidivism. Some studies have found that prisoners who adjust poorly to the prison structure are less likely to return to custody than are other inmates who are more institutionalized or 'prisonized' (Goodstein, 1979; Porporino & Zamble, 1984). Similarly, Goodstein (1979) found that those who do not subscribe to the rules and boundaries of the prison make the transition to the community with more ease. However, Ganzer and Sarason (1973) found that those who re-offend have marginal or poor institutional adjustment. This finding corresponds with Palmer and Wedge (1989) who found that recidivism is reduced with higher frequency of outside contacts and recreation, which presumably is related to 'good behavior'. That is, outside contacts and recreation are likely to be used as a positive consequence of obeying the rules and boundaries of the prison, and removed or limited with poor behavior.

INFORMATION GATHERING

As the research was exploratory and attempted to derive an understanding if the experiences of the young women, a suitable approach needed to be developed. While there are various scales to measure aspects of sense of community, these were not seen as suitable, both because there was no *a priori* research hypotheses, and because many of the people in Harris have limited literacy skills. Hence, semi-structured interviews were utilized, lasting up to 2 hours each.

Interviews provided an opportunity to achieve a greater understanding of the culture of Harris and the residents managed their time there (Rubin & Rubin, 1995). The interviews were phenomenological and ethnographic, focusing on individuals' perspectives and interpretations of their world (Miles & Huberman, 1994), and how they make sense of their lives (West, 1996). They allowed flexibility in the direction of the conversation dependent on what information arose during the course of the interview (Patton, 1990). No formal schedule was developed; instead, a guide to the general topics to be discussed was created, with the topics largely generated by the researcher's previous observations (Bowler, 1997) while working in the center.

Each participant was asked an initial question regarding how she felt about being at Harris, and further specific questions evolved from responses to each subsequent question. These subsequent questions addressed general underlying questions: 1) how do the young women perceive Harris; 2) do they feel any sort of attachment to Harris or the people in it; 3) what are their thoughts on leaving Harris; and 4) what are their thoughts regarding issues with reintegration into the external community.

Participants

Interviews were conducted with 13 residents of Harris. One was 16 years old, two were 17 years, three were 18 years, two were 19 years, and five were 20. Their sentences ranged from 5 months to 5 years, with an average length of 9.5 months, mostly at the lower end. Five of the clients were in Harris for the first time when interviewed, although three of them had spent time in the adult custodial system. Two clients were in for the second time, two for the third, and the other four had experienced at least four episodes of incarceration at Harris, with one of these also having spent some time in the adult system.

Six of the young women had no childhood contact with protective services. However, four of these had had episodes of homelessness and separation from the family prior to incarceration. The other seven had difficult family backgrounds, with histories of involvement with child protection services, periods of foster or government care, and little or no current family support or contact. Only 2 participants had no history of homelessness or family breakdown. Twelve of the interviewees were incarcerated for crimes related to substance abuse, including theft, burglary, armed robbery, and drug possession. The thirteenth client was in for a serious crime unrelated to substance use. None of them had completed their schooling, and none had been undertaking any sort of educational course prior to their admission to Harris.

RESULTS AND DISCUSSION

Despite the diversity in clients, the content of the interviews was remarkably uniform -- making the process of content analysis relatively simple. Of course, there were variations in responses, and the non-structured interview meant that different participants focused on different areas. However, all of participants addressed a similar range of issues (independent of questioning by the researcher) and opinions about Harris, sense of community and external environments were not widely divergent. Five clear themes emerged from the data, with the second theme having sub-themes (with only the first three themes discusses in this chapter):

- Psychological sense community within the facility;
- The experience of the external community, both positive and negative
  - ○ Positive external community
  - ○ Negative external community
    - ▪ Lack of sense of community external
    - ▪ Sense of community with a negative community externally
- The role of staff in creating a sense of attachment
- Issues with readjustment to the external community on release
- Overall impressions of the facility

Sense of Community Within the Facility

This theme included two main categories of responses -- those who felt a positive sense of community within Harris, and those who did not feel a sense of community, either positive or negative. A strong sense of community with Harris was indicated in general terms by almost all of the clients. This supports the contention by Rokach (1997) that for some people, "jail may offer a warm and supportive community" (p. 268), which can be difficult to leave. There is the development of a sense of community over time, as discussed by Pretty, et al. (1991), showing a progression from hating Harris to not wanting to leave. A link with recidivism is indicated, presumably to maintain the relationships while there (Baumeister & Leary, 1995).

For some participants, a sense of community, the feeling that Harris provided a home was a significant factor in their developing an attachment. For some clients, 'It was like a home away from home.' For others, it appeared to be their first experience of a home, the 'warm and supportive community' that Rokach (1997) describes.

A number of clients talked about a sense of safety at Harris, a critical component to feeling a sense of community (Chipuer & Pretty, 1997). Given that many of the participants had histories of homelessness, abuse and substance use, it is perhaps not surprising that to some, Harris appeared to offer a haven. A number of participants identified Harris as providing safety by providing an opportunity to stop substance abuse. Others also identified a sense of safety at Harris, although for some this appeared to be associated with stability rather than a homely environment or freedom from drug use. As many came from environments of violence, unpredictability, and transience, the desire for stability is a logical requirement for a sense of safety.

Safety is a critical factor in the development of sense of community. The very fact that they feel safe in Harris (for various reasons) indicates that they have some sense of community, and have not distanced themselves from those around them. Another indicator of sense of community is a feeling of comfort -- that is, that individuals feel a sense of membership, which provides emotional safety with a feeling of belonging, or fitting in (McMillan & Chavis, 1986). A number of the participants reported they felt sense of belonging at Harris.

It was expected that there would be an association between the level of attachment the residents felt to other women at Harris, and their sense of community. However, there were relatively few responses about other clients, despite questions related to how they felt about the other residents. Among the responses, there was a wide diversity regarding friendships and relationships to other clients, with some interviewees feeling close attachments, and some not reporting any meaningful connection with other clients. Those who appeared to feel connected to other clients related this to a sense of having something in common with them, supporting Rokach's (1997) contention that prisoners may form relationships because they feel something in common, with shared histories of offending and trauma. These shared histories may also contribute to a sense of belonging (McMillan & Chavis, 1986), with boundaries of belonging and identification, where those in custody clearly belong to a group of people with similar experiences and current circumstances. One client in particular summed up this sense of similarity, reporting that "We're all exactly the same." Other clients clearly identified how important similar experiences were to their ability to form relationships.

Some clients indicated that these friendships, while providing support during incarceration, could actually make it harder to reintegrate into the external community, with some suggesting the relationships formed in Harris contributed to recidivism. The sense of community some clients felt with other clients could have a potentially negative impact, supporting Brodsky's (1996) contention that a negative sense of community may actually be more adaptive than forming connections with a damaging or harmful community.

A number of other residents reported that they felt a sense of or community with the other clients while in Harris, but that those relationships were not likely to be maintained on release. Such temporary connections could serve the purpose of avoiding social alienation while in custody (Rokach, 1997), without providing any long-term support or connections. Alternatively, the decision these clients made to keep connections temporary or superficial is an example of a negative sense of community (Brodsky, 1996), whereby individuals deliberately maintain a negative relationship with a community that they perceive to be potentially damaging or non-beneficial.

A small number of participants did not appear to feel any meaningful connection with other clients, even superficially, suggesting that these clients did not feel a sense of community among the women at Harris. However, this lack of sense of community appears to be something different from

Brodsky's (1996) adaptive negative sense of community. This group of participants did not appear to be choosing to maintain their distance, instead they lacked a sense of community because of circumstances not of their choosing.

The idea of a potential negative impact of feeling a sense of community at Harris was not limited to discussions about relationships with other clients. A number of clients talked in more general terms about the perceived risks involved in forming any form of attachment while at Harris, either with clients, staff or the physical environment of the facility itself. They perceived that that forming a connection to Harris could be non-beneficial or even damaging.

In summary, it seems that the majority of participants did feel some sense of community at Harris, either with the other clients or more generally. However, a number of clients indicated that they saw this sense of community as having a negative impact, at least in some ways, in that it contributed to their desire to return to Harris after release. A minority of clients reported that they did not feel a sense of community or connection with other clients. For some this appeared to be a choice to develop a negative sense of community as defined by Brodsky (1996), while for others, it appeared that they were unable to form connections with other clients.

The Experience of the External Community

Positive External Community

The interviews showed that there was a clear subset of responses indicating that 7 of the 13 participants had a positive sense of community with their external community, primarily family. Not surprisingly, 6 of these 7 were the ones who had not been linked with child protection services. However, of them, at least 4 had undergone extended periods of homelessness prior to incarceration. Nevertheless, this group of clients all indicated the important role their families played in their lives, and how critical the support from their families was to their happiness.

Only two of the clients focused on the importance of friends. This was a surprising finding, given the general stereotype of adolescence, in which the peer group is perceived to be crucial. Perhaps this is a result of the tension many had experienced with their families due to their substance abuse, and the consequent fear of losing their support. It is possible that episodes of homelessness and separation from relatives had caused them to value their family more than the 'average' adolescent, who may take family for granted. Another factor in this emphasis on family may be, as discussed below, that many of the participants had spent a number of years in the drug-using scene, and did not perceive the resulting friendships to be 'real' or meaningful. As they were generally out of the social mainstreams, with most not having worked or attended school in a number of years, it may have been more difficult to meet and form connections with other teenagers.

Negative external community

All 13 participants, including those who had talked about the strong connections they had to family, commented on the lack of community they perceived in their external environments. Three clients did not perceive this lack of community in their own lives, but recognized that other clients came from backgrounds offering few supports or resources for members.

There was a relationship between a lack of external community and difficulties with leaving Harris. This has implications for recidivism if the clients would rather stay at Harris than be released, it follows that they may be more likely to re-offend to return to an environment where they felt wanted. This emotion has already been demonstrated in Theme 1, in which clients indicated they wanted to return to Harris on release.

Interviews with the participants supported these perceptions, with each of the clients identifying a negative experience of their external communities. There were two main types of negative experience: some clients felt a total lack of a sense of community; while other clients felt a sense of community with a community that they recognized as negative and harmful.

Many of the young women had experienced episodes of homelessness due, at least in part, to negative experiences of child protection services and poverty. Homelessness is also associated with less social support, reduced contact from communities of origin and greater incidence of mental health issues (Solarz & Bogat, 1990). Not surprisingly, a number of participants identified a lack of social support and contact with their communities of origin, and many linked this lack of connection to their substance use. However, it is not clear how much the substance use was caused by the lack of community, and how much it contributed. It is possible that some young people commence using drugs to manage a sense of isolation and sadness associated with family breakdown or trauma. Many of the participants in this study had experienced extremely traumatic and unstable childhoods, so it may be that they commenced drug use as a form of pain management.

Regardless of the initial cause of the drug use, it seems that for many of these young women it resulted in an increased lack of a sense of community. As mentioned in the section above, many of the young women indicated that this lack of community was particularly related to friendships, with most of the participants reporting that their friendships while on drugs had been superficial and impermanent.

Negative perceptions of external communities were not just limited to a sense of a lack of community. Some participants also recognized that they were connected to a community, but that the community was potentially damaging. While some of the young women indicated that they were trying to distance themselves from these harmful communities (Brodsky, 1996), they made it clear how difficult this was. Perhaps this is because they clearly did identify with the negative communities, feeling that they had something in common with the other members, a sense of membership that forms a critical part of any sense of community (McMillan & Chavis, 1986).

The Role of Staff in Creating a Sense of Attachment

The role of peers in Harris clients forming a sense of community has been discussed. However, staff also, potentially, play a significant role, participating in the lives of the young women in Harris. This role was clearly recognized by the 13 clients interviewed for this study. Each made reference to the significant positive role that staff members played in assisting them during their time at Harris. Most also indicated that this contributed to a sense of community at Harris, rather than just practical support such as assistance finding accommodation. Only one client limited her comments to the practical interventions that staff offered. Apart from that one comment, all discussion about staff members was positive.

Many clients reported significant levels of attachment to the staff, and felt staff provided them with many resources, and the ability to access those resources. It would seem, therefore, that staff contributed to clients' sense of being part of a competent community (Cottrell, 1976; Iscoe, 1974). Such a competent community would provide resources to help its members cope with the adversity of incarceration and limited positive experiences of external communities. It would seem that the staff assisted the residents of Harris to experience a competent community, despite being an oppressed group in the most literal of senses.

For many clients, one of the most important roles of the staff appeared to be the emotional support they offered, most visibly in the form of being someone the clients could talk to. Clients mentioned how important it was not only to feel able to talk, but to be able to do so without feeling judged or dismissed. Many of these positive reports also recognized the contribution that staff members made to the young women's ability to make a successful transition to the community. In Sonn and Fisher's (1998) words, the staff contributed to a competent community for the young women, by assisting them to develop ways to effectively cope with the challenges of living. However, at least one of the young women perceived this connection to staff as an additional pressure on release, because she did not want to personally disappoint them by relapsing yet, wanted to re-offend to return to Harris to be near them.

Perhaps clients maintained such relationships with staff because they did not feel such relationships were available in the external community. If they suffered persecution in the external community, which seems likely given their histories of crime and substance abuse, it is possible that they would prefer the supportive environment provided by Harris (Bishop, Jason, Ferrari, & Huang, 1998), with staff who did not judge and who had some understanding of the backgrounds they had come from. This attachment to staff, and the positive experiences they have provided, that are often in direct contrast to experiences the clients have had in the external community, clearly has implications for clients on release from Harris.

CONCLUSION

The Harris residents raised many of the areas of interest identified in the literature as issues relevant to their time in custody. Their histories of abuse, trauma and sexual assault were representative of incarcerated women around the world, as discussed in studies undertaken in Britain, Canada and the United States (Chesney-Lind, 1989; Davies & Cook, 1998; Funk, 1999; Jasper, et al., 1998; Widom & White, 1997). Most of those interviewed for this research were sentenced for crimes related to their substance abuse, which again mirrors a world wide trend that suggests that most incarcerated women are locked up for drug related crimes (Henderson, 1998).

Adjustment to Custody and Sense of Community at Harris

This study suggests a quite different process of adaptation to custody than earlier studies have found. Previous research has provided conflicting results regarding whether or not prisoners adapt to incarceration, how long that process takes and whether such an adaptation has positive effects (Paulus & Dzindolet, 1993; Ruback, Carr, & Hopper, 1986; Zamble & Porporino, 1990). This research, however, has found that the young women at Harris appear to adjust to incarceration extremely quickly. Even those clients only a few weeks into their first sentence reported feeling safe and comfortable at Harris, and those who had been there numerous times did not appear to be significantly more or less adapted than those who were undergoing their first period of incarceration. In other words, this study suggests that the young women at Harris seem not to require a period of adjustment to custody -- after the initial fear about what to expect they soon learn that they can feel comfortable within its walls.

This reported sense of comfort suggests that Harris may offer a safe place that provides protection and support for the young women incarcerated there. In many respects this safe place enables them to develop a strong positive sense of community. There do appear, however, to be variations in the strength of a sense of community when comparing those clients who had experienced multiple episodes of incarceration or were well into a long sentence to those in the early stages of a first sentence. Given that length of time in a residential setting is related to sense of community (Pretty et al., 1996), it is perhaps not surprising that those clients who had spent lengthy or multiple periods of time at Harris appeared to have a stronger sense of community within the facility. Nevertheless, all clients reported a sense of community within Harris to some degree.

The participants identified the sense of community on a number of levels. Previous research suggested relationships with other prisoners are likely to be formed for fear of social alienation (Rokach, 1997). However, relationships with other clients were a surprisingly small contributor to the development of a sense of community within Harris. This was surprising, given that the prisoners are adolescents, who are generally assumed to form stronger ties with peers than with adults. Only a small number of clients reported the role of peers was significant in their sense of belonging or attachment with Harris. Other participants suggested that they had chosen to develop a negative sense of community with other clients, by remaining distant because they perceived the community of young offenders to be potentially damaging. There was also a small group of young women that reported feeling a lack of community with other clients through no deliberate efforts on their part.

For the majority of clients, sense of community in Harris appeared to develop out of relationships with staff. Generally, these relationships appeared to be positive, contributing to an experience of stability in an environment where they felt they belonged and were cared for. As such, Harris can be defined as a competent community (Cottrell, 1976; Iscoe, 1974) which the residents have been able to form despite histories of marginalization and trauma, and which assists the individuals sentenced there to "cope positively" (Sonn & Fisher, 1998, p. 459). By forming such a sense of community at Harris, the young women have demonstrated that, with the assistance of staff, they have the capacity and resources to cope with adversity.

Many of those interviewed alluded to a sense of safety at Harris, which is critical to the formation of a sense of community (Chipuer & Pretty, 1997). These young offenders often had few experiences with safe environments, and recognized the benefits of the security and routine offered by Harris. Many of the participants reported they felt a stronger sense of belonging, attachment, or sense of community at Harris than they did when they were not in custody.

Recidivism and Reintegration

Although it is generally assumed that a strong sense of community will have positive impacts, the longer-term implications of strong attachments to Harris are of concern. Some participants reported finding it difficult to reintegrate into the external community because their attachment to Harris was so strong. For some, this difficulty was so great it contributed to a desire to re-offend in order to return to custody. This finding may support previous findings (e.g., Goodstein, 1979; Porporino & Zamble, 1984) that suggested that those who were less adapted to a custodial facility were also less likely to re-offend. For the young women leaving Harris, their difficulties with reintegration seemed linked to intense loneliness, which in itself indicates a significant problem in the general community. If young women can be so lonely they wish to return to relationships formed in custody, they clearly lack relationships that provide such a sense of belonging (Baumeister & Leary, 1995) in the external community. This is especially critical given the importance of such social bonds, particularly to adolescent females (Morris, 1964; Thoits, 1991). The desire to return to custody may also be influenced by the degree to which these adolescents have experienced persecution in the general community (Bishop, et al., 1998). Some of those interviewed identified such persecution, related to their drug use, offending, or histories of trauma.

A positive sense of community is something with which many of the participants had little previous experience. Many expressed a significant lack of external community, while others signified that the sense of community they did have had a negative impact. Those clients who reported a strong, positive external sense of community did not have the same concerns about reintegration into the general community as did the clients who reported a negative or null external sense of community. Except for one client, all of those who reported strong external communities were on their first sentence at Harris when interviewed. This suggests that those with a stronger external community are more likely not to be repeat offenders with multiple episodes of incarceration. In addition, those on their first sentence were more likely to be older, in their late teens or early twenties. In comparison, those with minimal external sense of community (often related to unstable and traumatic childhoods, with few consistent adults) tended to have their first sentence when they were much younger. However, some of this discrepancy in age between those on their first sentences and those with multiple incarcerations may simply be explained by the finding that older adolescents are less likely to re-offend anyway (Fendrich, 1991; Ganzer & Sarason, 1973).

Of course, there are many factors involved in the development of a strong sense of community that would also impact on an individual's ability to maintain a drug and crime free lifestyle. Other studies (e.g., Alder & Hunter, 1999; Stewart & Tattersall, 2000) have addressed and highlighted these issues for the young women in custody, issues such as abuse, sexual assault, poverty, and parental substance use and offending. If a young female is subjected to trauma in her community, she is less likely to form a strong attachment to that community, and is also more likely to experience instability or removal from that community. As other research has demonstrated, such trauma will also make her more likely to develop a substance dependency and delinquent behavior (Bailey, Smith, & Dolan, 2001; Bank & Burraston, 2001; Rosenbaum, 1989; Smith & Thornberry, 1995).

Implications

The issues for Harris are clearly extremely complex. It appears that many of the women incarcerated within its fences are extremely comfortable there, and may even be unwilling to be released. There are implications regarding the risk of recidivism, given the prevalence of comments such as 'I feel safe when I'm at Harris' and 'It's probably the most stable home I've ever had.' Clearly, the issues regarding the role of the institution and the role of external agencies become extremely complicated. Is the answer to make the facility so unpleasant that it will act as a disincentive to return to crime? Of course, such a question raises many more, with implications regarding human rights, including the right of these young women to be treated with dignity and respect, regardless of the crimes they have committed. Further, it is difficult to address any question of how to treat these clients without taking into account the horrendous abuse that many have suffered in their lives prior to incarceration. Is such abuse to be allowed to continue in custody? Obviously, the answer must be no. However, if Harris makes a decision not to allow deliberate abuse on these young women while they are in custody (apart from removing their liberty), the facility automatically becomes a safer, more caring and more positive place than any they have previously experienced.

Why is it that some of these young women feel safer in a custody center, and that they are more comfortable there than they are in the general community? What issues does this raise for our community? That anybody would prefer to be locked up is an indictment on the resources, both practical and emotional, that we make available to these disadvantaged and marginalized young women. The fact that so many of the participants in this study commented on the importance of staff members' willingness to talk and listen implies that there is a lack of such willingness among the general population. Perhaps rather than blaming the communities from which the young people originate, we should all be questioning our own role in the larger community. Perhaps it is our larger community that is non-competent, since we seem unable to provide the resources to assist all our members to cope positively with adversity. In fact, the issue may be even larger, since we seem unable even to provide these people with a sense of membership, or allow them any capacity to influence how that community functions.

NOTES

[i] Harris Custodial Facility (a fictional name) accommodates female offenders between the ages of 10 and 21 years sentenced for various offenses. Harris has a variety of support, counseling, education, and community transition programs for the residents.

[ii] Estimate provided in personal correspondence with Noelle de Clifford, Chief Executive Officer of Harris Custodial Facility in February 2001.

[iii] Estimate provided in personal correspondence with Noelle de Clifford, Chief Executive Officer of Harris Custodial Facility in February 2001.

[iv] Sheehan, M. (1998). *Working with young people who have experienced family violence.* Workshop presented to a group of youth workers, Victoria, Australia

REFERENCES

Alder, C., & Hunter, N. (1999). "Not worse, just different"?: Working with young women in the juvenile justice system. *Report of Findings 2: Young women's juvenile justice experiences.* Melbourne, Australia: Criminology Department, University of Melbourne.

Bailey, S., Smith, C., & Dolan, M. (2001). The social background and nature of 'children' who perpetrate violent crimes: A UK perspective. *Journal of Community Psychology, 29,* 305-317.

Bank, L., & Burraston, B. (2001). Abusive home environments as predictors of poor adjustment during adolescence and early adulthood. *Journal of Community Psychology, 29,* 195-217.

Baumeister, R. F., & Leary, M. R. (1995). The need to belong: Desire for interpersonal attachments as a fundamental human motivation. *Psychological Bulletin, 117,* 497-529.

Bell, C. C., & Jenkins, E. J. (1993). Community violence and children on Chicago's southside. *Psychiatry, 56,* 46-54.

Bishop, P. D., Jason, L. A., Ferrari, J. R., & Huang, C. (1998). A survival analysis of communal-living, self-help, addiction recovery participants. *American Journal of Community Psychology, 26,* 803-821.

Bowler, I. (1997). Problems with interviewing: Experiences with service providers and clients. In G. Miller and R. Dingwall (Eds.). *Context and method in qualitative research* (pp. 66-76). London: Sage Publications.

Brodsky, A. E. (1996). Resilient single mothers in risky neighborhoods: Negative psychological sense of community. *Journal of Community Psychology, 24,* 347-363.

Brodsky, A. E., O'Campo, P. J., & Aronson, R. E. (1999). PSOC in community contexts: Multi-level correlates of a measure of psychological sense of community in low-income, urban neighborhoods. *Journal of Community Psychology, 27,* 659-679.

Bukstel, L. H., & Kilmann, P. R. (1980). Psychological effects of imprisonment on confined individuals. *Psychological Bulletin, 88,* 469-493.

Chavis, D. M., & Newbrough, J. R. (1986). The meaning of 'Community' in community psychology. *Journal of Community Psychology, 14,* 335-340.

Chesney-Lind, M. (1989). Girls' crime and women's place: Toward a feminist model of female delinquency. *Crime and Delinquency, 35,* 5-29.

Chipuer, H. M., & Pretty, G. H. (1997). *Adolescent construction of the neighbourhood community.* Paper presented at the Young People and Their Environment conference, Queensland Public Health, Queensland, Australia.

Community Services Victoria. (1992). *Becoming stronger: An action plan for young women.* Melbourne, Australia: Community Services Victoria.

Cottrell, L. D. Jr. (1976). The competent community. In B. H. Kaplan, R. N. Wilson, & A. H. Leighton (Eds.). *Further explorations in social psychiatry.* New York: Basic Books.

Davidson, W. B., & Cotter, P. R. (1991). The relationship between sense of community and subjective well-being: A first look. *Journal of Community Psychology, 19,* 246-253.

Davies, S., & Cook, S. (1998). Women, imprisonment and post-release mortality. *Just Policy, 14,* 15-21.

Department of Justice. (1996). *The Victorian Prison Service in 1995.* Melbourne, Australia: Department of Justice.

Fendrich, M. (1991). Institutionalization and parole behavior: Assessing the influence of individual and family characteristics. *Journal of Community Psychology, 19,* 109-122.

Ford, N. (1999). The treatment of major depression in adolescents. *The Australian Journal of Psychopharmacology, 9,* 36-39.

Funk, S. J. (1999). Risk assessment for juveniles on probation: A focus on gender. *American Association for Correctional Psychology, 26(1),* 44-68.

Ganzer, V. J., & Sarason, I. G. (1973). Variables associated with recidivism among juvenile delinquents. *Journal of Consulting and Clinical Psychology, 40,* 1-5.

Grisso, T. (1999). Juvenile offenders and mental illness. *Psychiatry, Psychology and Law, 6,* 143-151.

Goodstein, L. (1979). Inmate adjustment to prison and the transition to community life. *Journal of Research in Crime and Delinquency, 16,* 246-272.

Hancock, L. (1986). Economic pragmatism and the ideology of sexism: Prison policy and women. *Women's Studies International Forum, 9,* 101-107.

Harding, R. (1990). *Review of suicide and suicide attempts by prisoners in the custody of the Office of Corrections, Victoria.* Melbourne, Australia: Office of Corrections.

Hartmann, D. J., Wolk, J. L., Johnston, J. S., & Colyer, C. J. (1997). Recidivism and substance abuse outcomes in a prison-based therapeutic community. *Federal Probation, 61,* 18-25.

Henderson, D. J. (1998). Drug abuse and incarcerated women: A research review. *Journal of Substance Abuse Treatment, 15,* 579-588.

Hokanson, J., Megargee, E., O'Hagan, S., & Perry, A. (1976). Behavioral, emotional, and autonomic reactions to stress among incarcerated youthful offenders. *Criminal Justice and Behaviour, 3,* 203-234.

Iscoe, I. (1974). Community psychology and the competent community. *American Psychologist, 29,* 607-613.

Jasper, A., Smith, C., & Bailey, S. (1998). One hundred girls in care referred to an adolescent forensic mental health service. *Journal of Adolescence, 21,* 555-568.

Kowalski, M., & Caputo, T. (1999). Recidivism in youth court: An examination of the impact of age, gender and prior record. *Canadian Journal of Criminology, 41,* 57-84.

Knutson, J. F. (1995). Psychological characteristics of maltreated children: Putative risk factors and consequences. *Annual Review of Psychology, 46,* 401-431.

Leibling, A. (1994). Suicide amongst women prisoners. *The Howard Journal, 33(1),* 1-9.

Maden, A., Swinton, M., & Gunn, J. (1994). Psychiatric disorder in women serving a prison sentence. *British Journal of Psychiatry, 164,* 44-54.

McCord, J. (1983). A forty year perspective on effects of child abuse and neglect. *Child Abuse and Neglect, 7,* 265-270.

McMillan, D., & Chavis, D. (1986). Sense of community: A definition and theory. *Journal of Community Psychology, 14,* 6-23.

Miles, M. B., & Huberman, A. M. (1994). *Qualitative data analysis: An expanded sourcebook.* Thousand Oaks, CA: Sage Publications.

Morris, A., & Wilkinson, C. (1995). Responding to female prisoners' needs. *The Prison Journal, 75,* 295-305

Morris, R. (1964). Female delinquency and relational problems. *Social Forces, 43,* 82-89.

Osofsky, J. D., Wewers, S., Hann, D. M., & Fick, A. C. (1993). Chronic community violence: What is happening to our children? *Psychiatry, 56,* 7-21.

Page, R. (1991). Loneliness as a risk factor in adolescent hopelessness. *Journal of Research in Personality. 25,* 189-195.

Palmer, T., & Wedge, R. (1989). California's juvenile probation camps: Findings and implications. *Crime and Delinquency, 35,* 234-253.

Patton, M. Q. (1990). *Qualitative evaluation methods.* Newbury Park, CA: Sage.

Paulus, P. B., & Dzindolet, M. T. (1993). Reactions of male and female inmates to prison confinement: Further Evidence for a two-component model. *Criminal Justice and Behaviour, 20,* 149-166.

Porporino, F. J., & Zamble, E. (1984). Coping with imprisonment. *Canadian Journal of Criminology, 26,* 403-421.

Pretty, G. M. H., Andrewes, L., & Collett, C. (1994). Exploring adolescents' sense of community and its relationship to loneliness. *Journal of Community Psychology, 22,* 346-358.

Pretty, G. M. H., Conroy, C., Dugay, J., Fowler K. & Williams, D. (1996). Sense of community and its relevance to adolescents of all ages. *Journal of Community Psychology, 24,* 365-379.

Rokach, A. (1997). Loneliness in jail: Coping strategies. *International Journal of Offender Therapy and Comparative Criminology, 41,* 260-271.

Rokach, A., & Koledin, S. (1997). Loneliness in jail: A study of the loneliness of incarcerated men. *International Journal of Offender Therapy and Comparative Criminology, 41,* 168-179.

Rosenbaum, J. L. (1989). Family dysfunction and female delinquency. *Crime and Delinquency, 35,* 31-44.

Ruback, R. B., Carr, T. S., & Hopper, C. H. (1986). Perceived control in prison: Its relation to reported crowding, stress, and symptoms. *Journal of Applied Social Psychology, 16,* 375-386.

Rubin, H. J., & Rubin, I. (1995). *Qualitative interviewing: The art of hearing data.* Thousand Oaks, CA: Sage Publications.

Sarri, R. C. (1983). Gender issue in juvenile justice. *Crime and Delinquency, 29,* 381-397.

Sheidow, A. J., Gorman-Smith, D., Tolan, P. H., & Henry, D. B. (2001). Family and community characteristics: Risk factors for violence exposure in inner-city youth. *Journal of Community Psychology, 29,* 345-360.

Singer, I., Bussey, J., Song, L., & Lunghofer, L. (1995). The psychosocial issues of women serving time in jail. *Social Work, 40,* 103-113.

Smith, C., & Thornberry, T.P. (1995). The relationship between childhood maltreatment and adolescent involvement in delinquency. *Criminology, 33,* 451-481.

Solarz, A., & Bogat, G. A. (1990). When social support fails: The homeless. *Journal of Community Psychology, 18,* 79-96.

Sonn, C. C., & Fisher, A. T. (1998). Sense of community: Community resilient responses to oppression and change. *Journal of Community Psychology, 26,* 457-472.

Stewart, H., & Tattersall, A. (2000). *Invisible young women: Hearing the stories of young women who present with violent, challenging and/or offending behaviour.* Victoria: Young Women's Project.

Thoits, P. (1991). On merging identity theory and stress research. *Social Psychology Quarterly 54,* 101-112.

West, C. (1996). Ethnography and orthography: A (modest) methodological proposal. *Journal of Contemporary Ethnography, 25,* 327-352.

Wexler, H., DeLeon, G., Thomas, G., Kressel, D.,'& Peters, J. (1999). The Amity Prison TC Evaluation. *Criminal Justice and Behaviour, 26,* 147-167.

Widom, C., & White, H. R. (1997). Problem behaviours in abused and neglected children grown up: prevalence and co-occurrence of substance abuse, crime and violence. *Criminal Behaviour and Mental Health, 7,* 287-310.

Wooldredge, J. D. (1999). Inmate experiences and psychological well-being. *Criminal Justice and Behaviour, 26,* 235-250.

Zamble, E., & Porporino, F. J. (1990). Coping with imprisonment. *Criminal Justice and Behaviour, 17,* 53-70.

Chapter 6

SENSE OF COMMUNITY AMONG OXFORD HOUSE RESIDENTS RECOVERING FROM SUBSTANCE ABUSE
Making a House A Home[i]

Joseph R. Ferrari, Leonard A. Jason, Bradley D. Olson, Margaret I. Davis, and Josefina Alvarez
DePaul University

INTRODUCTION

As noted throughout this book, the study of a *psychological sense of community* (PSOC) is an important area of interest to community psychologists. Much of this interest focuses on the theoretical model proposed by McMillan and Chavis (1986) in their refinement of Sarason's (1974) notion of community. While a growing body of research has also examined the sense of place a person may experience, research on PSOC examines a person's identification with others and a feeling of belongingness within a physical setting (see Chipuer & Pretty, 1999; Hill, 1996). Consequently, a person may experience multiple layers of PSOC, even while residing in the same physical setting (Brodsky & Marx, 2001). For instance, Davidson and Cotter (1998) assessed a PSOC among sub-groups of city residents based on demographics, home ownership, and level of civic involvement. Prezza and colleagues (Prezza & Constantini, 1998; Prezza, Amici, Roberti, & Tedeschi, 2001) reported levels of PSOC and overall life satisfaction among residents of towns and cities. Zaff and Devlin (1998) found that PSOC was strong among residents of garden apartments and high rises.

Some community psychologists argue that PSOC includes more than the confines of one's neighborhood (Glynn, 1981; 1986; Kingston, Mitchell, Florin, & Stevenson, 1999). Hyde (1998), using a large sample of urban adults, found that PSOC was stronger among women, persons with high rates of social contact with others, and a low rate of perceived distress encountered in their neighborhoods. Persons with a strong PSOC report a need for affiliations (Burroughs & Eby, 1998; Davidson, Cotter, & Stovall, 1991), sense of empowerment and perceived control over their lives (Chavis & Wandersman, 1990), self-control and self-esteem (Ferrari, Loftus, & Pesek, 1999), and self-disclosure to others (Zaff & Devlin, 1998). A strong PSOC also influences a person's tendency toward community volunteer service (Ferrari & Chapman, 1999) among both younger and older adults (Ferrari, 2000; Ferrari, Dobis, et al., 1999). Other studies, in contrast, found that a lack of a PSOC promotes dissatisfaction at work and high rates of employee grievances (Catano, Pretty, Southwell, & Cole, 1993), physical ailments among low income, urban residents (Brodsky, O'Campo, & Aronson, 1999), greater problems with health care costs, choices, and services (Ahern, Hendryx, & Siddharthan, 1996), and child-raising problems by minority single mothers (Brodsky, 1996).

Despite the plethora of research on PSOC (see also Chipuer & Pretty, 1999; McMillan, 1996), little attention has focused on how a perceived sense of community may impact on substance abuse recovery. Bishop, Chertok, and Jason (1997) found that a PSOC for recovering alcoholics was unrelated to their hope for the future, and may include a level of disharmony among group members. Bishop, Jason, Ferrari, and Huang (1998), however, reported that among continued residents of an alcohol treatment facility, over time, PSOC increased while disharmony among members decreased. This chapter focuses on alcohol and drug addiction recovery among men and women residing in a communal-living, self-help setting that promotes a PSOC toward sobriety called *Oxford House*.

We believe that the bonding and abstinence support within the sense of community of Oxford House that residents receive turns the "house" into a "home" for those persons invested in the lives of fellow residents. In this chapter we present a brief review of our recent research focusing on the Oxford House model for recovering substance abusers, demonstrating how a PSOC promoting social support for abstinence may facilitate addiction recovery.

Persons Recovering from Substance Abuse: The Oxford House Alternative

A review of the literature on the effectiveness of substance abuse programs indicate high recidivism rates for men and women within one year of inpatient treatment, with 52-75% of all participants dropping out during treatment (Montgomery, Miller, & Tonigan, 1993). Consequently, there is a tremendous need to develop, evaluate, and expand lower cost, non-medical, community-based care options for substance abuse patients (Jason, Olson,

Ferrari, & Davis, 2001). Related to this need, there is a rising interest in self-help groups (Humphreys, Mankowski, Moos, & Finney, 1999; McCrady & Miller; 1993; Tonigan, Toscova, & Miller, 1996) and in mutual-help influenced treatments because they offer an empowerment orientation and may be more cost-effective than more professionally directed treatments (Olson, Jason, Ferrari, & Hutcheson, 2002).

Oxford House, founded in 1975, illustrates a community-based approach that facilitates a PSOC toward substance abuse abstinence that is unlike traditional care. In usual after-care programs, trained professionals are necessary, and therapeutic communities have a maximum length of stay for residents. Oxford House offers a community where residents can live without the involvement of professional treatment staff and where there are no time restrictions on length of stay (Oxford House Manual, 1988). Because there is no maximum stay, unlike therapeutic communities, residents may have a greater opportunity to develop a sense of competence toward maintaining abstinence, and to bond in long-term relations with other residents. Similar to Alcoholics Anonymous (AA), members of an Oxford House receive abstinence support from peers; unlike AA, there is no single, set course for recovery that all members must follow (Nealon-Woods, Ferrari, & Jason, 1995). In fact, residents of Oxford House are free to decide personally whether to seek psychological or substance abuse treatment by professionals or by mutual support groups such as Narcotics Anonymous (NA). In short, Oxford House offers residents the "best" of options: freedom to decide whether to seek and choose which (if any) treatment they desire while receiving constant support and guidance within an abstinent communal setting fostering one's PSOC. The involvement of the individual in the course of treatment may encourage him/her to learn how to cope effectively and independently with stressful situations that promote substance abuse (Chazan, Levi, & Tal, 1989; Majer, Jason, Ferrari, Venable, & Olson, 2001). This sense of competence may reduce the risk of relapse when the person returns to former high-risk situations or family settings that may promote relapse.

Each House operates democratically with majority rule regarding membership (i.e., > 80% approval rate), although residents elect House officers (President, Secretary) every six months who facilitate the handling of clerical responsibilities (e.g., convene weekly House meetings, collect rent). House members maintain financial independence, with each resident paying rent and doing chores. Deviations from House financial responsibilities, disruptive, anti-social behaviors, or resuming drugs or alcohol use result in eviction (Jason, Pechota, Bowden, et al., 1994; Oxford House Manual, 1988).

In 1988, the Anti-Drug Abuse Act was passed by Congress, allocating federal funds to any state for the start-up of Oxford Houses. A group of recovering substance abusers, through the support of an established House, may request only up to $4,000 from their state in an interest-free loan to begin a new Oxford House. Repayment of loans is returned to the fund for start-up costs of additional Houses in that state. The houses are rented, multi-bedroom dwellings for same-sex occupants (range = 6-8 persons). At present, 70% are male Houses and 30% are female Houses; 55% of occupants are Caucasian, 35% are African-American, 5% are Hispanic, and 5% are other (e.g., Asian-Americans across 48 states). Grassroots movements helped expand the number of Houses to over 850 within the USA (J. Paul Molloy, Oxford House, Inc., personal communication, September, 2001). In the current cost-conscious environment, this network of Oxford Houses represents an inexpensive and effective setting that promotes abstinence.

Oxford House was established for substance abusers seeking a supportive, democratic, mutual-help setting where a PSOC with other recovering substance abusers may develop long-term abstinence skills (Jason, Olson, Ferrari, & Davis, 2002; Majer, et al., 2001). Each House is organized in a way that sets up a setting for recovery away from "using others." That is, residents of Oxford House "switch" membership from a community of peers who use or abuse drugs and alcohol to membership with abstinent peers seeking mutual support toward sobriety. Membership with similar others is a cornerstone to a PSOC (McMillan, 1996), and for recovering addicts that membership must include abstinent peers. The sense of community within Oxford House is lived out in a setting away from mainstream substance users. The residents develop skills where an abstinence culture can be lived and reinforced, thereby changing their setting for addiction. Similar to AA and other 12-Step programs, the Oxford House approach to recovery promotes total abstinence (as opposed to reduced harm or sustained periods of abstinence with moderate substance use permitted). While proponents of harm reduction and moderation management methods may consider this approach extreme, we believe that for many recovering addicts such a setting may be needed as they attempt to regain control over their lives. Also, social support from similar others in a communal setting may be perceived as another type of dependency which is encouraged in Oxford House. We propose that because of the mutual support, modeling of self-efficacy skills, and fellowship among House residents that a sense of "pro-dependency" toward recovery may be beneficial to residents (Nealon-Woods, et al., 1995). Learning to conform to a lifestyle of total substance abuse abstinence within the company of supportive others may result in a change in how residents of Oxford House construct their addiction and recovery (Olson, et al., 2002).

Investigators have examined how abstinent self-efficacy may affect long-term alcohol and drug-addition abstinence (see Marlatt & Gordon, 1985). Self-efficacy is a belief in one's ability to exercise control over events or to perform particular behaviors that result in effective management of future actions (Bandura, 1977). The development of self-efficacy has been implicated as a critical factor in resisting the urge to use drugs and alcohol in high-risk situations after treatment, and in maintaining long-term abstinence (Miller, Ross, Emmerson, & Todt, 1989). Thus, social factors or environments that promote the development of self-efficacy would appear to reduce the likelihood of substance abuse relapse (Majer, et al., 2001; Olson, et al., 2001).

We believe the Oxford House communal-living experience of abstinence social support nurtures a PSOC where abstinence self-efficacy may increase. For instance, newer residents may be exposed to a variety of high-risk situations for using drugs. Residents who have been members of the House for longer periods of time may act as successful role models for dealing with these high-risk situations. Receiving abstinence support from Oxford House members committed to the goal of long-term abstinence may enable substance abusers to engage in successful coping responses in these situations, increasing self-efficacy and thereby reducing the probability of relapse. Enhancing self-efficacy for coping in these and related situations may reduce the probability of future relapse.

Longabaugh, Beattie, Noel, Stout, and Molloy (1993) proposed that the presence or absence of social support advocating abstinence related to recovery from substance abuse. These relationships are moderated by social investment, defined as the extent to which a person values the abstinence support. In fact, Longabaugh, Wirtz, Beattie, Noel, and Stout (1995) reported that continued substance abuse abstinence at 18 months post-treatment was greatest among individuals with high social investment within networks supportive of their abstinence. As one might expect, then, successful substance abuse outcome is most likely when one has social support networks that advocate abstinence (i.e., abstinence support), and when one has high social investment in those networks.

An Oxford House experience may provide residents with a PSOC where peers can "teach" effective coping and controlling skills, be resources for information on how to maintain abstinence, and act as advocates for abstinence. To the extent that recovering substance abusers invest or commit themselves to an abstinent setting (Longabaugh, et al., 1993), support for abstinence from similar strengthens that person's substance abuse self-efficacy. Residents of Oxford House may gain abstinence support in these new environments and they may make a social commitment to those networks, which facilitates their abstinence self-efficacy. As social investment in abstinence support becomes stronger, increases in the person's abstinence self-efficacy may promote substance abuse abstinence. Abstinence support, theoretically, may strengthen one's own self-efficacy for abstinence (Beattie, Longabaugh, & Fava, 1992; Beattie, et al., 1993). The sense of community among abstinent others within and outside an Oxford House appears to be the type of environment necessary for the development of self-efficacy for substance abuse abstinence.

In relation to PSOC, personal investment with similar others creates a sense of "us" versus "them" (McMillan, 1996). We hypothesize that, consistent with Longabaugh, et al.'s (1993) model, the level of personal or social investment a person places on his/her abstinence support (from within and outside an Oxford House) impacts that network's influence. Abstinence support, theoretically, may strengthen one's own self-efficacy for successful substance use outcomes (Beattie et al., 1992; 1993). Therefore, as social investment in abstinence support becomes stronger, the PSOC increases, and increases in the person's abstinence self-efficacy promotes substance abuse abstinence. Residents of Oxford House come to view abstinent peers as "us" and persons who continue to abuse substances as "them." We propose that for Oxford Houses residents' abstinence support and social investment within that support (i.e., how much one values and is committed to that support) impacts on one's self-efficacy, which, in turn, impacts substance abuse abstinence.

It seems reasonable to expect that in social networks and activities that encourage substance abuse abstinence, former substance abusers living in an Oxford House may be able to focus on improving their self-efficacy. The values and goals that transcend individual participation and the perception that one is accepted by members of an ongoing group may result in optimism about the future and a lessening of stress (Bishop, et al., 1997). In short, living with abstinent others may create a PSOC with a common goal toward successful substance use outcomes within a self-help recovery environment (Coe & Ferrari, 2001; Jason, Ferrari, Smith, et al., 1997). Living with others who share a similar view toward abstinence validates one's perceptions and reinforces behavior change. In the next section, we outline briefly a series of research studies that examined the nature and characteristics of the Oxford House model of communal-living.

A Review of the Oxford House Research by DePaul University Researchers

One important goal of our first study on Oxford House (Jason, Ferrari, Groessl, Dvorchak, & Molloy, 1997) was to examine how the characteristics of residents compared with those of other substance abuse recovery programs as reported in the literature. A number of client-demographic similarities between different Oxford House samples were obtained across the six years and with different data collection methods. We obtained information from "Oxford House, Inc." a national nonprofit clearinghouse for information and referrals to the program. Brief survey or interview data on some residents living in select states (between 1988 and 1993) have been collected. It is important to note that these data were collected by convenience sampling of residents who happened to be present when a representative of Oxford House visited a local House.

Residents typically were never married (53%), young (early to mid-30s), Caucasian (58%), and male (70%). These findings are consistent with previous studies of substance abusers in recovery programs (Grant, Chou, & Pickering, 1992; Hasin & Glick, 1992). The majority of residents were educated at least through high school (71%), employed with monthly incomes sustaining an independent living (69%), poly-substance abusers of alcohol and other drugs (53%), and had experienced homelessness (64%). This client-demographic profile of Oxford House residents matched the typical profile characteristics reported on recovering substance abusers from more traditional programs (e.g., Armor, Polich, & Stambul, 1978; Beattie, et al., 1992).

Another of our studies examined the characteristics and perceptions of men from Illinois Oxford Houses (Jason, Ferrari, Smith, et al., 1997). When the first Illinois Oxford House opened in 1992, a team of investigators at DePaul University began assessing the characteristics of male Oxford House residents as they entered one of 11 newly formed houses. During the course of 18 months, investigators conducted face-to-face interviews with 134 men (M age = 33.5; SD = 9.4) who had between 2 weeks and 3 months living experience in an Oxford House (79% completion rate) and recorded their qualitative responses to the five items: (a) their personal benefits for joining an Oxford House, (b) their reasons for choosing a setting such as Oxford House to facilitate their recovery, (c) their prior knowledge of the Oxford House concept, (d) the perceived differences between living in an Oxford House compared with other living experiences, and (e) the characteristics that made Oxford Houses different from other treatment programs.

Each Illinois House held weekly business meetings in which the residents collected rent (M weekly rent = $70) and discussed household matters. The majority of participants were Caucasians (62.9%) who had never been married (56.1%). Latino residents were fluent in English. In terms of education, most of the sample of men in Illinois either had a high school education or less (47.3%) or had begun or completed college (49.7%). Most participants were employed (65.3%), with a mean income of $805.88 per month (range = $651.89-1150.00).

These men indicated that their knowledge before entering Oxford House included a strong fellowship (i.e., PSOC) with similar substance abusers, the enforcement of set rules on abstinence, and participation in the self-governance of their living experiences. Moreover, they reported that PSOC with similar others in a stable environment, plus self-paced time for personal psychological growth while abstinent, were the most important benefits to gain from living in an Oxford House. These men claimed that a PSOC and a structured setting where successful substance use outcomes were enforced were reasons for choosing to reside in a House. In addition, they believed Oxford House differed from other recovery programs they experienced because it allowed the development of a PSOC with similar others, stability in their life, and a period of time for personal growth and change to occur (see also Bishop, et al., 1997).

The implications of this study are that it demonstrates that abstinence support from similar others is perceived to be an important quality obtained by living in an Oxford House. The mutual-help aspect of Oxford House, coupled with its self-governed structure and stability, made it desirable to residents. The shared bonds and validation of experiences help residents to reconstruct their view of addiction and redefine their activity setting. In terms of developing a PSOC, it seems that living in a stable environment for recovering addicts is an important component.

In another study, we evaluated male residents after 6 months of residence in Oxford House (Smith, Ferrari, & Jason, 1995). Eighty-two percent of residents had reported a history of criminal involvement prior to entering Oxford House; however, at the six-month follow-up, no criminal activity was found among residents. Within this PSOC self-help living setting, recovering substance abusers were able to maintain employment and eliminate criminal activities over the six months, thereby reducing the need for government subsidies and interventions (Smith, et al., 1995). Most residents also reported use of 12-step programs, such as NA and AA, to assist in their maintenance of abstinence (Nealon-Woods, et al., 1995). Adjusting to a lifestyle free of criminal activity, maintaining employment, and seeking self-help methods toward recovery may promote increased personal responsibility and self-efficacy for residents in an Oxford House. The setting can be seen as supportive, protective, and nurturing help to reshape one's construction of their activity. The feelings of belongingness in an Oxford House may foster increased levels of self-worth and reinforce the belief that abstinence is appropriate and desirable.

We also used a structured diagnostic interview to investigate the prevalence of psychiatric co-morbidity among residents in several Oxford Houses from the mid-west (Majer, Jason, Ferrari, & North, in press). In that study, socio-demographic information and substance abuse treatment characteristics were obtained on each participant. Considerable psychiatric co-morbidity was present, consistent with other studies with substance abusers. Antisocial personality disorder, mood disorders, and anxiety disorders were the most frequently observed co-morbid disorders among these substance abusers, whose drugs of choice were cocaine, alcohol, and cannabis. Affective disorders were the most prevalent observed Axis I disorders among Oxford House participants, and there was no significant difference between men and women for major depression.

Bishop, et al. (1998) found that those who did not leave the house during the study period had stayed longer ($M = 349$ days) than those who were evicted for relapse ($M = 129$ days), and those evicted for disruptive behavior ($M = 159$ days). The houses included in this study had only recently opened, and it often takes about six to eight months for the initial residents of an Oxford House to develop a PSOC and cohesion. Their PSOC seemed to be evolving through their mutual support for abstinence. Because many of the residents of the Oxford House were first-time residents to enter, there was greater instability than had been reported at more long-standing Oxford Houses. Preliminary data collected by Oxford House Inc. (J. Paul Molloy, personal communication, May 1995) suggests that few residents are evicted from more established houses.

We also studied demographic characteristics of men and women residing for an average of three months in Oxford Houses (Ferrari, Curtin, Dvorchak, & Jason, 1997). Women were more likely to report sexual abuse as an adult, be diagnosed with eating disorders, engage in writing bad checks prior to recovery, and claim they sought Oxford House for a structured and safe setting. Men were more likely to have engaged in drug sales and residential theft prior to recovery, and sought Oxford House as an attempt to rebuild interpersonal relationships. Men and women did not differ in their co-dependency, as assessed by a psychometric measure, suggesting that the PSOC that may develop among residents is not a factor of interpersonal dependence.

In addition, we collected data through interviews and surveys from women with and without children entering one of several Oxford Houses (Ferrari, Jason, et al., 1999). We found that both groups of women reported the same expectations (i.e., that Oxford House would provide them with a healthy environment for their continued successful substance use outcomes while residing in a setting that promotes a strong PSOC with similar peers). Findings suggest that Oxford Houses offer women and women with children a setting where they can enhance their skills at long-term abstinence within a PSOC, and such settings also assist mothers in the care of their children. Unfortunately, there currently are only a little over a dozen Oxford Houses in the U.S. for women and children. Nevertheless, this study suggests that for women and women with children recovering from addiction the acquisition of similar members in their network of a PSOC validates their perceptions and may buffer them against relapse.

GENERAL CONCLUSION

These studies indicate that Oxford House residents reflect the profile of most other recovering substance abusers, yet living in a community of abstinent others makes their "house" a "home" through a PSOC. This PSOC seems suitable for diverse minority populations, such as women with children. Moreover, our initial studies indicate that Oxford House residents desire "safe and abstinent settings" that promote a PSOC where they can gain skills for long-term abstinence from their addiction. Abstinence may be prolonged as individuals acquire skills and strengthen self-efficacy necessary to control abstinence throughout life. Residents prefer a PSOC setting that includes only individuals who were like themselves -- person's recovering from substance abuse. Fellow residents may facilitate their coping and control of stressful life events that may prompt relapse.

In addition, from a public health perspective these studies suggest that the Oxford House model promoting a PSOC for substance abuse recovery has great potential. For example, within this mutual-help, communal living setting, recovering substance abusers were able to maintain employment and eliminate criminal activities, thereby reducing their need for government subsidies. Maintaining employment for recovering substance abusers may promote increased personal responsibility, which may increase self-efficacy beliefs. These studies, then, raise both theoretical and practical issues needing further evaluation on the PSOC and addiction recovery.

Future Oxford House Research and Implications

Presently, we are conducting two large-scale community research projects that investigate the processes of change that occur among Oxford House residents. In one project we are comparing across twelve-months the recovery processes of a random sample of Illinois Oxford House residents compared to usual care participants. The other project focuses on assessing, over one year, a random sample of Oxford House residents from across the United States. In both cases, abstinence social support and abstinence self-efficacy is examined in order to ascertain how a PSOC for recovery impacts on substance abuse. We believe that our collective body of research will add substantially to an understanding of the role of PSOC in addiction recovery and provide practical tools that may be generalized to other public health areas. (See Jason, et al., 2002, for a full discussion on the need for a second order change strategy to promote substance abuse treatment.)

Within these two community projects, we also are investigating how Oxford House residents view their sense of physical place. We are collecting data on the neighborhood setting characteristics where these Houses are located. To understand the processes of change within Oxford House (Olson, et al., 2001), we are collecting information on eviction rates within Houses, the rules and regulations that Houses use to manage their setting, and how House policies actually impact on target disruptive behaviors among residents. In relation to the concept of social support, we are examining resident's social ties (i.e., network size), as well as their perceived and received support levels. Other PSOC-related variables we are exploring include racial tolerance as it may develop among House members, altruistic acts between and among House members, conflict resolution skill-building through peer interactions in an Oxford House, interpersonal-romantic relationships experienced while living in a House, and changes in the nature of the community resources that facilitate recovery among House members. In addition, we are investigating psychosocial variables among Oxford

House members such as self-regulation, parenting skills, optimism and hopefulness about the future, illegal activities, and eating disorders, trauma experiences, and co-morbidity rates.

Taken together, we believe these studies provide a well-rounded, in-depth assessment of a promising mutual-help substance abuse program known as Oxford House. The Oxford House model's emphasis on peer relationships in a cost-effective setting may be useful in the design of other treatment programs. Moreover, Oxford House is an excellent "working model" for principles related to community psychology, such as the impact of a PSOC on individuals and groups.

NOTES

[i] Funding for this manuscript was made possible in part by an NIH–National Institute for Alcohol and Alcohol Abuse grant award (# AA 12218) and NIH-National Institute for Drug Abuse (#DA 13231). The authors express much gratitude to the men and women of Oxford House who devoted time and interest to participate in each of the research projects, as well as the numerous students and volunteers who assisted in data collection and analysis for these projects. The authors also thank Jason Oleniczak and Thara Nagarajan for assisting in preparing this chapter.

REFERENCES

Ahern, M. M., Hendryx, M. S., Siddharthan, K. (1996). The importance of sense of community on people's perceptions of their health-care experiences. *Medical Care, 34,* 911-923.

Armor, D. J., Polich, J. M., & Stambul, H. B. (1978). *Alcoholism and treatment.* Report R - 1739 -NIAAA. Santa Monica, CA: The Rand Corp.

Bandura, A. (1977). Self-efficacy: Toward a unifying theory of behavior change. *Psychological Review, 84,* 191-215.

Beattie, M. C., Longabaugh, R., Elliott, G., Stout, R. L., Fava, J., & Noel, N. E. (1993). Effects of the social environment on alcohol involvement and subjective well being prior to alcoholism treatment. *Journal of Studies on Alcohol, 54,* 283-296.

Beattie, M. C., Longabaugh, R., & Fava, J. (1992). Assessment of alcohol-related workplace activities: Development and testing of "Your Workplace." *Journal of Studies on Alcohol, 53,* 469-475.

Bishop, P. D., Chertok, F., & Jason, L. A. (1997). Measuring sense of community: Beyond local boundaries. *Journal of Primary Prevention, 18,* 193-212.

Bishop, P. D., Jason, L. A., Ferrari, J. R., & Huang, C. F. (1998). A survival analysis of communal-living, self-help, addiction recovery participants. *American Journal of Community Psychology, 26,* 803-821.

Brodsky, A. E. (1996). Resilient single mothers in risky neighborhoods: Negative psychological sense of community. *Journal of Community Psychology, 24,* 347-363.

Brodsky, A. E., O'Campo, P. J., & Aronson, R. E. (1999). PSOC in community context: Multi-level correlates of a measure of psychological sense of community in low-income, urban neighborhoods. *Journal of Community Psychology, 27,* 659-679.

Burroughs, S. M., & Eby, L. T. (1998). Psychological sense of community at work: A measurement system and explanatory framework. *Journal of Community Psychology, 26*, 509-532.

Catano, V. M., Pretty, G. M., Southwell, R. R., & Cole, G. K. (1993). Sense of community and union participation. *Psychological Reports, 72*, 333 -334.

Chavis, D. M., & Pretty, G. M. H. (1999). Sense of community: Advances in measurement and application. *Journal of Community Psychology, 27*, 635- 642.

Chavis, D. M., & Wandersman, A. (1990). Sense of community in the urban environment: A catalyst for participation and community development. *American Journal of Community Psychology, 18*, 55-81.

Chipuer, H. M., & Pretty, G. M. H. (1999). A review of the Sense of Community Index: Current uses, factor structure, reliability, and further development. *Journal of Community Psychology, 27*, 643-658.

Coe, M. S., & Ferrari, J. R. (2001). Halfway houses. In W. E. Craighood (Ed.) *Encyclopedia of Psychology and Neuroscience* (pp. 657-659). New York: John Wiley and Sons.

Davidson, W. B., & Cotter, P. R. (1998). Measurement of sense of community within the sphere of city. *Journal of Applied Social Psychology, 16*, 608- 619.

Davidson, W. B., Cotter, P. R., & Stovall, J. G. (1991). Social pre-dispositions for the development of sense of community. *Psychological Reports, 68*, 817-818.

Ferrari, J. R. (2000). Contributing to the community: The impact of service learning on students and community agencies. *Proceedings of the International Education Conference on Community Building in a Global Context.* ACEA/OCEAM

Ferrari, J. R., & Chapman, J. G. (1999). *Educating students to make a difference: Community-based service learning.* Binghamton, NY: Haworth Press.

Ferrari, J. R., Curtin, M., Dvorchak, P., & Jason, L. A. (1997). Recovering from alcoholism in communal-living settings: Exploring characteristics of African-American men and women. *Journal of Substance Abuse, 9*, 77-87.

Ferrari, J. R., Dobis, K., Kierawski, S., Boyer, P., Kardaras, E. I., Michna, D. M., & Wagner, J. M. (1999). Community volunteerism among college students and professional psychologists: Does taking them to the streets make-a-difference? *Journal of Prevention and Intervention in the Community, 18*, 35-51.

Ferrari, J. R., & Jason, L. A. (1994: October). *Oxford House: Promoting empowerment in a self-help community.* Paper presented at the annual ECO-Community Conference, Bowling Green State University, at Liberty Center, OH.

Ferrari, J. R., Jason, L. A., Nelson, R., Curtin-Davis, M., Marsh, P., & Smith, B. (1999). An exploratory analysis of women and men within a self-help, communal-living recovery settings: A new beginning in a new house. *American Journal of Drug and Alcohol Abuse, 25*, 305- 317.

Ferrari, J. R., Loftus, M. M., & Pesek, J. (1999). Young and older caregivers at homeless animal and human shelters: Selfish and selfless motives in helping others. *Journal of Social Distress and the Homeless, 8*, 37-49.

Glynn, T. J. (1981). Psychological sense of community: Measurement and application. *Human Relations, 34*, 789-818.

Glynn, T. J. (1986). Neighborhood and sense of community. *Journal of Community Psychology, 14*, 341-352.

Grant, B. F., Chou, S. P., Pickering, R. P. (1992). Empirical subtypes of DSM-III-R alcohol dependence: United States, 1988. *Drug and Alcohol Dependence, 30*, 75-84.

Hasin, D. S., & Glick, H. (1992). Severity of DSM-III-R alcohol dependence: United States, 1988. *British Journal of Addiction, 87*, 1725-1730.

Hill, J. L. (1996). Psychological sense of community: Suggestions for future research. *Journal of Community Psychology, 24*, 431-438.

Humphreys, K., Mankowski, E. S., Moos, R. H., & Finney, J. W. (1999). Do enhanced friendship networks and active coping mediate the effect of self-help groups on substance abuse? *Annals of Behavioral Medicine, 21*, 54-60.

Hyde, M. M. (1998). Local sentiments in urban neighborhoods: Multilevel models of sense of community and attachment to place. *Dissertation Abstracts International, 59*, 1354.

Jason, L. A., Ferrari, J. R., Dvorchak, P. A., Groessl, E. J., & Molloy, J. P. (1997). The characteristics of alcoholics in self-help residential treatment settings: A multi-site study of Oxford House. *Alcoholism Treatment Quarterly, 15*, 53- 63.

Jason, L. A., Ferrari, J. R., Smith, B., Marsh, P., Dvorchak, P. A., Groessl, E., Pechota, M. E., Curtin, M., Bishop, P. D., Grams, G., Kot, E., & Bowden, B. S. (1997). An exploratory study of male recovering substance abusers living in a self-help, self-governed setting. *Journal of Mental Health Administration, 24*, 332- 339.

Jason, L. A., Olson, B. D., Ferrari, J. R., & Davis, M. I. (2002). *Substance abuse: The need for second order change.* Manuscript under review.

Jason, L. A., Pechota, M. E., Bowden, B. S., Lahmar, K., Pokorny, S., Bishop, P., Quintana, E., Sangerman, C., Salina, D., Taylor, S., Lesondak, L., & Grams, G. (1994). Oxford House: Community living is community healing. *Addictions: Concepts and strategies for treatment.* (pp. 333-338). Gaithersburg, Md.: Aspen.

Kingston, S., Mitchell, R., Florin, P., & Stevenson, J. (1999). Sense of community in neighborhoods as a multi-level construct. *Journal of Community Psychology, 27*, 681- 694.

Longabaugh, R., Beattie, M., Noel, N., Stout, R.L., & Malloy, P. (1993). The effects of social investment on treatment outcome. *Journal of Studies on Alcohol, 54*, 465-478.

Longabaugh, R., Wirtz, P. W., Beattie, M. C., Noel, N., & Stout, R. (1995). Matching treatment focus to patient social investment and support: 18-month follow-up results. *Journal of Consulting and Clinical Psychology, 63*, 296-307.

Majer, J., Jason, L. A., Ferrari, J. R., & North, C. (in press). Co-morbidity among Oxford House residents: A preliminary outcome study. *Addictive Behaviors.*

Majer, J., Jason, L. A., Ferrari, J. R., Venable, L. B., & Olson, B. D. (2001). *Abstinence social support and abstinence self-efficacy among Oxford House residents: An initial study.* Manuscript under review.

Marlatt, G. A., & Gordon, J. R. (1985). *Relapse prevention: Maintenance strategies in addictive behavior change.* New York: Guilford Press.

McCrady, B. S., & Miller, W. R. (1993). *Research on Alcoholics Anonymous: Opportunities and alternatives.* New Brunswick, NJ: Rutgers University Press.

McMillan, D. W. (1996). Sense of community. *Journal of Community Psychology, 24*, 315- 325.

McMillan, D. W., & Chavis, D. M. (1986). Sense of community: A definition and theory. *Journal of Community Psychology, 14*, 6-23.

Miller, P. J., Ross, R. Y., Emmerson, R. Y., & Todt, E. H. (1989). Self-efficacy in alcoholism: Clinical validation of the Situational Confidence Questionnaire. *Addictive Behaviors, 14*, 217-224.

Montgomery, H. A., Miller, W. R., & Tonigan, J. S. (1993). Differences among AA groups: Implications for research. *Journal of Studies on Alcohol, 54*, 502-504.

Nealon-Woods, M. A., Ferrari, J. R., & Jason, L. A. (1995). Twelve-step program use among Oxford House residents: Spirituality vs. social support in sobriety. *Journal of Substance Abuse, 7*, 311-318.

Olson, B. D., Jason, L. A., Ferrari, J. R., & Hutcheson, T. D. (2002). *An application of the transtheoretical model to mutual help.* Submitted for publication.

Oxford House, Inc. (1988). *Oxford House Manual.* Silver Springs, MD.

Prezza, M., & Constantini, S. (1998). Sense of community and life satisfaction: Investigation in three different territorial contexts. *Journal of Community and Applied Social Psychology, 8*, 181-194.

Prezza, M., Amici, M., Roberti, T., & Tedeschi, G. (2001). Sense of community referred to the whole town: Its relations with neighboring, loneliness, life satisfaction, and area of residence. *Journal of Community Psychology, 29*, 29-52.

Roberts, R. N. (1999). Supporting families with children in a community. In R. N. Roberts & P. R. Magrab (Eds*). Where children live: Solutions for serving young children and their families* (pp. 31-72). Stamford, CT: Ablex Publications.

Sarason, S. B. (1974). *The psychological sense of community: Prospects for a community psychology.* San Francisco: Jossey-Bass.

Smith, B., Ferrari, J. R., & Jason, L. A. (1995, April). *Age-related differences among addicts in recovery: Effects of communal-living on abuse recov*ery. Paper presented at the annual meeting of the Eastern Psychological Association, Boston, MA.

Tonigan, J. S., Toscova, R., & Miller, W. R. (1996). Meta-analysis of the literature on Alcoholics Anonymous: Sample and study characteristics moderate findings. *Journal of Studies on Alcohol, 57,* 65-72.

Zaff, J., & Devlin, A. S. (1998). Sense of community in housing for the elderly. *Journal of Community Psychology, 26,* 381-397.

Chapter 7

SENSE OF COMMUNITY IN A UNIVERSITY SETTING
Campus as Workplace

Beverly B. Mahan, Wendy M. Garrard, Susan E. Lewis, and John R. Newbrough
Vanderbilt University

INTRODUCTION

The term sense of community (SOC) is used liberally in both the popular press and psychology, sociology, and management literatures to characterize a variety of social settings, including families, neighborhoods, schools, organizations, cities and rural areas, businesses and industries. Various instruments have been developed to measure sense of community in a variety of settings, and it has been documented among adults, adolescents, and pre-adolescents. It is apparent from these references that the authors judge sense of community as something to be desired, something for which to strive. It seems as if everyone knows what sense of community is, and most everyone seems to want it.

Despite the ubiquitous use of the phrase, there remain many questions regarding the meaning and application of sense of community in diverse settings and populations. It is a challenge to assess SOC in a manner that is grounded in community theory, while at the same time making no assumptions about the similarities in dimensions and correlates from setting to setting. Various efforts to assess SOC have been based on differing theoretical foundations, which prevent comparisons between results, and limits theory building and testing (Chipuer & Pretty, 1999).

The authors were part of a community research group (CRG) known for its work on sense of community (e.g., Chavis & Newbrough, 1986; McMillan & Chavis, 1986; Newbrough & Chavis, 1986). They encountered an opportunity to explore the relationship between sense of community and trust on the campus of a research university where the chief executive officer (the Dean) was new and wanted to involve the faculty in strategic planning. This dean encountered a belief that faculty morale was low and that this was a factor in the daily round of work. As part of the strategic planning process, the dean decided that there should be an initial assessment of morale of the faculty and staff. This could then serve as a benchmark for later assessments that might show whether the planning affected the morale. Morale on this campus was approached in sense of community terms as "campus as community" had been a theme of a prior study by the faculty senate.

THE CAMPUS AS COMMUNITY

Our inquiry into sense of community in the university workplace and the relationship between SOC and trust is built on the theoretical foundation laid by McMillan and Chavis (1986), as recommended by Chipuer and Pretty (1999). The earliest inquiry into sense of community used neighborhood as the referent. Shortly afterwards, researchers began to broaden their conceptualization of community beyond the neighborhood to include cities, schools, etc.

Communities are social phenomena with central characteristics that bring the people and organizations together. Typically, they are characterized as being either location-based or interest-based settings. Location-based communities are often residential and have the primary subgroup designated as a neighborhood. When the setting is a workplace, location within a common building or on a common floor can serve as the central characteristic. Interest communities are more likely to be identified by an activity center, such as a religious community (church), or a function, like a professional organization. The university, however, can be considered a combination of both location and interest-based communities.

The university is a centrally important institution in the society and is organized around two goals: (1) the discovery of knowledge through the nurturance of individual talent, and (2) the passing on of knowledge through teaching. Like all social institutions, morale is an important aspect of the experience, and the level of morale greatly affects performance. Morale at educational institutions can be described as "school spirit" and is associated with student morale and sports activities. Yet, the campus is also a workplace, one to which concepts from organizational psychology and the construct of sense of community (SOC) can be applied.

Hill (1996) noted that sense of community is setting specific. Therefore, the researcher must understand the unique characteristics of the setting before initiating a research project, so that setting specific correlates can be included in an assessment of sense of community. There are elements common to most universities, such as mission, purpose, and organizational structure, which distinguish them from other businesses and industries. There are also distinctive features of individual settings that may moderate sense of community among the members, such as history, rituals, and leadership style. Examination of both the generic and unique nature of a setting is important in the design of an inquiry and interpretation of the results. As an example, Burroughs and Eby (1998) included the common elements of membership, influence, needs meeting, and shared emotional connection (theorized by McMillan and Chavis, 1986) in their assessment of sense of community among adults in various work settings. In addition, they tested the hypothesis that individual, group, and organizational characteristics serve as antecedents of sense of community in the workplace. The results supported their hypothesis, and highlighted the specific correlates of sense of community that are unique to the work setting.

There are several characteristics that most universities have in common, but that also distinguish them from many other work settings. The organizational structure of universities is both flat and vertical. There are executive functions performed by the various administrators. These positions begin at the departmental level (e.g., chair or head) and proceed upward (vertically) to the level of college deans and beyond. Within the departments, however, the organization is basically flat. There is a status structure, but the work is not typically organized by status. Faculty members are each organizations unto themselves. Each is expected organize, obtain funding for, conduct, analyze, and disseminate findings of a research program. There are, typically, minimal direct supervisory relationships within departments.

The work of the university serves both a service delivery and a product-producing function. Its service is to the students, as well as to the community in which it is situated, and to the broader academic communities to which it belongs. The products produced by the university are methodological approaches to inquiry, knowledge as contained in papers and reports, and faculty and students equipped with that knowledge.

The work of others who have examined sense of community in the workplace provide interesting reference points and directions for our study. Royal and Rossi (1996) found that associations with smaller subunits within the organization were associated with greater SOC. We sought to expand this idea by examining SOC in each of a set of nested communities within the work setting, namely the university, school, department, and work group as referent. We expected an inverse relationship between the size of the referent and sense of community.

Theoretical issues involving the role of gender and job status in the development and maintenance of sense of community have not been resolved, as previous studies have produced mixed results. For example, regarding gender, Pretty and McCarthy (1991) found that SOC at work varied according to gender differences. Specifically, peer support from, and involvement with, others were the primary predictors of SOC for male managers. The predictors of SOC for female managers were supervisor support, involvement, and work pressure, which had a positive impact for men, and a negative impact for women. Lambert and Hopkins (1995) found a number of gender differences related to workplace SOC. For women, having influence in decision-making, formal work support such as benefits, and family supportive policies were more important than they were to men. In contrast, supervisor and work group support were more important to men than women.

Pretty and McCarthy (1991) found no significant status differences in SOC, but they did find that the predictors of SOC differed for managers and non-managers. Royal and Rossi (1996) reported no status differences and did not speculate on that finding. The Burroughs and Eby (1998) results indicated no length of service or workgroup size differences in SOC. Although length of residency is linked to neighborhood sense of community, length of service in the workplace has only been found to be associated with SOC for male managers (Burroughts & Eby, 1998; Pretty & McCarthy, 1991; Royal & Rossi, 1996). Similarly, while job status might seem to provide employees with varying degrees of influence and, thus, could be associated with SOC, neither the Pretty and McCarthy, nor Royal and Rossi studies found an association between job status and SOC in the workplace. However, sense of community may be negatively related to worker burnout (Pretty, McCarthy, & Catano, 1992). Overall, the lack of consistency in findings suggests, among other things, that setting differences may influence the impact of individual characteristics on SOC. These mixed results were the basis for our inquiry into the group (gender, job status, and work referent) differences in SOC in this academic workplace setting.

Trust within the University

A very relevant construct in the university workplace is trust. Trust is necessary in any inquiring system with a horizontal structure. That is, in order to ask the unasked questions, probe the unknown, and challenge the known, the academician must be able to trust the support of colleagues, the university, and the greater academy. In order to be self-directed, the members have to have a strong sense of trust as well as a common bond. Without this basic level of trust, the difficult questions are not asked, the limits are not tested, and innovations are not dared. The system of granting tenure to researchers and teachers was established in part to protect those who produce knowledge, to ensure the support of the institution for the individual inquirer (Finkin, 1996).

In university settings, where power differentials are the norm, where a hierarchy is well established and recognized by all, trust must be established between individuals at every level of the hierarchy before mutual influence can take place. When trust is not a part of the work environment, and influence is not available to all, then a sense of community among faculty, staff, and administrators is weakened, resulting in a lack of community for some, and alienation for others. There may be human capital costs associated with this lack of community in terms of personnel turnover, a compromised ability of departments to attract and retain highly sought-after faculty, and ultimately a perception of decreased credibility of the institution in the eyes of the students it serves. Following two focus groups and pilot testing of survey items, it was clear to the authors that lack of trust between some employees was a unique characteristic of this university setting.

Sense of Community and Trust

McMillan and Chavis (1986) did not use the term trust in setting forth a definition and theory of sense of community. Instead, in discussing the membership element, they offered that membership boundaries "provide members with the emotional safety necessary for needs and feelings to be exposed and for intimacy to develop" (p. 9). A benefit, and requirement, of membership in a community is emotional safety. Conversely, describing the investment component of the shared emotional connection element, McMillan and Chavis argued that shared emotional connection requires some amount of emotional risk taking. The amount of interpersonal emotional risk taken directly affects one's sense of community. Although not named explicitly, trust was an integral part of their theory of sense of community.

A review of the literature suggested that intimacy is built on trust, and the capacity of the individual and the community to trust and be trustworthy determines the level of SOC members have with the community. Trust is a multidimensional construct, with most research converging on competence, openness, concern, and reliability as the four dimensions of organizational trust (Mishra, 1996). Emerson (1981) defined organizational trust as a non-economic exchange between workers and the organization. Tway and Davis (1993) conceptualized trust as the state of readiness for unguarded interaction with someone or something. Etzioni (1988) argued that trust is fundamental to all market transactions. The substantial literature on organizational trust identifies it as a key element in the interaction-influence process of organizational life (Likert, 1967). Speaking to the community side of the equation, Harris (1993) argued that trust is highly influential in group formation and maintenance.

Interestingly, in a 1996 revisit of the theory, McMillan renamed and reordered the original elements of sense of community. The influence component became trust, which requires order in the form of social norms and rules, decision making procedures based on the greater good rather than personal gain, and reciprocal influence between members. McMillan redefined sense of community in part as "a feeling that there is an authority structure that can be trusted" (p.315), connecting with the hierarchy and status variables so relevant in university settings. Asked to comment on the role of trust in sense of community, Chavis indicated that it is implicit in the membership component of SOC, synonymous with the security and safety afforded in membership (Chavis, personal communication, May 11, 1999). Together, the originators of the SOC model found trust a vital ingredient in the membership, influence, and emotional connection elements of SOC.

The benefits that grow out of trusting relationships, and the costs of mistrust, can be clearly illustrated in the workplace setting. The relevance of exploring the relationship between SOC and trust in the workplace is supported by research findings that suggest that distrust and suspicion are common in organizations (PEW, 1998; Sitkin & Roth, 1993). In addition, the public trust in both private and public institutions has been declining for years (Kramer, 1999). Therefore, it seemed to the authors that any inquiry into sense of community in the workplace should account for the role of trust.

We considered several possibilities regarding the relationship of trust to sense of community. One is that there is no relationship between the two constructs. A second possibility is that trust and sense of community are one and the same. A third possibility is that trust is an element of sense of community, like membership or influence. In this case, trust would be a necessary, but not completely sufficient, foundation upon which sense of community rests. An analogy would be reading comprehension, which is an element or component of general intelligence. Such a relationship between the constructs could be established through tests of convergent validity. A fourth possibility is that trust and sense of community are different, but related constructs, in the same way that weight and height are separate but highly related constructs. A primary goal of our inquiry, in addition to examining the nature of sense of community among faculty and staff of the university workplace, was to determine the nature of the relationship between workplace SOC and trust.

Measuring Sense of Community and Trust in the University Workplace

The Sense of Community Index (SCI) has proven to be a practical survey instrument (Perkins, Florin, Rich, Wandersman, & Chavis, 1990). However, identification of and empirical support for the elements of SOC have been more mixed. In a review of the SCI, Chipuer and Pretty (1999) reported reliabilities ranging from .64 to.80, and support for three of the four elements of SOC theorized by McMillan and Chavis (1986) when adapting the SCI to the workplace. The strengths of the SCI are that it is an established scale with "strong validity" (Chavis, personal communication, May 11, 1999), and more than 15 years of use and refinement. In order to examine the relationships between SOC and trust among college faculty and staff, 11 of the 12 SCI items were included in the survey[i] instrument. The one remaining

SCI item ("I recognize most people from my neighborhood.") was excluded because it did not directly translate to the academic setting. It was reasoned that SOC in this setting should not be expected to be strongly related to visual recognition of others. The wording of all the items was adapted to reflect the academic setting. For example, "supervisor," and "manager" were replaced by "colleague/co-worker." Each item was given a uniform stem that led to the response choices. For example, the SCI item, "It is very important for me to live in this neighborhood" was changed to, "It is very important for me to work at..."

Five items were written by the authors and the CRG to assess trust in this setting. Each reflected the interpersonal aspect of organizational trust, while at the same time allowing the respondents to define the construct for themselves. The five held face validity. The items were designed to assess the giving and receiving of trust with colleagues, superiors, and subordinates in the workplace, not to thoroughly cover all aspects of trust as reported in the literature. The responses to the five trust items were aggregated, and that one score inserted as a substitute for the twelfth SCI item.

Each item stem was followed by five response choices reflecting five work settings: the university, the school, my department, my research center, and my work or research group. None of the choices was defined for the respondent. In particular, work or research group was most subject to individual interpretation. The respondents were asked to indicate their level of agreement with each item stem relative to each work environment. If they were not affiliated with a particular work setting, such as a research center, they were to leave that response category blank. There were so few responses at the research center level that analyses were not possible.

Seven demographic items referring to department, research center, and specific program affiliation, job status, and gender were included. A line was provided after each item for the respondents to add comments that would elaborate, explain, or contextualize their responses. Feedback from the pilot stage resulted in the deletion of other demographic items to further ensure the anonymity of respondents. For example, we were not able to gather data on length of service, intent to leave, or ethnicity. However, this reluctance on the part of some faculty and staff validated our plan to explore trust in this setting.

A total of 152 completed surveys were returned. Although demographic information was not provided by all respondents, available information indicated that 77 staff members (84% response rate) and 72 faculty members (74% response rate) completed surveys. This represented 63% of the tenured and 68% of the non-tenured faculty at the school during the time period covered by the study. The female faculty respondents accounted for 54% of the faculty respondents, and the male faculty 46%. In comparison, females made up 48% and males 52% of all school faculty during the same time period covered by the study. The university could not provide demographic data on the school staff, so it was not possible to determine whether the staff respondents were representative of all school staff.

THE FINDINGS

The CRG was interested in whether there were any setting differences in SOC, and hypothesized that the more proximal the setting, the higher the SOC. Because all respondents were from within one school, their university level SOC is difficult to interpret without a comparison group of others within the university, but outside the school. It was the case that some staff members of the school previously had held other positions within the university and, therefore, had a frame of reference for assessing sense of community in the university and school. However, this was not the case for other staff members or the faculty.

For the aggregate respondents of faculty and staff, the central tendency for SOC did increase as the setting became more proximal, with the highest values of SOC observed in the work group setting (Figure 1).

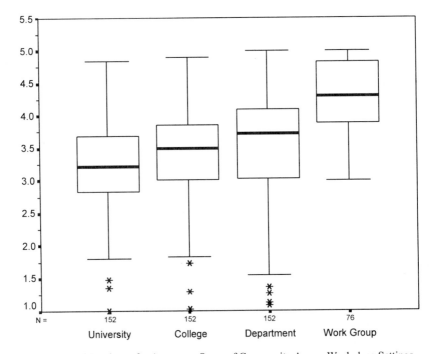

Figure 1. Central Tendency for Aggregate Sense of Community Across Workplace Settings

Initial analyses indicated significant differences between faculty and staff at all four work settings: University ($F_{(1, 149)}$ = 11.915, p = .001), School ($F_{(1, 149)}$ = 6.527, p = .012), Department ($F_{(1, 149)}$ = 38.950, p = .001), and Work Group ($F_{(1, 149)}$ = 8.270, p = .005). The correlations among the global scores ranged from .712 to .499 for the University, School, and Department levels, and the Work Group ranging from .071 to .291. A between groups multivariate F including all four work·settings revealed a significant overall effect for job status (Wilk's Λ = .623; $F_{(8, 124)}$ = 4.133, p = .000), but no gender effect or interaction. Univariate F's show that job status contributes significantly at the levels of Department ($F_{(2, 65)}$ = 5.458, p = .006) and Work Group ($F_{(2, 65)}$ = 6.852, p = .002).

Looking at Figure 2, we see that there are differences in the findings depending on the job status of respondents. In general, mean staff scores for SOC were higher than faculty for the university, school, and department setting, but faculty scores were higher than staff in the work group setting.

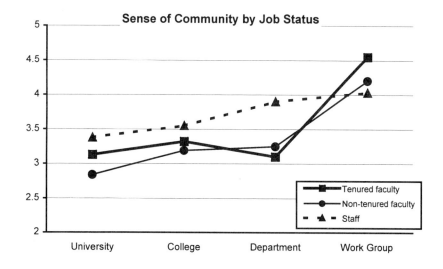

Figure 2. Mean Sense of Community for Selected Groups Across Workplace Settings (All items were measured using a numerical scale of 1 to 5.)

Although there were no significant differences due to gender, or a job status by gender interaction, it is important to consider whether the differences in proportions of males and females may play a role in the differences attributed to job status. Approximately two-thirds of the tenured faculty were male, and females comprised about two-thirds of non-tenured faculty and staff. To better understand how SOC may be influenced by gender, the disaggregated means were examined for males and females by staff, tenured faculty, and non-tenured faculty.

Figure 3 illustrates that female staff report a slightly higher SOC than male staff; non-tenured male faculty consistently score in the highest range for faculty in all settings, and non-tenured females report a relatively low SOC across all settings. Finally, we note that only tenured faculty (males and females alike) show a decrease in SOC from school to department setting, and the highest scores for SOC in the work group setting are reported by all tenured faculty along with non-tenured males.

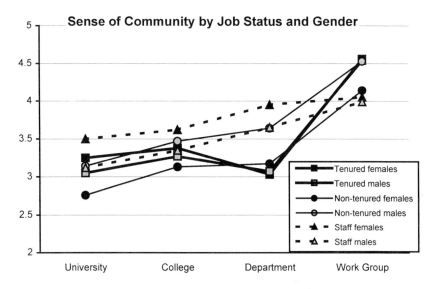

Figure 3. Mean Sense of Community for Selected Groups by Gender
(All items were measured using a numerical scale of 1 to 5.)

We reason that the department is a very different experience for faculty and staff. There is a clear hierarchy and structure among the staff that link them together. They are more likely than faculty to interact with each other, with faculty, and students on a daily basis. On the other hand, faculty members are more autonomous within the department. On any given day, they may have no contact with others in the department, or perhaps only those in their office suite. Instead, faculty bonds are more likely to be with those in other locations who share a discipline or research interest. The competition within the department for resources may be the antithesis of sense of community. Still, without data from other universities, it is not possible to know whether this dip in SOC scores at the department level is unique to this particular university.

The work group had the highest number of missing cases, suggesting that some respondents did not identify with a work group. Those missing tended to be women and staff. Thus, the work group respondents were composed of more males and faculty than found at other setting levels. The high mean score at the work group level was due in part to 20 scores that clustered at the ceiling. These scores came mostly from tenured faculty, equal parts male and female, who rated the importance of research very highly. Often, tenured faculty work groups are made up of one or a few faculty and those students who participate in their research projects. Non-tenured faculty and staff typically do not have an analogous work group. It is important to note, however, that the staff merely leveled off at the work group level, as did both male and female non-tenured faculty.

We were intrigued by the subgroup differences in SOC related to job status and gender at the Department level. Previous studies found mixed gender results for sense of community and trust at work. In our study, males and faculty were generally below the overall mean, except in the work group setting, while females and staff were generally above the overall mean, except in the work group. Most of the staff in this sample were female (58 females out of 73 staff), so a "female influence" for higher SOC in staff would be reasonable. Non-tenured faculty were also predominantly female (18 out of 26), so if females tended to demonstrate higher SOC as a rule, if follows that a similar influence would be observed in non-tenured faculty, but this was not the case. Female, non-tenured faculty were consistently among the lowest scorers in all settings. Perhaps this is a reflection of the fact that females were less likely to be tenured in this setting, and they perceived the work environment as less supportive or secure. There may be a more complex dynamic operating in conjunction with job status and gender. Unfortunately, due to the disproportionate number of males and females across the staff and faculty breakouts, it is impossible to disentangle the covariation of job status and gender in this sample.

Our hypothesis regarding job status differences was that SOC would mirror the status hierarchy, that tenured faculty would have the highest SOC and staff the lowest. We reasoned that tenured faculty have the most influence, the highest salaries, have specific and specialized professional needs that can best be met in a university setting, and have emotional connections with colleagues based on both the shared setting and disciplinary bonds. Conversely, we expected that lower status and benefits, and job skills that could be employed in any variety of settings, would result in lower SOC among staff. Continuing with this logic, we expected that non-tenured faculty SOC would fall between tenured faculty and staff. Finally, we held no *a priori* hypothesis regarding departmental differences.

Contrary to our expectations regarding job status differences, the mean staff SOC was higher than faculty at all but the work group setting, and all differences were significant. Breaking faculty into tenured and non-tenured groups resulted in small sub-sample sizes for the non-tenured group in particular, resulting in a loss of power to determine significance. The mean SOC for each group is interesting and not as predicted, nonetheless. Again, non-tenured females (n = 18) were different from other faculty and staff by a lower score at the university, school, and workgroup level. This group ran against the other faculty, except at the department level, and consistently against the female staff trends. Finally, we found no significant department differences in SOC between any subgroup.

Trust

A major area of interest for us was the concept of trust, specifically interpersonal trust in the workplace. Based on a literature review, as well as faculty and staff responses gathered in focus groups and pilot testing, we were intent on including items in our survey that specifically addressed interpersonal trust in the workplace. What we found was that the trust items were highly correlated with the SOC items, ranging from .80 to .92 across setting referents. As expected, due to the high correlation, the exploratory analysis yielded a similar pattern of findings across settings for the averaged trust items that were added to the SOC. The correlations among the global scores ranged from .737 to .423 among the University, School and Department levels, with the correlations involving the Work Group ranging from -.056 to .006. The multivariate F for trust across all four settings indicated an overall significance for job status (Wilk's $\Lambda = .559$; $F_{(8, 102)} = 4.307$, $p = .000$), but no gender effect or interaction. The univariate F's show that job status contributes significantly at the Department ($F_{(2, 54)} = 5.128$, $p = .009$), and Work Group ($F_{(2, 54)} = 5.596$, $p = .006$) levels. Post hoc comparisons show that staff scored significantly higher than tenured faculty at the Department level (mean difference = .935, $95\%CI = .301$ to 1.570). At the Work Group level there was a mean difference of .512 ($95\%CI = .171$ to .853) between tenured faculty and staff, with tenured faculty obtaining the higher value. Also, there was a significant mean difference of .428 ($95\%CI = .025$ to .831 between non-tenured faculty and staff at the Work Group level.

To confirm our hypothesis that trust is a related but distinct construct, the findings would have had to establish the divergent validity of trust. However, the findings offered no evidence of divergent validity. The trust measure behaved exactly like the SOC measure, and did not significantly diverge at any point, for any subgroup. We could only conclude that trust and sense of community are bundled together, that trust covaries with SOC across gender and job status groups.

Broadening the Understanding of Sense of Community

Exploring sense of community outside the neighborhood has led researchers to conclude that different referents highlight a variety of dimensions of SOC, such as fun and safety (Pretty, et al., 1996), job satisfaction (Burroughs & Eby, 1998), and trust. Re-examining the theory of sense of community in light of these complicated setting differences results in its refinement and enhancement. For example, the finding that SOC differs according to referent within the workplace implies that it may also differ according to various neighborhood referents. Reconsidering the neighborhood results in this light suggests that block, or even section of a block SOC may have a different meaning from a global neighborhood SOC. The pattern of increasing SOC as the referent becomes smaller, and socially closer, did not hold at the work group setting for staff, and was less dramatic for non-tenured faculty. This may be explained by the fact that the work group is qualitatively different from other referents, in that people enter into these subgroups voluntarily around a shared interest or project. Members can change workgroups, perhaps when the project is completed or interests change. There may be less of a hierarchical structure within workgroups, which promotes equal influence among members. On the whole, our findings relative to referent are consistent with those of previous researchers, and underscore the importance of organizational structure to workplace SOC.

Hierarchy is less of an issue in the workgroup than in other workplace settings. It is not known whether status differences between neighbors, such as those created by socioeconomics, create differential dependencies on the neighborhood. The McMillan and Chavis (1986) model of sense of community may be most applicable to those communities without varying status and dependency levels among members. When status and dependency differences are present in a community, it seems that additional elements of SOC must be considered. It is likely that even those elements of SOC that community referents such as neighborhood and workplace hold in common, be they membership, influence, need meeting, emotional connection, or trust, are manifested differently in each setting. In the case of trust, the literature seems to agree that it is a basic requirement for all healthy human relationships, and is, therefore, a part of SOC in the neighborhood as well as the workplace. Nevertheless, the trust requirements between neighbors are not the same as those between a department chair and the dean, or between collaborators on a research project.

Regarding status differences alone, the findings of this study were contrary to those reported in the literature, with staff reporting higher SOC than faculty. The gender and status variables were confounded, with the men in this setting holding most of the high status tenured faculty positions, and the women holding the majority of low status staff positions. These findings challenge some assumptions about the role of status and influence in sense of community, that greater status is associated with greater sense of community. Likewise, the literature identified job status as a predictor of trust, but the findings of this study suggested that for some subgroups, high status was correlated with less trust and less status was associated with greater trust.

Trust and SOC in the Workplace

Given the finding that trust is an element of workplace SOC, it is important to consider what meaning it holds in the various workplace settings. The organizational trust literature makes clear that there are several dimensions of trust, though there is no consensus on what those might be. It is possible, for instance, that trust in the fulfillment of transactional (economic) contracts differentially affects SOC at the university through workgroup levels. These distinctions between the varying impacts of the elements on SOC become especially important when considering intervention efforts, regardless of the community referent. It is important not only to establish the role of trust in sense of community, but that of other elements suggested in the literature as well, such as physical environment and management style.

As trust is a part of workplace sense of community, it follows that trust may mediate job status and SOC. Perhaps persons in lower status jobs feel trusted by those with greater status to uphold the day-to-day operation. Perhaps they feel no competition for their job and are not responsible for competing for resources, which in turn creates for them a more trusting work environment. A rival explanation is that those in lower status jobs have no expectation of being in control or exerting influence, thus, their expectations are met, resulting in greater SOC. On the other hand, those in higher status jobs may be more likely to hold expectations about control and influence within their work environment, which if not met, may reduce SOC.

Intervention

As is the case with many psychological constructs, sense of community is difficult to quantify. No one has ever suggested that there is an optimum amount of sense of community one should have; neither has any instrument provided a threshold below which a sense of community intervention is indicated. Nevertheless, assessment is often conducted not only to understand a present condition, but also to direct an intervention for change in that condition. Given our role as consultants to the dean in the matter of faculty and staff morale, we were very interested in considering what our results suggested as possible next steps to improve sense of community. One might conclude that a viable strategy would be to import the features of the workgroup, which reported positive SOC, into other settings. However, there is evidence that such an approach will fail (Stewart, 1996). The nature of the workgroup is that its members feel responsible only to themselves, and as a group are resistant to management from outside. Attempts to impose characteristics of the workgroup on other subgroups within an organization are more likely to disrupt the SOC of the workgroup and fail to strengthen the SOC of other groups. A more sound approach may be to encourage the development of workgroups, or communities of practice, so that everyone has a place in which they can collaborate, influence, meet needs and have needs met. Such an organizational structure is relatively flat, spreading decision-making power across the membership. To enter into such an arrangement would require a foundation of trust among members, and unique supervisory skills within the leadership.

Research has identified skilled supervisors, mentoring, and need meeting in the form of access to resources, including information and people, as the reasons workers take, stay, and feel supported in a job (Fitz-Ens & Phillips, 1999). Need meeting has an obvious connection to sense of community. Mentoring provides a personal connection with another member, as well as guidance into the rituals and customs of the organization, and as such can be easily associated with SOC. Supervisory skill is more difficult to link with the elements of SOC, and is not adequately assessed in the SOC instrument. However, attention to these three features of the workplace, skilled supervisors, mentoring, and need meeting, may be an effective intervention strategy.

Finally, responses to individual items in the assessment may direct an intervention. The findings indicated that all SOC items tapped into the general sense of community construct. Therefore, responses to particular items may serve as indicators of barriers to SOC among workers. For example, if respondents generally disagree with the items, "Genuine appreciation for my work is often expressed," and "Criticisms are offered in a positive and constructive way," then training of employees can target these specific areas.

Application of Findings Beyond SOC

For a practical application, tying outcomes to SOC in the workplace would be very powerful. For example, intent to stay/leave data may connect with SOC. If it can be established that those with a high SOC intend to stay with the organization, and those with low SOC intend to leave, then SOC can be linked to the administrative costs associated with rehiring and training employees, as well as the benefits of retaining senior employees. Particularly in the academic workplace, the retention of senior faculty may result in a steady flow of grant money to the university. In addition, a correlation between faculty SOC and student evaluations of faculty members would indicate the effect of faculty SOC in the classroom, on students, and on student-teacher relationships.

The costs and benefits associated with faculty SOC relative to students may include future giving to the institution by alumni. Finally, SOC may indirectly contribute to the accreditation of programs within the university through reduced turnover, retention of senior faculty, and positive student evaluations of faculty. Establishing a connection between these examples of economic capital and SOC will address the issue raised by some as to the importance, or necessity, of establishing, increasing, or maintaining, SOC in the workplace.

From a more theoretical perspective, the setting specific nature of sense of community within the organization raises questions about the elements of SOC at each setting level. Are SOC differences the result of something more than size of referent? What constitutes sense of community within a large university, for example, and does it differ from the important elements of SOC at the department level? Perhaps opportunities to influence the larger organization are more limited than in the department, while emotional connections may be more easily made in the department where personal interaction occurs regularly.

The finding that people in different job status categories have different SOC experiences in the organization raises questions about the effect on SOC of transactions between people. How does the level of SOC in one subgroup affect that in others? If classroom teachers do not feel a sense of community in their school, is it still possible for the students to have a strong SOC? Students may have connections from their neighborhoods or dorms that carry over into school. Teachers of the same race or religious practice may have a sense of community based outside of work that serves as a foundation for the establishment of SOC for that subgroup within the school. Beyond the effect of varying levels of SOC between groups within an organization, what is the effect of differing SOC levels on the community as a whole? How much variance within can a community tolerate?

There are those who question the need for SOC at work. Some argue that competition is necessary to succeed in a research university setting, and that SOC is antithetical to competition. Comments of this nature reflect the interaction between trust and SOC. Several respondents in this study rejected the desirability of SOC at work, saying, "I don't want SOC," or "Why do we need SOC?" Yet no one said, "I don't want trust," or "Trust doesn't matter". Perhaps this was because SOC was not defined for respondents, so they were expressing a fear of the unknown, or a resistance to some forced interaction and loss of choice. Or perhaps a lack of trust left no foundation on which to build a sense of community. Whatever the source of the aversion, it is important to consider that in some situations, it would be a mistake to assume that all members desire a sense of community. In fact, there may be active resistance to the establishment or maintenance of sense of community.

There seems to be a receptive audience for and a high tide of interest in this area of research, from schools for children and adults, to non-profit organizations, municipalities, and the corporation. The opportunity is ripe for making significant strides in understanding the complex nature of sense of community at work, and using that knowledge to improve the lives of individuals, as well as the products and services of organizations and communities.

NOTES

i The 11 SCI items and 5 trust items were part of a 53-item survey that also included 3 open-ended questions. Only the results obtained with the SCI and trust items are reported here. For a discussion of the findings from the full instrument, see Mahan (2000).

REFERENCES

Burroughs, S., & Eby, L. (1998). Psychological sense of community at work: A measurement system and explanatory framework. *Journal of Community Psychology, 26*, 509-532.

Chavis, D. M., & Newbrough, J. R. (1986). The meaning of "community" in community psychology. *Journal of Community Psychology, 14*, 335-340.

Chipuer, H. M., & Pretty, G. M. H. (1999). A review of the Sense of Community Index: Current uses, factor structure, reliability, and further development. *Journal of Community Psychology, 27*, 643-658.

Emerson, R. W. (1981). *Essays: First & second series*. Franklin Center, PA: Franklin Library.

Etzioni, A. (1988). *The moral dimension: Toward a new economics*. New York: Free Press.

Finkin, M. W. (1996). *The case for tenure*. Ithaca, NY: ILR Press.

Fitz-Ens, J. & Phillips, J. (1999). *New dimensions in human resources*. New York: AMACOM.

Harris, G. M. (1993). *Trust and betrayal in the workplace: The subordinates' point of view*. Unpublished doctoral dissertation, The University of Tulsa, Tulsa, OK.

Hill, J. L. (1996). Psychological sense of community: Suggestions for future research. *Journal of Community Psychology, 24*, 431-438.

Kramer, R. (1999). Trust and distrust in organizations: Emerging perspectives, enduring questions. *Annual Review of Psychology, 50*, 569-598.

Lambert, S. J., & Hopkins, K. (1995). Occupational conditions and workers' sense of community: Variations by gender and race. *American Journal of Community Psychology, 23*, 151-179.

Likert, R. (1967). *The human organization*. New York: McGraw-Hill.

Mahan, B. B. (2000). *An exploratory study of the relationship of sense of community and trust in the university workplace*. Unpublished doctoral dissertation. Vanderbilt University.

Mahler, J. (1988). The quest for organizational meaning: Identifying and interpreting the symbolism in organizational stories. *Administration and Society, 20*, 344-368.

McMillan, D. W. (1996). Sense of community. *Journal of Community Psychology, 24*, 315-325.

McMillan, D. M., & Chavis, D. W. (1986). Sense of community: A definition and theory. *Journal of Community Psychology, 14*, 6-23.

Mishra, A. K. (1996). Organizational responses to crisis: The centrality of trust. In R. M. Kramer & T. R. Tyler (Eds.), *Trust in organizations: Frontiers of theory and research*. Thousand Oaks, CA: Sage Publications.

Moore, K. M., & Gardner, P. D. (1992). *Faculty in a time of change: Job satisfaction and career mobility*. East Lansing, MI: Collegiate Employment Research Institute.

Newbrough, J. R., & Chavis, D. M. (1986). Psychological sense of community, I: Foreword. *Journal of Community Psychology, 14*, 3-5.

PEW Research Center for People and the Press. (1998). *Deconstructing distrust: How Americans view government*. Washington, DC: PEW.

Perkins, D., Florin, P., Rich, R., Wandersman, A., & Chavis, D. (1990). Participation and the social and physical environment of residential blocks: Crime and community context. *American Journal of Community Psychology, 18*, 83-115.

Pretty, G. M. H., & McCarthy, M. (1991). Exploring psychological sense of community among women and men of the corporation. *Journal of Community Psychology, 19*, 351-361.

Pretty, G. M. H., McCarthy, M., & Catano, V. (1992). Psychological environments and burnout: Gender considerations in the corporation. *Journal of Organizational Behavior, 13*, 701-711.

Pretty, G. M. H., Conroy, C., Dugay, J., Fowler, K., & Williams, D. (1996). Sense of community and its relevance to adolescents of all ages. *Journal of Community Psychology, 24*, 365-379.

Royal, M. A., & Rossi, R. J. (1996). Individual-level correlates of sense of community: Findings from the workplace and school. *Journal of Community Psychology, 24*, 395-416.

Sitkin, S. B., & Roth, N. L. (1993). Explaining the limited effectiveness of legalistic "remedies" for trust/distrust. *Organization Science, 4*, 367-392.

Stewart, T. A. (1996, August 5). The invisible key to success. *Forbes*, pp. 173-175.

Tway, D. C., & Davis, L. N. (1993). Leadership as trust building -- Communication and trust. *Proceedings of the Eighth Annual Texas Conference on Organizations* (pp. 48-52). Lago Vista, TX: The University of Texas at Austin.

Chapter 8

BEING CHURCH AND COMMUNITY
Psychological Sense of Community in a Local Parish

Ron Miers and Adrian T Fisher
Victoria University

INTRODUCTION

The nature of communities, how they form, and how they function are questions that underpin much of the research in sense of community. In his description of communities, Heller (1989) proposed that they are formed to serve one of three functions -- they were locational (based on place), relational (based on a shared interest, issues, etc.), or they form so that the members can exercise joint power. Church parishes, as embodiments of religious communities, incorporate elements of both the location and relational functions; with the adherence to a super-ordinate structure and goals, and a transcendent aim, represented by the broader church and its body of beliefs and liturgies.

Most parishes have developed, in western countries, as the place of worship central to a residential area. Hence, they are subject to demographic and social shifts, with their viability subject to the numbers of active parishioners. Local parishes face many of the challenges that have recently befallen other communities with the loss of participants, changing demographics in the local neighborhood, and an erosion of the basis of faith upon which liturgy and action are based (Dokecki, Newbrough, & O'Gorman, 2001).

A more recent phenomenon has seen some parishes formed through types of missionary outreach with social action goals as core representations in their charters. Parishes that have been developed through a focus on activist goals, in addition to locational and relational elements, can face extra challenges because of the passage of time, the nature of the privilege that underpinned their original founding, and the necessity to replace departing members and, especially, founding leaders as they moved on or retire.

In this chapter, we consider a parish whose founding reflected the coming together of members to share their power with those seen as less privileged. It is used to examine the ways in which the social ideals, charismatic leadership, and changes in socio-economics and demographics are able to challenge the bases of the parish, and the struggle that is needed to define new directions and meaning for the community.

Church Community

A Christian Biblical image of community is based in the emergence of tribes or clans in the Old Testament writings, and was closely related to the land, geographic regions, and bloodlines (Bright, 1960). The Biblical texts reflect a later theological interpretation of the formation of the nation of Israel as a political, social, and racial entity (Ackroyd, 1968). These theological emphases and developments led to an increased emphasis on the local church as a community. As a result, some local church leaders began to refer to themselves as the "Church Community" which emphasizes the type of place the local church is envisaged to be. Community was, however, rarely if ever defined; so a broad understanding of community with elements of belonging, support and participation has been reflected in liturgy (Falla, 1981).

The New Testament writers deliberately used the word 'church' to refer to the followers of Jesus as distinct from the Jewish Synagogue. The word 'church' historically referred to the citizens called out and gathered together in assembly (Coenen, 1979). Members of this community (church) were the saints, brothers. Emphasis was on the community identity rather than the individuals who made it up. The life of the early church was seen to be communal; they enjoyed κοινωνια (fellowship) a word that is rooted in the ideal of participation, sharing in common, communal, communion, a connection with, participation with others. "It denotes the unanimity and unity brought about by the Spirit. The individual was completely upheld by the community" (Schattermann, 1979, p. 642). Thus, the church may be described as an organism, "a community of cells and organs, the whole giving meaning, form, and purpose to each of its members" (Driver, 1981, p. 146).

Developments in the critical analysis of the New Testament texts have given rise to the view that the gospels and other writings arose in the context of specific communities of Christians (Brown, 1979). Perhaps largely geographic, these communities gathered around specific theological (faith) positions and, in some cases, the teachings of the charismatic teachers who inspired them (Brown, 1984). With clearly drawn boundaries of belief some communities defined themselves in opposition to other churches (Brown, 1979; Brown & Meier, 1983). Such developments challenge an understanding of an homogeneous New Testament church as a model for each local church today. In light of this interpretation of the New Testament churches community has elements of place and belief (interest, relationships).

Sense of Community and Church

Following on from Sarason's (1974) statement of the place of sense of community, Chavis and Newbrough (1986) suggested "that a sense of community is the organizing concept for the psychological study of community" (p. 335). With a move away from the conception of community as referring primarily to place, community can be observed to exist in settings and systems other than residential locales. Community, therefore, "should be defined as any set of social relations that are bound together by a sense of community" (p. 335). Using this definition, the presence of a sense of community could be understood as marking the existence of, or even creating, community -- and particularly understand the nature of the church parish as a community with multiple levels of location, relationships and power.

An effective conception of community today must take into account any changes in the social environment. Sarason (1974) proposed that the neighborhood, the local social setting, as the most logical place to foster a sense of community. Glynn (1986) suggested that, although our conceptions of community are changing, the neighborhood continues to contribute significantly to the development and maintenance of a sense of community. He warns that this conception must not be raised to the level of an ideal, and that the concept of community cannot be based too concretely in geography.

The intentional development of community may be a legitimate goal of intervention and prevention strategies (Chavis & Newbrough, 1986). The model is cited as a framework for these strategies. Community development itself then becomes "a process that stimulates opportunities for membership, for influence, for mutual needs to be met, and for shared emotional ties and support" (p. 337). In current times, the development of parishes includes not only those with a locational base, but also reflects those intentional communities focusing upon social justice and missionary outreach to areas which are socially underprivileged.

The concept of the group of individuals is important in Chavis and Newbrough's (1986) formulation. Development, sense of community, and empowerment do not exist for their own sake, but to facilitate the growth of people and communities, which in turn may lead to health and the ability to deal with problems. Chavis and Newbrough suggest a grand vision for community as an important element in the development of systems and environments promoting the health of humans. They examine research suggesting a sense of community contributes to health, coping, problem-solving and more positive development of neighborhood environments.

Religion has been suggested as a valuable resource for well-being by providing prevention in psychological health and as a resource for healing (Maton & Wells, 1995). Organized religion may also be a resource for social action and the development of social policy, possessing the human resources to address issues of social problems and conditions (Maton & Wells, 1995; Pargament & Park, 1995). Religion has been suggested as a valuable resource for well-being by providing prevention in psychological health and as a resource for healing (Maton & Wells, 1995). Flowing from their perception that research on the relationship between religion and health has tended to focus on issues such as group identity and religious behaviors that lead to health rather than beliefs and their related cognitions, Dull and Skokan (1995) suggested a model in which religious belief systems may be incorporated into a system of cognition that has an influence on physical health.

A revival of spiritual direction has benefited from the discipline of psychology, with a metaphor of practice similar to that of therapy and counseling (Jones, 1985; Kelsey, 1984). The, potentially, negative influences of religion have been acknowledged by Maton and Wells (1995), but they suggest a broad beneficial effect of religious commitment in areas such as prevention, healing, and empowerment.

A conceptual link exists between empowerment and sense of community. Both appear to be interdependent. A sense of community may give community members the sense of control and social support necessary for development (Chavis & Newbrough, 1986). At the same time empowerment is an important aspect of a sense of community. Maton and Salem's (1995) model of support suggests empowerment is related to a sense of community. Their investigation suggested empowerment in a community setting has four organizational features: (1) a belief system that inspires growth, is strengths-based, and focused beyond the self; (2) role-structures that provide opportunities for participation, development, and growth; (3) a support system that encompasses all members, is peer-based, and provides a sense of community; and, (4) leadership that is inspirational, talented, shared and committed.

Newbrough (1995) wrote that community is "an endangered part of modern society" (p. 24). The perceived loss of community values is lamented by some, community is seen to provide people with a structure and a reference point for their lives (Glynn, 1986; Newbrough, 1995; Putnam, 2000; Sarason, 1986, 2001). Newbrough (1995) suggested a new approach or theory of community is needed to address the negative impact of the fragmentation of community -- what he refers to as the "Third Position" (p. 25).

The "First Position" is the collective identity where individual interests were secondary. The community is most important. The "Second

Position" is the antithesis of the first where individual liberty and privacy were the basis for relationships in the community (Newbrough, 1995). The movement from the first to the second position is clear in the history of the Western world. Newbrough's (1995) Third Position is a synthesis of the first two, with the introduction of the concept of *Equality* to hold them in balance, resulting in "The Just Community" (p. 14). The third position is a process guiding interventions aimed at transforming and creating *Just Communities*.

Such a community can become competent to manage and change itself in a systematic way. It learns through experience, with a leadership that guides and is responsive to feedback from its members and environment, while at the same time continuing traditions that are important to the community. Communication, therefore, becomes important to the development of community, communication as conversation. Community is the narrative, the story of the development of the interaction among individuals (Dokecki, et al., 2001). Newbrough (1995), therefore, suggested that the development of such communities could provide the foundation for a society "that can function as a human system" (p. 24).

Newbrough's later collaborative work has sought to build on the perceived relationship between the psychological sense of community and the spiritual sense of community (Dokecki, et al., 2001). Influenced by Latin American liberation theology, Dokecki, et al. used increasingly theological and cosmological terminology to describe their approach to an active-reflective study in a North American Catholic Church. The study involved a consultation process with four phases over seven years. Three phases had passed, Opening Consultation, Core Team formation, and the beginning of ' Small Basic Communities or groups within the church as the basis of community. The fourth phase, in process, posed the question of service and the Parish as a 'Community of Communities' (Dokecki, et al., 2001; Newbrough, 1995). It was suggested that membership of the small groups would make individuals feel at home in the larger group.

CHURCH SETTING AND STUDY CONTEXT

The history of Mount of Olives Baptist Community (MOBC)[i] shows some evidence of elements of Maton and Salem's (1995) model of empowerment; charismatic leadership, a philosophy of participation and consensus, and social action. It has also emphasized the concept of intentional community, with members living in close proximity to each other, suggesting elements in McMillan and Chavis' (1986) model of psychological sense of community. Hence, the name Mount of Olives Baptist Community rather than Church.

MOBC was established in the early 1980's through the amalgamation of two Baptist churches in industrial/working class suburbs. A third Baptist church split over the amalgamation issue with some members choosing to join the MOBC and some remaining in the original church. This amalgamation grew from the conclusions of a report to the Conference of Baptist Churches. The report recommended the rationalization of the six Baptist churches in the area.

MOBC sought to implement many of the report's recommendations. Among these were to break with the largely middle-class ways and reflect the region in which the churches existed. An emphasis was placed on the family and structures that ease pressures rather than create them. The small group was seen as a basis and building block of the church's life. Most importantly, small groups were to be the center of church life providing the caring and nurturing necessary for members and the church as a whole. The report encouraged church members from resource rich suburbs to move into the area to fill the gaps in leadership and as the workers necessary to reverse the decline in membership.

A charismatic pastor moved from the eastern suburbs to lead the new church, and the first author of this chapter became a paid pastor for several years in the establishment phase. The church emphasized intentional community, sharing of possessions in order to free finances to assist those who had less. Young (20's) Christians moved into the area to join the church. A range of initiatives, notably addressing health, housing, and unemployment, was established in line with recommendations of the report.

Between 1992 and 1995, three long-standing pastors moved from their positions. During late 1996 and early 1997, the church experienced what was described as a "crisis in leadership." Communication by the leadership to members suggested conflict had emerged which was not resolvable without outside intervention. The events that precipitated the "crisis" were not disclosed and speculation developed around the issue. There were various theories about dwindling attendances, or whether they are dwindling at all, and low financial giving.

The advent of this "crisis" suggested that this was an historically appropriate time for the present project. Emotions appeared to have been running high. Discussions with some of the leaders revealed that each of them had a theory. The present research also aimed to provide the opportunity to gather data regarding some of the feelings expressed by members of the church. It was expected that the results of this research would provide an insight into the group's understanding of itself as a group and an indication of its sense of community. Community was something spoken about as a goal by the leaders in the church, but not measured by other than various anecdotal reports.

It was envisaged that the present research would benefit from the opportunity to test McMillan and Chavis' (1986) model in an applied, local, community setting, and to bring the benefits of this model to bear on that setting. The history of Mount of Olives Baptist Community shows some evidence of elements of Maton and Salem's (1995) model of empowerment;

charismatic leadership, a philosophy of participation and consensus, and social action. It has also emphasized the concept of intentional community, with members living in close proximity to each other, suggesting elements in McMillan and Chavis' (1986) model of psychological sense of community.

The study aimed to provide the context for individuals to express some of their feelings about their history in the church, and to play a part the church's ongoing program of review in which this project would be a part. It was felt that the confidential and anonymous nature of the questionnaire would facilitate open responses to the statements presented in them. The project will provide a report to church leaders containing an examination of the above elements in the light of research and theory. This report will also present an indication of members' feelings and the possibilities for future directions arising from the research.

RESEARCH APPROACH AND INFORMATION GAINED

In order to gain a clear picture of the perceptions of the crisis, and the ways in which it was having impacts on various groups within the parish, a multi-method approach was utilized. By so doing, different types of information could be gained from the different constituencies, these could then be triangulated in order to provide a source of information to the parish to find ways forward from the precarious position in which it found itself. The research process involved two major components: in-depth interviews with members of the leadership team of the parish (pastors and deacons) to tap into their knowledge and interpretations of the situation that was facing the parish and to identify possible solutions to these, and a survey of parishioners. This survey included sense of community questions, based on the Sense of Community Index (Chavis, Hogge, McMillan & Wandersman, 1986) as well as some questions replicating the wider survey of Baptist parishes in the state, the National Church Life Survey (Kaldor, Bellamy, Correy & Powell, 1992; Kaldor, Powell, Bellamy, Castle, Correy & Moore, 1995), and specific open and closed ended questions specifically designed for this survey.

This multi-method approach was chosen as it was seen as the best way in which to gain substantive and grounded data that could used in describing how people had seen the parish develop, what changes they perceived as having come about across time, and in canvassing different ways in which the parish could develop in the future. The questioning was designed to match the social justice stance that was the official underpinning of the parish, and the sense of community that was supposed to have developed across time.

Sense of Community in the Parish

As the notion of a parish is based on both locational and relational community organization, the measure of sense of community was seen as a crucial element to measure using the SCI. However, such a measure does not provide much information on its own. As the research was sparked by the supposed problems with the leadership of the parish, the SCI scores were related to a number of variables measuring other aspects of community and the relationship between members, the parish, and the parish leadership drawn from the National Church Life Survey, see Table 1.

Not surprisingly, there were moderate to strong correlations between the SCI total score, SCI sub-scales, and participants' self-report sense of belonging. Higher SCI scores were associated with participants' agreement with the statement "I feel a sense of 'belonging' to MOBC." There were weak to moderate positive correlations between the SCI and participants' perception of their influence on decision making at the church. Higher SCI total and SCI sub-scale scores were associated with participants' agreement with a statement of their influence on decisions at the church.

Given the idea that there was a 'crisis of leadership' in the parish, there were significant moderate positive correlations between the SCI total and participants' confidence in the leaders. High scores on the SCI were associated with agreement with a statement of confidence in the leadership team's ability to lead the church to achieve goals that had been set. Significant negative with a statement suggesting they felt excluded from participating in areas of the church's life that were important to them.

There were significant weak to high correlations between SCI and sub-scale scores and participants' frequency of church attendance. High scores on the SCI and sub-scales were associated with more frequent attendance at worship services. There was also a moderate correlation between contact with people from MOBC and frequency of attendance at Worship.

Significant weak to moderate positive correlations resulted between the SCI and its sub-scales and participants' belief that intentional community was important. High scores on the SCI and its sub-scales were associated with agreement with the statement that deliberately being 'community' is an important part of life as a church at MOBC.

Perceptions About the parish

Participants were asked to respond in any way they wished to three questions designed to elicit broad comment about the church: "In your opinion, what are the five best things about MOBC?" and "In your opinion, what are the five worst things about MOBC?" "What are the FIVE most important issues/questions MOBC must face in the immediate future?" As

Table 1. Correlations of SCI Scores with Self-Report Measures of Community Life

Variable	Sense of Belonging	Influence Decisions	Confidence in leadership	Feel excluded from participation	Contact with people from MOBC	Frequency of Attendance
SCI	.73**	.54**	.57**	-.55**	.41**	.59**
Membership	.80**	.56**	.43**	-.55**	.56**	.72**
Influence	.49**	.48**	.50**	-.38**	.23	.32*
Integration & Fulfillment of Needs	.51**	.32*	.54**	-.49**	.14	.42**
Shared Emotional Connection	.69**	.48**	.45**	-.49**	.46**	.57**

n=54

**p<.01 * p<.05

each item could have multiple responses the total number would add to more than the sample. Responses to each item were collated and sorted according to theme. Table 2 presents participants' responses to each of these questions, shown in order of frequency of elicitation from the parishioners.

Table 2. Themes for the Best, Worst and Issues About the Church (frequency order)

BEST	WORST	ISSUES TO FACE
Friendships/People	People	Reference to recent conflict
Worship	Relationships	Finance
Empowerment	Commitment	Leadership
Openness	Leadership	Mission
Community	Pastors	Commitment
Small groups	Directions/Future Directions	Spirituality
Theology	Politics	Support
Leadership	Worship	Homosexuality
Past history/ values/ projects	Buildings	General conflict
Caring/addressing needs of members	Mission	Future directions
Children	Young people/Youth	Children
Spirituality	Reference to Past/ Projects	Nature of the Church
Mission	People who have left/drifted away	Growth
Commitment	Time/Busyness	People left out
Alternative to other/ traditional church models.	Finance	Property
	Faith	Time
	Middle Class	Community
	Spirituality (lack of)	

In light of the ideas of sense of community underpinning the life of a parish, there were interesting and important contrasts shown in these results. Perhaps the most important of these is the appearance of "People" as the highest rating theme in both best and worst columns. On the positive side, 42 responses referred to people at Mount of Olives, 14 of which referred directly to friends; 28 of the 42 referred in varying ways to the people at the church. The common theme was of the people and how the participant appreciated them for who they are and what they do: they were "people," "wide range of different types of people and ideas," "some very talented people," "number of people I feel I can trust and turn to for help if needed," "some of the people."

Openness was also a theme in its own right although somewhat different to those comments grouped under empowerment. Thirteen responses referred to MOBC as open to people and ideas: "been welcome," "fitting in," "willingness to try new ideas," "tolerance." Thirteen responses also grouped around the theme of community. These referred to a sense of belonging, the use of the image of family to describe MOBC and community as a description of what is best about the church: "the feeling of belonging," "singles made a part of family," "community life," "community".

As with the "best" things about the church the largest worst themes to emerge referred to "People" with 22 responses. Comments within this theme were diverse. The community was described as not welcoming ("introverted as a group and reserved towards newcomers") and not tolerant at times. Participants indicated they did not like what some members of the community said or did ("people wanting power for themselves," "people complaining"). Although similar in theme relationships were grouped separately, occurring in 18 responses. These generally referred to the breakdown of relationships within the MOBC: "that some people cannot come to terms with hurts, resentments, etc. -- carry grudges, cannot forgive and cannot give credit where credit is due." Conflict and relationship breakdowns were seen as not resolved. Together references to people and relationships totaled 40 responses, a similar result as in the "best" things about the church.

This issue also appeared as a lower level theme in the issues that needed to be addressed by the parish in the future. General issues of support for members or newcomers were present in 12 responses. These were diverse including comments such as "Pastoral Visiting Group," "togetherness," "understanding," "be more relevant to people's needs in the church," to one response indicating a lack of support. In these responses, the members of the church expressed an indication of some of the problems they perceive within the church in the relationships between people, as well as some means of remedying these.

Given the leadership issues that were the underpinnings of the research, another set of themes emerged across the three headings. On the positive side, a theme of empowerment emerged from comments about the community's openness to people and their particular experiences. These ranged from what may be described as an atmosphere "the freedom to think differently," "no one dominating authority" to active empowering of people through participation "affirming a variety of people", and "sharing of roles."

Comments involving the leadership of the community were made in 14 responses. Of these five did not feel leaders received enough support ("lack of support for leaders coupled with high expectations of them"). The majority of responses (nine) indicated a "lack of leadership" or problems in the leaders themselves ("lack of truth," "manipulation," "conflict"). Responses involving pastors also formed a group of 14. These in turn formed three sub-groups. Six responses suggested expectations of pastors were too high or unrealistic ("high expectations of pastors," "inability to adjust expectations of pastors to financial support we give them"). Three responses referred to individual pastors' lack of experience, or their sex. Five to a lack of clarity regarding issues of boundaries for pastors including, but not limited to the recent past conflict within the leadership team ("lack of clarity about ethical issues").

Participants suggested there was a "lack of commitment," criticism rather than contributing ("some/many people who are quick to criticize but don't actually put in and commit") by members of the community (15 responses). The directions in which the community was heading received 12 responses. The majority of these (8) indicated that the MOBC lacked direction ("lack of direction and purpose," "its penchant for following fads"). Others suggested "tiredness and apathy," or that the church "needed to develop."

In order to deal with the recent conflict within the leadership team, 21 responses were made. Most of these referred to the need to deal with the issues arising from recent events as perceived by the respondent. The issues were described as the need to resolve "current conflict within its leadership," resolve "the question of pastoral integrity," to deal "with the fallout from the recent crisis in the leadership." Also important in this context was the need "to confront and deal with what is really happening among relationships at the church," rebuilding trust, a better understanding of "the nature of intimacy in Christian relationships."

Leadership also received 20 responses which fell into three general areas: leadership generally, deacons and pastors. General comments referred to expectations of leaders, who exercise power within the church community. Respect and trust of leaders were seen as issues to be addressed. Comments on pastors indicated the need to support them, clarify their role within the church and the need for them to take leadership. Support of deacons, the time involved and the level of involvement by members were also deemed important issues to address.

Related to the perceptions of leadership was the viability of the parish. Finance was seen as important with 20 responses. The majority (15) simply referred to "finance" generally, the need for the church to live within its means or future financial viability. Five responses referred to "financial support of Pastors/Workers" their time fractions, and the amount of work able to be done within the time paid for by the membership.

In examining this leadership theme, there appears to be a significant split within the parish. There are those who are praising the leadership team, at the same time as they criticize other parishioners for lack of support and commitment. Another group seems to take a negative view of the leaders themselves, while there is quite a strong sense of the need for renewal and new direction. The comments about "tiredness and apathy" seem to capture the problem of the 15-year history of the parish, with the founders having moved on, and the original principles on which the church was built as being less immediate or relevant to the current life of members.

This may be seen from the responses about the future directions of the parish. These directions and relevance of the parish was explored in several themes related to future issues. Seventeen responses indicated mission, or the church's role in the wider community was an important issue to face. Ten of these referred to the community outside and around the church ("Its role in the local community," "relevance to the community"). Other responses referred to mission generally, as a concept to be understood by the church ("developing its understanding of mission -- personal and programmatic").

Commitment was an issue for 15 responses. This was seen to be an understanding what commitment to the church and membership of the church community might mean. Some participants perceived a lack of commitment as the issue and the need to gain a level of energy or commitment to the community. A reference to what may generally be classified under Spirituality was present in 14 responses. "The place of God" in members' lives, "prayer," "growth," discipleship, God, Jesus, or direct references to spirituality were present in 10 of the 14 responses.

Leadership Team Responses

As the issue of leadership was both the catalyst for the research and a significant area identified in the questionnaires, the leadership team was interviewed. The team consisted of two pastors and five deacons. All saw themselves as leaders, with two ambivalent about their participation in the role.

Due to the resignation of both pastors prior to interviews with the leadership team all felt the future directions were tied up with the appointment of a new pastor or pastors. The immediate future was seen as "difficult," "anywhere," "no idea, difficult to say right now." Similarly, the most important issue facing the church was seen to be pastoral leadership. There was some prior work to be done, on a "model" of pastoral leadership, to see that "financial constraints" are taken into account.

These sets of comments clearly match the findings from the members of the parish. Because of the current circumstances, there was a lot of uncertainty and ambivalence about the state of the parish and how it could develop and proceed into the future. That the leadership team felt both constrained by the finances of the parish, as well as having considerable difficulty in articulating a clear direction into the future, mapped onto a number of the issues raised by parishioners, even leading to the question of the viability of the parish.

In the absence of a new leader, the roles and perceptions of the leadership team are crucial for holding together the parish. Formal authority was seen to lie with the Community as a whole (expressed in the regular Community Meeting), Pastors, and Deacons. No clear hierarchical order emerged in their responses. One responded in terms of the leadership team, and two expressed their perception of confusion among members on the question. All emphasized the role of the members of the community (congregational government). The relationships among the leadership team, specifically between pastors and deacons, was described as a "partnership," "working together as a team." There were variations in comments regarding differing functions. The pastors performed "higher" functions; yet the deacons have an "element of supervisor/management" in their role. Pastors may be "agenda setting" or "charismatic." The relationship is determined by the personalities in the leadership team.

Most saw their role as leaders in terms of facilitation, they were "facilitating and encouraging," to equip the community to discover and realize its vision This involved "listening to people and to feed back to the community," "pulling together options rather than making decisions." Making sure decisions are made, but not necessarily making those decisions. One of the seven interviewed felt it was the leadership team's role to make decisions, another saw their role in terms of dealing with administrative issues to free the pastors to provide spiritual leadership.

All saw that leadership roles in the church were taken on by both the leadership team and by individual members who provided leadership to the church through their "example," and "innovation." For example, an individual working in a particular area or task within the church may also exercise leadership: SKC (Sunday Kids Club), FRENDS (older age small group), worship group.

From the interview with the leadership team a number of issues emerged. They saw their roles as important in the parish, of course. However, their ability to put into place vision and action for the future was severely constrained. Some were ambivalent about their positions in the leadership, some seemed to be waiting for a new, senior person to be appointed (perhaps another charismatic leader resembling the founding pastor). All believed in the importance of the parish and the work they were undertaking, but how to bring the rest of the parishioners with them was not an issue they had resolved. This jeopardized the place of the parish and the reasons for which people would remain as members.

DISCUSSION

Resulting from the three types of data collection, there are strong elements in common, and which may be applied to a better understanding of both the parish, and of sense of community. These are reflective of themes that hark back to the history of the parish, which reflect on current problems and dilemmas, and which are important to the survival of the parish itself.

The conflict around the leadership, and the alternative constructions of the nature of leadership in the parish, directly address the future of the parish, as well as the ideas of the past. The original charismatic pastor provides a focal point for many in the community, and the ideas of directions and decision-making styles that could be present. Interviews with the leadership team also supported a general ambivalence about leadership. They suggested a lack of clarity regarding their roles, and a hesitancy in making decisions. This was, of course, coupled with the serious financial issues facing the parish.

The concept of the leadership as facilitating may lead to this general lack of clarity. The leadership team expressed their understanding of leadership with reference to the role of the community members and informal leaders, the congregation. This concept of community leadership and decision making may contribute to the ambivalence, or confusion around the role of formal leaders, and how the deacons relate to the pastors as co-leaders of the community. There may be a need for future work to develop clarity about the role of leaders and leadership in the community.

The formal leaders were able to articulate the shared nature of leadership and the congregation's role but appeared uncertain or, perhaps, unwilling to explore the extent of their authority as leaders. The community's commitment to leaders as facilitators and participation at this level may suggest interaction between the members' influence on the community and the community's influence on the individual member (Pretty, 1990), but in practice may simply lead to a perception of a lack of action. More 'action' oriented themes such as finance and mission were seen as important issues to be addressed in the immediate future.

Leadership in the parish was caught between elements of Maton and Salem's (1995) model for empowerment. Two parts of the model were in a state of flux, and two were being put into place. Because the charismatic leader was gone and the leadership team was waiting for a replacement, and the foundation belief systems of mission and social justice had become dated, there was need for new personnel and directions to be developed. On the other hand, the leadership team was attempting to develop participatory role structures for informal leadership, and there was a clear sense of community among members.

Participants primarily became involved in MOBC through existing members or friends, and came from active involvement in other churches, mainly Baptist churches. As such, it reflects Sarason's (2001) indication that church membership is a major way of feeling a part of a thing that was larger than themselves and which served to give direction in life. A large number had been a part of the community for a many years (73.6% for six years, or more). A strong sense of belonging by members who had been living in the area and participating in the community for a long period of time suggested a stable membership. From these results, the balance that a parish community achieves between locational and relational membership is demonstrated, with the relational aspects further reinforced by the liturgy and attendance at services.

Participants reported they felt a sense of belonging to the church and there was evidence of a significant relationship between the Sense of Community Index sub-scale membership and a sense of belonging. Formal membership was high, suggesting personal investment in the community by participants. Quality and type of contact may be important to a shared emotional connection (McMillan & Chavis, 1986). The themes of friendship and people emerged as participants' most frequent responses to the best things about the community suggest the importance of a shared emotional connection to a sense of community. However, that the same themes emerged as the worst things about the church points to some ambiguity, perhaps even confusion, among participants regarding relationships with other members.

The relationship dimensions of the SCI, membership and shared emotional connection, showed evidence of stronger relationships with other self-report measures of community life. The membership element contributed strongly to an overall sense of community. Participants' sense of membership of the community appeared to be strong. They felt it was important to live close to each other and lived close to the church buildings suggesting the physical boundaries around the community were developed. These same people, for whom membership was important, had been a part of the community for a long time.

With this high sense of membership and belonging came a negative impact for the parish. The ongoing recruitment and replacement of members became problematic. While the members value their interactions with one another, there was a clear indication that newcomers were not welcomed as openly as they should. This was seen as an immediate problem, as well as issue for the future -- without new members joining the parish, it must have a very limited future. The membership dimension of the McMillan and Chavis (1986) model of sense of community incorporates a boundary notion -- indicative of those who are in and those who are out. For a church parish, such as Mount of Olives, the imposition of a relatively hard boundary seems to have provided a club for those who were early members, have been born in or sponsored in. For the health and continuation of the parish, such a hard boundary appears to be far from appropriate as new members are required to join to maintain the strength of the parish.

In some ways, the hard boundaries appear to match some of the early ideas of the parish as a locational community, the experience of κοινωνια (fellowship) that flowed from a physical closeness, combined with the experience of the church and its practices. At MOBC, there are clear experiences of this fellowship, combined with a physical proximity by living in a local area. However, other experiences are not as representative of the experience as it would be desirable. The parish had been established on social justice principles, but with a charismatic pastor as the clear leader. The present situation showed major concerns, and some diffusion of the responsibility for the leadership of the parish. While the pastors indicated that there should be a sharing of responsibility, the parishioners -- and some of the leadership group, itself -- saw a need for the concentration of the authority in a small group with formal responsibility. Few people were involved in ministry or mission activities apart from small groups. Those who were involved participated in more than one activity suggesting a core group of workers. This may suggest that community members saw little reward in participation or that they did not see their needs being met through the "official" activities investigated in this study.

The results also suggest that values are not all shared at MOBC. Participants judged commitment by other members to be low. Commitment emerged strongly as one of the worst things about the church and was low as a theme in the best. That participants were willing to make a judgment about other members' commitment supports the themes developing around relationships in this study. The sort of uncertainly around values and future directions evident in responses may contribute to a perception of a lack of commitment by members. Responses to the item asking about the community's future directions suggested there was no clear consensus among participants about the goals and future directions of the community. More than a quarter of participants indicated they did not know what the community's goals were.

Relationships emerged throughout the study both as strength and an issue needing to be addressed. These results suggest support for Dokecki, et al.'s (2001) formulation of community. Communication becomes an important part of the development of community, specifically conversation, narrative, the story of the relationships of the individuals who make up the community.

Understood in this sense communication may provide a platform for understanding and quantifying the opportunities for membership, influence, mutual meeting of members' needs and opportunities for shared ties and support. There needs to be the provision of opportunities for individual members to tell their stories, and for the community as a whole to articulate its history, its current position and future directions. Leadership may arise that can model and provide opportunities for this communication. Not facilitating opportunities but empowering members to do so (Maton & Salem, 1995).

Dokecki, et al. (2001) applied and developed their model in a Roman Catholic Church of basic communities or small groups, with the parish as Community of Communities. This model would intuitively appear to fit best within a Catholic Church with ritual and liturgy playing a more important part in drawing people together than in a Baptist Church. With just over half the participants in the present study in small groups one would have expected them to rate higher as one of the best things about the church if they were to be playing a pivotal role in the community. It may be that much of the participants' experience of people and relationships has been in small groups and that here is one place the ambivalence may be experienced. These groups may also be the place for future healing to take place.

Dokecki, et al.'s (2001) early phases of development emphasized communication and relationships and developed clear leadership. The question of "service" was not posed until the fourth phase of their study. The researcher's understanding of the development of small groups at MOBC suggests some early confusion between small groups and mission (service) groups. There has perhaps been ambiguity around the purpose of the small group that may have inhibited their role in the development of this community.

The results of this study suggest that sense of community is a useful concept for understanding the life of a local church community and the Sense of Community Index is a useful tool when used in conjunction with other measures of community life. MOBC appears as a community with a strong history and core membership -- almost reminiscent of Bright's (1960) idea of geography and bloodlines as determinant of parish. Members participate actively in the life of the community and formal leadership is clear and has the support of members. However, a clear future orientation and growth commitment was not as evident.

The results emerging from the present study suggest that relationships amongst members would benefit from further development. Relationships, leadership and future goals and directions emerged as issues needing to be addressed. The conflict in the leadership team in the months prior to the study may have influenced the results. It may have positively brought issues and conflicts to the surface so that they influenced participants' responses. On the other hand this conflict may have colored participants' perception of their experience of the community and biased the study. Future development of the community may benefit from the application of McMillan and Chavis' (1986) model of psychological sense of community and Dokecki, et al.'s (2001) model of communication in the development of community and the benefits membership may promote in its members.

NOTES

[i] Mount of Olives is a pseudonym to protect the privacy of the parish and parishioners.

REFERENCES

Ackroyd, P. (1968). *Exile and restoration*, London: SCM.

Bright, J. (1960). *A history of Israel* (2nd ed), London: SCM.

Brown, R. (1979). *The community of the beloved disciple*. New York: Paulist Press.

Brown, R. (1984). *The churches the apostles left behind*. New York: Paulist Press.

Brown, R. & Meier, J. P. (1983). *Antioch and Rome*. New York: Paulist Press.

Chavis, D. M., & Newbrough, J. R. (1986). The meaning of "Community" in community psychology. *Journal of Community Psychology, 14*, 335-340.

Chavis, D. M., Hogge, J. H., McMillan, D. W., & Wandersman, A. (1986) Sense of community through Brunswik's lens: A first look. *Journal of Community Psychology, 14*, 24-40.

Coenen, L. (1979). Church, Synagogue. *The new international dictionary of new testament theology*, Volume 1. (ed. C. Brown). Grand Rapids, MI: Zondervan.

Dokecki, P. R., Newbrough, J. R., & O'Gorman, R. T. (2001). Toward a community-oriented action research framework for spirituality: Community psychological and theological perspectives. *Journal of Community Psychology, 29*, 497-518.

Driver, T. (1981). *Christ in changing world*. London: SCM.

Dull, V. T., & Skokan, L. A. (1995). A cognitive model of religion's influence on health. *Journal of Social Issues, 51*, 49-64.

Falla, T. C. (1981). *Be our freedom lord: Responsive prayers and readings for contemporary worship*. Adelaide, Australia: Lutheran Publishing House.

Glynn, T. J. (1986). Neighborhood and sense of community. *Journal of Community Psychology, 14*, 341-352.

Heller, K. (1989). Return to community. *American Journal of Community Psychology, 17*, 1-15.

Jones, A. (1985). *Soul making: The desert way of spirituality*. London, UK: SCM.

Kaldor, P., Bellamy, J., Correy, M., & Powell, R. (1992) *First look in the mirror: Initial findings of the 1991 national church life survey*. Homebush West, NSW, Australia: Lancer.

Kaldor, P., Powell, R., Bellamy, J., Castle, K., Correy, M., & Moore, S. (1995) *Views from the pews: Australian church attenders speak out*. Adelaide, Australia: Open Book.

Kelsey, M. T. (1984). *Companions on the inner way: The art of spiritual guidance*. New York: Crossroad.

Maton, K. I., & Salem, D. A. (1995). Organizational characteristics of empowering community settings: A multiple case study approach. *American Journal of Community Psychology, 23*, 631-656.

Maton, K. I., & Wells, E. A. (1995). Religion as a community resource for well-being: Prevention, healing, and empowerment pathways. *Journal of Social Issues, 51*, 177-193.

McMillan, D. W., & Chavis, D. M. (1986). Sense of community: A definition and theory. *Journal of Community Psychology, 14*, 6-23.

Newbrough, J. R. (1995). Toward community: A third position. *American Journal of Community Psychology, 23*, 9-37.

Pargament, K. I., & Park, C. L. (1995). Merely a defense? The variety of religious means and ends. *Journal of Social Issues, 51,* 13-32.

Pretty, G. M. H. (1990). Relating psychological sense of community to social climate characteristics. *Journal of Community Psychology, 18,* 60-65.

Putnam, R. D. (2000). *Bowling alone: The collapse and revival of American community.* New York: Simon and Schuster.

Sarason, S. B. (1974). *The psychological sense of community: Perspectives for community psychology.* San Francisco: Jossey bass.

Sarason, S. B. (1986). Commentary: The emergence of a conceptual centre. *Journal of Community Psychology, 14,* 405-407.

Sarason, S. B. (2001). Concepts of spirituality and community psychology. *Journal of Community Psychology, 29,* 599-604.

Schattermann, J. (1979). κοινωνια. *The new international dictionary of new testament theology,* Volume 1. (ed. C. Brown). Grand Rapids, MI: Zondervan.

Chapter 9

SENSE OF COMMUNITY IN THE SCHOOL
Listening to Students' Voices

Helen Vrailas Bateman[i]
Vanderbilt University

INTRODUCTION

The importance of creating and sustaining learning communities in which all members are valued can be traced to Vygotsky's theory in which culture plays a central role in developmental processes. Vygotsky (1978) suggested that all learning is culturally mediated, historically developing, and arising from cultural activity. Leontiev describes Vygotsky's cultural method of thinking as developing in a system of human relationships:

> if we removed human activity from the system of social relationships, it would not exist...the human individual's activity is a system of social relations. It does not exist without these reactions (Leontiev, 1981, pp. 46-47).

According to the situated learning theorists, learning is a social practice in which learning, thinking, and knowing involve the whole person (e.g., cognition, emotion, and social relations) and membership and active participation in various communities of practice (Lave & Wenger, 1991). Such a reciprocal and active relationship between learners and their place and participation in their communities of practice, calls for providing supportive, enriched, and flexible community settings for people to learn in. Having strong social networks within a classroom, within a school, and between classrooms and outside resources should provide students with multiple sources of knowledge, that can then facilitate multiple and flexible zones of proximal development (Moll & Greenberg, 1995).

In addition to multiple "rich" funds of knowledge, strong learning communities can also provide learners with considerable support by providing settings in which students are not afraid to ask questions, to attempt solving difficult problems, or to occasionally fail. Such social networks can be thought of as communities of learners (Bateman, 1998; Bateman, Bransford, Goldman, & Newbrough, 1999; Cognition and Technology Group at Vanderbilt, 1994). Successful learning communities should provide students with multiple opportunities for active participation (Lave & Wenger, 1991; Vygotksy, 1981). Such communities of practice provide learners with a gradual intrinsic motivation to move to increasing levels of participation in the community, thus becoming an active member of the community of learners (Lave & Wenger, 1991).

This research program builds on the aforementioned theoretical perspectives on the nature of learning by examining -- through a series of empirical studies -- students' psychological sense of community in classroom and school settings. In order to examine the central role that community processes play in students' classroom and school settings we adopted the McMillan and Chavis (1986) model of sense of community. Our research findings support the notion that community processes play a central role in students' emotional, social, and cognitive development in classroom settings, and suggest that certain characteristics of classroom learning environments are positively associated with students' sense of community.

In this chapter we will briefly discuss a study that examines students' sense of community in three different types of school settings, and the common threads running across our research findings at the school and at the classroom level.

Related Research

Students' engagement

An increasing body of research supports the significant role that students' level of engagement, sense of belonging, and sense of community play in their academic, social, and emotional adjustment to classrooms and school settings (Osterman, 2000). Finn (1992), Finn and Rock (1997) and Newmann (1981, 1995) suggest that students' engagement in high-level participatory activities in the school and classroom is particularly beneficial in secondary school students. Finn and Rock found that active participation in the classroom, especially at a higher level is a significant predictor of students' academic achievement, and of identification with the school community. Finn and colleagues identified lack of participation and engagement in the school and classroom at all levels as the single most important antecedent of at-risk-behavior and academic failure, even when controlling for socioeconomic status, race, and ethnicity. Finn and colleagues reported that small size classes and schools seem to enhance students' engagement by providing more opportunities for classroom and school participation.

This body of work supports the hypotheses that certain aspects of participatory behavior, such as students' influence over the content and context of learning in the classroom and students' engagement with learning goals, are critical elements in students' academic success. Wehlage (1989), Newmann (1981; 1998) and Wehlage and colleagues (1989) have concluded that academic engagement, involvement, and participation are the critical factors in prevention of school dropout and have called for educational reform that focuses or increases student engagement for all students. Factors affecting engagement are a) the need for competence, b) the quality of school membership, c) the quality of the academic work, with an emphasis on intrinsic motivation, d) sense of influence (ownership) on the conception, execution, and evaluation of the work itself, e) authenticity of task, that makes academic tasks more meaningful, useful, and valuable, and f) social support within the classrooms from teachers and peers that create a community in which taking risks and making mistakes in the learning process is accepted and supported.

Wehlage and Rutter (1983) suggest that in order to successfully address the large number of dropouts and indifferent students, schools should provide a learning community that combines more opportunities for all students to learn through personalized teaching and a caring relationship with a high degree of structure and with clear but attainable goals for students to achieve. While proficiency in traditional academic subjects is very important, proficiency in other domains should also be encouraged. According to Wehlage and Rutter (1983): such diverse opportunities for success and development can change the view that many youth now have that "school is not for me" (p. 51).

Students' Sense of Community or Belonging

Several studies have demonstrated students "sense of school" and/or classroom community as being associated with higher levels of happiness and coping efficacy, social skills, intrinsic motivation, self-esteem, academic self-efficacy, and interest in academic activities (Battistich, Solomon, Watson, & Schaps, 1997; Battistich, Solomon, Kim, Watson, & Schaps, 1995). Royal and Rossi (1996) found that students' school sense of community was related to student involvement in school activities, in addition to being negatively associated with truancy, disruptive classroom behavior, and experiences with burnout in school. Other researchers have found that school communities that provide students with school and/or classroom sense of belonging and educational engagement and support have been found to be most effective in retaining high-risk youths and have been associated with students' school motivation, interest, and expectations of success in academic work (Goodenow, 1993a, 1993b; Wehlage, et al., 1989)

Students' Sense of Community: Research Using the McMillan and Chavis Model

Pretty and her colleagues (Pretty, Conroy, Dugay, & Fowler, 1996; Pretty, Andrews, & Collett, 1994), using the McMillan and Chavis (1986) model of psychological sense of community, examined young adults and adolescents in universities and schools. Results from Pretty's work indicate that school sense of community was significantly and negatively correlated with loneliness, and indicated that, at least for adolescents, a lack of school community seems to be strongly related to feelings of loneliness and social isolation. Sense of community in the school was positively correlated with higher levels of happiness and coping efficacy, and with lower levels of worry. In all age groups of young adolescents, a psychological sense of community was positively correlated with social support.

Bateman (1998) found that students' psychological sense of community in the classroom was positively associated with students' social skills, conflict-resolution skills, academic self-efficacy, academic achievement, task-mastery/learning goals, interest in complex-problem solving, and safety in the classroom. She also found that psychological sense of community in the classroom was negatively associated with students' level of antisocial behavior in the classroom.

Bateman, Goldman, Newbrough, and Bransford (1998) examined a collaborative/constructivist learning environment -- Schools For Thought (SFT) -- and its contribution to students' sense of community (PSC) and social skills. SFT is consistent with a constructivist approach to learning (Bransford, Goldman, & Husselbring, 1995; Brown & Campione, 1996; Scardamalia & Bereiter, 1991), and is characterized by educational principles of: a) the importance of sustained thinking about authentic problems as a basis for extended and deep inquiry in various domains such as mathematics, science, and social studies; b) classroom instruction that promotes collaborative and active student involvement in planning and organizing research and problem-solving activities; c) formative assessment and revision opportunities for students; and d) the creation, through collaboration, of a sense of community. Bateman, et al. (1998) demonstrated that SFT students had significantly higher levels of sense of community in the classroom than students in traditional classrooms. Further, it was found that students in constructivist/collaborative learning environments reported: a) having a higher sense of influence in the classroom, and b) having their needs fulfilled and better integrated in their classroom learning (Bateman, Newbrough, Goldman, & Bransford, 1999). Our findings at the classroom level strongly support the views that emphasize the social nature of learning and the significance of students' reciprocal and active role in a classroom-based learning community.

In previous studies, Bateman (1998) found psychological sense of community in the school to be significantly and positively associated with students' social skills, collaborative solutions to conflict situations, academic competence, and student's academic achievement. Conversely, students' sense of community in the school was significantly and negatively associated with students' reports of peer antisocial behavior. This research offers strong support to the hypothesis that students' psychological sense of community in the school is an important factor in students' social and academic success in a school setting The study briefly discussed below has as its goal to extend our investigation of school-level sense of community by asking the question: *What are some of the school environment characteristics that seem to promote students' sense of community?*

METHOD

The study examined some of the parameters associated with 6th-grade students' psychological sense of community in the school: school-orientation, school-related activities, after-school clubs, and school safety. Three different middle schools were involved in the study. All were public schools located in an inner-city urban community, in a large mid-western city in the United States. While none of the schools had academic pre-requisites, one (A) had a specific magnet focus on science and school B was a performing arts magnet. School C was designated a "community" school, community referring to after school-hours classes offered to adult at the school. Students in school A and B were selected by a lottery, whereas school C was by district.

The overall size of all three schools was similar as previous research indicates that school size is important factor, with students in small schools being active participants in the school community more often than in large schools (Barker & Gump, 1964).

A total of 462 sixth-grade students participated in the study. Racial composition for the 6th grade students who participated in the study was similar across all three schools with African-American students being the highest percentage, and Caucasian students the second highest. Hispanic and Asian students comprised a very small percentage for all schools. School A had a large number of special needs students.

Design and Procedure

Students in the schools completed a pencil and paper survey. In addition to the survey data, the investigator visited all three schools, toured the facilities, and talked with students, teachers, and principals. Information was collected regarding each school's structure, goals, daily student routine, and school-related activities. The student surveys consisted of:

Psychological Sense of Community in the School Index (PSCSI). Students' psychological sense of community in the school was assessed using a 12-item scale derived from the original "Sense of Community" (SCI) index (Chavis, 1986), as well as from the Pretty, et al. (1994) scale on school sense of community. Minor rewording of items was necessary in order to create a more age-appropriate measure for 6th grade students. The scale was also converted from a dichotomous "Yes" or "No" scale to a Likert-type of scale with values ranging from 1--not at all to 4--a lot.

Open-Ended Questions. Students were asked to write about *their favorite school activities.* The broad nature of these questions allowed students to mention a wider spectrum of school-related activities (including, but not limited to, learning activities). The open-ended questions were analyzed in two waves. Firstly, answers were read by two coders and salient categories were identified from the open-ended responses. Secondly, the entire text of each answer was used to deepen and enhance our understanding of how students perceived the activities they mentioned. Such secondary analysis enabled us to better understand some of the etiology behind students' choices as well as some of the specific characteristics of some of these activities.

Activities Questions. In addition to the open-ended questions, students were asked to respond whether, during the academic year, they did or did not participate in: a) after-school clubs, b) school-team sports, and c) band/choir. Students were asked to further elaborate by itemizing the specific activities they participated in.

Safety Questions. Finally, students were asked to rate how safe they felt in their classroom and in their school.

RESULTS

In response to Question 1 (i.e., students' reported favorite school activities), students in school B reported a greater range of favorite school activities than students in the other two schools. Such activities included spirit squads, school-wide assembly, carnivals, drill team, flag team, student council, and others. Overall, students in school B responded with the largest number of favorite school activities (n=29), students in school A with the second largest number of favorite school activities (n=24), and school C with the lowest number of favorite school activities (n=17).

A closer examination of the qualitative responses reveals another important dimension in the differences between schools -- students in school B describe *multiple activities that involve the entire school population and not just students in their grade.* Such activities include daily school assemblies, school-wide performances in drama and music/band, and school-wide carnivals. Students from the other two schools mentioned activities almost exclusively limited to 6th grade students (often only to students in their class). It is apparent from their responses that students in school B had the greatest amount of exposure to activities that involve the entire student body of the school. It is also apparent that these were activities the students rated as among their favorite.

In addition to the open-ended questions, students were asked to respond if, during the academic year, they participated in: a) after-school clubs, b) school-team sports, or c) band/choir. Figure 1 depicts the percentage of students from all three schools that reported participating in after-school clubs, school team sports, and band/choir. The most salient difference between schools is the percentage of students that reported participating in after-school clubs. Students in schools A and B -- reported participating in after-school clubs twice as frequently as students in school C.

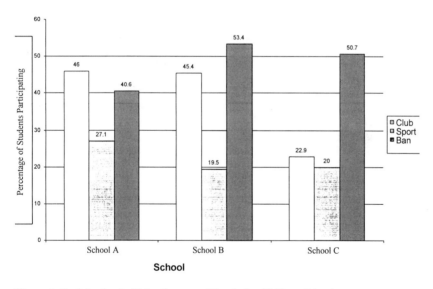

Figure 1. Participation in Clubs, Sports, and Bands for All Three Schools

In addition to being asked if they participated in these activities or not, students were asked to write down the clubs they participated in. Students were also asked to write down any school-related activities they participated in that may not necessarily fit the categories, above. These responses indicate students in school C report having the fewest after-school clubs to choose from (only two were mentioned). Conversely, students in school B report having the highest number of after-school clubs. Students in school B were more likely to mention school-related activities that they were engaged in, but which did not fit the aforementioned categories. Activities involved performances in drama, instrumental music, cheerleading, peer tutoring, and student government.

Quantitative and qualitative analyses of the "Yes" or "No" questions confirm the information supplied by the students in their open-ended questions. Students in school B engaged in, and enjoyed, participating in the most school-related activities, while students in school A reported the second highest level of participation, and students in school C reported the lowest level of participation. Differences between schools extend beyond the sheer number of school-related activities and after-school clubs available to the specific nature and duration of these clubs.

Students' sense of community in the school and school safety were significantly correlated ($r = .38$, $p < .001$). This relationship is congruent with previous findings (Bateman, 1998, 1999). In order to compare school safety and sense of community in the school in all three schools, two multiple comparisons were conducted using the Tukey procedure with school as the between subjects factor. Students' sense of safety in schools A and B was significantly higher than students' sense of safety in school C ($p < .05$). There was no significant difference in students' sense of safety in the school between schools A and B.

Students' psychological sense of community in school B was significantly higher when compared to students' psychological sense of community in schools A and C ($p < .05$), see Table 1. The difference in students' sense of community in schools A and C was not significant (although school A had the second highest sense of community in the group).

Table 1. Means and Standard deviations for Psychological Sense of Community in the School (PSCS) and school safety by different schools

			School		
Outcome Variable	n		A	B	C
PSC	402	M	2.69	2.80	2.55
		SD	.47	.43	.46
School Safety	412	M	3.68	3.80	3.16
		SD	1.26	1.21	1.44

In an attempt to exclude population differences in gender or race composition between schools as accounting for the differences in safety, we also conducted a hierarchical Regression Analysis with school safety as the dependent variable in which we entered gender and race in Step 1 and sense of community in the school in Step 2 (See Table 2). Results suggest *that psychological sense of community in the school is a significant predictor of students' safety after controlling for gender and race differences.*

Table 2. Summary of Hierarchical Regression Analysis for Variables Predicting Safety in the School (n= 411)

Variable	B	SEB	ß
Step 1			
Gender	.031	.14	.01
Race	.054	.11	.02
Step 2			
Sense of Community in the School	1.10	.13	.39**

Note. R2 = NS for Step 1; ΔR2 = .15 for Step 2 (p < .001). **p < .05.

In order to better understand the nature of the differences between students' sense of community in school A and students' sense of community in schools B and C, we examined the role that the four dimensions of psychological sense of community play in the differences between schools (Bateman, 1998). We found that students in schools A and B reported significantly higher "Integration and Fulfillment of Needs" when compared to students in school C ($p < .05$), see Table 3. "Membership" levels reported by students in schools A and B were also found to be significantly higher when compared with students in school C ($p < .05$). In addition, students in school B reported significantly higher levels of "Membership" than students in school A ($p < .05$). No two schools were found to be significantly different, at the .05 level, in students' reports of "Emotional Connection" and "Sense of Influence".

DISCUSSION

The lack of difference in size between the three schools -- all three schools are regarded as "medium" size middle schools (500-600 students), the overall similarities in other characteristics of the student body (race, and gender), as well as their lack of academic prerequisites for student preselection suggest that the differences between schools in students' sense of community can be attributed to a certain extent on other factors.

Table 3. Means and Standard deviations for Psychological Sense of Community in the School (PSCS) subscales by different schools

PSCS Subscales	n	School A	B	C
"Needs"	398			
M		2.83	2.83	
2.61				
SD		.54	.58	.77
"Membership"	405			
M		2.75	2.95	
2.45				
SD		.70	.61	.65
"Influence"	406			
M		2.49	2.54	
2.55				
SD		.61	.63	.70
"Emotional Conn."	405			
M		2.68	2.76	
2.63				
SD		.62	.61	.64

Students in schools A and B (the magnet schools) report school-related activities which often translate to higher visibility and participatory patterns of their schools in the broader community, and to more opportunities for the students to represent their schools to showcase their learning in other community settings. The science magnet school students reported repeated opportunities to visit and collaborate with the city's science museum as well as repeated opportunities to participate in various city- and state-wide science fairs and competitions. Similarly, students in the performing arts magnet reported repeated opportunities to participate in concerts and plays that were performed in their city -- in other schools, universities, and performing arts centers. Pride in the opportunity to participate in activities in which they could showcase not only their own abilities but also their school's collective accomplishments is evident in their reports. Students in the third school however, did not report participating in any city- or state-wide activities sponsored by their school. Students' in school C report, for the most part, participation in activities restricted to classes within the regular school day.

Another important factor that may contribute to students' sense of community in the school is student participation in after-school clubs taking place in the school. A significant difference was found between the two magnet schools and the third middle school in the number of after school activities and/or clubs students reported participating in over the year. Students in both magnet schools (A and B) reported participating in after-school clubs twice as frequently as students in school C.

It is possible that participation in after-school clubs promotes students' sense of community in the school by various mechanisms. The presence of enjoyable activities that students can select to participate in (rather than mandatory participation) may enable students to have a sense of influence and a higher sense of fulfillment of needs in their school setting. Such clubs also enable students from different classes and, in some cases, from different grades to meet and work together, thus exposing a student to a greater number of people from his school and therefore increasing his/her sense of membership.

After-school clubs also typically contain more collaborative or team projects with definite goals and team end products without the pressure of a "grade" evaluation at the end. Students in these clubs engage in collaborative, hands-on learning activities that are meaningful to them. These types of activities have been associated with higher sense of community (Bateman, 1999). The small number of student participants in each club gives more opportunities to all students to actively participate in club activities.

These results seem consistent with existing research on the effect of after-school clubs on students' academic performance (Beck, 1999) that suggests that public school-based after-school clubs benefit the students by offering both structure and autonomous space, cultural consistency, child-centered leadership, a core of committed adults, and a safe environment. Posner and Vandell's (1999) longitudinal study examining the effects of after-school clubs in low-income children found that time spent on formal after-school activities was associated with better school adjustment.

The variety and the nature of after-school activities/clubs offered in a given school seem to be factors in students' school sense of community. Students in schools A and B report participating in a wide variety of after-school clubs for prolonged periods of time. A pattern of varied participation in school-related activities sustained over significant periods of time throughout the academic year offers more students an opportunity to find an activity they are truly interested in and feel they can do well. After-school clubs often give students the opportunity to share their work with other communities. Students in after-school clubs in school A created a Web-based science project and shared their findings on a national scale, going to Washington, DC, to demonstrate their creations.

After-school clubs can also play an important role in deepening and enriching the educational experiences of students in a school, dramatically broadening their horizons, and enabling them to develop expertise in an area they are interested in and to share this expertise with the school community, or even with broader communities. Such activities, in turn, would increase students' psychological sense of community in the school, by increasing their sense of membership in the broader school community, their sense that their learning and social needs are met, their sense that they have some influence over their school-related experiences, and ultimately their emotional connection to the school community.

In further examining differences between the three schools, we note that school B students have a significantly higher sense of community in the school than school A students. In comparing student essay responses from schools A and B, we note that students in school B mention a wider range of school activities they enjoy participating in. Most of the activities that students in school B mention are activities that are shared in a school-wide context. More specifically the sixth-graders in school B discuss the daily school-wide assembly as a place in which they both watch performances by students in other grades and perform for students in other grades. Other such activities mentioned include carnivals, flag team, spirit squad (cheerleading), tutoring, and student council. All these activities enable sixth-grade students to come into frequent contact with or collaboration with students from other grades.

Students in school A, in contrast, do not mention school-wide assemblies and activities shared with the entire school population as part of their daily life in the school. This factor may account for the some of differences in reported sense of community in the school between the two magnet schools (A and B). If students are relatively isolated from the rest of the school body for most of the academic year, school community will not be as powerful as in schools in which students come into frequent contact with peers from other grades.

The nature of this contact between students, however, is equally critical. When students from all three schools were asked how safe they felt in their school, students in schools A and B felt significantly safer than students in school C. The pattern of these results corresponds with students' sense of community in the school and supports the hypothesis that students' sense of community in the school is positively associated to students' feeling safe in their school (Bateman, 1998). These data suggest that increased contact between students across grades may increase students' sense of community in the school under certain circumstances, namely when this contact is regulated in that it is channeled through proactive, fairly well-structured, goal-oriented activities, school-wide activities in which students across different grades may participate. Such activities can range from presentation of one's work to the entire school (in the form of displays, concerts, and plays) to collaborations that include students from different grades (in the form of tutoring, mentoring, school carnivals, school-wide concerts, plays, or sporting events).

On the other hand, unregulated and unsupervised contact between students of all grades can lead to student concerns about safety. Students' comments on things they'd like to see changed in their schools illustrate such concerns. Students report bullying, fighting, and illegal activities such as smoking cigarettes in the school corridors, recess areas, and playgrounds as among of the things they'd like to see changed in their schools. Students ask for better adult supervision in these areas and stricter measures in dealing with repeated offenders as some of the ways these behaviors can be reduced.

Another factor that may account for the differences in sense of community between the two magnet schools beyond the frequency of across-grade activities between students may be the specific content area of these activities. School B as a performing-arts magnet provided students with more opportunities to participate in art-related activities, such as drama, dance, visual arts, and music. Such activities, most of the time, involve active collaboration between students. In addition, they provide students with different abilities the opportunity to become experts in school-related activities and to share their expertise with the entire school.

These multiple and diverse opportunities enable all students to find an area in which they are really good, to excel in it, and to share this excellence with members of their school community, as well as with members of other communities. This contributes to a strong sense of community in the school for more students. More research is needed in order to further investigate the community-building role of the arts in classroom and school settings.

CONCLUSION

Practical /Policy Implications

School environments are complex, multidimensional systems. No one study can capture all the dimensions of a school environment that can foster students' psychological sense of community in the school. By conducting studies that offer us detailed information about various school characteristics that contribute to students' sense of community in the school we can design better school communities in which all students, not just a select few, can be valued members.

In this study, by utilizing students' reports, we have begun to identify certain school-environment characteristics that seem to be associated with students' psychological sense of community in the school. We find that schools with a higher student sense of community tend to offer a wide variety of learning activities for the students, and frequent opportunities for students to participate in school activities shared with the entire school. They also provide more opportunities for students to participate in school activities in city- or community-wide events. High levels of students' sense of community seem to be associated with accessible and diverse after-school clubs and with an environment in which issues of student safety are successfully addressed outside as well as inside the classroom.

In thinking of our classroom-based and our school-based findings, collectively, we can identify several common characteristics that are associated with higher levels of community for students at both the classroom and the school level:

- *Multiple opportunities for collaboration* between members of the community appear as a central theme in both environments. This type of collaboration appears to be most effective when it involves active participation opportunities for all members in multiple learning media
- *Connections with multiple communities* (in and outside the school). This type of active connection to multiple communities has many functions, enabling students to engage in authentic learning tasks, learning apprenticeships, and sharing of learning tools and products
- *Active student participation.* Students are given multiple opportunities to actively participate in their communities (in academic and non-academic activities)
- *Meaningful activities.* Students are able to engage in activities that are inherently meaningful, relevant to their learning needs and enjoyable
- *Safe environment.* Students feel they are in a community in which there is mutual respect, adherence to classroom and school norms, and low levels of antisocial and delinquent behavior.

This study has several limitations. We are unable to account for the possible role that school selection and school spirit may play. More specifically, students in both magnet schools self-selected their schools, and it is quite possible that such self-selection processes coupled with a school-wide academic focus might account for students' increased opportunities to engage in learning activities they find inherently more interesting at a deeper level. The relative "prestige" of a magnet type of school might also contribute to students' higher levels of school spirit and membership. It is important to note, however, that students' responses were never tied to their school's purported "reputation"; rather to personal experiences and specific activities they enjoyed at their school during the academic year. Future studies need to examine in more depth the issues of school choice and magnet school environments and their influence on students' sense of community.

Theoretical Implications

The conceptualization and research methodology of this study utilizes the gestalt theoretical perspective of "person-in context". Students' social and academic development is considered inextricably linked to the social context in which this development occurs. By collecting students' reports on their personal experiences in their schools, we are tapping into their perceptions of their school environments as it affects their lives and those of their peers, and, conversely, into their perceptions of how they and their peers shape their school environment.

Barker's (1968) concept of graduated "zones of penetration" that range from being a passive onlooker (zone 1) to being the leader (zone 6) can be used to illustrate that school environments with high sense of community are environments in which students are offered multiple opportunities to increase their zone of participation. These increased opportunities for most students to be "active performers", "co-leaders", or even "sole-leaders" in school-related activities can also be interpreted as supporting Barker and Gump's (1964) "responsibility theory". In our case, the overall size of all three schools was the same, but each school community provided different opportunities for students to take on roles of greater responsibility.

Our findings extend the notion that small schools promote higher levels of student' participation in responsible roles by demonstrating that variety, availability, and relevance of student activities in a school have an equally powerful effect on community-building processes, regardless of school size. These multiple school-based activity and learning opportunities, however, appear to be most effective in building community when they are at some point and, to various degrees, shared with the entire school community and with the larger communities to which the students belong. Following Bronfenbrenner's (1979) model of nested ecological structures, Figure 2 presents a schematic model of our findings. The lettered squares represent different types of school-based activities that students and/or others can engage in. The arrows represent the sharing or presentation of activity outcomes outside the immediate system (e.g., a type of inter-system exchange that excludes active participation in the activity).

In our model, student activities differ along dimensions:

- The level of involvement of students from a single grade, students from all grades, or students and members of communities outside the school.
- The degree to which they share or showcase products or outcomes within a single grade, with students from all grades, or with students and communities outside the school.

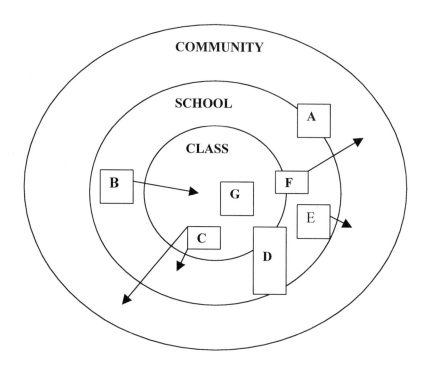

Figure 2. Model of Participatory Patterns of School-Based Activities

Results from our study suggest that, while all types of school-based activities that actively engage students will promote students' sense of community, *activities that enable students to come into contact with students from other grades and with the larger community seem to be most effective* (e.g., activity G of Figure 2 would be the least effective). Our data do not enable us to address the differences in effectiveness between activities that are simply presented to school-wide or community-wide audiences and activities in which members of school-wide and/or broader communities are participating (e.g., are activities D or F stronger facilitators of school community?). Future research is needed to help us answer this question.

Finally, our studies have provided further validation for the McMillan and Chavis (1986) model of psychological sense of community. Validation for the model and its measurement is provided by the convergence of multiple indices indicating that the level of psychological sense of community reported by students in each school was congruent with the overall data patterns provided by students. In addition, the use of the four dimensions of sense of community enabled us to better understand and explain the differences between schools. The explanatory power of the

McMillan and Chavis (1986) model makes it an optimal tool in our quest to evaluate, understand, inform, and strengthen our school communities.

NOTES

[i] This study was supported by a fellowship grant from the J. S. McDonnell Foundation. I would like to thank J. D. Bransford and J. R. Newbrough for their outstanding mentoring and support during the two-year fellowship, and Susan R. Goldman for her encouragement and advice. I would also like to thank the administrators, teachers, and students of the St. Louis, MO public schools for their selfless and enthusiastic participation in this study.

REFERENCES

Barker, R. (1968). *Ecological Psychology: Concepts and methods for studying the environment of human behavior.* Stanford, CA: Stanford University Press.

Barker, R., & Gump, P. (Eds). (1964). *Big school, small school.* Stanford, CA: Stanford University Press.

Bateman, H. V. (1998). *Psychological sense of community in the classroom: Relationships to students' social and academic skills and social behavior.* Unpublished doctoral dissertation, Vanderbilt University, Nashville, TN.

Bateman, H. V. (2001). *Creating a psychological sense of community in the classroom: Effects on students' social skills, and social behavior.* Manuscript in preparation.

Bateman, H. V., Goldman, S. R., Newbrough, J. R., & Bransford, J. D. (1998). Students' sense of community in constructivist/collaborative learning environments. *Proceedings of the Twentieth Annual Meeting of the Cognitive Science Society* (pp. 126-131). Mahwah, NJ: Lawrence Erlbaum.

Bateman, H. V., Goldman, S. R., Newbrough, J. R., Bransford, J. D., & the Cognition and Technology Group at Vanderbilt. (1997, August). *Fostering social skills and prosocial behavior through learning communities.* Paper presented in the seventh biennial conference of the European Association for Research on Learning and Instruction, Athens, Greece.

Bateman, H. V., Newbrough, J. R., & Goldman, S. R. (1997, May). *Psychological sense of community in the classroom: Relationships to students' social and academic skills and social behavior.* Paper presented in the sixth biennial conference on Community Research and Action, Columbia, SC.

Bateman, H. V., Newbrough, J. R., Goldman, S. R., Bransford, J. D. (1999, April). *Elements of students' sense of community in the classroom.* Paper presented at the annual meeting of the American Educational Research Association, Montreal, Canada.

Battistich, V., Solomon, D., Kim, D., Watson, M., & Schaps, E. (1995). Schools as communities, poverty levels of student populations, and students' attitudes, motives, and performance: A multilevel analysis. *American Educational Research Journal, 32,* 627 658.

Battistich, V., Solomon, D., Watson, M., & Schaps, E. (1997). Caring school communities. *Educational Psychologist, 32,* 137-151.

Beck, E. L. (1999). Prevention and intervention programming: Lessons from an after-school program. *Urban Review, 31,* 107-124.

Bransford, J. D., Brown, A. L., & Cocking, R.R. (1999). *How people learn: Brain, mind, experience, and school.* Washington, DC: National Academic Press.

Bransford, J. D., Goldman, S. R., & Hasselbring, T. S. (1995, April). *Marrying constructivist and skills-based approaches: Could we, should we, and can technology help?* Symposium presented at the annual meeting of the American Educational Research Association, San Francisco.

Bronfenbrenner, U. (1979). *The ecology of human development.* Cambridge, MA: Harvard University Press.

Brown, A. L., & Campione, J. C. (1996). Psychological learning theory and the design of innovative environments: On procedures, principles and systems. In L. Schauble & R. Glaser (Eds.) *Contributions of instructional innovation to understanding learning.* Hillsdale, NJ: Earlbaum.

Chavis, D. M., Hogge, J.H., McMillan, D. W., & Wandersman, A. (1986). Sense of community through Brunswik's lens: A first look. *Journal of Community Psychology, 14*, 24-40.

Cognition and Technology Group at Vanderbilt. (1994). From visual word problems to learning communities: Changing conceptions of cognitive research. In K. McGilly (Ed.), *Classroom lessons: Integrating cognitive theory and classroom practice* (pp. 157-200). Cambridge, MA: MIT Press.

Doolittle, R., & MacDonald, D. (1978). Communication and a sense of community in a metropolitan neighborhood: A factor analytic examination. *Community Quarterly, 26*, 2-7.

Finn, J. D. (1989). Withdrawing from school. *Review of Educational Research, 59*, 117-142.

Finn, J. D. (1992, April). Participation among 8th grade students at risk. Paper presented at the meeting of the American Educational Research Association, San Francisco.

Finn, J. D., & Rock, D. A. (1997). Academic success among students at risk for school failure. *Journal of Applied Psychology, 82*, 221-234.

Fyson, S. J. (1996). *Community, alienation and middle school.* Paper presented in the sixth A.N.Z., C.P. conference. Melbourne, Australia.

Glynn, T. (1981). Psychological sense of community: Measurement and application. *Human Relations, 34*, 789-818.

Goodenow, C. (1993a). Classroom belonging among early adolescent students. *Journal of Early Adolescence, 13*, 21-43.

Goodenow, C. (1993b). The psychological sense of school membership among adolescents: Scale development and educational correlates. *Psychology in the Schools, 30*, 79-90.

Lave, J., & Wenger, J. (1991). *Situated learning: Legitimate peripheral participation.* Cambridge, UK: Cambridge University Press.

Leontiev, A. N. (1981). *Problems in the development of mind.* Moscow: Progress.

McMillan, D. W., & Chavis, D. M. (1986). Sense of community: A definition and theory. *Journal of Community Psychology, 14*, 6-23.

Moll, L. C., & Greenberg, J. B. (1995). Creating zones of possibilities: Combining social contexts for instruction. In L.C. Moll (Ed.)., *Vygotsky and education: Instructional implications and applications of sociohistorical psychology* (pp. 319-348). Cambridge, UK: Cambridge University Press.

Nash, J. K., & Fraser, M. W. (1998). After-school care for children: A resilience-based approach. *Families in Society, 79*, 370-383.

Newbrough, J. R., & Chavis, D. M. (1986). Psychological sense of community, I: Foreword. *Journal of Community Psychology, 14*, 3-5.

Newmann, F. M. (1998). How secondary schools contribute to academic success. In K. Borman, & B. Schneider (Eds.), *The adolescent years: Social influences and educational challenges: Ninety-seventh yearbook of the National Society for the Study of Education, Part I.* Chicago, IL: The National Society for the Study of Education.

Newmann, F. M. (1981). Reducing student alienation in high schools: Implications of theory. *Harvard Educational Review, 51*, 546-564.

Newmann, F. M. & Wehlage, G. G (1995) *Successful school restructuring: A report to the public and educators by the Center on Organization and Restructuring of Schools.* Madison, WI: Center on Organization and Restructuring of Schools, University of Wisconsin-Madison.

Osterman, K. F (2000). Students' need for belonging in the school community. *Review of Educational Research, 70*, 323-367.

Posner, J. K. & Vandell, D. L. (1999). After-school activities and the development of low-income urban children: A longitudinal study. *Developmental Psychology, 35*, 868-879.

Pretty, G. M. H., Conroy, C., Dugay, J., Fowler, K. (1996). Sense of community and its relevance to adolescents of all ages. *Journal of Community Psychology, 24*, 365-379.

Pretty, G. M. H., Andrews, L., & Collett, C. (1994). Exploring adolescent's sense of community and its relationship to loneliness. *Journal of Community Psychology, 22*, 346-358.

Royal, M. A., & Rossi, R. J. (1996). Individual-level correlates of sense of community: Findings from workplace and school. *Journal of Community Psychology, 24,* 395-416.

Sarason, S. B. (1974). *The psychological sense of community: Prospects for a community psychology.* San Francisco: Jossey-Bass.

Scardamalia, M., & Bereiter, C. (1991). Higher levels of agency for children in knowledge building: A challenge for the design of new knowledge media. *Journal of the Learning Sciences, 1,* 37-68.

Vygotsky, L. S. (1978). *Mind in society: The development of higher psychological processes.* Cambridge, MA: Harvard University Press.

Wehlage, G. G. (1989). Engagement, not remediation or higher standards. In J. M. Lakebrink (Ed.), *Children at risk.* Springfield, IL: Charles C Thomas Publisher.

Wehlage, G. G. & Rutter, R. A. (1983). *Dropping out: How much do schools contribute to the problem?* Madison, WI: Wisconsin Center for Education Research, University of Wisconsin-Madison.

Wehlage, G. G., Rutter, R. A., Smith, G. A., Leski, N., & Fernandez, R. R. (1989). *Reducing the risk: Schools as communities of support.* Philadelphia, PA: Falmer Press.

Wertsch, J. V., Tulviste, P., & Hagstrom, F. (1993). A sociocultural approach to agency. In E. A. Forman, N. Minick, and A.C. Stone (Eds.), *Contexts for learning: Sociocultural dynamics in children's development.* New York: Oxford University Press.

PART IV

SPECIFIC GROUPS

Chapter 10

YOUNG PEOPLE'S DEVELOPMENT OF THE COMMUNITY-MINDED SELF
Considering Community Identity, Community Attachment and Sense of Community

Grace M. H. Pretty
University of Southern Queensland

INTRODUCTION

This chapter considers a young person's perceptions of and experiences in the residential community and how these might contribute to the maturation of a community-minded self. The discussion is guided by an integration of perspectives from social, environmental, developmental and community psychology. The discussion of social identity and self-categorization theories suggests how *place identity*, an environmental psychology concept, becomes a contextual aspect of self-identity development. Sense of community and community attachment are described as concepts that capture the community experiences and relationships that foster community identity as an aspect of self-identity through processes of social cohesion and social identity. In addition to proposing theoretical links between these concepts, supportive findings from community studies with adolescents are reviewed, along with the challenges and possibilities of creating a lifespan perspective of how people come to identify with community. The overall aims of the chapter are to make the case that adolescents should not be omitted from our research on residential community phenomena, and to encourage future investigations by reviewing relevant theoretical and empirical literature and describing challenges and possibilities for the field.

In this chapter, the word *community* defines a specific geographical residential location where boundaries are identifiable by its inhabitants.

Some of the theoretical and empirical work reviewed in the chapter has been conceptualized as relating to place rather than community. However, this work is considered to be applicable to discussions of community in that communities are considered to have all the multidimensional physical and psychological environmental attributes of place, including that which influences the meaning occupants give to it through personal, social, and cultural processes (Altman & Low, 1992).

Young People: The Silent Residents in Residential Community Research

In 1966, Margaret Mead suggested "The neighborhood is the place where children are brought up to become members of their own society. Inevitably, within a neighborhood, children encounter various older adults from whose experience they learn how to adapt themselves to the kind of society into which they are growing (Mead, 1984; p 3). While there has been much effort to uncover individual and group differences in young people's well-being related to socio-economic factors and the adequacy of residential environments (see Leventhal & Brooks-Gunn, 2000 for a review), these researchers have not included young people's voices in explorations of the psychological dimensions of residential community living. For example, from the earliest studies that informed our conceptual models of sense of community (Glynn, 1981; McMillan & Chavis, 1986) to more recent research (Brodsky & Marx, 2001; Prezza, Amici, Roberti, & Tedeschi, 2001) 90% of researchers have typically excluded participants younger than 18 years of age. Similarly, participants in sociological and psychological investigations of community attachment and other community sentiments have excluded young people from their samples (Cuba & Hummon, 1993; Goudy, 1990a, 1990b; Mesch & Manor, 1998; O'Brien, Hassinger, & Dershem, 1994; Puddifoot, 1994; Riger & Lavrakas, 1981; Stinner, VanLoon, Chung, & Byun, 1990).

This is not to say that there are no environmental studies that have been conducted from a young person's perspective. Youth have assessed micro-level contexts of community systems, such as family and school environments (Seidman, et al, 1995), and social support and peer networks (Barone, Iscoe, Trickett, & Schmid, 1998). These represent a "series of nested communities" (Brodsky & Marx, 2001, p.162) the hierarchy of communities within which every day life takes place (Hunter & Riger, 1986). However, few have considered the next level of community hierarchy, the residential neighborhoods and towns constructed and governed by adults. For this reason, it is unknown the extent to which the residential community is a useful site within which to explore adolescents' construction of self-identity.

The basis for the omission of young people in residential community research has not been addressed directly. However, it may be understood in terms of assumptions regarding the developmental nature of young people's awareness and understanding of phenomena from a community level. This is reflected in the first published psychological research article on sense of community and young people (Adelson & O'Neil, 1966), wherein the researchers concluded that at this age residents do not have a consciousness of group membership at the geopolitical community level. In more recent environmental research, temporal and spatial boundary factors described by researchers studying residential locales in terms of favourite places and the home dwelling (Korpela, 1989; Malinowski & Thurber, 1996), and others who have considered developmental issues in place attachment (Fried, 2000; Giuliani & Feldman, 1993; Hay, 1998) may reflect a question of the utility of including residential neighborhood in this research. The concern here is the relative amount of time adolescents spend in neighborhood locales compared to school and other activity settings that are often located distances from their homes.

The issues of adolescents' neighborhood awareness and involvement becomes especially important when we consider the social psychological theories of group membership that have influenced the conceptual models of community that have guided this research to date; in particular, the social cohesion theory of social group membership (Shaw, 1976). This theory assumes that without actual engagement with a social group (i.e., neighborhood) one will not come to affiliate oneself with that group. This theory of social groups is implicated in many of the concepts that describe dimensions of community experience, for example, neighboring, attachment, and sense of community. The theory maintains that individuals affiliate with a group for the satisfaction of particular needs, such as attainment of particular goals or consensual validation of values, ideas, etc. A group structure, where members have a sense of belonging, evolves from this mutual interaction, influence and interdependence. What matters is that individuals feel positively about each other. Hence, if one considered community affiliation and belonging to be contingent on these factors, one could assume that adolescents would not likely develop affiliations with the residential community as their needs and goal-directed behaviors are situated primarily in micro-level systems, their family, school and recreational environments; and most of their activity is situated within formal settings such as schools, rather than the larger residential community.

A different perspective might be taken, however, if social identification theory was used to explain the psychological processes of how an individual comes to associate oneself as a group member. Social identity theory (Tajfel & Turner, 1986) proposes that group formation is a transition from personal to social identity, and that the subjective sense of togetherness, or "we-ness", which indicates the formation of a group, in this case a community, (see Weisenfeld, 1996), is not dependent on the behavioral-affective processes implicated in the social cohesion theory, but on perceptual or cognitive processes. Social identification theory stresses that members of a social group may share little more than a collective perception of their own social unity, which can be sufficient for them to act as a group. The process of identification with a group does not begin with the question "do I like these other people enough to associate my self with them?", but rather with the question "who am I?". I am not suggesting here that social cohesion factors do not play a role in community identity, attachment or sense of community, but that these phenomena are not dependent on them. If we take this position, then the argument that young people are sensitive to these processes in residential environments has more credibility.

A description of processes of self -identity formation is offered next as background to the subsequent discussion and research suggesting the possible links between it and adolescents' community perceptions and experiences.

Residential Community as a Site of "Who Am I?"

In answering the "who am I?" question, an individual engages in a process of locating oneself within a system of social categories. This process of self-perception and social categorization of self (Turner, 1985) becomes internalized as a component of social identity which is "the individual's knowledge that he (*sic*) belongs to certain social groups together with some emotional and value significance to him of the group membership" (Tajfel, 1972, p 31). The shared characteristics of the group as a social category are subjectively attributed to one's individual self. From this theoretical perspective, this is how an individual assumes the mindfulness of a group, or how the group becomes part of the individual. Hence, group behavior is understood as an individual's acting in terms of a shared social identity. Over time, personal identity becomes intertwined with social identity. The processes of self-perception and self-categorization create identity and generate behaviors that are congruent with this identity.

Environmental psychologists take exception to social identity theory (e.g., Bonnes & Secchiaroli, 1995), partly because it does not recognize the importance of the physical and social environments in which self-perception and self-categorization take place. Because these processes occur within physical environmental contexts, the question "where am I?" coincides with the question "who am I?" As suggested by Cuba and Hummon (1998) "place identity answers the question Who am I? by countering Where am I? or Where do I belong?" (p. 112). The self-perception and categorization occurring within the construction of self-identity include perceptions of the territorial markers around experience. The physical residential community is one such marker that can implicitly communicate personal and social identity (Brown, 1987). This is how community as place becomes inherent in constructions of self, or to use social identity language, how community becomes part of the individual, and generates behaviors that are congruent with this identity.

An extensive review of the social-environmental perspectives on the development of self-identity is beyond the scope of this chapter. However, a sketch of the following work (Proshansky, Fabian, & Kaminoff, 1983; Sarbin, 1983; Twigger-Ross & Uzzell, 1996; and more recently, Breakwell, 2000; Gustafson, 2000; Fried, 2000) is useful in considering how community perceptions and experiences, particularly sense of community and attachment, can be significant factors in the maturation of the adolescent's community-minded self.

The processes by which place identity becomes implicated in the construction of self-identity have been the subject of much speculation by the above theorists. In short, they agree that place identity is a cognitive structure which contributes to the global self-identification process There is consensus that "I" and "me" statements are always constructed within contexts. Together these statements tell stories of person-in-environment experiences that include people, and the natural and built environment. Put another way, place identity is constructed from acts of locating oneself in a geographical ecology, as "locales are imbued with personal and social meanings, and ...serve in turn as an important sign or locus of the self" (Hummon, 1992, p. 258). As people go about daily routines, and experience exceptional circumstances, they situate themselves within a geographical context; everything happens "somewhere," and the "somewhere" becomes part of the constructed event, and impinges on the self-categorization related to that event. Hence, a physical locale, such as a residential community, can have personal meanings that are constructed such that the experiences and images of the place constitute a symbolic extension of the self (Hummon, 1992; Proshansky, et al., 1983; Sarbin, 1983). The self thus becomes situated within social spatial landscapes, which, in turn, become associated with remembered events, private and public. Hence, people become emotionally attached and behaviorally committed to such places, such as the neighborhood within which one is growing up.

During the construction of self-identity, people engage in dialogues with the environment. They ask explicit and implicit questions about themselves verbally in conversations. For example, consider the adolescent attempting to say something at a community meeting; implicitly she is asking "Do I have a place here, do I belong?" Such questions about self are also asked through physical interactions with the environment; "By picking up this litter in the park, I care about my community?" The responses we receive to these inquiries. inform the answers we construct to the question "who am I?" relative to "where am I?" In the above examples, different conclusions regarding contextual-related identities may be reached if, for example, the discussion occurred in the family home, or the litter was in the yard of a friend.

In this way, aspects of one's identity evolve from the continuing interplay between environment and self. An adolescent's experiences in the neighborhood provide information as to his or her identity as a community member. For example, consider a young person giving a friendly wave to an adult neighbor (an example of asking a "who am I" question through a physical action). If this gesture is positively acknowledged, then the response informs the youth of their identity within the neighborhood; in this instance, as one who is a neighbor, one who is part of the residential community.

A youth's self-perception and categorization as a community member, then, depends on the meanings given to the personal collages of images and emotions that accumulate from experiences in their neighborhood. These experiences may not involve the same degree of need fulfillment and goal-oriented behavior exhibited by adults, but may reflect simple acts of association and recognition, as suggested by social identity theory.

While not considering residential community specifically as a research site, investigators have made convincing propositions regarding the significance of place in the dynamic construction of self identity in general (Giuliani & Feldman, 1993; Proshansky, et al., 1983; Proshansky & Fabian, 1987; Sarbin, 1983), and to that which occurs specifically during childhood and adolescent stages (Chawla, 1992; Chipuer, et al., 1999; Elder, King, & Conger, 1996; Fried, 2000; Hart, 1979; Hay, 1998; Korpela, 1989). This work provides theoretical and empirical foundations to further research that establishes the residential community as a place wherein community identity is constructed during the formative years of adolescence. The beginnings of such research will be reviewed next.

Evidence that Residential Communities are Implicated in Adolescents' Self Identity

There is little empirical evidence of adolescent identity with the residential community. Much of what does exist in adolescent research concentrates on special or preferred places (Chawla, 1992; Korpela, 1989; Malinowski & Thurber, 1996). However, findings from a few investigations suggest that the residential community is implicated in young people's development of self-identity.

Campbell's (1995) research in South Africa indicates how members of the residential community may be overlooked as reference persons influencing youth's self categorization. She found that, in addition to references to group memberships identifiable in terms of specific characteristics, such as church members, family, educators, friends, gender, race, etc., participants also identified a group of "ordinary" residents that Campbell describes as follows, "after it appeared that while a large number of responses were not associated with any explicitly named group membership (such as Family or Comrades), they did appear to be associated with connotations of a reliable and respectable community member, …regarding themselves as one of the people" (p 154).

Elder, et al. (1996) interviewed young people in 8th and 11th grades in rural communities threatened by economic decline. Their findings showed several sources of identity with community, including social (presence of family) and physical environment features. Furthermore, young people's identity with community entered into decisions that had implications for future adult identity. Youths' preferences for future jobs were related to whether particular career choices would affect their ability to remain in their community of origin.

My colleagues and I have found similar connections between young people and their residential communities. We conducted hundreds of individual interviews (Chipuer, et al., 1999; Pretty & Chipuer, 1996) and many focus groups with young people (Laurent, 2001). Their descriptions of every-day acts that occur within their neighborhoods imply identity of self with respect to the community. Their discourses contain "I" and "me" statements which clearly situate aspects if their identity within neighborhoods. For example, one of the most important experiences that tended to be described by young people, with notable affect, is to know and be known by name by the people who lived around them. Such statements refer to experiences with adults, other than family and friends. As one 14 year old boy commented "some people don't even say hello when I say hello to them." Our interviews provide further evidence to Campbell's (1995), in that persons constructed as part of the "we" in adolescents' community identity include adults in addition to family, peers and those from other settings such as school. In our focus groups and interviews, while young people across all ages indicated the importance of having people in their neighborhood of their own age, they indicated that they also valued adults' attention and inclusion. Anecdotes about neighborhood get-togethers where youth were included were fondly described. A 13 year old commented "we all got together and had a large BBQ with all the neighbors...it is a really good neighborhood to organize something like that" a 15 year old describes a similar neighborhood gathering, "and we were allowed to stay with the adults, we didn't have to eat separately and play on our own." These comments clearly indicate that the youth themselves recognize the value of the identification processes with neighborhood adults to which Margaret Mead had earlier referred.

There have also been attempts to capture youths' identity with community using self report measures adapted from place identity methods developed for adults by Cuba and Hummon (1993) and Puddifoot (1994). Pennant (2000) approached adolescents in general community settings (fast food restaurants, movie theaters, skateboard parks, malls) to complete a questionnaire asking "Do you feel at home..." Different locales were indicated for residential dwelling, street, neighborhood, town and region. Similarly, they were asked where they would identify as being from. Findings showed that when indicating locales of identification, young people discriminated between two; territories that contained their residential dwelling, street and neighborhood (suburb), and territories in which these were geographically nested, the town and region. One interpretation of this data is that neighborhood is included in young people's conception of home. As an aside, it is interesting that these findings are similar to Harris and Brown (1996) who found a lack of territorial distinction amongst adults regarding home and block. Taken together, the findings of Pennant and Harris and Brown suggest that when exploring the fundamental significance of "home" experiences in the development of self identity, as suggested by Sixsmith (1986) and Smith, (1994), neighborhood environment should be included.

In a study using similar methodology, Kotroni (2000) found that adolescent males living in rural and urban communities also distinguished identity in terms of geographical locale. Identity with residential dwelling, street, neighborhood was most salient for younger participants, while identity with the town and region was most prominent for older participants. Urban dwellers were more likely to identify with localized residential surroundings of street and neighborhood than rural dwellers, who identified with the greater geographical surroundings of the rural town.

The above research findings suggest that the residential community warrants further investigation as a site of young people's development of self- identity. In considering what kinds of community perceptions and experiences we might be looking for that impact on community identity as part of self -identity, community attachment and sense of community are useful concepts to guide such research. Within all of the studies reviewed above, dimensions from these two constructs are implicated in the descriptions of community experience related to community identity. This discussion now turns to the consideration of these concepts from the theoretical perspectives of social cohesion and social identity, and in terms of the empirical support for their relevance to adolescents.

Community Attachment

Initial sociological studies to uncover the dynamics of community attachment (i.e., Gerson, Stueve, & Fisher, 1977; Kasarda, & Janowitz, 1972) defined it in terms of two dimensions; subjective feeling toward the geographical locale of neighborhood (implying the inclusion of natural and built environments for a wholistic construct of people - in - environment) and commitment to neighboring by contributing personal resources. From a psychological perspective, behavioral indicators of bonding and commitment, and the emotions associated with it, are central to the concept of attachment (Altman & Low, 1992).

Studies of adult communities (Brown & Perkins, 1992; Goudy, 1990 a, b; O'Brien, Hassinger, & Dershem, 1994; Rubinstein & Parmelee, 1992; Sampson, 1988; Stinner, et al., 1990) indicate that community attachment is multidimensional, and that these dimensions can be both interdependent and independent. For example, while one may develop attachment over time, it is also the case that one may continue to stay in a location because one is attached. While it was initially hypothesized that emotional attachment occurs as a result of behavioral involvement, it became apparent that one was not dependent on the other. For example, one may have considerable social involvement in a neighborhood, such as being an active member of Neighborhood Watch to protect one's financial investment, but not actually like the neighbors or the neighborhood, and hence, not be emotionally attached. One may have strong feelings about the physical surroundings because of personal meaning associated with the land, trees, wildlife, etc., but not be willing to commit to neighborly behavior with human inhabitants. In terms of how attachment might be related to identification with community, the focus on behavioral commitment and affect reflects a social cohesion theoretical explanation.

Cuba and Hummon (1993) suggested that place attachment can be indicative of place identity, as discourses around the sentiment one has for a place often reveals the extent to which one identifies with it. Hummon (1992) had earlier suggested a lifespan orientation to understanding such aspects of community attachment and identity. Since then, several theorists and researchers have proposed links between them. Fried (2000) suggests that we might appreciate the significant psychological implications of place attachment if we consider it in relation to the work from attachment theory within developmental psychology. It points to the deeper meaning of having available close, local relationships to people and, by extension, to places of relational interaction. Borrowing from attachment theory Fried maintains that attachment to the community can be understood in terms of "remaining within a protective range of familiar places...that it (*sic*) encourages greater freedom of behavior, exploration, confidence and affective responsiveness" (p. 195). This was suggested earlier by Brown and Perkins (1992), who maintained that attachment supports a sense of stability and predictability within an environment, which consequently promotes and sustains a stable sense of self.

Despite discussion of a lifespan perspective and, as with community identity, evidence of adolescents' attachment to the residential community is sparse. From her research findings, Chawla (1992) suggests that "children are attached to a place when they show happiness at being in it and regret or distress at leaving it, and when they value it not only for the satisfaction of physical needs but for its intrinsic qualities" (p. 64). Evidence of such sentiments are found in the work of Elder, et al. (1996) which indicated how young people considered their ties with their community when deliberating leaving to take advantage of job and educational opportunities. Research on homesickness in adolescents attending boarding school also indicates attachment to the physical environment, as well as to family and friends, and is further indicative of their attachment to residential communities. For example, my colleague Heather Chipuer and I were interested to hear several 16 year old adolescents from a very remote town in Western Australia describe how they had insisted on returning to their town after being "sent" to boarding school in the "big smoke" of Perth. "I missed going down to the river to fish," "I missed the bush around my house," "I wanted the peace and quiet where I live." Laurent (2001) reports similar comments from rural youth talking about what made them feel at home, "Well, I live on a property...I don't think I would ever live, sort of, in a subdivided area where you put your hand out the window and touch the house next door..." As Korpela (1989) found, in the essays of 12 and 17 year old youth, physical environments contribute to many aspects of self-regulation, including pleasure and distress. Particular locales were sites for clearing the mind and calming down, while others prompted feelings of happiness. From this research, we can extrapolate the probable associations between behavioral and emotive aspects of self, and social and physical factors of the residential community.

However, as mentioned earlier, investigations with adults indicate that one does not necessarily feel attachment to a place with which one identifies. An interesting finding of both the Pennant (2000) and Kotroni (2000) studies, described above, suggests this may also apply to young people. Participants' responses on indicators of place identity were not always related to indicators of place attachment or sense of community. Laurent also found that young people distinguish between identity and attachment, "I feel like I belong here (identity), but I don't necessarily like or enjoy Toowoomba (attachment) ... but it is where I consider home (identity)." Clearly, there are some interesting intimations of possible differences in youths' identity and attachment to residential community to prompt further research.

This discussion next considers sense of community as another concept that can inform investigations of youths' identity with community.

SENSE OF COMMUNITY

Some of the identity we have to place arises out of a shared public meaning regarding community experiences and images, which are established through consensual agreement as to what has happened to "us," or what is "ours." As much as the "I" is situated within the community "we," association with place is mediated by perceiving oneself to be part of the "we," or, in other words, if we have a sense of belonging to the community.

Sarason (1974) described this "sense" as the extent to which a person feels part of a readily available, supportive and dependable structure; that one belongs somewhere. One model of sense of community (McMillan & Chavis, 1986) further delineates its content in terms of affective, cognitive and behavioral components (shared emotional connection, membership and sense of belonging, influence, and integration and fulfillment of needs). When one has a sense that one belongs to an identified community, one can anticipate receiving from the community those resources that he/she perceives to be present in the community. One then reciprocates by responding in kind when the community requires something of his/her resources. In other words, people care for, and are cared for by, those with whom they feel they belong.

In proposing the link between sense of community and community identity, the dimensions of this concept echo principles of social cohesion as well as social identity and self-categorization theories. The goal-directed and need satisfaction behaviors implied in Sarason's definition, and McMillan and Chavis' model, are at the center of community membership. The positive affect associated with community is related to its functional nature. These behavioral and affective components reflect social cohesion theory. However, it is also important to note the particular use of the word "sense," implying cognitive dimensions of community. It suggests the possibility that one may have a sense of something, even though one may not have had actual experience of it. In this way, sense of community implies the possibilities and potential that one associates with being a member of community. Hence, the self-perception that one fits in with these possibilities, and the categorization of one's self within the community, results in community becoming an aspect of one's social, and, hence, personal identity. This reflects social identity and self-categorization theories.

Unlike community identity and community attachment, there have been studies specifically of adolescents' sense of residential community. My colleagues and I found that youth attend to, consider, and evaluate many aspects of their residential neighborhoods and towns, and that their perceptions and experiences are identifiable in terms of the sense of community concept (Pretty, et al., 1994, 1996; Chipuer, et al., 1999). Using various self-report measures of sense of community, these studies show relationships between sense of community and many aspects of adolescent well-being. Recent research (Pretty, Rapley, & Bramston, in press) shows that the sensitivity of young people to their community surroundings is not dependent on having particular levels of cognitive functioning. Matched on many contextual and personal factors that might influence community access and participation, young people, with and without an intellectual disability, showed little difference in perceptions of community characteristics defining sense of community. Conversations with hundreds of young people (Pretty & Chipuer, 1996; Laurent, 2001) show that they know what it means to have a sense of community, describing it as, for example, "nice people who respect you and care about what you do," "everybody would do things that are worthwhile doing together," "you are in a community that you can talk to and share things with", "you feel you are involved in the community and that you are aware of what is going on around you," "like a family... people you can trust when you need help," "people who live together, talk, are friendly to one another and work together," "people working together to achieve something. People with similar morals and wants," and "cooperation, understanding, leadership, everybody would be equal." When asked whether they had actually experienced what they were describing, of those young people who indicated that that hadn't, some maintained that they "just knew" their neighborhood was "that kind of place," while others indicated they "just knew" that it wasn't. These youth, as Sarason (1974) predicted, knew when they had it and when they didn't.

The extent to which these perceptions of sense of community are related to the evolution of young people's community-minded self-identity is still an empirical question. Kotroni (2000) found that some items indicative of the membership dimension on the Sense of Community Index (Chavis, Wandersman, McMillan, & Hogge, 1986) are positively and significantly related to place identity indicators. However, other items indicative of the influence and reinforcement of needs dimensions were not.

SUMMARY

This chapter has presented a review of conceptual and empirical work supporting the possibility that adolescents' self-identity could subsume community as an aspect of social identity. It also described how community attachment and sense of community can be considered as examples of the processes involved in this identity construction. While the constructs of community identity, community attachment and sense of community have been described here as separate but related dimensions, they present theoretically and empirically as different ways of thinking about the same phenomenon, self-in-community. Each concept exists and has meaning partly by its relationship to the other. The chapter now turns to the difficulties of distinguishing between these concepts, both conceptually and empirically, as this is one of the biggest challenges facing researchers pursuing the question of community identity.

Conceptual and Methodological Challenges for Future Investigation

There is considerable overlap between the kinds of feelings, thoughts and behaviors included in the theoretical description of identity, attachment, and sense of community, which makes it very difficult to construct empirical indicators which have clear and distinctive construct validity (Jorgensen & Stedman, 2001; Lalli, 1992; Puddifoot, 1996). Factors such as emotional ties, bonds, affiliation, behavioral commitment, satisfaction and belonging are loosely associated with each concept. For example, the dimensions of McMillan and Chavis (1986) model of sense of community can be interpreted to reflect aspects of community identity and community attachment. This is not surprising as McMillan's ideas were influenced by sociological and anthropological literature across all of these areas (as reported by McMillan and Chavis, 1986). Indeed much of the psychological investigations of sense of community can also be interpreted as implicitly describing community identity and community attachment. Glynn (1981), Davidson and Cotter (1986), and Buckner (1988) have included components of these concepts in their models, and related items in their measures of sense of community. Responses to these items can be interpreted as indicative of participants' identification with subjective feeling and behavioral commitment toward their community (attachment), as much as their sense of community.

This lack of conceptual clarity is reflected in other research. For example, Cuba and Hummon (1993) describe emotional ties and affiliation with place as aspects of identity, whereas others (Altman & Low, 1992) use these same factors to describe attachment. Shamai (1991) distinguishes between belonging and affiliation, and bonding, however, Puddifoot (1996) identifies these as common aspects of community identity, making no distinction. In the sociological literature, community attachment is defined in terms of bonding, behavioral commitment, and satisfaction (Goudy, 1990a; Stinner, et al., 1990), and affiliation and belonging (O'Brien, et al., 1994).

However, some researchers have attempted to conceptually and empirically differentiate these aspects of community experience. For example, Bonnes and Secchiaroli (1995) propose that, conceptually, attachment implies an individualistic perspective, concerned with an individual's emotional and behavioral commitment, or bonding, with place. This individualistic orientation contrasts with the sense of community concept where the meanings of place are common amongst its inhabitants, including affective, cognitive and behavioral components of shared experiences. Identity has an individualistic aspect, in terms of the development of the self-in-place identity, and a communal aspect, which encompasses the processes of social identity. The latter describe the shared collective dimensions of place that become integrated within one's individual identity. Community identity is associated with individual as well as shared dimensions of community sentiment.

Shamai (1991) distinguishes belonging (affiliation), attachment (special affinity) and commitment (ready to do something for the place) on the basis of levels of intensity of feeling. He suggests that these different sentiments may reflect stages from not having a sense of belonging to sacrifice for a place. He developed a measure on the basis of these definitions and found that people do distinguish between these different place sentiments. Jorgansen and Stedman (2001) proposed that the dimensions of identity and attachment reflect different domains of attitude; beliefs about the relationship between self and place (place identity) and feelings toward the place (place attachment). These form the basis of the subscales of his measure of sense of place. Taking a different tack, my colleagues and I (Pretty, Chipuer, & Bramston, 2001) chose subscales of existing community measures, on the basis that there was no overlap in item content between them, in our attempt to identify distinguishing features of the three concepts of community identity, community attachment and sense of community. We found that adolescents indicating low and high identity with their rural community (indicated from select items from the Community Satisfaction Scale, Bardo and Bardo, 1983) could be discriminated on the basis of sense of community indicators (perceptions of fitting in to the community, as indicated by the sense of community subscale of the Neighborhood Cohesion Instrument (Buckner, 1998), while attachment indicators (neighboring behavior and expressions of affective sentiment toward community residents, as indicated by the sense of community subscale of the Neighborhood Cohesion Instrument and the friendship subscale of the Neighborhood Youth Index (Chipuer, et al., 1999)) did not. Hence, for future research endeavors there are several survey models on which to build reliable and conceptually valid methodologies.

Another way of investigating the relationship between these constructs is to listen to the discourses of the adolescents themselves. Several researchers have described the richness of opportunities to understand community phenomenon in general (Rappaport, 2000; Rapley & Pretty, 1999), and the construction of place identity in particular (Dixon & Durrheim, 2000), through discourse with residents. As indicated earlier in this chapter, conversations with young people have proved to be very insightful in the research of my colleagues and I, as well as that of Campbell (1995) and Elder, et al. (1996). Similar insights have been found in adolescents' writings (Korpela, 1989). Such qualitative methodologies may be more in keeping with the earlier studies of sense of place phenomena where phenomenologists, such as Relph (1977), cautioned against the positivist tradition of dissecting sense of place phenomena into precisely defined and measurable dimensions. Future investigations would benefit from the use of mixed methods to articulate and explore how youths' community perceptions and experiences may influence their construction of a community-minded sense of self.

Finally, I would like to address why, from a practical perspective, researchers should pursue the different aspects of adolescents' community perceptions and experiences. This chapter concludes with the consideration of these issues.

Understanding Youth-In-Community and Creating It

Within our western society there is an age at which we expect the adolescent to adopt the attitudes and behaviors of a community-minded person. We hope young people will engage in community service, such as volunteer groups, neighborhood watch, and environmental protection organizations, and that when of age they will participate in elections and other civic processes. While the exact influences on young people in their adolescence to become community-minded adults are not clear, the efforts of parents, and other significant adults in education settings to shape this aspect of the maturational process is paramount (Flanagan, Bowes, Jonsson, Csapo, & Sheblanova, 1998; Rosenthal, Fiering, & Lewis, 1998; Yates & Youniss, 1998). However, these researchers are still explaining minimum amounts of variance in community-minded behavior, such as youths' inclination to volunteer, with variables such as family factors and educational programming. Perhaps, considering youths' experiences and perceptions of their residential community, community identity, sense of community and community attachment could contribute to this research.

Some writers, such as Comerci (1989), describe the exclusion of youth from much of the adult community and worry about the effects of the decline in meaningful adult-adolescent interactions as people have less time for their families and neighbors. Many young people in our research (Pretty & Chipuer, 1996) made it clear that, while they want to have their own spaces, they don't want to be segregated always into "youth only" places. Comerci strongly maintains the role of the adults in many aspects of young people's later responsible and pro-community behavior. He further distinguishes between the role of familial relations and professionals, and the adult community in general in doing this.

However, our interviews with young community residents regarding their life-in-community revealed some disturbing indications of why it may be difficult for them, and why they may choose not to identify with the adult community in general. It is interesting that many of their discourses did not include "I" and "me" statements, indicating a lack of personal identity in their description of their community. Also, there were many examples of young people's experiences in community that might prevent the development of their sense of community, which may impede their identity with the community, and thus the development of their community-minded self and its community minded behavior.

Young people describe difficulties in forming attachment to place (Pretty & Chipuer, 1996). For example, participants commented "people are always moving, so you never get to know anyone really well." Others complained that "everyone in my neighborhood pretty well keeps to themselves", "people don't interact a lot with one another, they just think about themselves and nobody else...people should respect each other a bit more," "people need to listen to one another more" and "you don't really know what your neighbors are like, whether or not you can trust them." Many young people's comments expressed dismay in that "people in my neighborhood don't have much to do with each other, people don't go out and socialize with neighbors." Comments also reflected their lack of experience of people having influence over, or making a contribution to, the community. As one young resident phrased it "I'm just a kid; there's nothing I can do." "I don't think they (my neighbors) could really do that much because they don't really talk to each other that much to get anything organized." Some observed that "we're not part of the community, we're usually considered part of the problem in our town," and "no one wants us hanging around anywhere there's adults." These comments need to be understood in terms of events occurring in the towns at the time the interviews were taking place. There had been many headlines in local newspapers and numerous interviews on radio and television regarding the "youth problem" that had arisen in relation to episodes of vandalism and groups of youth in local malls. One solution being proposed by the local counsel was to build a youth center farther out of the central business district where young people would be able to "have their own place to do their own thing". One young person interpreted that for me as "being put in their place, away from adults." Clearly such experiences of adults' constructions of youth-in-community can jeopardize identity of community as part of self.

A further example of concerns for the future of the inclusion of young people in the residential community comes from responses I received following an ABC (Australian Broadcasting Corporation) radio interview regarding my youth and community research. A frustrated mother of a 14 year-old boy argued, "I don't have time to get to know my neighbors or many other people in this town, so I'm not letting my kid talk to or help out people I don't know." An elderly resident from a small country town in northern Queensland related how he had been admonished by another older gent during a stroll around their neighborhood. The caller had greeted a few teenage girls he met on the footpath with the tip of his hat and a good day. His friend told him he shouldn't do that because if something were to happen to those girls he would be a suspect if people saw him talking to them. So, if these are representative of adult community voices regarding inclusion of young people in every day life, how will the developing community-minded self be nurtured? Obviously there are changes in the social climate of our social fabric that will make Margaret Mead's call to draw on neighborhood as an active site for young people's socialization more difficult to pursue

It seems that it has become the responsibility primarily of our schools to instill the attitudes and skills required of the community-minded citizen. Here again, there are limitations as to what our education systems can accomplish in generalizing school community behavior to the larger residential community. Sergiovanni (1994) suggests that schools have been relatively unsuccessful in achieving this because they have been created out of a theory and practice of formal organizations, rather than out of theory and practice of community development. Furthermore, there is the question of whether inclusion in and identity with sub-communities, such as schools, formal youth groups and organized sport, will later translate into a sense of self that incorporates positive identity toward the larger community. The comments of one 16 year-old suggests not, "adults include young people either when they have to deal with them because they are family, or when they are being paid to deal with them."

As proposed by social environmental theory, reviewed earlier, it seems that the physical context within which adult interactions occur partly define the meaning the adolescent gives the interaction. That is, an adult initiated interaction with a young person in a school or community youth center or sports ground context is different (a behavior prescribed by the context) from interactions within a non-age or activity specific setting, such as the residential neighborhood. It is an empirical question as to whether experiences that jeopardize a young person's identity within the neighborhood will influence his adult identity and its related behavior as a neighbor in later adult life. We also don't know whether more community affirming experiences in other contexts, such as school, will compensate for the lack of mentoring in neighboring behavior within the residential community. Considering recent research indicating "layers of identity" within a community (Brodsky & Marx, 2001), it seems that one does not necessarily generalize from one to the other. Hence the necessity of longitudinal investigations of community perceptions, experiences and behavior within layers of community contexts is evident.

CONCLUSION

It is important to recognize that community minded attitudes and behaviors are not outcomes of psychological processes automatically inherent in an adolescent's maturity into adulthood. They do not materialize with the school graduation certificate, nor when the person reaches the legal or voting age and is expected to invest interest and resources in the community. This chapter is a proposal that they may be constructed, as part of one's self-identity, through the affective, cognitive, and behavioral processes of community identity, community attachment, and sense of community. There are theoretical and empirical foundations to pursue this question, researchers just need to take up the challenge.

REFERENCES

Adelson, J., & O'Neil, R. P. (1966). Growth of political ideas in adolescence: The sense of community. *Journal of Personality and Social Psychology, 4,* 295-306.

Altman, I., & Low, S. M. (Eds.). (1992). *Place attachment.* New York: Plenum.

Bardo, J. & Bardo, D. (1983). A re-examination of subjective components of community satisfaction in a British new town. *The Journal of Social Psychology, 120,* 35-43.

Barone, C., Iscoe, E., Trickett, E., & Schmid,K. (1998). An ecologically differentiated, multifactorial model of adolescent network orientation. *American Journal of Community Psychology, 26,* 403-423.

Bonnes, M., & Secchiaroli, G. (1995). Environmental Psychology. London, UK: Sage.

Breakwell, G. M. (2000). Social representational constraints upon identity. In K. Deaux and G. Philogene (Eds) *Representations of the Social.* Oxford, UK: Blackwell.

Brodsky, A., & Marx, C. (2001). Layers of identity: Multiple psychological senses of community within a community setting. *Journal of Community Psychology, 29,* 161-178.

Brown, B. B. (1987). Territoriality. In D. Stokols and I. Altman, (Eds). *Handbook of environmental psychology,* (pp. 505-531). New York: Wiley.

Brown, B. B., & Perkins, D. D. (1992). Disruptions in place attachment. In I. Altman and S. M. Low (Eds.). *Place attachment.* New York: Plenum Press.

Buckner, J. (1988). The development of an instrument to measure neighborhood cohesion. *American Journal of Community Psychology, 16,* 771-791.

Campbell, C. M. (1995). The social identity of township youth: An extension of Social Identity Theory (Part 1). *South African Journal of Psychology, 25,* 150-159.

Chavis, D., & Wandersman, A. (1990). Sense of community in the urban environment: A catalyst for participation and community development. *American Journal of Community Psychology, 18,* 55-81.

Chawla, L. (1992). Childhood place attachments. In I. Altman and S. M. Low (Eds.). *Place attachment.* New York: Plenum Press.

Chipuer, H. M., & Pretty, G. H. (2000). Facets of adolescents' loneliness: A study of rural and urban Australian youth. *Australian Psychologist, 35,* 233-237.

Chipuer, H.M., Pretty, G. H., Delorey, E., Miller, M., Powers, T., Rumstein, O., Barnes, A., Cordasic, N., & Laurent, L. (1999). The Neighbourhood Youth Inventory: Development and validation. *Journal of Community and Applied Social Psychology, 9,* 355-368.

Comerci, G. (1989). Society/Community and the adolescent: How much the problem, how much the solution. *Journal of Early Adolescence, 9,* 8-12.

Cuba, L., & Hummon, D. M. (1993). A place to call home: Identification with dwelling, community, and region. *Sociological Quarterly, 34,* 111-131.

Davidson, W., & Cotter, P. (1986). Measurement of sense of community within the sphere of city. Journal of Applied Social Psychology, 16, 608-619.

Elder, G. H., King, V., & Conger, R. D. (1996). Attachment to place and migration prospects: A developmental perspective. *Journal of Research on Adolescence, 6,* 397-425.

Flanagan, C., Bowes, J., Jonsson, B., Csapo, B., & Sheblanova, E. (1998). Ties that bind: Correlates of adolescents' civic commitments in seven countries. *Journal of Social Issues, 54,* 457-476.

Fried, M. (2000). Continuities and discontinuities of place. *Journal of Environmental Psychology, 20,* 193-205.

Gerson, K., Stueveu, C. A., & Fisher, C. S. (1977). Attachment to place. In C. S. Fisher, R. M. Jackson, C. A. Stueve, K. Gerson, L. M. Jones, and M. Baldassare (Eds.), *Networks and places: Social relations in the urban setting.* New York: Free Press.

Glynn, T. J. (1981). Psychological sense of community: Measurement and application. *Human Relations, 34,* 780-818.

Goudy, W. (1990a). Community attachment in rural regions. *Rural Sociology, 55,* 178-198.

Goudy, W. (1990b). The ideal and the actual community: Evaluations from small-town residents. *Journal of Community Psychology, 18,* 277-288.

Giuliani, M. V., & Feldman, R. (1993). Place attachment in a developmental and cultural context. *Journal of Environmental Psychology, 13,* 267-274.

Gustafson, P. (2000). Meanings of place: Everyday experience and theoretical conceptualizations. *Journal of Environmental Psychology, 21,* 5-16.

Harris, P., & Brown, B. (1996). The home and identity display: Interpreting resident territoriality from home exteriors. *Journal of Environmental Psychology, 16,* 187-203.

Hart, R. A. (1979). *Children's experience of place.* New York: Irvington.

Hay, R. (1998). Sense of place in developmental context. *Journal of Environmental Psychology, 18,* 5-29.

Hummon, D. M. (1992). Community attachment: Local sentiment and sense of place. In I. Altman and S. M. Low (Eds.), *Place attachment,* (pp. 253-277). New York: Plenum Press.

Hunter, A., & Riger, S. (1986). The meaning of community in community mental health. *Journal of Community Psychology, 14,* 55-71.

Jorgensen, B. S., & Stedman, R. C. (2001). Sense of place as an attitude: Lakeshore owners attitudes toward their properties. *Journal of Experimental Psychology, 21,* 233-248.

Kasarda, J & Janowitz, M. (1974). Community attachment in mass society. *American Sociological Review, 39,* 328-39.

Korpela, K. M. (1989). Place identity as a product of environmental self-regulation. *Journal of Environmental Psychology, 9,* 241-256.

Kotroni, J., (2000). *Community and context: Perceptions of male adolescents in rural and urban Australia.* Unpublished Masters Dissertation, The University of Southern Queensland.

Lalli, M. (1992). Urban-related identity: Theory, measurement, and empirical findings. *Journal of Environmental Psychology, 12,* 285-303.

Laurent, K (2001). *Adolescents' attachment to and identification with their community.* Paper presented at the Seventh Trans-Tasman Conference in Community Psychology, Melbourne, Australia.

Leventhal, T. & Brooks-Gunn, J. (2000). The neighborhoods they live in: The effects of neighborhood residence on child and adolescent outcomes. *Psychological Bulletin, 126,* 309-337.

Malinowski, J. C., & Thurber, C. A. (1996). Developmental shifts in the place preferences of boys aged 8-16 years. *Journal of Experimental Psychology, 16,* 45-54.

McMillan, D., & Chavis, D. (1986). Sense of community: A definition and theory. *Journal of Community Psychology, 14,* 6-23.

Mesch, G. S., & Manor, O. (1998). Social ties, environmental perception, and local attachment. *Environment and Behavior, 30,* 504-519.

Mead, M. (1984). Neighborhoods and human needs. *Children's Environments Quarterly, 1(4),* 3-5.

O'Brien, D., Hassinger, E., & Dershem,L. (1994). Community attachment and depression among residents in two rural Midwestern communities. *Rural Sociology, 59,* 255-265.

Pennant, L. (2000). *Exploring the relationship between place identity and psychological sense of community in a sample of adolescents.* Unpublished Masters Dissertation, The University of Southern Queensland.

Prezza, M., Amici, M., Roberti, T., & Tedeschi, G (2001). Sense of community referred to the whole town: Its relations with neighboring, loneliness, life satisfaction and area of residence. *Journal of Community Psychology, 29,* 29-52.

Proshansky, H. M., & Fabian, A. K. (1987). The development of place identity in the child. In C. S. Weinstein and T. G. David (Eds), *Spaces for children.* New York: Plenum.

Proshansky, H. M., Fabian, A. K., & Kaminoff, R. (1983). Place identity: Physical world socialization of the self. *Journal of Environmental Psychology, 3,* 57-83.

Pretty, G. & Chipuer, H. (1996). The development of neighborhood and school psychological sense of community among adolescents. *International Journal of Psychology, 31,* 324.143

Pretty, G. H., Andrewes, L., & Collett, C. (1994). Exploring adolescents' sense of community and its relationship to loneliness. *Journal of Community Psychology, 22,* 346- 358.

Pretty, G., Rapley, M., & Bramston, P. (In press). Neighborhood and community experience, and the quality of life of rural adolescents with and without an intellectual disability. *Journal of Intellectual and Developmental Disability.*

Pretty, G., Chipuer, H., & Bramston, P. (2001). *Sense of place amongst adolescents and adults in two rural Australian towns: The discriminating features of place attachment, sense of community and place dependence in relation to place identity.* Unpublished manuscript, University of Southern Queensland.

Pretty, G.H., Conroy, C., Dugay, J., Fowler, K., & Williams, D. (1996). Sense of community and its relevance to adolescents of all ages. *Journal of Community Psychology, 24,* 365-379.

Puddifoot, J. E. (1994). Community identity and sense of belonging in a town in North-East England. *Journal of Social Psychology, 134,* 601-608.

Puddifoot, J. E. (1995). Dimensions of community identity. *Journal of Community and Applied Social Psychology, 5,* 357-370.

Rapley, M., & Pretty, G. (1999). Playing Procrustes: The interactional production of a "psychological sense of community." *Journal of Community Psychology 27,* 695-715.

Rappaport, J. (2000). Community narratives: Tales of terror and joy. *American Journal of Community Psychology, 28,* 1-24.

Relph, E. (1976). Place and placelessness. London: Pion.

Riger, S., & Lavrakas, P. (1981). Community ties: Patterns of attachment and social interaction in urban neighborhoods. *American Journal of Community Psychology, 9,* 55- 66.

Rosenthal, S., Fiering, C., & Lewis, M. (1998). Political volunteering from late adolescence to young adulthood: Patterns and predictors. *Journal of Social Issues, 54,* 477-494.

Rubinstein, R., & Parmelee, P. (1992). Attachment to place and the representation of the life course by the elderly. In I. Altman and S. M. Low (Eds.). *Place attachment.* New York: Plenum Press.

Sampson, R. (1988). Local friendship ties and community attachment in mass society: A multilevel systematic model. *American Sociological Review 53,* 766-779.

Sarason, S. B. (1974). *The psychological sense of community: Prospects for a community psychology.* San Francisco: Jossey-Bass.

Sarbin, T. R. (1983). Place identity as a component of self: An addendum. *Journal of Environmental Psychology, 3,* 337-342.

Sergiovanni, T. J. (1994). *Building community in schools.* San Francisco: Jossey Bass

Seidman, E., Allen, L., Aber, J., Mitchell, C., Feinman, J., Yoshikawa, H., Comtois, K, Golz, J., Miller, R., Ortiz-Torres, B., & Roper, G. (1995). Development and validation of adolescent-perceived microsystem scales: Social support, daily hassles, and involvement. *American Journal of Community Psychology, 23,* 355-388.

Shamai, S. (1991). Sense of place: An empirical measurement. *Geoforum, 22,* 347-358.

Shaw, M. E. (1976). *Group dynamics,* 2nd Edition. New Delhi: Tata McGraw Hill.

Sixsmith, J. (1986). The meaning of home: An exploratory study of environmental experience. *Journal of Environmental Psychology, 6*, 281-298.

Smith, S. G. (1994). The essential qualities of a home. *Journal of Environmental Psychology, 14*, 31-46.

Stinner, W., VanLoon, M., Chung, S., & Byun, Y. (1990). Community size, individual social position, and community attachment. *Rural Sociology, 55*, 494-521.

Tajfel, H. (1972). La categoisation sociale. In S. Moscovici (Ed), *Introduction a la psychologie sociale*, (pp. 272-302). Paris: Larousse. (English Manuscript).

Tajfel, H., & Turner, J. C. (1986). The social identity theory of intergroup behavior. In S. Worchel and W. G. Austin (Eds), *Psychology of intergroup relations* (2nd ed., pp. 7-24), Chicago: Nelson-Hall.

Turner, J. C. (1985). Social categorization and the self-concept: A social cognitive theory of group behavior. In E. J. Lawler (Ed), *Advances in group processes* (Vol 2., pp.77-122). Greenwich, CT: JAI Press.

Twigger-Ross, C. L., & Uzzell, D. L. (1996). Place and identity processes. *Journal of Environmental Psychology, 16*, 205-220.

Weisenfeld, E. (1996). The concept of "we": A community social psychology myth? *Journal of Community Psychology, 24*, 337-346.

Yates, M., & Youniss, J. (1998). Community service and political identity development in adolescence. *Journal of Social Issues, 54*, 495-512.

Chapter 11

IMMIGRANT ADAPTATION
Understanding the Process Through Sense of Community

Christopher C. Sonn
Edith Cowan University

INTRODUCTION

Immigration and cross-cultural transition are strong features of modern societies. It has been suggested that immigration is one of the main processes that have contributed to the culturally pluralistic nature of many nations (Berry, 1998; Blauner, 1972). Immigration, voluntary or involuntary, is a transition that often entails the severing of community ties, the loss of social networks and familiar bonds -- it can mean the loss of taken for granted sources and systems of meaning. Many have discussed the negative social and psychological challenges and outcomes associated with immigration and settlement in unfamiliar environments (e. g., Berry, 1984; 1986; 1997; Birman, 1994; Furnham & Bochner, 1986; Ogbu, 1994; Segall, Dasen, Berry, & Poortinga, 1999).

Although the process of immigration-adaptation is a challenging experience, it can also mean hope for a better future, safety, and security for many individuals and groups. Indeed, individuals and groups may not always respond in negative ways and instead may adapt social and support systems based on the home culture to the new culture. These social and support systems can be construed as relational communities that facilitate the continuity of cultural identities and sense of community that are important for social and psychological well-being and adaptation to the new country. In a sense, immigrant-adaptation can be construed as a process of community making that involves the negotiating and integration of cultural systems and identities developed in one context to a new context and the development of ties with the new country. Viewing the adaptation process in this manner means individuals and groups are positioned as dynamic and not passive recipients of acculturative forces.

In this chapter, I use research with immigrant groups in Australia to explore the role of sense of community in immigrant adaptation. It is suggested that immigrant adaptation can be viewed as a process of community-making that can be understood by using the notion sense of community (SOC). Sense of community reflects feelings of belonging and identification with and participation in communities (Sarason, 1974). Conceptualizing immigrant settlement as a process of community making allows us to explore the nature and meaning of sense of community from the perspective of groups that have experienced rapid change. Immigrant groups may transfer the SOC developed in one context to another through social and support systems and this may have implications for their adaptation. Additionally, these groups provide the opportunity to understand the range of forces that impact community and the way in which they respond and provide its members with opportunities for belonging and identification.

IMMIGRANT ADAPTATION

Immigration means change; it implies disruptions to interpersonal systems and social networks, and challenges to systems of meaning. It means adaptation to the new contexts that involves the integration of identities and social and cultural systems into that context. In essence, immigration, and the ensuing intercultural contact, can involve challenges to social identities and community that are reflected in identification and well-being.

The settlement experiences for immigrant communities have been explored through different theoretical and conceptual frameworks including acculturation, social identity theory, and family values (Sam, 2000; Smith, 1991). Researchers have offered models to capture the individual and community responses to intergroup contact (e. g., Berry, 1984, 1997, 1998; Birman, 1994; Bulhan, 1985; Tajfel, 1981). Berry's (1997) model of acculturation and immigrant adaptation contains four common responses to intercultural contact, including integration, assimilation, separation, and marginalization. These responses are characterized by shifts in attitudes and behavior toward one's own and other communities. For example, group members may move away from their community of origin toward the host community, or they may move towards their own community and away from the host community.

The different responses are characterized by different mental health outcomes with integration being the most favorable and marginalization the least. There is general agreement among these models that those who are rooted in their home culture report better social and psychological well-being compared to those who are not (Lafromboise, Coleman, & Gerton, 1993). For example, McCubbin, Futrell, Thompson, and Thompson (1998) discussed research showing that participation in ethnic community activities and strength of ethnic identification has positive links with self-esteem and well-being. Ghaffarian (1998) also found support for the bicultural hypothesis -- those who hold onto their home culture while adopting the host culture report better health outcomes.

Birman (1994) offered an expanded typology of acculturation and adaptation strategies that stress the importance of understanding the process in context. In her model, identity options are integrated with attitudes and behavioral indicators to understand the complexity of the acculturation experience. In addition, she argued that adaptation strategies are influenced by broader contextual factors that have implications for social and psychological responses of individuals and groups. These contextual features include attitudes and policies of the host community toward the immigrant group, understandings of ethnicity and race, and other social, economic, and political factors. She concluded by stating that, in some circumstances, assimilation may be a better option than biculturalism because of broader social and political realities and the survival of the group. That is to say that social and political structures and processes and experiences of social exclusion impact communities' responses to transition and intercultural contact.

The important role of contextual factors in the shaping the settlement experience cannot be over-emphasized. It is equally important to consider the experiences, resources, and competencies of immigrant communities as they negotiate the new context and settlement process. These experiences, resources, and competencies may reflect important aspects of SOC that are central to the adaptation of a community to a new place. However, it seems that there is still a need to improve our understanding of the complexity of the process, the sociocultural systems, resources, and histories that immigrant communities bring with them, and the implications of these for adaptation. Overlooking the internal experiences, competencies, and social resources that communities may hold can result in a misinterpretation of settlement experiences and overlooking of existing strengths and resources that are important in the settlement process.

Immigrant Groups and Social Settings

An important adaptive feature of the settlement process is the formation of ethnic groups (Horenczyk, 1997). Within the broader ethnic community there are settings where people participate in cultural activities and retell stories. In Sarason's (1974) terms, these settings provide structure and meaning to the lives of members. The social settings in these groups function as social support and fulfill important social and psychological functions for group members and can be construed as relational communities. Cox (1989) suggested: "Within the familiar surroundings of the ethnic group, the immigrant or minority group member will usually find acceptance, common interests, opportunities to give and receive and a sense of belonging." (p. 147). Such networks provide opportunities for SOC, and in turn, are related to lowered probability of mental and physical illness (Furnham & Bochner, 1986). Sonn and Fisher (1998) stated that these settings play an important protective role for individuals and groups experiencing change, adversity, or other challenges. In their research, participants mentioned family and friendship networks, sporting clubs, and church-based groups as important settings in which they can socialize with similar others. Sonn and Fisher suggested that these the settings can be viewed as activity settings (O'Donnell, Tharp, & Wilson, 1993) that afford contexts in which valued cultural identities are propagated and the realities of the new context negotiated.

Activity settings are the basis for social processes common to participants that lead to shared systems of meaning and understanding, experiences, and ways of relating to the world. Expanding on Barker's notion of behavior settings, O'Donnell, et al. (1993) contended that activity settings differ from behavior settings by "including an account of subjective experience, cognition, and characteristics of individuals, by having specific relationships to other activity settings," (O'Donnell, et al. 1993, p. 504). Gallimore, Goldenberg, and Weisner (1993) and Gallimore and Goldenberg (1993) offered their understanding of activity settings, which is couched in ecocultural theory, suggesting that they are in part social constructions, and they moderate and mediate the impacts of social systems on people. Thus, activity settings provide the contexts in which various histories, experiences, and ideologies converge and people make sense of their individual and cultural identities and everyday experiences.

Applying Sense of Community

The psychological sense of community (SOC) framework provides a useful tool for understanding community and community change including immigration. Sarason (1974) introduced the notion SOC and emphasized the importance of connectedness to a larger dependable collectivity for the well-being of individuals and groups. His articulation of SOC is concerned with the embeddedness of people in systems and the importance of these systems in providing material and psychological resources that are important for well-being. In his view there is a dialectical relationship between community functioning and SOC.

McMillan and Chavis (1986) formulated a definition and theory of SOC that contains the elements membership, integration and fulfillment of needs, influence, and shared emotional connection that can be applied to both relational and geographical communities. Membership contains the attributes boundaries, personal investment, sense of belonging and identification, and emotional safety. The elements of the model work together and are context dependent; some elements may be more important than others. The SOC framework is concerned with identifying the structures and processes in communities that provide opportunities for belonging and identification and meaningful participation. This model is contextual and the elements reflect person-environment transactions.

The literature shows that a large proportion of the research have used the Sense of Community Index (SCI, Chavis, Hogge, McMillan, & Wandersman, 1986) derived from the SOC model to explore the correlates and antecedents of SOC (Chipuer & Pretty, 1999). This avenue for investigation has been very fruitful revealing that the SCI is a useful and reliable measure for exploring SOC in different settings, that SOC is related to different aspects of social and psychological functioning, and that both individual and community level factors are associated with variations in SOC (e. g., Brodsky, O'Campo, & Aronson, 1999; Kingston, Mitchell, Florin, & Stevenson, 1999).

Although this research has been very fruitful, we have not been able to fully appreciate the complex and diverse nature of community has not been fully appreciated because our the focus has largely been on understanding SOC as an individual psychological phenomenon within a North American context (Sonn, Bishop, & Drew, 1999). Community and SOC has not been viewed as emerging from the transactions between people and the broader social, historical, and cultural contexts. Viewing SOC in this way is consistent with the transactional or contextual view articulated by Altman (1993) who state that a "transactional perspective adopts the position that *people and psychological processes are embedded in and inseparable from their physical and social context*" (p. 140, italics in original). It is also akin to Newbrough's (1995) third position. This is a process orientation concerned with understanding and building communities that balances the needs of the individual and the collective.

In both of these orientations, the various contexts such as culture, history, community structure and social class shape social and psychological experiences. Significance is attributed to people and groups' capacities to reconstruct communities and to utilize social and cultural resources in their environments to make meaning of their social realities.

THE RESEARCH

Grounded in this orientation, I have focused on exploring sense of community and its role in the adaptation of immigrants in Australia. My colleagues and I (Sonn & Fisher, 1996; Sonn & Fisher, 2000; Sonn, Fisher, & Bustello, 1998) have been interested in the factors that facilitate and inhibit SOC and settlement. Data have been collected from two immigrant communities, coloured South Africans (Sonn, 1996; Sonn & Fisher, 1996) and Chileans (Sonn, et al., 1998), in separate studies. In both studies, participants were interviewed using a semi-structured guide that was developed using the SOC model.

Survey data was collected from a total of 97 participants in the South African group. The survey contained an adapted version of the Sense of Community Index, the General Health Questionnaire 30 item version (McDowell & Newell, 1987), ethnic identification and demographics (Sonn, 1996). Adaptation of the SCI for data collection with the South African community was facilitated by interview data collected as part of that research. Examples of adapted items included: "Very few South Africans in Australia know me," "Most South Africans in Australia share the same values about family togetherness," and "It does not matter to me what South Africans think of me when I socialise with them." Additional items included: "I feel the South African group I socialise with accepts me as a member" and "South Africans are very supportive in times of emotional challenges." The data from both studies are used in the following discussion to explore the nature and meaning of SOC, its links with ethnic identification and well-being, and the implications of within group diversity for the formation of settings and adaptation.

The Nature and Meaning of SOC

The settings in immigrant groups are central to the adaptation process in that they provide a vehicle for the transfer of SOC from one context to another. The findings suggests that a shared emotional connection based a shared history, experiences, and common country origin is central to the SOC. Immigrant and ethnic groups are often organized around shared stories and common symbols that people have transferred from the home culture.

Nagel (1994) wrote about the ways in which ethnic and cultural identities are negotiated and revived. She stated that "culture is constructed in much the same way as ethnic boundaries are built, by the actions of individuals and groups and their interactions with the larger society" (Nagel, 1994; p. 162). This understanding of the process is consistent with person-in-context models and allows for immigrant groups to be viewed as agentic and active in the acculturation and settlement processes. Nagel suggested that groups can reconstruct and create their culture through processes of revival and cultural reconstruction. Cultural revisions and revivals occur when aspects of culture are changed and new practices and processes created. The revival of culture and making of identities is an important aspect of the settlement process and a significant variable for the well-being of group members.

Common symbols and shared histories are central to making settings and in providing a shared emotional connection with the community of origin. For example, in the research with Chilean immigrants common symbol systems, shared cultural values, and boundaries such as the Spanish language, Catholicism, familialism, and shared historical events such as the Chilean Independence celebrations were identified by participants as important to their belonging and identification with the Chilean community (Sonn, et al., 1998). These aspects are markers of the ethnic community, they are shared by members and provide dimensions for group membership and social inclusion. They are also important in that they reflect significant social and cultural resources that have emotional and symbolic significance for community members in that they provide an anchor for individual relatedness.

The data that we collected suggested that participation in cultural activities and socializing in settings (Gallimore & Goldenberg, 1993; O'Donnell, et al., 1993) were important for linking people with the community of origin. For example, a participant stated that: "Independence day is very special for us. I love to celebrate that. We dance the Quecca [a national dance]." Another suggested that: "We have our national day and we celebrate. In Chile we can celebrate for a week sometimes". It was also said that:

> It is great [Social Club]. We feel alright, we like to join with the different people from Latin America. We speak Spanish, we all have the same thinking. We all have different cultures but I think it is a little bit the same. The main thing is we all speak Spanish.

Immigration is a major change that may bring to the forefront some of the taken for granted cultural learning that provide the basis for communality or intersubjectivity (O'Donnell, et al., 1993). These shared phenomena that may reflect shared cultural resources and learning can be thought of as tacit knowledge (Altheide & Johnson, 1994) that provide the basis for making meaning in and responding to the demands of the new country.

Factor analyses of South African immigrants' responses to the SCI revealed four factors that were labeled Shared Emotional Connection, Integration and Fulfillment of Needs, Influence, and Social Support. Oblique rotation (Oblimin) was used in the factor analysis because the elements of the model are theorized as interdependent (McMillan & Chavis, 1986). Shared Emotional Connection was the strongest factor for the group and together with social support accounted for 45.9% of the overall variance. Questions assessing importance of maintaining traditions, feelings of comfort with other South Africans, developing social ties with other South Africans, and preferring to socialize with other South Africans, loaded onto the factor and suggested a sense of familiarity and shared history. In Australia, coloured South Africans are faced with challenges to adapt to the new environment. These challenges, demands of the new context, and the support provided by fellow South Africans both contribute to the development of SOC. Shared emotional connection is based on a shared history and common understandings of what it meant to be coloured in South Africa. Through social systems people had the chance to rebuild and revitalize the cultural roots they established in South African society. In these settings they had the opportunity to reconstruct what it meant to be South African in the Australian context. Thus, these social settings provide opportunities for people to rebuild a SOC and incorporate new symbols, norms and stories into their own community identity.

These shared cultural understandings, symbols, and histories are important aspects of the shared emotional connection which McMillan and Chavis (1986) hypothesized as the catalyst for SOC. Shared emotional connection contains common symbols, shared history, and quality social networks that fosters shared emotional connection. The shared emotional bond that they describe can be likened to Tönnies (1955, 1974) *Gemeinschaft*, Leighton's (1959) shared sentiments, and Nobles' (1990) notion of experiential communality. *Gemeinschaft* is based on "well-defined habits of reunion and shared custom." (Tönnies, 1974, p. 10) and experiential communality is "the sharing of a particular experience by a group of people. ..." (Nobles, 1990, p. 49). The shared emotional connection reflects shared history and systems of meaning, and experiences that people may have internalized because of time spent together in a specific social-cultural contexts.

Aspects underpinning the shared emotional connection may be taken for granted and implicit, but it may come to the forefront in the face of change and adversity. According to Weisenfeld (1996), these shared symbols and systems of meaning can be construed as macro belongings because they are meaningful to all members of a social group or community and not easily disrupted by everyday change. However, during times of major change such as dislocation significant and meaningful rituals, symbols, and stories may be drawn upon as resources that are important for the survival and continuity of community identities.

Sense of Community and Ethnic Identification

SOC is linked with group membership and participation in settings. These settings provide opportunities for the fulfillment if needs and the development and continuity of ethnic identities. In fact, for immigrants ethnic groups are often the primary community and a major source for values, identities, and cultural scripts for living. Spencer and Markstrom-Adams (1991) defined ethnicity as: "a characteristic of shared unique cultural traditions and a heritage that persists across generations" (p. 292). Shared symbols, values, and experiences are significant aspects of ethnicity in that they provide the basis for cultural identity. It has been noted that important part of the acculturation and settlement processes involves the revision of symbols and retelling of stories and experiences internalized in the home culture.

These social processes are important for the continuity of ethnic and cultural identities. Indeed, the participation in cultural activities and the shared construction of meaning in social settings is important for belonging and identification. The shared connection based on experiences in the home and new country and the valuing of shared symbols and systems of meaning is an important feature of SOC. In the research with South African immigrants (Sonn, 1996) it was found that shared emotional connection is an important predictor of ethnic identity. Shared Emotional Connection reflected a sense of familiarity and relatedness with other South Africans. Regression analyses revealed that the Shared Emotional Connection was a strong predictor of both ethnic and national identification explaining 19% of the variance for ethnic identification and 11% for national identification. Influence and Integration and Fulfillment of Needs contributed 6% each to the equation that predicted ethnic identification (coloured South African). The overall equation accounted for 31% of the overall variance. Social support contributed to the prediction of national identity (South African).

It was argued that the links with ethnic identification may reflect the importance of the social identity to the ingroup. Coloured is not necessarily meaningful to the broader community and South African as, a social identity marker, is used with outsiders to the group. Additionally, in the new cultural context the label coloured may not have the same negative connotations that it may have carried in South Africa. Here people have the opportunity for reconstructing the meaning of the label and own it -- it serves as a marker to identify self to similar others.

Sense of Community and Well-being

The research literature in cultural and ethnic psychology show involvement in cultural activities in different settings fosters belonging and identification with similar others (McCubbin, et al., 1998), which, in turn, may enhance the potential for positive adaptation. There are also strong suggestions in the literature that SOC is important for psychological well-being. In fact, researchers have shown that aspects of SOC are related to different facets of psychological functioning (Chavis, 1983;Chipuer & Pretty, 1999; Cohen & Wills, 1985; Chipuer & Pretty, 1999). In our research we assessed psychological well-being using the General Health Questionnaire version 30. This measure contains subscales that assess anxiety, depression, and social functioning that together capture general health. Correlational analysis revealed moderate significant relationships between shared emotional connection and the GHQ-30 $(r = .24$ and anxiety $(r = .27)$. Social support also correlated moderately with the GHQ-30 $(r = -.28)$, depression($r = -.39)$ and social functioning $(r = -.32)$. It is important to note that because of the scoring of the GHQ-30 higher scores indicate poorer general health. Regression analysis showed that only social support loaded as a significant predictor of well-being. Social support reflected the group as an extraindividual factor (Felton & Shinn, 1992).

This finding is consistent with other researchers who have found that the SCI did not relate as an overall indicator to well-being. Instead, the subscales of the measure may be better indicators of psychological well-being. In this case, SOC may not be important for psychological well-being as measured by the GHQ and may well be related to some other aspect of quality of life.

Further analysis sought to clarify if there would be difference in psychological well-being for those who scored high and those who scored low on the SCI. Oneway ANOVA's revealed no significant differences in levels (Low, Medium, and High) of SOC and psychological well-being in our sample. However, correlational analysis revealed significant relationships between subscales of the SCI and the GHQ.

Although the immigrant group often represent the primary community, people may be members of multiple communities and they may have different needs met in different settings. There may be multiple sources of community and SOC may not be directly related to well-being and may, instead, be associated with settings outside the immigrant community. Hunter and Riger (1986) suggested that people may be members of multiple, yet interrelated communities in which different needs are met. The ethnic community may be one that meets specific needs related to social identity.

Immigrants often leave their country of origin in search of better futures for themselves and their children. Their leaving can be understood as an effort to resist oppression, exclusion, or other negative experiences. In the new countries they are often freer to participate in the mainstream society and realize economic and material goals and aspirations. The opportunities to meet material goals and to contribute to the broader community may well be important to psychological well-being. The fact that they have these opportunities for participation may be important for their identification with the host community, while the settings within the immigrant community provide the context for ethnic identity development. In this way, immigrants may form bonds with both their own community and the host community.

Threats to cultural identities and well-being may be tied to the actual and perceived experiences of inclusion and exclusion including racism and prejudice. That is, forces that devalue and threaten cultural and ethnic identities may impact community functioning and be reflected in the social and psychological adaptations. These experiences of inclusion and exclusion may in fact have implications for SOC and psychological well-being.

Diversity and Sense of Community

The shared histories, values and common symbol systems are important aspects of the experience of SOC. These, in essence, can be viewed as central features of ethnic and cultural communities that provide sources of meaning. However, this does not mean that immigrant and ethnic groups are homogeneous, that all members participate in the same social settings, and that SOC has the same meaning or are derived from the same sources for all members of a community. Although, a community may have a shared cultural background and history their communities are complex and diverse. In fact, it has been suggested that it is quite misleading to use proxy variables such as country to depict ethnic groups because it oversimplifies the cultural and social diversity of these communities (Bhatia & Ram, 2001; Hermans & Kempen, 1998). Thus, there are other important dimensions of diversity that must be considered because these have implications for community functioning and adaptation. If we do not consider these we may contribute to the stereotyping and unwitting homogenization of groups. Trickett (1994) stated that, "In discussing diversity in terms of groups, however, it is clear that the potential for stereotyping is present unless the diversity within diversity is clearly accounted for" (p. 585).

Dimensions of diversity reflect different social identities and social structures and the ways groups are positioned within a broader social ecology. Weisenfeld (1996) referred to these identities as microbelongings, the multiple collective identities that may impact community and the experience of community. These dimensions refer to other group memberships that one may hold within an ethnic community and the broader social ecology. That is, political affiliations, socioeconomic status, religion, age, gender, and immigration status may all have implications for our experiences and perceptions of and participation in community.

For example, in research with Chilean immigrants it was evident that there was a general sense that all members of the community shared a history and cultural background, but within the community it seemed there were strong differences in terms of political allegiances, immigration history, and socioeconomic background that impacted the nature of the adaptation and the settings in which people participate. For example, a participant observed that:

> If you think back to the '70s during the social depression [in Chile], people who were very much right wing left the country on their own. They were professional people and educated people...they did what they had to do and so when other people came with government assistance they were very reluctant to mix with them.

Although people shared cultural roots that are important to the community, different social and political factors that impacted community in the home country impact community functioning and have implications for the settlement in the new country. The political realities that triggered the waves of immigration following the coming to power of the Socialist government led by Salvadore Allende and the coup that saw the coming to power of Augusto Pinochet have implications for sense of community and adaptation.

The multiple community memberships that people hold may be observed under different circumstances. In fact, the recent media coverage about the possible prosecution of Augusto Pinochet, showed that many expatriate Chileans responded very differently to the issue. Although people ostensibly identified with the broader Chilean community, the varied responses to the issue reflected quite different political allegiances and community memberships. That is, within that community there are different groupings that serve as referents for sense of community including a soccer club that is largely Chilean and a social club that has a broader Latin American membership. Participation in these are impacted by microbelongings.

Data in the South African research also show that SOC may be perceived and experienced differently and vary for different members in a community. For example, although analysis of data showed no significant difference in scores on the SCI (high, medium, and low -- based on a percentile split of SCI scores) between those who migrated to Australia as adults and those who came as children with their parents, cluster analysis of data revealed that different generations may perceive and experience SOC differently. The cluster analysis of the SCI revealed that the nature and meaning of SOC was quite different for those who came to Australia as adults and those who came with their parents. For the adults, SOC was underpinned by items related to values, family togetherness, and socializing with other South Africans. For those who came as children, the symbolic identification with the home country was reflected in the importance of retaining the culture and traditions and for socializing with other South Africans. This suggested that the perceptions and experiences of group membership and community may be quite different for different groups within a community. In this case generational differences may impact the experiences and perceptions of community for members in a group.

In essence, this shows that cultural understandings and meanings provide the basis for a shared emotional connection and identification with the home country and may be important for identity and community. However, the way in which SOC is expressed and conceived in communities are impacted by social and political realities of the home country. The social, political, and economic structures that impacted community in the home country have important implications for the experience of community in the new country. In fact, these different community memberships may contribute to the creation of settings within the broader community that reflect social and economic differences. This reality impacts the nature and experience of SOC and social and psychological processes related to adaptation and community. It is essential that we are attuned to these factors because an idealized and homogenized conception of ethnic communities can result in us overlooking the multiple other memberships that may impact community functioning and adaptation.

CONCLUDING COMMENTS

Immigration and adaptation is a challenging process. In this chapter it was suggested that we can view immigrant adaptation as community making and that the SOC model can be used to explore adaptation. By using the SOC framework in a transactional orientation people and social systems as inseparable. Individuals and groups are positioned as resourceful and agentic not just as passive recipients of acculturative forces. The centrality of community structures in impacting social and psychological processes are acknowledged so to the fact that nature and meaning of SOC will be different for different groups.

In our local research to date, social settings within immigrant communities have been identified as performing protective and integrative functions. These settings can be conceptualized as activity settings that provide the spaces in which people jointly construct and negotiate shared understandings and meanings of community and identity -- they provide the basis for SOC. Participation in the settings, cultural activities, and other events foster belonging, identification and connectedness. In one sense it protects groups members and provides them with opportunities for meaningful participation. In another, it links them with the broader social and cultural context.

We, Adrian Fisher and I, have (Fisher & Sonn, 1999; Sonn & Fisher, 1998) suggested that communities can respond to change in resilient ways. Among other responses, they suggested that groups can create settings away from the mainstream that provide group members with opportunities for participation, social identities and roles, and the propagation of cultural values. These settings can include family networks, church and social groups, sporting clubs, and other settings. Similar settings can be observed in immigrant communities that provide context for community resilience -- an active adaptation to change.

We should continue to investigate the nature and structure of settings within communities because they may provide the sites for community building activities. We also need to explore the way in which social and political forces in host countries impact communities because these have implications for the survival of communities. I recognize that the settings may also be construed as exclusionary. However, only by understanding the nature of the settings and the functions they fulfill will we be able to optimize their potential for people and reduce the potential for harm following exclusion.

In terms of the McMillan and Chavis (1986) model, these social systems provide opportunities for quality interaction. The shared symbols and shared histories that are central to shared emotional connection are propagated in those settings and provide the basis for identity continuity and maintenance. This is not to say that it becomes only a process of reminiscing and romanticizing about the past and the home country. Rather, there is an active process of retelling about the home community as part of the remaking and integration of identities into the new community. It is like Nagel (1994) and others (e.g., Bhatia & Ram, 2001) have suggested, the histories, and memories, and stories are negotiated in the new context and become resources that provide meaning for people as they imagine new futures for future generations.

Furthermore, the research also revealed that as a global assessment the SCI does not correlate with an indicator of well-being. Rather, subscales of the SCI, in particular shared emotional connection and social support had significant correlations with the GHQ. This suggests that aspects of sense of community such as emotional attachment and perceptions of social support may be more important for well-being.

In the research reported above, we have collected both quantitative and qualitative data have been collected. The qualitative data has allowed us to grounding understandings of SOC in the realities of different communities. This has made it possible to identify the nature and meaning of community and the different social and psychological processes involved in SOC and adaptation. It is essential that we adapt our instruments and anchor them in the realities of the groups we work with. There is a wealth of literature in community psychology that explores the challenges associated with understanding the person in context that is consistent with the third position (Newbrough, 1995) and transactional models (Mankowski & Rappaport, 1995; Rappaport, 1995). These emphasize the need to use multiple forms of data collection and levels of analysis in addition to importance of understanding phenomena as they are reflected in the everyday realities of the individuals and communities.

Importantly, the cultural grounding of the instruments are necessary so to the efforts to assess the phenomenon at multiple levels (Tolan, Keys, Chertok, & Jason, 1990). By exploring SOC in communities we will also need to confront questions related to epistemology that may well challenge us to recognize the political and discursive or socially constructed nature of SOC. By considering epistemological issues as an integral part of our action and research cycle in our pursuit to understand and to promote SOC we will take another step toward culturally grounding the research. In doing this we will move beyond providing surface level adaptations of our instruments and begin to ask questions about the political nature of our research processes as well as the political nature of community. This may be very useful and allow us to capitalize on the SOC framework as a guide for intervention and SOC as an indicator of the success of those interventions.

REFERENCES

Altheide, D. L., & Johnson, J. M. (1994). Criteria for assessing interpretive validity in qualitative research. In N. K. Denzin & L. Y. S. (Eds.), *Handbook of qualitative research* (pp. 485 - 499). Thousand Oaks, CA: Sage.

Altman, I. (1993). Challenges and opportunities of a transactional world view: Case study of contemporary Mormon polygynous families. *American Journal of Community Psychology, 21*, 135-156.

Berry, J. W. (1984). Cultural relations in plural societies: Alternatives to segregation and their sociopsychological implications. In N. Miller and M. B. Brewer (Eds.), *Groups in contact: The psychology of desegregation* (pp. 11-27). Orlando, Fl: Academic Press.

Berry, J. W. (1986). Multiculturalism and psychology in plural societies. In L. H. Ekstrand (Ed.), *Ethnic minorities and immigrants in a cross-cultural perspective* (pp. 35-51). Lisse, The Netherlands: Swets & Zeitlinger.

Berry, J. W. (1997). Immigration, acculturation, and adaptation. *Applied Psychology: An*

International Review, 46, 5-34.

Berry, J. W. (1998). Intercultural relations in plural societies. *Canadian Psychology, 40*, 12-21.

Bhatia, S., & Ram, A. (2001). Rethinking 'acculturation' in relation to diasporic cultures and postcolonial identities. *Human Development, 44*, 1-18.

Birman, D. (1994). Acculturation and human diversity in a multicultural society. In E. J. Trickett, R. J. Watts, & D. Birman (Eds.), *Human diversity: Perspectives of people in context* (pp. 261-284). San Francisco: Jossey Bass.

Blauner, R. (1972). *Racial oppression in America.* New York: Harper Row.

Bulhan, H. A. (1985). *Frantz Fanon and the psychology of oppression.* New York: Plenum Press.

Brodsky, A. E., O'Campo, P. J., & Aronson, R. E. (1999). PSOC in community context: Multi-level correlates of a measure of psychological sense of community in low-income, urban neighborhoods. *Journal of Community Psychology, 27*, 681-694.

Chavis, D. M. (1983) Sense of community in the urban environment: Benefits for human and neighborhood development. *Dissertation Abstracts International* (Doctor of Philosophy George Peabody College for Teachers Vanderbilt University), *45*, 03B, p.1058.

Chavis, D. M., Hogge, J. H., McMillan, D. W., & Wandersman, A. (1986). Sense of community through Brunswik's lens: A first look. *Journal of Community Psychology, 14*, 24-40.

Chipuer, H. M., & Pretty, G. M. H. (1999). A review of the sense of community index: Current uses, factor structure, reliability, and further development. *Journal of Community Psychology, 27*, 643-658.

Cohen, S., & Wills, T. A. (1985). Stress, social support, and the buffering hypothesis. *Psychological Bulletin, 98,* 310-357.

Cox, D. R. (1989). *Welfare practice in a multicultural society.* Sydney, Australia: Prentice Hall.

Felton, B. J., & Shinn, M. (1992). Social integration and social support: Moving "social support" beyond the individual level. *Journal of Community Psychology, 20*, 103-115.

Fisher, A. T., & Sonn, C. C. (1999). Aspiration to community: Community responses to rejection. *Journal of Community Psychology, 27*, 715-725.

Furnham, A., & Bochner, S. (1986). *Culture shock: Psychological responses to unfamiliar environments.* London, UK: Methuen.

Gallimore, R., & Goldenberg, C. (1993). Activity settings of early literacy: Home and school factors in children's emergent literacy. In E. A. Forman, N. Minick, & C. A. Stone (Eds.), *Contexts for learning: Sociocultural dynamics in children's development* (pp. 315-335). New York: Oxford University Press.

Gallimore, R., Goldenberg, C. N., & Weisner, T. S. (1993). The social construction and subjective reality of activity settings: Implications for community psychology. *American Journal of Community Psychology, 21*, 537-559.

Ghaffarian, S. (1998). The acculturation of Iranian immigrants in the United States and the implications for mental health. *The Journal of Social Psychology, 138*, 645-655.

Hermans, H. J. M., & Kempen, H. J. G. (1998). Moving cultures: The perilous problem of cultural dichotomies in a globalizing society. *American Psychologist, 53*, 1111-1120.

Horenczyk, G. (1997). Immigrants' perceptions of host attitudes and their reconstruction of cultural groups. *Applied Psychology: An International Review, 46*, 34-36.

Hunter, A., & Riger, S. (1986). The meaning of community in community mental health. *Journal of Community Psychology, 14*, 55-71.

Kingston, S., Mitchell, R., Florin, P., & Stevenson, J. (1999). Sense of community in neighborhoods as multi-level construct. *Journal of Community Psychology, 27*, 681-

694.

Lafromboise, T., Coleman, H., & Gerton, J. (1993). Psychological impact of biculturalism: Evidence and theory. *Psychological Bulletin, 114*, 395-412.

Leighton, A. (1959). *My name is legion: Foundations for a theory of man in relation to culture*. New York: Basic Books.

Mankowski, E., & Rappaport, J. (1995). Stories, identity, and the psychological sense of community. In J. R. S. Wyer (Ed.), *Knowledge and memory: The real story. Advances in social cognition (no. 8)* (pp. 211-226). Hillsdale, NJ: Lawrence Erlbaum Associates.

McCubbin, H. I., Futrell, J. A., Thompson, E. A., & Thompson, A. I. (1998). Resilient families in an ethnic and cultural context. In H. I. McCubbin, E. A. Thompson, A. I. Thompson, & J. A. Futrell (Eds.), *Resiliency in African-American families* (pp.329-351). Thousand Oaks, CA: Sage.

McDowell, I, & Newell, C. (1987). *Measuring Health: A guide to rating scales and questionnaires*. Oxford, UK: Oxford University Press.

McMillan, D. W. (1996). Sense of community. *Journal of Community Psychology, 24*, 315-325.

McMillan, D. W., & Chavis, D. M. (1986). Sense of community: A definition and theory. *Journal of Community Psychology, 14*, 6-23.

Nagel, J. (1994). Constructing ethnicity: Creating and recreating ethnic identity and culture. *Social Problems, 41*, 152-176.

Newbrough, J. R. (1995). Toward community: A third position. *American Journal of Community Psychology, 23*, 9-37.

Nobles, W. N. (1990). African philosophy: Foundations for black psychology. In R. Jones (Ed.), *Black psychology* (3rd ed.) (pp. 41-57). Berkeley, CA: Cobb & Henry.

O'Donnell, C. R., Tharp, R. G., & Wilson, K. (1993). Activity settings as the unit of analysis: A theoretical basis for community intervention and development. *American Journal of Community Psychology, 21*, 501- 520.

Ogbu, J. U. (1994). From cultural differences to differences in cultural frame of reference. In P. M. Greenfield, & R. R. Cocking, (Eds.), *Crosscultural roots of minority child development* (pp.365-391). Hillsdale, NJ: Lawrence Erlbaum.

Rappaport, J. (1995). Empowerment meets narrative: Listening to stories and creating settings. *American Journal of Community Psychology, 23*, 795-807.

Sam, D. L. (2000). Psychological adaptation of adolescents with immigrant backgrounds. *The Journal of Social Psychology, 140*, 5-25.

Sarason, S. (1974). *Psychological sense of community: Prospects for a community psychology*. San Francisco: Jossey Bass.

Segall, M. H., Dasen, P. R., Berry, J. W., & Poortinga, Y H. (1999). *Human behavior in global perspective: An introduction to cross-cultural psychology* (2nd ed.). London, UK: Allan & Bacon.

Smith, E. J. (1991). Ethnic identity development: Toward the development of a theory within the context of majority/minority status. *Journal of Counseling and Development, 70*, 181-188.

Sonn, C. C. (1996). *The role of psychological sense of community among coloured South African immigrants*. Unpublished Doctoral Thesis, Victoria University of Technology, Melbourne, Australia.

Sonn, C. C., & Fisher, A. T. (1996). Sense of community in a politically constructed group. *Journal of Community Psychology, 24*, 417-430.

Sonn, C. C., & Fisher, A. T. (1998). Sense of community: Community resilient responses to oppression and change. *Journal of Community Psychology, 26*, 457-471.

Sonn, C., Fisher, A. T., & Bustello, S. (July, 1998). *Sense of community: A different way to understand immigrant adaptation*. Paper presented at the 6th Australia-

Aotearoa/New Zealand Community Psychology Conference, KiriKiriroa/Hamilton, Aotearoa/New Zealand.

Sonn, C. C., Bishop, B. J., & Drew, N. M. (1999). Sense of community: Issues and considerations from a cross-cultural perspective. *Community, Work, and Family, 2,* 205-218.

Sonn, C. C., & Fisher, A. T. (2000). Oppression: Moving beyond the dominant-nondominant dichotomy. *The Community Psychologist, 34,* 32-34.

Spencer, M. B., & Markstrom-Adams, C. (1990). Identity processes among racial and ethnic minority children in America. *Child Development, 61,* 290-310.

Tajfel, H. (1981). *Human groups and social categories.* Cambridge, UK: Cambridge University Press.

Tönnies, F. (1955). *Community and association.* Norfolk, UK: Lowe & Brydone.

Tönnies, F. (1974). Gemeinschaft and Gesellschaft. In C. Bell & H. Newby (Eds.), *The sociology of community: A selection of readings* (pp. 5-12). London, UK: Frank Cass and Company.

Trickett, E. J. (1994). Human diversity and community psychology: Where ecology and empowerment meet. *American Journal of Community Psychology, 22,* 583-592.

Tolan, P., Keys, C. Chertok, F., & Jason, L. (1990). Researching community psychology: Issues of theory and methods. Washington, DC: American Psychological Association.

Weisenfeld, E. (1996). The concept of "We": A community social psychology myth? *Journal of Community Psychology, 24,* 337-363.

Chapter 12

MOOING TILL THE COWS COME HOME[i]
The Search For Sense Of Community In Virtual Environments

Lynne D. Roberts, Leigh M. Smith, and Clare Pollock
Curtin University

INTRODUCTION

As social beings, we strive to obtain a sense of community in our lives. Place-based communities have been seen as the main source sense of community. Today, however, place-based communities do not always meet this need. Individuals may feel isolated and alienated within their place-based communities. Large cities, by virtue of their size alone, may not offer the idealized sense of community associated in people's minds with small villages and towns. What are the alternatives? One arena in which people are experimenting with new forms of community is cyberspace. Communication technology advances have enabled the establishment of virtual environments where geographically dispersed individuals interact to form communities.

McMillan and Chavis (1986) defined sense of community as "a feeling that members have of belonging, a feeling that members matter to one another and to the group, and a shared faith that member's needs will be met through their commitment to be together" (p. 9). In this chapter we use the definition and four elements of sense of community outlined by McMillan and Chavis to examine sense of community within a type of virtual environment known as a MOO (Multi-User Dimension or Dungeon, Object Oriented).

From Place-Based To Virtual Communities

Sense of community has traditionally been associated with groupings of people from discrete geographical areas (e.g., villages, suburbs, towns, and cities). Community psychologists have reported a growing disillusionment amongst people in their search for a sense of community and community values in place-based communities (Dunham, 1977, 1986; Glynn, 1986; Sarason, 1974). Sarason (1974) stated his belief that "the dilution or absence of the psychological sense of community is the most destructive dynamic in the lives of people in our society" (p. viii). The hypothesized declining sense of community in place-based communities has been linked to the social development of western societies, increasing industrialization, and increasingly centralized bureaucracies and government (Glynn, 1986). However, as Hill (1996) noted, there is a lack of longitudinal research documenting this hypothesized decline in sense of community.

Disillusionment has resulted in individuals searching for a sense of community in areas other than their geographical community, reflecting a movement from place, or structurally-based communities to process-based communities (Dunham 1977, 1986), or non-place communities (Webber, 1964). Consistent with this, research in sense of community has expanded from places of residence, to non-residential places where people interact. Dunham (1986) attributed this movement to the effects of the industrial revolution, increasing scientific knowledge, and technological advances enabling rapid communication across distance. Recent technological advances enabling the widespread usage of computer-mediated communication (CMC) have opened up the possibility of process-based communities that are not dependent upon the geographical location of members. The potential for transglobal virtual communities now exists.

Transglobal virtual communities are dependent upon communication technologies such as satellites, computers and telephones. Jones (1995a) argued that there are two motives driving the development of transglobal virtual communities: the search for new communities, and the capability of current technologies to create them. CMC can be used to communicate either asynchronously (delayed) or synchronously ('real time') with one another, by text, voice, or image. Jones (1995a) coined the term "CyberSociety" to describe these new forms of mediated community enabled by CMC (p. 2). As Jones, (1995b) explained:

> CMC, of course, is not just a tool: it is at once technology, medium, and engine of social relations. It not only structures social relations, it is the space within which the social relations occur and the tool that individuals use to enter the space. It is more than the context within which social relations occur (although it is that, too) for it is commented on and imaginatively constructed by symbolic processes initiated and maintained by individuals and groups (p.16).

CMC then, forms the basis of transglobal virtual communities.

Virtual communities are dynamic communities accessed via CMC and based on shared interests, rather than shared locations (Little, 1993; Wellman & Gulia, 1999). A commonly used definition of virtual communities is offered by Rheingold (1994): "social aggregations that emerge from the Net when enough people carry on public discussions long enough, with sufficient human feeling, to form webs of personal relationships in cyberspace" (p. 5). Virtual communities are social constructions. The term 'virtual community' is used to describe the 'place' or 'space' where people interact on a regular basis. Even these words are misrepresentations. There are no defined spaces or places in cyberspace. Virtual environments have no geographical boundaries or proxemics (Aoki, 1995; Carlstrom, 1992) and reflect an information reality, rather than a physical reality. Indeed, from a symbolic-interactionist perspective, reality itself is socially constructed (Berger & Luckmann, 1966) and all communities are social constructions emerging from shared communication and interaction (Hunter & Riger, 1986). Communities are imagined in the sense that community members "will never know most of their fellow members, meet them, or even hear of them, yet in the minds of each lives the image of their communion" (Anderson, 1991: p. 6). Virtual communities are not physical communities, but exist in the minds of those who inhabit them.

Despite the widespread use of the term virtual community, debate continues over whether communities can, and do, exist in cyberspace. The term virtual community has been applied by researchers to a range of virtual environments including newsgroups, Internet Relay Chat (IRC) and Multi-User Dungeons or Dimensions (MUDs) (see, for example Baym, 1995; Clodius, 1997; Hampton, 1996; Patterson, 1996; Phillips, 1996; Reid, 1991, 1995). Early proponents of virtual communities (e.g., Rheingold, 1994) expressed hopes for more democratic human relationships within these communities. Opponents argued that there is more to community than a group of people interacting via text (e.g., Kling, 1996). Even those who used the word 'community' to describe computer-mediated communication environments may doubt the value of virtual communities, having claimed they are poor substitutes for place-based communities (McBeath & Webb, 1995; Stoll, 1995). Wellman and Gulia (1999, p. 167) described the debate as "Manichean, presentist, unscholarly and parochial." The current discussion on whether communities exist ignores the historical context of debate on the existence and nature of communities. The Internet is discussed in isolation as a separate reality, without recognition of the possible overlap between people's everyday and virtual lives. Kot (1999) noted that the debate paralleled the movement in sense of community research from place-based definitions to functional components.

A body of field research is emerging that suggests that individuals are experiencing a sense of community in a range of virtual environments. The development of sense of community has been reported in IRC (Reid,

1991; Surrat, 1996), MUDs (Clodius, 1997; Hampton, 1996), email discussion groups (Kot, 1999), bulletin boards (Dunham, Hurshman, Litwin, Gusella, Ellsworth, & Dodd, 1998), computer-supported distance learning programs (Haythornthwaite, Kazmer, & Robins, 2000), on-line support groups (Glasser Das, 1999) and newsgroups (Baym, 1995; Phillips, 1996; Watson, 1997).

In addition to experiencing sense of community within a specific virtual environment, some people may experience a generalized sense of community while on-line. Almost half of the respondents to the GVU 8th WWW User Survey (1997) reported feeling more connected to people since coming on-line. The feeling of connection increased with Internet experience. Women were more likely to feel connected with their families and with people with similar life experiences, while men were more likely to feel connected to people with similar hobbies or professions.

MOOs

Of all the virtual environments, MOOs have been described as providing the closest resemblance to traditional communities on the Internet (Falk, 1995). MOOs are socially oriented MUDs based on object oriented programming and providing a database of rooms, descriptions, and objects that are usable and extensible by all players (Curtis, 1992; Curtis & Nicholls, 1993). Individuals from disparate geographic locations can connect simultaneously to a MOO via computer and modem to engage in real time text-based (typed) communication with one another.

MOO communities develop their own cultures, norms, and systems of social regulation (Reid, 1995). Individuals create their own character(s), clothing and accessories, build their own homes and interact with other community members on an ongoing basis. Turkle (1995) claimed that virtual environments such as MOOs fulfill the need for Goldenburg's notion of a "great, good place," providing central meeting places that are no longer available in the offline world. Despite claims of MOOs as communities, a literature search of on-line and paper journals revealed no systematic research investigating sense of community in MOOs.

MOOs vary in their purpose, size, and requirements for identifying information. Allen (1996) identified four genres of MOOs: social, adventure, professional, and special interest. In addition, most MOOs have a stated theme that newcomers are encouraged to read prior to requesting the allocation of a character, and expected to adhere to once a character is granted. Some MOOs have more stringent entry requirements than others, and request 'real life' identifying information, such as name and address, and the reason for requesting a MOO character. The number of individuals with characters on a MOO varies widely. MOOs range from private MOOs set up for the use of the owner and their invited friends, to large public MOOs with several thousand members that are accessible by anyone with telnet access.

On social MOOs, users are known only by the character name they have chosen, the self-description they have created, and what they choose to disclose about themselves. Allen (1996) described MOO characters as providing both anonymity and pseudonymity. MOO users have *anonymity* in the sense that there is no direct link between the MOO character and the individual. Only 'wizards' (the administrators of the MOO) have legitimate access to information that links the MOO character to the individual (e.g., email addresses). However, hackers have been known to access and distribute this information. Information about the real life identity of a MOOer may be spread through gossip or obtained through electronic surveillance. MOO characters have *pseudonymity* in the sense that the character itself develops a reputation with ongoing use. The combination of pseudonymity and anonymity allow the individual to maintain ongoing relationships with other MOO users in MOO space while maintaining the illusion of anonymity.

We chose to examine sense of community within publicly accessible social MOOs. The research findings presented here form part of a larger study examining the effects of computer-mediated communication on social interaction in MOOs (see Roberts, Smith, & Pollock, 1996).

METHOD

The research was conducted using grounded theory methodology (Glaser & Strauss, 1967): a qualitative research methodology that uses systematic procedures to develop inductively derived theory grounded in the data collected about the phenomena of interest. In accordance with grounded theory methodology, theoretical sampling (sampling based on selecting participants according to their knowledge of the phenomena of interest, and their ability to reflect upon and verbalize their experiences) was used to ensure a wide variety of MOO users were interviewed. The researcher took on the character of "Questioner" and a "Research Room" on the MOOs.

In total, 58 individuals were interviewed about their MOOing experiences. Fifty-four interviews were conducted on eight social MOOs using typed CMC. Interviews were semi-structured and lasted between one and three hours. With the research participants' permission, all interviews were recorded using the logging facility of MUTT-Lite software (Free, 1995). Four interviews with local MOO users were conducted face-to-face, audio recorded, and transcribed.

As part of the interview, MOO users (with the exception of 'guests' and individuals new to MOOs) were asked if they thought the MOO they were on had a sense of community. The researcher offered no definition of sense of community. Where the answer was affirmative, MOO users were asked what, to them, gave the MOO a sense of community. They were also asked if other MOOs they frequented had a sense of community, and whether this sense of community was the same across MOOs.

In addition to interviews, postings to MOO-mailing lists, help files, and MOO documentation relating to social interaction on MOOs were included in the data collection process. Permission was requested and obtained for the use of all postings included in the analysis. Data were entered into the QSR NUD*IST program (QSR NUD*IST, 1995) with an utterance (for interviews) or paragraph (for all other material) as the unit of analysis. Data were coded and categorized based on the constant comparison of data. A category labeled sense of community was developed.

Upon completion of the research, all MOO users who had participated in the research were sent a MOO-mail contained the World Wide Web address of a site containing a summary of the research findings, and invited to provide feedback. The feedback obtained was incorporated into the research findings.

Research Participants

Research participants were past or present users of MOOs. The following statistics are designed to provide a demographic picture of the 'real' and 'virtual' lives of the MOO users interviewed. As theoretical (as opposed to random) sampling was used, no claim is made that the MOO users interviewed comprise a representative sample of the MOOing population.

The demographics of MOO users 'real lives' are based on self-reports. No identifying information such as name or address was sought. This was an intentional strategy designed to increase the likelihood of obtaining 'truthful' answers by reducing fears of reports of MOO activities having repercussions on the individuals' off-line lives. No attempt was made to verify the demographic information received.

MOO users interviewed ranged in self-reported age between 14 and 50 years ($M = 26$ years, $SD = 8.5$, Median = 23). Forty (69%) stated their biological sex was male, 16 (23%) female, and two (3%) described their sex as 'spivak' (indeterminate). While 64% of the participants resided in the United States of America, nine different countries were represented in the sample. All but four (93%) of the interviewees had completed, or were currently enrolled in, tertiary education. Of the four that hadn't, two were currently in secondary school and had plans to continue their education at university. Twelve participants had post-graduate qualifications, or were enrolled in postgraduate studies. The emerging picture of MOO users interviewed is that of a predominantly male, young, highly educated group of North Americans.

In addition to 'real life' demographics, it is necessary to examine the demographics of MOO characters. Each individual has complete control over the description and gender of their MOO character(s). As gender is self-selected on the MOO, it is necessary to distinguish between biological sex and MOO gender. Sixty-two percent of the research participants interviewed gendered their main character male, 21% female, and 17% had adopted an 'alternative' MOO gender (spivak, plural, or neuter). The number of different characters an individual used ranged from none (guests awaiting the creation of their first character) to 35 (*Median* = 2). Some chose to use the same character on all MOOs they frequented (that is, use the same character name and description), while others used multiple characters within, and between, MOOs. Those interviewed varied in their MOOing histories and current MOOing behaviors. The length of time since first MOOed (i.e., the 'MOO age' of the character) ranged from 1 day to five years (*M* = 17 months, *SD* = 12 months). The average stated time spent MOOing each week ranged from nil (an ex-MOOer) to 75 hours per week (*M* = 25 hours per week, *SD* = 18 hours per week). The number of MOOs frequented by an individual ranged from one to 54 MOOs (*Median, Mode* = 3).

RESEARCH FINDINGS

Two types of results are presented here. First, we detail research participants' views on whether MOOs have a sense of community. Second, the contents of the sense of community category developed in this study are compared with the elements of sense of community described by McMillan and Chavis (1986). The results are presented in the form of quotes from interviews and MOO-mailing lists interwoven with research findings. Names of MOO users and MOOs have been removed. Where necessary explanatory notes have been included in bracketed text within quotes. Unless otherwise indicated, all quotes are from interviews. A common characteristic of MOO speech is to 'talk' (type) in phrases connected with ellipses. As such, ellipses (with varying numbers of 'dots') used in quotes do not indicate that material has been cut by the authors, but reflect actual speech patterns on MOOs.

Do MOOs Have A Sense Of Community?

The MOO users interviewed had varying perceptions of sense of community. These ranged from there being no sense of community on MOOs to claims that a MOO *is* a community. Of the 47 MOO users who were asked specific questions about sense of community, four (8.5%) felt that MOOs did not have a sense of community, six (12.8%) were unsure, and 37 (78.7%) responded that MOOs did have a sense of community. Typical responses for each of these categories are shown below. Users from the three response groups did not significantly differ in the number of MOOs used, hours spent MOOing per week, or MOOing history.

Three MOO users stated that they did not feel a sense of community on any of the MOOs they frequented. The other MOOer who felt the MOO did not have a true sense of community explained:

> the sense of community is actually false.. if you know what I mean. It's more like a dysfunctional family.. well there is a heck of a lot of drama behind the scenes.. like my house used to be.. I come from a Latin family so I recognize horrid useless drama when I see it.

Some MOO users thought that MOOs might have a sense of community, but seemed uncertain as to the extent of this, and whether it was more groupings of friends rather than a community:

> they should have, they should feel like small towns. In truth i think that these small towns dismember into much smaller 'friends circles.' and then there is the obvious fact that most 'dedicated' MOOers have characters on just about every MOO.

Another MOOer commented that while there may be a sense of community on MOOs, they had not personally experienced it:

> perhaps but if so then I don't really think I've been a part of it to any great degree. I've just tended to know a few people around the edges.

The majority of users stated that some, or all, MOOs have a sense of community. MOO users tended to use their conception of community and sense of community in 'real-life' as the basis for judging sense of community on MOOs. For example:

> 'community' as we say would mean as we live now with jobs, homes, possibly families..we have forms of governments, etc. The MOO offers most of this..it offers homes, friends, and wizards [administrators on MOOs].

Some MOO users experienced a level of sense of community on MOOs that is greater than that experienced in their real lives. Pravatiner (1996), in a posting to an on-line discussion list, claimed that "they (MOOs) have provided me with the greatest sense of community I have experienced in a long while, and some of my closest friends ever."

MOO users varied in their views about the extent of sense of community within, and across, MOOs. Some MOO users felt that the sense of community experienced by MOO users crossed MOO boundaries. This was enhanced by individual MOO users having characters on several MOOs. While some felt that there was a sense of community across MOOs, others felt that each MOO had its own sense of community. The differing sense of community between MOOs was often likened to the difference in sense of communities between cities:

> Yes, each moo has a different feel and environment, much akin to moving from one city to another.

> people in small towns and large cities both have senses of community -- moos are like that too ... both personal community of whatever size and identification with the larger entity.

Some MOO users felt that rather than communities across MOOs, there were multiple communities within a single MOO:

> I think that we want to have a sense of community but that in the long run there are too many people to have one unified community. I know there are communities there, and I know that they overlap, but I also know that some people exist who don't fit into other people's communities at all.

> I know there are communities in here, people into moo sex, the living room crowd, the rpg [role play gaming] crowd, the political class.

Whether a MOO is seen as a single community, or a group of communities depends partly on the size of the MOO. Smaller MOOs were generally seen as friendlier, with a closer sense of community than larger MOOs:

> The MOOs with a 'small-town' atmosphere tend to be fun, lively, happening places. ...The huge ones like [MOO A] and [MOO B] are too big, there's not enough sense of community, and consequently they tend to suck, frankly.

While many individuals have characters on multiple MOOs, most have a MOO that they designate as their 'home MOO' and feel a special attachment to:

> community on a moo is like IPR [in physical reality] ... peer groups ... home groups ... whole world identity ...there's one big difference imho [in my humble opinion] ...any moo is accessible by any person ... so it takes a very strong link to become 'world associated' ... most

people call one moo their 'home moo' ...but that isn't moo based ..
normally there's an interpersonal reason for its choice ...the place
where your love is .. where most of your friends are .. or in some
cases .. the place where you built for a purpose or are proud of your
work.

Sense of community is a subjective experience, and as these results
indicate, individuals experienced sense of community in MOOs in different
ways. The majority of the MOO users interviewed experienced at least some
sense of community on at least some MOOs. Sense of community was
experienced within groups, within MOOs, or across MOOs. Sense of
community was strongest on the individual's home MOO, and in some cases
exceeded the sense of community experienced in off-line communities.

Elements of Sense of Community

This section examines MOOs in terms of the four elements of sense
of community outlined by McMillan and Chavis (1986): membership,
influence, integration and fulfillment of needs, and shared emotional
connection.

Membership

On MOOs, boundaries are enforced between members (those who
have characters) and non-members (those who use guest characters). To
attain membership of a MOO, one must have access to a computer and
modem, and apply for membership. Some MOOs require a reason for
joining, while others outline conditions that must be met. Even when a
character has been created for an individual, membership is not automatic.
The individual must make a personal investment in the MOO to learn the
basic programming skills required to describe, gender, and clothe their
character; the commands to create a home; the commands used to enable
their character to communicate and express emotions; and the commands to
move around the MOO. Even then, full acceptance as a member of the
community may not be felt.

Boundaries are also set to provide an environment of emotional
safety for members to share and grow closer to one another (McMillan &
Chavis, 1986). The combination of anonymity and physical distance between
MOO users provides a perceived safe environment in which to self-disclose
(Reid, 1995). Threats to this anonymity are treated seriously. Members of
Lambda MOO voted to have the following message displayed on the log-in
screen:

NOTICE FOR JOURNALISTS AND RESEARCHERS:
The citizens of LambdaMOO request that you ask for permission from all direct participants before quoting any material collected here. (Lambda MOO log in screen, 2 June 1996.)

While having no legal backing, the notice serves to reinforce boundaries, and provide the perception of a protective environment. In addition, MOO users have access to a number of commands that increase their feeling of safety. The commands @gag and @refuse can be used to block messages from specified players. Rooms can be 'swept' to ensure no 'listening devices' (bugs) are in place. Various commands can be used to 'lock' rooms, to eject other MOO users from rooms, and to banish guests from the MOO. In combination, these things increase the perception of a 'safe' environment for personal disclosure.

Scapegoating works to reinforce established boundaries. Deviants from expected behavioral/communication norms (and these norms vary widely between MOOs) may be 'toaded' (character is turned into a toad and the typist banned from the MOO permanently), 'newted' (temporarily suspended from the MOO), lose their 'prog bit' (resulting in loss of ability to program on the MOO), or have other punishments applied. For example, a player who changed other MOO users' character descriptions and messages was punished by having their character made accessible and changeable by any other character on the MOO. As one MOOer commented:

> I think like any community there is an attempt of sorts to align the community to someone's standards, yes? Or they want to change the community to their standards by getting rid of that which offends them and won't change to their standards.

Sense of belonging and identification with the community enhance feelings of membership (McMillan & Chavis, 1986). Some MOO users described sense of community in terms of the feeling of belonging:

> part of it has to do with a relatively regular set of people participating/playing -- that group can shift, but if you don't have some sense of continuity and belonging, you're not likely to feel there's a community there...

> I think that there is a certain inherent loyalty you feel towards others after playing for so long. I think that eventually you do feel that you're part of the group.

Use of a common symbol system aids sense of belonging in communities (McMillan & Chavis, 1986). MOOs share a common programming language (object-oriented programming). The use of this programming language both creates boundaries between MOO users and users of other types of MUDs, and dissolves boundaries between MOOs. All communication occurs using a common language in a common text-based environment, resulting in a "common culture" (Reid, 1995, p. 173). Within MOOs, feature objects can be programmed to shortcut speech. A one or two word command can generate a phrase, a sentence or a series of paragraphs. Multi-layered conversations are common, due to the delay in waiting for typed responses and system lag. MOO users use ascii-text emoticons (e.g., ':)' seen sideways represents a smiling face, or 'smilie') and the emote command to express emotions. This text-based communication has been described as 'written speech' (Marvin, 1995) and includes the use of paralanguage and MOOisms. As one MOOer noted:

> some of the bashers [MOO users who meet in real-life for parties known as 'MOO bashes'] and I seem to communicate largely with shared idioms and expletives. :>.

Influence

McMillan and Chavis (1986) highlight the role of bi-directional influence between community and member as an important element of sense of community. Internet users have a culture of helping one another on a voluntary basis (Wellman & Gulia, 1999). Many MOO users take on positions of responsibility and influence within MOOs. Experienced MOO users may become wizards, members of review boards, arbitrators, or help staff for new MOO users. MOO users are often categorized by others in terms of their influence: "Of course, these societies also have the criminals (evil deviant hackers), and the popular kids (the wizards)." MOO users who become wizards gain power and influence within the MOO, but this power comes with the responsibility for running of the MOO.

Helping other MOO users can take the form of a formal help system, or ad-hoc help offered to a new MOOer by an experienced MOOer. One MOOer described the category of "kind old fart [moo-old]," the experienced MOOer who helps new MOO users on an informal basis and "tries to help ppl [people] through the early stages .. listens to ppl's problems .. agony aunt ..in away .. and plumber/car mechanic too .. not just social help... 'mechanical help' too."

Another form of influence within the community is obtained by becoming active in MOO politics. For political MOO users, a MOO represents a new form of society where new forms of governance can be tried. For example, at the time of this research one MOO experimented with an elected monarchy, another MOO had a form of democracy. Politically motivated MOO users may spend many hours learning the history of the politics of their MOO, forming allegiances with like-minded people, and planning strategies. One MOOer described their entry into MOO politics as:

> I read and read and read up on history and *lists [MOO mailing-lists] like *soc [a socially oriented mailing list] and *arbitration. After that I formed up ideas about the incomplete change of [MOO] from wizocracy to some form of democracy.... At first I bickered little on *soc. It was going nowhere so I learnt how to switch conversations onto topics and play up on people's fears on democracy and stuff. Eventually I just formed a group to spam in order to cause commotion."

Not all MOO users take an active role or seek influence in the MOO community. As one casual MOOer observed, "the running and politics of moo's is of little to no interest for me, like I said its mainly just light entertainment for me I think." This highlights an ongoing tension in MOOs, the perceived dichotomy of MOO as a game versus MOO as a community. A MOOer, in a posting to a MOO-mailing list announcing their decision to stop MOOing, described their feelings about MOO community:

> I hope all of you will think about what you're building here, because it is for all practical purposes, a community, even though it is in a text form. You will argue...you will disagree...you will be offended...but you will also be amused, delighted, and supported by your friends on here. Think about the big picture, if only for a moment. What you are all doing here isn't trivial, even though some of you think it is. Remember, on the other side, there's another person just like you with the same feelings, insecurities, and hopes. As Eric Bogosian said in _Talk_Radio_, "Sticks and stones may break your bones, but words cause permanent damage." True, but they also heal, soothe, and encourage. Consider that next time you type in your thoughts.

Collective action increases the sense of ownership of a community (McMillan & Chavis, 1986). The petition process at Lambda MOO is an example of collective action at work. In order to make changes to the MOO, any MOOer with voting rights has the right to create a petition. Ten MOO users must sign the petition, before it can be submitted to the wizards for vetting. The original petitioner needs to collect signatures from at least 10% of active eligible voters before the petition is transformed into a ballot for all eligible MOO users to vote on. The rationale given for this was:

> A lot of signatures are required to turn a petition into an open ballot, but this seemed reasonable; after all, if you want to change the rules

of the universe, you really ought to need the support of a fair fraction of those who will have to live under those rules. It was Haakon's (the Arch Wizard of Lambda MOO) expectation that you'd need to do some real footwork to get an open ballot on your issue, talking to a lot of players that you don't know and getting the issue discussed pretty broadly. Think of this process as paralleling that of getting a voter-sponsored initiative on the ballot in the real world (Lambda MOO Help files: Help Petition-Process).

MOO users need to work collectively to achieve change in their community. Despite the complexity of the petition process, at the time of this research one hundred and twenty one petitions had achieved ballot status and been voted on at Lambda since the system was introduced. One MOOer noted that a lack of collective action results in MOOs that have no sense of community: "other moos seemed like places of conversing between people [like me], not involved communal effort."

Integration and Fulfillment of Needs

Sense of community is reliant on individual members of a community having their needs met by the community, and in turn meeting the needs of other community members. Effective reinforcers for membership in a community include the status of membership, community success, and the competence of community members (McMillan & Chavis, 1986). The status of membership in MOOs is high. MOO users are highly educated, intelligent, have high socio-economic status, and are mostly male.

Shared values perform an integrative function in communities (McMillan & Chavis, 1986). MOOs have a relatively homogeneous population in comparison to place-based communities, with members having much in common. Underpinning this is the shared value of choosing to take part in a virtual community. MOOs are seen as communities of choice. An active decision is made to become part of the community, and to remain within the community.

no matter what..we all have the common denominator of being net users.. we have figured out how to get here.. and we stayed. So in a sense we have chosen to be part of a community.

Strong communities have members that meet others' and their own needs (McMillan & Chavis, 1986). MOO users meet each others' needs by being a source of emotional support on the MOO:

Hmmm ...I would think that they [MOO friendships] are as strong as any other... I mean I can talk to them and they are there to help me when I need to talk to someone... For example... my father is very close to dying right now... they have all talked with me about it and have been a great deal of comfort to me.

MOO users may contact each other outside of the MOO environment to provide additional support: "A lot of them (MOO friends) have been here for me when my rl friends weren't ... they either were here for me on here, or they called me when they knew I needed them." MOO users will protect other community members against threats from 'outsiders':

well, for example, with the guests who gang up on me....people come from all over the moo to fight for each other if we need it. Even people who didn't really know me that well came, just because someone was beating up on another person.

In addition, MOO users may provide off-line support to meet other community members needs. During their interviews, MOO users mentioned loaning goods such as books and disks to other MOO users, sending money to MOO users in need, and helping other MOO users with their academic work and programming problems.

Shared Emotional Connection

MOO users share a common environment, the perception of a common place, and a shared history; folklore about MOOing and MOO users continues to grow. MOO users spend time together interacting and sharing virtual experiences: "folks on MOOs do things together, there are arguments and agreements, animosity, even MOOlove, weddings, sex etc etc." Over time, a MOO culture has emerged:

I notice the sense of community in shared culture. Shared jokes among players, shared experiences, people knowing each other and making friends.

The contact hypothesis suggests that the more people interact, the closer they become to each other (McMillan & Chavis, 1986). MOOs are purely social environments. Individuals connect to MOOs in order to interact with each other. In interviews, the most commonly cited initial motivation for MOOing was to meet people from around the world. However, the most commonly cited current motivation for MOOing was to meet the individual's existing MOO friends. Through social interaction on MOOs, MOO users are forming intense personal relationships with one another, as exemplified by this comment "many of the most gratifying social relationships I've ever had have been in MOOspace" ... "closest I've ever come to real intimacy is on moos." As described by the MOO users, these relationships often surpass the depth and intimacy of 'real life' relationships. Walther (1996) described this phenomenon as 'hyperpersonal communication.' As one MOOer noted:

> I think that here you actually are getting more of a mental connection which is much stronger and longer lasting than physical.

This positive interaction between members enhances community cohesion on MOOs.

SUMMARY OF RESEARCH FINDINGS

Findings from this study suggest that sense of community can exist without the need for a community to be place-based, and without the need for face-to-face interaction. Most of the MOO users interviewed believed there was a sense of community within MOOs. The four central elements of sense of community identified by McMillan and Chavis (1986); membership, influence, integration and fulfillment of needs, and shared emotional connection were present within MOO communities. MOO users' perceptions of the level at which sense of community occurs varied. For some MOO users, individual MOOs form part of a larger community, while for others each MOO is a distinct community within itself. A third group of MOO users perceived multiple communities within MOOs. These points of view are not necessarily incompatible, and have their counterparts in off-line life. For example, in place-based communities we may speak of sense of community within a suburb, a city and a nation. However, not all MOO users feel part of the community. This parallels place-based communities, where not all community members feel part of the community, despite living within the community.

Are MOOs Communities?

Are MOOs communities? Certainly MOOs differ from place-based communities in a number of ways. First, MOOs are relatively homogenous in terms of age, education, and socioeconomic status of members. Few children or older members of society actively participate in social MOOs. Individuals, rather than families, frequent MOOs. Second, MOOs represent an environment of choice, rather than an environment of necessity. MOO users can access and leave the MOO whenever they wish. If problems arise within a MOO, the individual needs only to type @quit to remove themself from the MOO. They need never return. Third, the virtual environment within which MOOs exist, combined with anonymity, provide the individual with freedom to explore aspects of the self and create new identities whenever required without fear of repercussions in 'real life.' These three factors combined produce an environment that on the surface appears to require limited commitment from users. Despite this, MOOs emerged in this research as virtual communities with the power to engender sense of community in members.

MOOs provide neither utopian nor dystopian communities. Individuals bring to the MOO environment their beliefs and values, although they may choose to suspend these. Clear evidence of conflict within MOOs was found. MOO users openly disagreed with others in their postings to MOO mailing lists, and heated discussions often erupted in public areas on MOOs. In interviews users reported cases of virtual harassment, sexual harassment, virtual rape, and virtual stalking. As with place-based communities, MOOs offer both rewards and problems for members.

Relationship Between Virtual and Place-based Communities

This research found that many individuals experienced a psychological sense of community within MOOs. What effect is this likely to have upon place-based communities for the individuals involved? This may depend upon the perceived level of overlap between place-based and virtual communities. Aoki (1995) described three types of virtual communities: those with complete, partial, and no overlap with place-based communities. We would like to suggest one further possibility: the replacement of place-based community with virtual community. Each of these four possibilities is explicated below.

Separate Virtual and Place-Based Communities

Some MOO users kept their virtual and 'real' worlds separate. This may be a conscious effort to ensure there is no overlap between virtual and real life, or due to circumstances (e.g., geographical isolation). For these MOO users, there is no overlap between place and virtual community, and activities in virtuality are not seen as impacting on their place-based community. However, it is possible that long periods of time spent in cyberspace may reduce the amount of time devoted to place-based community activities.

Overlapping Virtual and Place-Based Communities

Perhaps the most likely relationship between virtual and place communities for a MOOer is the overlapping virtual and place communities. Members of an individual's place community may be introduced to MOOing, or the individual may meet members of their place-based community on MOOs, or choose to meet MOO users in off-line settings. For instance, one MOOer who was introduced to MOOing by friends, and has since introduced other friends to MOOing described the interweaving of virtual and place-based friendships as:

> and now it as much a part of my life as other sets of friends who exist irl [in real life]....the boundaries are much more blurred now...esp as in rl meet more and more MOOers ... where I live all the MOOers or many of them now socialie together in rl as well...I doubt we would have met otherwise...most are at uni, but we are from diverse faculties.

The interweaving of place and virtual communities can result in the perception of MOOing as part of 'real life':

> MOOing is central to my RL. I _do_ a lot of things here. Politics, relationships, programming, building, networking, etc. I've had job leads on [MOO], I've given job leads to others, on [MOO] and on [MOO]... when I indulge in psychoactives, MOOing is central to the universes I visit... when I dream, I sometimes MOO... sometimes I have sex dreams about MOO-sex... it's all terribly intertwined.

For individuals with overlapping virtual and place communities, psychological sense of community and participation in multiple communities may be enhanced by the growth of friendships across mediums: "I think it is just a wonderful extension of one's rl community." Wellman and Gulia (1999) noted that the ease of participation in virtual worlds enables individuals to belong to several virtual communities according to their interests, building personal communities based on a network of interpersonal ties.

Virtual Community as Part of Place-Based Community

Some virtual communities, referred to as community-based computer networks, are set up to support place-based communities. The aim of community-based computer networks is the strengthening of community through increased communication and access to information (Beamish, 1995). None of the MOOs where interviews were conducted met this criterion. Examples of virtual communities that are part of geographical communities are the WELL community in San Francisco, the TWICS community in Tokyo, the CIX community in London, CalvaCom in Paris, Cleveland Free-Net, and the Blacksburg electronic village (Beamish, 1995; Rheingold, 1994). As Rheingold (1994) noted about his own virtual community "The WELL felt like an authentic community to me from the start because it was grounded in my everyday physical world" (p. 2). Early research in this area suggests that these virtual communities have the greatest potential for increasing sense of community in place-based communities.

Virtual Community as Replacement For Place-Based Community

Fourteen percent of the MOO users interviewed spent more than 50 hours per week in virtual environments. Extended participation in virtual environments may leave little time for involvement in place-based communities. For many of the 'heavy' MOO users, the sense of community experienced in MOOs has become an important part of their life:

> Being on line is part of my everyday life now. I don't think I can last long without logging on at least once a day or something like that. I suppose it increases my circle of friends and it is a good way of meeting friends and I don't go anywhere to go socializing in real life either, so I suppose that is my way of meeting people.

For these individuals, sense of community within virtual communities may replace sense of community in place-based communities. Perhaps replacement is the wrong word. As one MOOer noted: "maybe we embrace the moo because of that sense of community...we certainly lack cohesive community in the west now....many people are very isolated." MOOs have the potential to provide a sense of community for those individuals who are not experiencing it in their place-based communities. Turkle (1995) claimed that MUDs can compensate for things missing in an individual's life, or serve as places of resistance to many forms of alienation and the violence they impose. However, she cautioned: "Instead of solving real problems, are we choosing to love in unreal places? Women and men tell me that the rooms and mazes on MUDs are safer than city streets, virtual sex is safer than sex anywhere, MUD friendships are more intense than real ones, and when things don't work out you can always leave" (p. 244). Extended periods in virtual communities may reduce civic activities in place-based communities.

The four models outlined suggest that virtual sense of community will have differential effects on place-based communities according to the degree of overlap of communities. Where there is little or no overlap of virtual and place-based communities, sense of community in place-based communities is likely to remain the same, although community participation may diminish. Where there is a high degree of overlap, the sense of community experienced in the virtual community has the potential to increase the sense of community experienced in the place-based community.

FUTURE RESEARCH

This research raises as many questions as it answers. Do virtual environments other than MOOs have the potential to provide a psychological sense of community for their users? How will the widespread use of video and audio affect sense of community in virtual environments? How will place-based communities be affected if more individuals elect to spend their time and effort in virtual environments? What effects will prolonged periods in cyberspace have on the individual and their perceptions of community? Longitudinal research is required to further examine the relationships between sense of community and participation in place-based and virtual environments.

In summary, we have argued that MOOs are communities. It is not necessary for a community to be place-based, or for face-to-face interaction to occur for sense of community to build. The majority of MOO users interviewed reported experiencing a sense of community within social MOOs. The sense of community experienced was congruent with McMillan and Chavis's (1986) definition and model of psychological sense of community. Evidence of membership, influence, integration and fulfillment of needs, and shared emotional connection were found in interviews with MOO users, and in an examination of MOO documentation and postings to MOO mailing lists. Four possible relationships between place-based and virtual communities were outlined: separate place and virtual communities; overlapping place and virtual communities; virtual communities as part of place communities; and virtual communities as a replacement for place communities. MOOs hold different meanings for different individuals, and are used in differing ways. In a world where place-based communities fail to meet some individual's needs for a sense of community, MOOs offer an alternative. We will leave the last word on sense of community on MOOs to one of the MOO users interviewed:

> It's a virtual medium, but not a fantasy...people online are real...not computers...the computers are only the means by which we communicate.

NOTES

[i] This paper is partially based on a paper by the same title presented at the 6th National Australian and New Zealand Community Psychology Conference: Promoting Action Research and Social Justice, Toodyay, Western Australia, 7th-9th June 1996. We thank Dr. Ros Morrow and Dr Chris Sonn for their comments on an early draft of this paper.

REFERENCES

Allen, C. L. (1996). *Virtual Identities: The social construction of cybered selves.* Unpublished doctoral dissertation, Northwestern University, Evanston, Illinois.

Anderson, B. (1991). *Imagined communities* London: Verso.

Aoki, K. (1995). Virtual communities: Reflections on the origin and spread of nationalism. in Japan: Their cultures and infrastructure. *Asia-Pacific Exchange (Electronic) Journal, 2*(1). Retrieved January 25, 1996 from the World Wide Web: http://www.apa.org/monitor/peacea.html.

Baym, N. K. (1995). The emergence of community in computer-mediated communication. In S. G. Jones (Ed.), *CyberSociety: Computer-mediated communication and community* (pp. 138-151). Thousand Oaks, CA: Sage Publications.

Beamish, A. (1995). *Communities on-line: Community-based computer networks.* Unpublished masters thesis, Massachusetts Institute of Technology, Boston.

Berger, P. L., & Luckmann, T. (1973). *The social construction of reality.* Hammondsworth, Middlesex : Penguin University Books.

Carlstrom, E-L. (1992). *Better living through language. The communicative implications of a text-only virtual environment. Welcome to Lambda MOO!* Retrieved January 25, 1996 using FTP: parcftp.xerox.com:/pub/MOO/papers/communicative.txt.

Clodius, J. (1997, January). *Creating a community of interest: "Self" and "Other" on DragonMud.* Paper presented at the Combined Conference on MUDs, Jackson Hole, Wyoming.

Curtis, P. (1992). *Mudding: Social phenomenon in text-based virtual realities.* Proceedings of Directions and Implications of Advanced Computing (DIAC'92) Symposium, Berkeley, California, May 2-3, 1992. Retrieved January 25, 1996 using FTP: parcftp.xerox.com, pub/MOO/papers/DIAC92.

Curtis, P., & Nichols, D. A. (1993). *MUDs grow up: Social virtual reality in the real world* Retrieved January 25 1996 ftp: parcftp.xerox.com:/pub/MOO/papers/MUDSgrowup

Dunham, H. W. (1977). Community as process: Maintaining the delicate balance. *American Journal of Community Psychology, 5,* 257-268.

Dunham, H. W. (1986). The community today: Place or process. *Journal of Community Psychology, 14,* 399-404.

Dunham, P. J., Hurshman, A., Litwin, E., Gusella, J., Ellsworth, C., & Dodd, P. W. D. (1998). Computer-mediated social support: Single young mothers as a model system. *American Journal of Community Psychology, 26,* 281-306.

Falk, J. (1995). *The meaning of the Web.* Paper presented at AusWeb 1995, Sydney, Australia. Retrieved October 30, 2000 from the World Wide Web: http://www.scu.edu.au/sponsored/ausweb/ausweb95/papers/sociology/falk.

Free, R. M. (1995). *Multi-User Trivial Terminal –Mutt™ Lite –Version 0.1k.* Retrieved January 25, 1996: http://www.graphcomp.com/mutt/help.html

Glaser, B. G., & Strauss, A. (1967). *The discovery of grounded theory: Strategies for qualitative research.* Chicago: Aldine Publishing Co.

Glasser Das, A. R. (1999) *The new face of self-help: Online support for anxiety disorders.* Dissertation Abstracts International: Section B: the Sciences & Engineering. Vol 59(7-B), Jan 1999, 3691.

Glynn, T. J. (1986). Neighborhood and sense of community. *Journal of Community Psychology, 14,* 341-352.

GVU (1997). *Graphic, Visualization, & Usability Center's (GVU) 8th WWW User Survey.* Retrieved January 25, 1999 from the World Wide Web: http://www.cc.gatech.edu/gvu/user_surveys/survey-1997-10/

Hampton, K. N. (1996). *Community, chaos and the Internet.* Unpublished honors thesis, University of Calgary, Canada.

Haythornthwaite, C., Kazmer, M. M., & Robins, J. (2000). Community development among distance learners: Temporal and technological dimensions. *Journal of Computer Mediated Communication, 6*(1). Retrieved October 21, 2000 from the World Wide Web: http://www.ascusc.org/jcmc/vol6/issue1/haythornthwaite.html

Hill, J. L. (1996). Psychological sense of community: Suggestions for future research. *Journal of Community Psychology, 24,* 431-438.

Hunter, A., & Riger, S. (1986). The meaning of community in community mental health. *Journal of Community Psychology, 14,* 55-71.

Jones, S. G. (1995a). *CyberSociety: Computer-mediated communication and community.* Thousand Oaks, CA: Sage Publications.

Jones, S. G. (1995b). Understanding community in the information age. In S. G. Jones (Ed.), *CyberSociety: Computer-mediated communication and community* (pp. 10-35). Thousand Oaks, CA: Sage Publications.

Kling, S. A. (1996). Social relationships in electronic forums: Hangouts, salons, workplaces and communities. In R. Kling (Ed.), *Computerization and Controversy: Value conflicts and social choices* (2nd ed., pp. 426-454). San Diego: Academic Press.

Kot, E. M. (1999). *Psychological sense of community and electronic mail.* Dissertation Abstracts International: Section B: the Sciences & Engineering. Vol 59(7-B), Jan 1999, 3699.

Little, S. E. (1993, Sept). Cyberspace versus citizenship: IT and emerging non space communities. *AJIS,* 38-45.

Marvin, L-E. (1995). Spoof, spam, lurk and lag: The aesthetics of text-based virtual realities. *Journal of Computer-Mediated Communication, 1*(2). Retrieved October 30, 2000 from the World Wide Web: http://cwis.usc.edu/dept/annenberg/vol1/issue2/

McBeath, G. B., & Webb, S. A. (1995, April). *Cities, subjectivity and cyberspace.* Paper presented at The British Sociological Association Annual Conference 1995 "Contested Cities", University of Leicester, England.

McMillan, D. W., & Chavis, D. M (1986). Sense of community: A definition and theory. *Journal of Community Psychology, 14,* 6-23.

Patterson, H. (1996). *Computer-mediated groups: A study of culture in newsgroups.* Unpublished Ph.D. dissertation. Texas A & M University, Texas. Retrieved October 30, 2000 from the World Wide Web: http://www.sci.tamucc.edu/~hollyp/pubs/dis/dissert.html

Phillips, D. J. (1996). Defending the boundaries: Identifying and countering threats in a usenet newsgroup. *The Information Society, 12,* 39-62.

Pravatiner, M. (1996, May). *A year as a MOOer--give or take.* Posting to Cybermind: Philosophy and Psychology of Cyberspace Mailing List [On-line]. Retrieved July 31, 1996 from the World Wide Web: http://www.cybermind.org.hk/archive/cybermind.0596/1202.html

QSR NUD*IST (Application Software Package). (1995). Melbourne: Qualitative Solutions and Research.

Reid, E. (1991). *Electropolis: Communication and community on Internet Relay Chat.* Adapted from an Honours thesis, University of Melbourne, Australia. Retrieved October 30, 2000 from the World Wide Web: http://www.aluluei.com/.

Reid, E. (1995). Virtual worlds: Culture and imagination. In S. G. Jones (Ed.), *CyberSociety: Computer-mediated communication and community* (pp. 164-183). Thousand Oaks, CA: Sage Publications.

Rheingold, H. (1994). *The virtual community.* London: Secker & Warburg.

Roberts, L. D., Smith, L. M., & Pollock. C. M. (1996, September). *A model of social interaction via computer-mediated communication in real-time text-based virtual environments.* Paper presented at the 31st Annual Conference of the Australian Psychological Society, *Sydney, Australia.*

Sarason, S. B. (1974). *The psychological sense of community: Prospects for a community psychology.* San Francisco: Jossey-Bass.

Stoll, C. (1995). *Silicon snake oil.* London: MacMillan.

Surrat, C. G. (1996). The sociology of everyday life in computer-mediated communities (Doctoral dissertation, Arizona State University). *Dissertation Abstracts International, DAI-A 57/03,* 1346.

Turkle, S. (1995). *Life on the screen: Identity in the age of the internet.* New York: Simon & Schuster.

Walther, J. B. (1996). Computer-mediated communication: Impersonal, interpersonal and hyperpersonal interaction. *Communication Research, 23,* 3-43.

Watson, N. (1997). Why we argue about virtual community: A case study of the Phish.Net fan community. In S. G. Jones (Ed.), *Virtual culture: Identity and communication in society* (pp. 102-132). London, UK: Sage Publications.

Webber, M. M. (1964). The urban place and nonplace urban realm. In M. M. Webber, J. W. Dyckman, D. L. Foley, A. Z. Guttenberg, W. L. C. Wheaton & C. B Whurster (Eds.), Explorations into urban structure (pp. 79-153). Philadelphia, PA: University of Pennsylvania Press.

Wellman, B. G., & Gulia, M. (1999). Net surfers don't ride alone: Virtual communities as communities. In P. Kollock and M. Smith (Eds.), *Communities in Cyberspace* (pp. 167-194). London, UK: Routledge.

Chapter 13

CONTEMPORARY ABORIGINAL PERCEPTIONS OF COMMUNITY[i]

Pat Dudgeon, John Mallard, Darlene Oxenham, and John Fielder
Curtin University

INTRODUCTION

Aboriginal Australian people have lived on the continent for over 40,000 years. They were a hunting-gathering people, with a total population, prior to colonization, estimated to be at least 300,000 people, and possibly as high as 1,000,000 (Bourke, 1994). From the onset of colonization in 1788, as was the case for many other Indigenous peoples, the subsequent centuries were characterized by genocide; by forced removal from land, peoples, families; by enslavement; and by assimilation and destruction of cultural ways. Despite this, the fact that Indigenous people have sustained their identity, and are experiencing a cultural renaissance, is a testimony to the determination of the human spirit.

Background and Context

This chapter explores contemporary Australian Aboriginal[ii] perceptions of "community." By exploring what contemporary Aboriginal people understand community to be, we aim to contribute to community psychologists' endeavors to work in empowering and culturally appropriate ways, and to be aware of the social and political complexity, and cultural diversity, of Aboriginal communities in Australia.

Beliefs and assumptions about the Aboriginal community are broadly framed by historically available dominant discourses on Aboriginal people. Muecke (1992) identifies these as either racist, romantic, or anthropological. However, over the past 20 to 30 years, Aboriginal people's own lived experiences of community have gained mainstream public recognition. Gradually, Aboriginal voices and resistant Aboriginal discourses are being listened to and acknowledged in their own right. In this chapter, we seek to foreground emergent and critically reflective Aboriginal discourses on community, and on associated issues such as identity, kinship, diversity, and difference.

Rather than simply drawing on existing literature and "text-book" theory about community and Aboriginal people, we conducted interviews with local, Perth Aboriginal community members, particularly leaders and academics. These participants are considered to be key cultural informants and are mainly university-educated men and women with strong community roles, and they come from different regions in Western Australia. They are Ted Wilkes, Nellie Green, John Mallard, Joan Winch, Pat Torres, Jill Abdullah, Pat Dudgeon, Kim Collard, Dawn Gilchrist, and Darlene Oxenham. Their voices are used to emphasize and illustrate issues from an indigenous Australian standpoint.

The viewpoints presented demonstrate that there is no definitive position on the notion of "community," rather confirming the diversity and pluralism among what is broadly termed "the Aboriginal community" by Indigenous people in Australia. At the same time, however, some core values, beliefs, and attitudes about community do emerge amid these insights on the significance of community. Ted Wilkes emphasizes this very inclusive and unified sense of community:

> *The Aboriginal community can be interpreted as geographical, social, and political. It places Aboriginal people as part of, but different from, the rest of Australian society. Aboriginal people identify themselves with the idea of being a part of a "community," it gives us a sense of unity and strength. Sometimes issues based groups are perceived as a community – but that is not the case, it is a re-configuration of some parts of the existing community. When I think f the notion of Aboriginal community, I think of us all together as a political and cultural group. It includes everyone no matter what "faction" or local group they are affiliated with, or which part of our diversity they live in. It is a national concept.*

The Aboriginal Community: Kinship and Connections

A key starting point in many Indigenous Australian people's perceptions of, and responses to, the nature of community is to emphasize the sophisticated kinship patterns and importance of family connections. The National Aboriginal Education Committee (NAEC, 1986) identify kinship as the foundation of relationships at a broader community level:

> In the main, Aboriginal society is structured around the community. There exists very strong kinship ties within each of the communities and within each of the categories [which we will outline later]. These kinship ties overlap the various categories thus forming very strong relationships among all Aboriginal people of this country (p. 10).

Within a "traditional" context, Aboriginal people associated with, and in, social groups primarily based on familial relationships. The defining dimensions of Aboriginal conceptions of community are a sense of belonging, based along family lines, and "country" or area of origin. From this base, several levels of association arise: family; local level linked to country; and Aboriginal community in general, which sometimes includes local, state and national layers. As Lucas, et al. (1998) point out, community can be referred to in a whole range of different ways and contexts.

So, this dimension of community based on *filiation* and "country" can be differentiated from forms of community based on *affiliation* -- more political and issue-based formations of community. But, it is this primary family and clan connection to a geographically defined area that explains why Aboriginal people identify themselves in terms of belonging to specific "country."

Aboriginal perceptions of "community" have two main facets: physical groupings and psychological belonging to a particular group(s). For some, the concept may also hold a political dimension, a vision of the entire cultural group of Aboriginal people working against oppression and towards self-determination -- a more abstract sense of community. More abstract perceptions of community, such as this, are derived from where people are situated, and also from their movement across groupings, and representation at various forums.

Pat Torres outlines some of the key dimensions of community, and acknowledges that there are factors that unite, but also factors that create tensions amongst, Aboriginal people:

> *There are lots of levels to the idea of what constitutes community-based on language, culture and historical circumstances, and spiritual connections (especially for people not attached to a land base). I guess community is about the common things which bind people. And when you're talking in terms of the bigger community, it's the common effects of colonization, the common effects of being an oppressed people, and how we've been influenced by that history of colonization.*

> *So it's those things that unite us -- the common things. Then, at another level, when you go down to the smaller units, what constitutes community is your heritage: so your own bloodlines, your own kinship groups, your own family's immediate connections ...We found, as a women's group, when talking about preserving language, culture, and oral histories in order to empower the Yawuru community, it was very uniting. And you had very few people oppose that idea, because everyone wanted to know about their stories: they wanted to know their country, they wanted to know the sites, and stuff like that, and there was a lot of support. So, in one sense, that historical and oral history and language stuff can be the issues that bring the community together.*

> *... Alternatively, I guess what fragments the country or the peoples is when Native Title creates groups that are exclusive, where they say things like, "Only people who practice Law and are black-skinned are the ones who have the right to speak for country." That creates fragmentation, and that's something we've definitely faced in the Broome region for the last five years ...*

The existence of conflict and fragmentation is a reality for any community. Hopes of reclaiming land through *Native Title* -- the historic High Court ruling that recognized Indigenous Australian people's occupation and ownership of land prior to colonization (*Mabo and others v State of Queensland* [No 2] (1992) 175 CLR 1) -- have also been accompanied by significant tensions to do with belonging, connections, cultural continuity, knowledge and leadership. The issue of political leadership is another vehicle that can cause considerable conflict within the Aboriginal community, both at local and national levels.

There is an ongoing struggle to build a sense of community in the face of many social, historical and political forces that have created significant trauma and breakdown in the culture and community, which is clearly linked to colonization and the systematic erosion of culture and community (Trudgen, 2000).

Community: Whose Conceptions?

The purpose of this chapter is to present contemporary Aboriginal understandings of community, thus ascribing Aboriginal meaning to the concept. As "the community" has now become a commonly used term by Aboriginal Australians, practitioners working with Aboriginal people will be required to have an awareness of the Aboriginal community if they are to work effectively with Aboriginal people.

When exploring the notion of the Aboriginal community, two factors need to be considered. Firstly, many Aboriginal people feel that this notion is just another western concept that has been imposed by non-Aboriginal people. Secondly, and despite this, it would appear that the concept of "community" has special significance to Aboriginal people. Aboriginal people have adopted, modified, and internalized the western notion of community and attributed meaning to it. Mindful of these two factors, we will explore the sense of community in contemporary Australian Aboriginal life in a way that captures the ambivalence that is typical of the psychological experiences of community in a range of diverse Indigenous groups.

This ambivalence derives from the different conceptions of "community," and the competing interests that frame its usage. When the term "community" is used in the context of Indigenous social organization, the connotations are invariably of homogeneous identity, shared interests, and positive forms of collectivity. Popularized notions of the unity and harmony of "traditional" communities are counterposed against the individualistic, or atomized, forms of social organization in mainstream western culture, and the fragmented and conflictual nature of modern life (Pettman, 1992, p. 122). In terms of Indigenous social organization, an understanding of the amorphous and ambivalent dimension of community allows for a positive valuing of cultural traditions which privilege collectivity and cooperation over individuality and competition, but without erasing the ongoing social tensions of realizing and reproducing these values. Initially, however, we will explain why there is a danger in over-simplifying and idealizing traditional Indigenous community life.

Community, Aboriginality and Dominant Discourses

Dodson (1994), a national Australian Indigenous leader, has pointed out that the romanticization of Indigenous people's social formations often functions to satisfy the interests of various non-Aboriginal stakeholders, rather than to work towards a better understanding of the complexity and nuances of "traditional" community life.

> At times, Indigenous people have been used to affirm the superiority of the colonisers, and to provide confirmation of the value of progress ... At other times, Indigenous people are used to create a counterpoint against which the dominant society can critique itself, becoming living embodiments of the romantic ideal, which offers a desolate society the hope of redemption and of recapturing what it has lost in its march forward. Those who wish to present a critique of individualism point out that Aboriginality is about community; those who wish to highlight the detrimental effects of industrialisation on the environment point to Indigenous people as the original conservationists. We present a remaining, though strategically distant, image of what has been lost, and what could be regained (Dodson, 1994, p. 8).

He does not deny that there is some "truth" in such notions, but his main point is to demonstrate that Aboriginality is frequently deployed as an object "... to be manipulated and used to further the aspirations of other people" (Dodson, 1994, p. 8). What often is excluded, then, are Aboriginal people's own perceptions:

> Alongside the colonial discourses in Australia, we have always had our own Aboriginal discourses in which we have continued to create our own representations, and to re-create identities which escaped the policing of the authorised versions. They are Aboriginalities that arise from our experience of ourselves and our communities (Dodson 1994, p. 9).

Our objective is not to deny the strength of Indigenous collectivity, which has been maintained and developed over thousands of years, but to challenge idealized constructions of Indigenous unity and harmony, following the lead of the Koori (south-eastern Australian Aboriginal) writer, Kevin Gilbert (1977):

> ... the majority of Aboriginals are deeply ashamed of what they know is the truth about their people today. So, together with many sympathetic whites, they embrace and propagate a number of myths about themselves: that Aboriginals share freely; that they have a strong feeling of community ... (p. 1).

Gilbert's statement is contentious, and one that certainly challenges the notion that stronger community ties are inherent to Aboriginal people. It is important to note that, when he refers to "the truth about their people today," he alludes to the social and cultural dislocation and degradation that afflicts so many Aboriginal people as a result of colonization (1977, p. 1).

In the text *A Dialogue On Indigenous Identity: Warts 'n' All* (Oxenham, et al., 1999), Gilbert's (1977) comment is used as a springboard for discussion about identity issues. One of the key points to emerge in the dialogue in this book is the way in which understandings of identity are inextricably linked to understandings of community. Individual identity -- or a sense of self or subjectivity -- is embedded within a sense of belonging to something larger than the self (family, community, society, culture, nation, etc.) (Gergen & Shotter, 1989). This notion of social subjectivity is also implicit in Langton's (1993) conception of Aboriginality as "a field of intersubjectivity" (p. 33). All people's identity, including descriptors of identity such as "whiteness" and "Aboriginality," is part of the way social subjects are "remade over and over again in a process of dialogue, of imagination, of representation and interpretation" (Langton 1993, p. 33). Such constructivist notions of identity are central to community psychology, which is an important development that challenges psychology's narrow and individualistic notions of "self" and "identity" (Sonn & Bishop, 2000).

The dominant culture, however, tends to use "Aboriginal community" in virtually the same way as "Aboriginal people." It is used as a signifier of cultural or ethnic identity -- an identity that is defined by its difference to what is often described as the broader mainstream community (Attwood, 1989). In general, cultural or ethnic signifiers for "the white community" or "mainstream community" are not required. However, even though minority or ethnic groups are subsumed within the broader markers of national, state and regional identity, these groups identify themselves differently to the way they are defined by the dominant culture. Minority groups within the dominant culture, generally, are very conscious of alternative or resistant conceptions of identity (their own self-identification as opposed to those imposed upon them). There is an awareness that their difference and distinctiveness is masked by an imagined sameness which is formed in the image of the dominant group. This idealized image is imperialist and assimilationist in the sense that assumptions about normalized human cultural standards are defined by the dominant culture.

Marginalized groups, such as the Aboriginal community, resist inclusion based on assimilationist attitudes and practices that actively exclude cultural difference. Joan Winch explains a resistant dimension:

> *My idea of community is people who share likewise interests. So, the reason we talk about the Aboriginal community is because ... we feel marginalised. And so, rather like gypsies, we stick together. Therefore you are a stronger group–to be able to talk about your feelings, and whatever. That's what I consider community to be: people with likewise ideas.*

Community: Western Connotations and Contestations

Many theorists (e.g., Ife, 1995; Joseph, 1998; Pettman, 1992; Wark,

1999; Williams, 1988), point out that the notion of "community" is highly problematic. Ife (1995) proposes; "it is, therefore, incumbent on anyone wishing to use the word to provide some clarification as to the meaning to be ascribed to it" (p. 90). It is important then to pay very close attention to the way the signifier "community" is used both to unite and embrace, and to differentiate and exclude.

Community is a very elastic term, which tends to get pulled and stretched in all sorts of directions to suit the interests and intentions of the user. In this sense, it is important to be aware of the way people deploy the term in different ways. Ife (1995) asserts that:

> ... [C]ommunity is essentially a subjective experience, which defies objective definition. It is felt and experienced, rather than measured and defined. Because of its subjective nature, it is not particularly helpful to think of community as "existing," or to "operationalise" community in such a way that we can measure it. It is more appropriate to allow people to develop their own understanding of what community means for them, in their own context (p. 93).

While this subjective experience of community does need to be taken into account, it is very important to understand the broad historical and cultural currency the word has gained. This helps to contextualize contemporary connotations of the term, and the ways in which the term is politically manipulated. Williams (1988) points out that "Community can be the warmly persuasive word to describe an existing set of relationships, or the warmly persuasive word to describe an alternative set of relationships ... it seems never to be used unfavourably" (p. 76). Similarly, Joseph (1998) suggests "There is a tendency ... to work with an idealized model of community as representing an area of shared experience and harmony" (p. 79). Wark (1999) argues that "Community is something of a 'motherhood' term in Australian political culture, conjuring up images of a small town life where everybody knows everybody and there's always someone special to lend a helping hand" (p. 269).

What is clear, then, is that tensions, ambiguities and contradictions are embedded in the way "community" is used -- no matter who deploys the term, and no matter the context. Wark's (1999) point is that, in contemporary political discourse, community is frequently appealed to as an antidote to the problems of modern/postmodern life, where the coldness and alienation of scientific and technological progress is contrasted against the warmth of a utopian sense of "common unity." Such rhetoric may be used by either progressive or reactionary forces, sometimes as part of the moral panic about the threat to private property and possessions, and sometimes as part of fears about the dis-integrating effects of global capitalism on social life. So, community is not only simply a subjective phenomenon: it is a highly politicized notion -- whether used consciously or unconsciously.

The "Traditional" as Counterpoint to "Modernity"

The notion of traditional communities can be applied to western social patterns, which are typically referred to as part of a nostalgic and idealized past, as highlighted earlier by Dodson (1994). This provides an interesting comparison to notions about traditional Indigenous communities. The main difference between the two is that assumptions about the "civility" of traditional western communities are part of racist discourses that construct traditional Indigenous communities as "primitive."

It is important to make the general point that forms of social life which can very broadly be termed "traditional" forms of social organization are defined against forms of social life that have emerged within what is often referred to as "modernity" (Bauman, 1991). The more abstract notion of modernity as the lived experience of modern life is probably best understood in terms of the social and cultural impact of modernization in the west. The modernization process includes, among other things, the historical emergence of urbanization, industrialization, automation, commodification/ mass production, technologization, and globalization (Frow, 1991).

One significant feature of the modernization process in the west is the way the individual has become the focus of a highly atomized social life. This is typified in the way the 20th century became preoccupied by the workings of the mind -- a mind that is understood in narrowly western ways. Despite the power of the myth of individualism in contemporary western culture, it is important to acknowledge that the individual is enmeshed in an intricate web of community connections and constraints.

To avoid essentializing community as, somehow, inherent to Indigeneity, or individualized identity as inherent to an undifferentiated and alienated post-industrial existence, it is an important conceptual strategy to understand identity as, to some degree, "imagined." Anderson (1991), in his analysis of the notion of the nation, suggests that such broad understandings of community, identity, and belonging are "... imagined because the members of even the smallest nation will never know most of their fellow-members, meet them, or even hear of them, yet in the minds of each lives the image of their community" (p. 6). In this sense, individualism is also imagined, for it functions as a powerful modern myth in that it is a naturalized "truth" of modernity -- a truth people live by. Similarly, community or collectivity is seen as a "truth" traditional people live by -- a myth that informs perceptions of social life. Describing these ideas as myths does not diminish the reality of these different patterns of existence. The point is that dichotmomies, such as "self-other" and "individual-collective," are often absolutized rather than being understood as dialogical interrelationships.

Assumptions of absolute difference tend to result in two polarized positions: either romanticizing Indigeneity as an idealized manifestation of the "traditional" in a reaction to the western myths of enlightened progress, civility, cultural sophistication, and economic development; or, alternatively, disparaging Indigeneity as fossilized "primitive culture," forever consigned to the past. At the same time, however, it is quite clear that the tendency to romanticize community is informed by specific social and historical changes that have fragmented modernized urban social life, radically transformed social structures, and opened up new forms of public lived experience.

There are some key conceptual claims that we propose at this point. Firstly, neither collectivity nor individuality is totally realizable: all forms of social subjectivity involve some combined notion of self-identity and collective-identity. Secondly, all cultures, in one way or another, negotiate some mixture of individual identity and collective identity. And, thirdly, contradictions, anomalies and tensions inevitably inhabit cultural myths: there is never seamless, uniform, or absolute consonance.

These claims are stated prior to continuing the exploration of very positive and real manifestations of contemporary community for Indigenous people to ensure the topic is approached on the basis of critical self-reflection. Moreover, there is a need to guard against essentializing primitive collectivity on the one hand and modern individualism on the other.

The Aboriginal Community and Control

The way the term "community" is deployed in reference to Aboriginal groups is by no means neutral or apolitical, especially when governments are deliberating on service delivery and funding. Ted Wilkes states: *Wadjella people and their systems manipulate the word "community" for their own ends. It is cheaper to call a group of 500 or more black or brown skinned human beings a community, than a town!* Economic imperatives and agendas often underpin negative images of Aboriginal people generally. Many Aboriginal people share Wilkes' skeptical view of government commitment to resource provision. To examine how such a view may have come about we need to examine community formation in its historical context.

Traditional social groupings of Aboriginal people were fragmented by the process of colonization, and by subsequent government policies. In the report, *Community-Based Planning*, the Aboriginal and Torres Strait Islander Commission (ATSIC) (1993) states that:

> Europeans dominated Australia's Aboriginal peoples with very specific policies that sought assimilation and the suppression of Aboriginal political life. They dispersed or concentrated tribal groups into settlements, which were later termed "communities" (p. 1).

Thus, Aboriginal people, often from different tribal/language groupings, were brought together (sometimes forcibly) because it allowed for greater control over the Aboriginal population. At a later point, the assumption was made (predominantly by non-Aboriginal administrators) that this grouping was homogeneous, possibly with a common sense of purpose. Although this was the reality at one level, it masked other complex and important nuances. Accordingly, John Mallard suggests this:

> *It is useful to think of the community not as a homogenous mass, but a layered series of delicate networks; each network defined by a particular issue. This issue may arise from the community or the individual. So, when working with "the Aboriginal community," it may sound obvious, but it is important to think before you act, to be aware of the complexity and multi-layered levels of the community.*

Before you address an issue with a group, consider the data surrounding that issue, identify those members of the community group that are involved in it, and then approach them. In this way you have defined the section of the community that you want to reach and you can get to the right people quickly.

This assumption of homogeneity can easily serve the interests of powerful non-Aboriginal groups, for talking to one representative of *the* "Aboriginal community" can be touted as verification of community consultation and/or consent. Mallard's reference to an issues-based notion of community highlights the political dimension to the way the term is used.

So, the power relations embedded in the various strategic deployments of the term "the Aboriginal community" foregrounds the need for more self-reflexive and provisional usage -- especially by non-Aboriginal people. Pettman (1992) identifies some of the different usages of community as, broadly, as "the nation," as well as to more specific "small, settled localities," "special interest groups" and "target groups" (pp. 122-123). Target groups are often "identified for government management of difference and provision of services" (Pettman, 1992, p. 123). It is easy to see that the Aboriginal community, from the perspective of governance, often means "target group." The report, *Our Future, Our Selves*, published by the House of Representatives Standing Committee on Aboriginal Affairs (1990) described government-directed new settlements as:

> ... artificial communities [which had] been created for the purposes of non-Aboriginal administrative convenience rather than as distinctively Aboriginal communities in accord with traditional Aboriginal social organisation and shared beliefs and interests" (p. 16).

Not only did these artificial communities allow greater control over the Aboriginal population, but they were also very convenient for administrative purposes. No doubt, dealing with a population contained in the same geographical location is easier than dealing with a population dispersed over a large area.

Thus, "community" was initially an imposed notion for the purpose of control over, and management of, the Aboriginal population. This included disruption to Aboriginal social, political and religious life; and the relocation of distinct Aboriginal groups from different areas. This construction of "community" did not recognize differences between Aboriginal groups (for example, language differences as well as social and spiritual differences). Nowadays it could also include the difference between traditional owners of "country" and long-term residents (over a number of generations).

There were traditional group structures in existence in the areas where missions and governments intervened, and these structures were generally challenged and changed in quite a destructive way. However, despite the negative effects of such religious and governmental impositions as missions and reserves, there were some positive outcomes in terms of the formation of extended affiliations and networks between different

Aboriginal groups. In this sense, some contemporary formations of community derive from old reserves, missions and new camps.

Despite the fact that some communities are the result of government intervention, Indigenous people have maintained considerable control and continuity. Smith (1999), a Maori researcher argues that community is an imposition by colonial administration to control Indigenous peoples, but states that despite this, communities have "made" themselves. "Indigenous communities have made even their most isolated and marginalized spaces a home place imbued with spiritual significance and Indigenous identity" (Smith, 1999, p. 126). Smith distinguishes different aspects of community that may be defined or imagined in multiple ways, such as physical, political, social, psychological, historical, linguistic, economic, cultural and spiritual places.

Types of Community

Aboriginal community groups vary considerably in their economic, social and geographical circumstances. The NAEC (1986) developed a model of Aboriginal society that included four broad categories of the Aboriginal community, which were; traditionally oriented, rural non-traditional, urban and urban dispersed communities. Seven types of living situations were also outlined such as, traditionally oriented, outstations, and rural non-traditional. The descriptions presented in Table 1 are derived from the four categories of Aboriginal communities and the seven types of living situations constructed by the NAEC.

The types of communities identified above underscore the diversity of Aboriginal communities, and Dawn Gilchrist points out that Indigenous Australians may have connections with several different communities:

> *People try to give us this tag "Aboriginal community" but don't realise there's a lot of diversity associated with that term. Your existence is established and nurtured by your sense of community. I was born into my family on Bidgemia Station, Gascoyne Junction (WA), My people are Ingada and Wadjari. I'm isolated from that community in that I married and moved away but I never lose sight of where I came from. It takes courage to leave home, to take that first step outside and make a difference, as it does for whitefellas to shift from their "comfort zone" into the Aboriginal community.*
>
> *I now belong to several other communities. I have a strong sense of community in my church, in that I spend a lot of time with those people, but it is the Gascoyne community that I'm connected to culturally.*

Community and Service Delivery

Under the recent government self-management and self-determination policies, resources have been directed towards community-

Table 1. Types of Aboriginal Communities

Traditionally oriented communities (e.g., Papunya, Fitzroy Crossing, Aurukun, Yirrkala, and Yam Island)
A community of people:
- with a high degree of observance of traditional institutions, but not necessarily of one tribal grouping;
- who live together in cultural groupings within settlements that have been established since the coming of Europeans into their region;
- who have the greatest geographic and social separation from mainstream Australian society, although they some degree of economic connection.

Homeland centres (Outstations, e.g., Strelley, Yandeyarra, Blackstone and Jarlmadangah Burru).
Settlements:
- to which Aboriginal people have moved at their own initiative;
- where they are self-governing;
- that are often geographically separated from rural/town centers, although they have some degree of economic connection.

Non-traditional communities/fringe dwellers (e.g., Merribank, Hermannsburg, Point Pearce and Bagot)
A community of people:
- living in what were state government reserves or missions;
- that has some geographic, and considerable social separation from mainstream Australian society.

Metropolitan urban communities. (e.g., Redfern, Lockridge, and St. Kilda.)
Aboriginal People:
- living within major cities in locations that are identified as having high proportions of Aboriginal residents; or,
- living within a closely connected group of dwellings.
- geographically and economically linked to mainstream Australia, but because of their community social organization, may have considerable social separation.

Metropolitan urban dispersed
Aboriginal people:
- living in major capital cities, who, while they may have close ties and connections with people living within the same metropolitan urban area, may themselves live in suburbs or locations not identified as part of an urban Aboriginal community;
- socially, economically, and geographically linked to mainstream Australia.

---

based organizations. The community has tended to be defined in terms of a geographically bounded group of people. Organizations are funded to deliver services and support to the local Aboriginal population. There is an implication that the services will be delivered equitably to all the community residents. The House of Representatives Standing Committee on Aboriginal Affairs' report, *Our Future, Our Selves* (1990), proposes that the concept of community requires critical definition to expose realistic shortcomings as community organizations may not represent or resource all members as the implicit understandings and meanings behind the concept of community implies.

While considering the notion of Aboriginal community as a self-governing social unit, Smith (1989) suggests that:

> If "community" continues to be used as a fundamental tenet of Aboriginal policy and service delivery, then questions which hang over the term and its vague use must be addressed. In addition those who continue to use the term must respond to criticism which suggests the term could be used for political expediency (p. 20).

Thus, a critical definition of "community" in an Aboriginal context may require clarification of the processes and intent of service delivery, as well as the relationship between the dictates of government administration and Aboriginal cultural life. It may also include clarifying the relationship between "community" and community development, as over the past few years community development methods have become a highly desired way to meet immediate and future community needs.

The interface between the government administrative domain and the Aboriginal cultural domain, ranges from quite an extensive and complex interaction in urban areas to a limited interaction in remote regions, brokered by Council representatives. In the latter, a division has been maintained by some cultural groups as desirable for the protection and well-being of their cultural domain (Tonkinson, 1992, cited in Rowse, 1995).

One example of this is the Jigalong community, a Western Desert group that has been researched by anthropologist Tonkinson over a 30-year period. Their reaction to the opportunities presented by policies and processes of self-determination has formed the basis of a series of ongoing papers:

> The Jigalong mob found in 1970 that the non-Aboriginal administration with which they had had to deal since 1946 had changed suddenly from a mission regime, antagonistic to Aboriginal Law and paternalistic in supervision, to a secular regime which validated their law and encouraged their making decisions about Jigalong's future. How the Jigalong mob have made sense of, and responded to that change has been Tonkinson's theme. ... According to Tonkinson this new agenda has not been taken on by Jigalong people. Rather, they have tried to maintain their compartmentalisation of worlds to which they have become accustomed in the mission days (Rowse, 1995, pp. 31-32).

Community Development

In recent years, the application of the Western concepts of community within the context of "community development," as related to Aboriginal cultural groupings, has come under scrutiny and some debate has resulted. It is important not to assume a necessary correspondence between Aboriginal notions of community and the concept of community implicit in community development. While "community" may refer to the internal identity of a cultural group per se, the term community development "... is a way of working that aims to change a system" (Kelly & Sewell, 1988, p. 93).

Ife (1995) while examining the meaning and characteristics of "community" and "development" in terms of community development, states that the concept of community is a fundamental concept for any "community development" perspective. Moreover:

> Community is consistent with empowerment models of change, as it provides a framework for people to take effective decisions, and also with a needs-based perspective, as it can enable people more readily to define and articulate their felt needs and aspirations (Ife, 1995, p. 89).

As already outlined, the government reports, *Community-Based Planning* (1993) and *Our Future, Our Selves* (1990) make reference to "community" as an imposed notion, largely to expedite administrative relations and services between government and Aboriginal people. The imposed notion of community did not reflect traditional aspects of Aboriginal cultural organization. However, Linda Smith (1999) states that Indigenous people have infused their communities with significance and meaning. In addition, Ife (1995) suggests that the people themselves develop their own understandings of what community means for them. In light of this we now turn to a description of various forms of Aboriginal communities.

Western notions and Aboriginal notions of community differ in that the Aboriginal notion of community includes the recognition that to be a member of the Aboriginal community one has to be Aboriginal, identify as such, and be known to the group.

Community and Commitment

Contemporary Aboriginal communities are dynamic and flexible, including many networks, politics, (set and shifting) affiliations, and other layers of significance (Smith, 1999). Members of these communities may have various responsibilities and obligations that confirm and reinforce their membership within these communities. These may include:

- responsibilities to be seen to be involved and active within the community;
- responsibility to support community activities;
- obligations to family;
- a sense of responsibility or commitment to use ones skills for

the benefit of the community;
- affiliations to family, and broader kin relations (including families become connected through marriage);
- affiliations to factions/sectors within the community (family, work, tribal group, country of origin, politics);
- affiliations to particular organizations. Feelings of loyalty and ownership sometimes extends to the organization one works for, and in some ways maybe reflective of Aboriginal cultural practices in that it has become another way of knowing and identifying individuals. Often, members of the community associate the employee with a particular organization and this may become part of the individual's identity and even carry over to social situations;
- politics, of which there are many layers. Examples of this are representation: who should speak and on what matters; and recognizing, that at times, we may be both "insiders" and "outsiders" as within Aboriginal communities there are varying degrees of inclusiveness.

Darlene Oxenham emphasizes the importance of connections and commitment to one's community of origin, to one's "country":

Community" has particular meaning for Aboriginal people. I usually locate the meaning of "community" in a localised setting, for instance, the Aboriginal community of Perth or the Nyoongar community of the southwest. In this way certain factors are enshrined in the concept of community. For example, location or "country" is identified along with particular family groups and/or language groups. Each Aboriginal person will identify with one or more communities depending on their birth place and family networks Other things that should be considered when talking about community is that there are sometimes boundaries to community. By this, I mean that even though as an Aboriginal person I am part of the Aboriginal community in Perth, I am not a Nyoongar and this may mean there are constraints on me at times. For example, some matters or events that occur may only relate to Nyoongars and so it would be not be appropriate for me to have input into these things or speak on them.

Other considerations that influence degrees of responsibility and obligation include the length of time an individual has been resident in a place, the individual's connectedness to the community through direct kin relationships and marriage, and the sense of accountability the individual has back to the community.

Community and Identity

To demonstrate the Aboriginal identity is closely tied to "community" it is worth looking at how this issue arises in *A Dialogue on*

Indigenous Identity: Warts "n" All (1999). Collard makes this point about identity and community:

> I looked at the definition of Aboriginality which came out in 1972 or 1973 and it says in there, *community acceptance* -- so another question arises -- what is community? Community is so broad and yet it's a generic description or descriptor of all Indigenous people. I mean, what we have to do is to break that down even further to a local context (Oxenham, et al., 1999, p. 61, italics added).

For such a key contemporary issue -- the issue of Aboriginal identity in an era when people are struggling to re-connect with family and a broader sense of Aboriginality after the fragmentation, dislocation and disintegration of assimilationist policies such as the removal of children -- this very broad notion of community is problematic, and creates conflict and confusion. Precisely which "community" body or representative has the right to confirm someone's identity?

Later in *A Dialogue on Indigenous Identity*, Oxenham and Dudgeon explore some of the tension connected with the struggle for consensus on such complex issues as community.

> *Darlene*: But see, this is the dilemma. Often we're forced into this situation where we have to present some sort of united front, and this also comes back to identity. I think many of us are looking for unity; on a political basis, we argue for a united Aboriginal identity or some sort of pan-Aboriginality across Australia. So we're looking for unity and within that unity looking for some sort of similarities or commonalties. I guess this is why we come back to making judgements about one–another whether that person is Aboriginal, or whether they think they're white, or whether they lived as an Aboriginal person or not. We're forced, in many situations, to present that united front. Those spokespeople -- often it's the media that actually sets them up as **the** spokesperson for **the** Noongar community, and, you know, and you can have a variety of different people depending on who is reporting at the time. But in many other ways we're actually very, very separate family groupings; and a lot of people will now say, if you're going to do any consultations, do it on a family basis. But then that doesn't sit comfortably with me as well; because then it just feels like we're so fragmented that we're actually not a community, we're not a cultural group as such.
>
> So I guess I'm looking for "a truth" and I'm looking for that truth to encompass some sort of pan-Aboriginality. So I am making the assumption that there is an essence of Aboriginal. Assuming that there are some things that generally apply to all of us, that there are commonalties and similarities, whilst recognising some diversity amongst us as a cultural group. But it doesn't feel like to me at times–that you can have those two things–that they are so much in contradiction with one another that you can't. I personally place importance on us as a cultural group. If we're all claiming to be Aboriginal, then my hope would be to find out what the

commonalties are amongst us, and not look at the diversity, not look at the differences amongst us. Because as soon as we start really looking at the differences amongst us, it seems to fragment us, and then I think that it undermines our unity as a cultural group. Does that make sense?

    Pat: Yes, but why shouldn't we be [different]. Also I think we are unified: there are some fundamental and universal things we all subscribe to–the common flag is one of them, and knowing that we have a shared history as a colonised people and a whole variety of things–but having differences or looking at our differences and fragmentations, is that such a big problem? I mean white society isn't unified! (Oxenham et al. 1999, pp. 101-102).

Identity and community, then, do not guarantee unity, univocality, or unanimity. Diversity and difference are always negotiated within communities and absolute unity or commonality is frequently an ideal that masks the political nature of all forms of social organization (such issues are discussed at greater length in Dudgeon's (2000a) article "Indigenous Identity"). Nevertheless, what the kind of dialogue in *A Dialogue on Indigenous Identity* shows is the way that such issues can benefit from frank and open discussion founded on respect for different perspectives.

Community and the Politics of Representation

In her work on "dealing with difference" Pettman (1992) examines the construction of community and the politics of representation:

> Community and category claims are part of "the struggle to come into representation" (Hall, 1988b), which involves naming oneself, recognizing shared experiences of oppression or exploitation, mobilizing and claiming against the state. It means getting access, a hearing and funding, which may depend on being able to demonstrate a constituency–often then called a community. There are many questions here about whose community. What are the conditions for individuals to enter it, or remain members? Who can speak on its behalf? (p. 123).

Representation is an important consideration within the Aboriginal construction of community. Jill Abdullah offers her perceptions of the meaning and construction of Aboriginal community.

> *As a Nyoongar woman, I am a member of the Nyoongar community. The concept of Aboriginal community I have is a fairly fluid one. It has a local, family and national aspect. It can take into account different levels. For instance, I consider myself a part of the community in the area where I live–both the Aboriginal and non-Aboriginal community. I have contact with the other Aboriginal people of that area through various committees we participate in to address Aboriginal concerns. I am a Nyoongar so my family is here*

*in Perth. I consider my family to be a community that I am a part of.
I also consider myself to be a part of the broader Perth Aboriginal
community that is made up of all different groups.*

*I see the different layers of community as something like this: family
(immediate and extended); local; general; broader; across
regions/state; and, national. In relation to the family above, this also
consists of layers of which could be referred to as community, that
is, immediate family or extended family depending on the issue/s.
The layers of the definition of community can be related to issues
that are specific.I think that non-Aboriginal people have a sense of
community too. In Western society it is based upon lifestyle or
interest groups. In the Aboriginal domain it is based on race and our
shared experiences. Both concepts of community, that is, Aboriginal
and non-Aboriginal, have a notion of representing the larger
collective but they may not necessarily achieve this. Perceptions and
values are other variables in differentiating the two concepts of
community. Aboriginal people tend to be more conscious of who
they can "speak" for, or represent. This perception and awareness
about who one can speak for expands as one moves into a variety of
forums. The more forums and especially at national levels, the more
broader one's notions of Aboriginality become. Each person has
different perceptions of community, given their personal experience.*

Both Abdullah and Winch also point out that there is a definite
cultural and political protocol to speaking on behalf of the Aboriginal
community, so "community" has distinct political as well as cultural
dimensions amongst Aboriginal people.

*I would say you can't speak on behalf of the Aboriginal community
because it's very diverse: within each group there are family
groups, and you have strong family groups–and there are. And I
would say that if something happens within a family group, well the
person that's considered the head of the family group is the person
that has their say: they're the spokesperson as far as I'm concerned.*

A number of research participants have pointed out that identity and
representation hinges on positionality within families foremost, and,
following on from Mallard's comment earlier, that broader political
representation is more of an issue-based process. Nellie Green identifies the
issue of representation as one of the most divisive within Aboriginal
communities:

*I think this coming together is actually about common goals and
aspirations, and trying to identify appropriate strategies to have
adequate representation–a strong voice. Issues like culture bring us
together–the things our tradition, our people, were really strongly
grounded in, like art (painting, dancing, singing, storytelling),
sharing things like that. And, the notion of respect for elders. All
that becomes problematic in who has the right to be an authority or*

to be a voice for particular issues, because we find in Perth that there's always been that anomaly of, "Well, you don't speak for me." The issue of "self-appointed" elders or spokespeople, and I think that fragments our community, and it's something politicians and the government loves to see, because the worst thing for them is for us to be one people, one community. Also, socioeconomic issues, like unemployment and youth crime, and things like that. I think too, the need to right all the wrongs that have been brought about due to institutionalized oppression and things like that–"bringing them back home" and "the stolen children"–and trying to work out how we can make people feel better about their sense of community.

CONCLUSION

This paper has provided an overview of what the term "Aboriginal community" means to Aboriginal people. Although we have acknowledged that "the community" is a notion that has been imposed upon Aboriginal people over the past century, we have also shown how we have internalized the concept and given it our own meanings that include cultural ways of association beyond family. These meanings are elastic and may reconfigure according to the issue at hand.

The Aboriginal concept of community can have political, social and geographic connotations, but at its most fundamental level it has widespread currency as signifying belonging to a group of Aboriginal people. There are distinct elements to this sense of belonging within an Aboriginal domain that differ from social relationships in mainstream western culture.

Overall, despite the imposition of this notion within the various dominant discourses on Aboriginality, Indigenous communities have actively maintained their own group formations and have challenged dominant social and cultural discourses with resistant Aboriginal discourses.

Community is ultimately a broad and fluid concept shared by Aboriginal people and those who work in the domain, and Kim Collard emphasizes this when he points out a connection between culture and community:

Community is like culture: it does not remain static, and to assume we are one fixed and homogenous group of people overlooks the many different and complex levels and dimensions to "community". At the same time, there are some shared values, beliefs and attitudes that interconnect Indigenous Australian people–spiritually, politically, and historically.

Within this broad understanding of belonging and collectivity, Pat Dudgeon emphasizes the need for all to find their own voice grounded within their community:

A sense of community in Aboriginal terms seems to be about identity and networks of belonging and participation–which usually primarily comes through family connections. Just as identity can not be taken away, neither can membership of the Aboriginal community be revoked. Membership can be strengthened through certain activities, but can not be forfeited.

Within this sense of community, there are degrees of authority to speak on behalf of the community. I was talking to an Indigenous friend the other day who was challenged by other people about her right to speak on behalf of the Aboriginal community on a particular occasion. Her networks and participation in the community are quite strong, and subsequently, she came to the realisation that if she couldn't speak on behalf of the community on that specific occasion, she would never be able to. The incident provided an opportunity for her to reflect and re-invest herself with appropriate personal authority. Hence, it would appear that, within the community, authority is not only bestowed, but at the same time, it can also be claimed.

Finally, those intending to work with Indigenous Australians need to be aware of the diversity and complexity of contemporary communities, and to be sensitive to the cultural and political protocols and alliances, just as one would in negotiating the complex community formation of modern western institutions. As Dudgeon (2000b, p. 344) points out, it is advisable to be aware of cultural protocols and "community politics", and "... as a new practitioner, it is important to be seen to be operating with impartiality ..." This paper does not give specific advice on how to work with Aboriginal communities, for there are other texts that can assist practitioners in this way, for example, Forrest and Sherwood (1988) and Dudgeon, Garvey and Pickett (2000). The primary point that this paper has made is that there are distinct cultural psychological perceptions about community that need to be taken into account.

NOTES

[i] An earlier version of this chapter appears in P. Dudgeon, D. Garvey & H. Pickett (Eds.), (2000). *Working with Indigenous Australians: A handbook for psychologists*. Perth: Gunada Press.
[ii] The information for this paper is derived from mainland Aboriginal experiences, and, therefore, the term "Aboriginal" people will be used on most occasions. "Indigenous Australians" refers to two cultural groups -- mainland Aboriginal people and the people of the Torres Strait Islands.

REFERENCES

Aboriginal and Torres Strait Islander Commission. (1993). *Community based planning: Principles and practices*. Canberra: Australian Government Publishing Service.
Anderson, B. (1983). *Imagined communities: Reflections on the origin and spread of nationalism*. London: Verso.
Attwood, B. (1989). *Them making of the Aborigines*. Sydney: Allen & Unwin.

Australian National Aboriginal Education Committee. (1986). *Policy statement on teacher education for Aborigines and Torres Strait Islanders.* Canberra: Australian Government Publishing Service.

Bauman, Z. (1991). *Modernity and ambivalence.* Ithaca, New York: Cornell University Press.

Bishop, B., & Sonn, C. (2000). Community psychology as a framework for working with Indigenous and other disenfranchised communities. In P. Dudgeon, D. Garvey, & H. Pickett (Eds.), *Working with Indigenous Australians: A handbook for psychologists* (pp. 293-304). Perth, Australia: Gunada Press.

Bourke, E. (1994). Australia's first peoples: Identity and population. In C. Bourke, E. Bourke, & B. Edwards (Eds.), *Aboriginal Australia.* St Lucia, Queensland: University of Queensland Press.

Dodson, M. (1994). The end in the beginning: Re(de)fining Aboriginality. *Australian Aboriginal Studies.* No. 1.

Dudgeon, P. Garvey, D., & H. Pickett (Eds.), (2000). *Working with Indigenous Australians: A handbook for psychologists.* Perth, Australia: Gunada Press.

Dudgeon, P. (2000a). Indigenous identity. In P. Dudgeon, D. Garvey & H. Pickett (Eds.), *Working with Indigenous Australians: A handbook for psychologists* (pp. 43-51). Perth, Australia: Gunada Press.

Dudgeon, P. (2000b). Working with Aboriginal communities: The challenges. In P. Dudgeon, D. Garvey & H. Pickett (Eds.), *Working with Indigenous Australians: A handbook for psychologists* (pp. 341-48). Perth, Australia: Gunada Press.

Forrest, S. & Sherwood, J. (1988). Working with Aborigines in remote areas. Perth: Western Australian College of Advanced Education.

Frow, J. (1991). *What was postmodernism?* Sydney: Local Consumption Press.

Gergen, K. J. & Shotter, J. (1989). Texts of identity. London, UK: Sage.

Gilbert, K. (1977). *Living black.* Harmondsworth, UK: Penguin.

House of Representatives Standing Committee on Aboriginal Affairs. (1990). *Our future, our selves.* Canberra: Australian Government Publishing Service.

Ife, J. (1995). *Community development: Creating community alternatives - vision, analysis and practice.* New South Wales: Addison Wesley Longman.

Joseph, S. (1998). *Interrogating culture: Critical perspectives on contemporary social theory.* New Delhi: Sage.

Kelly, T. & Sewell, S. (1988). *Head, heart and hands: Dimensions of community building.* Brisbane, Australia: Boolarong Publications.

Langton, M. (1993*). "Well, I heard it on the radio and I saw it on the television ... "* Woolloomooloo, NSW: Australian Film Commission.

Lucas, T. et al. (1998). *A sense of community: An exploratory study.* Perth, Australia: Centre for Aboriginal Studies, Curtin University.

Mabo and others v State of Queensland [No 2] (1992) 175 CLR 1.

Muecke, S. (1992). *Textual spaces: Aboriginality & cultural studies.* Sydney, New South Wales: Allen & Unwin.

Oxenham, D., et al. (1999). *A dialogue on Indigenous identity: Warts 'n' all.* Perth, Western Australia: Gunada Press.

Pettman, J. (1992). *Living in the margins: Racism, sexism and feminism in Australia.* Sydney, New South Wales: Allen & Unwin.

Rowse, T. (1995). *Remote possibilities - the Aboriginal domain and the administrative imagination.* Darwin: North Australian Research Unit, Australian National University.

Smith, B. (1989). *The concept of community in Aboriginal policy and service delivery,* Occasional Paper 1, North Australian Research Unit. Darwin: North Australian Development Unit, Department of Social Security.

Smith, L. T. (1999). *Decolonizing methodologies: Research and Indigenous peoples.* London: Zed Books.

Trudgen, R. I. (2000). *Why warriors lie down and die.* Darwin: Aboriginal Resource & Development Inc.

Wark, M. (1999). *Celebrities, culture and cyberspace: The light on the hill in a postmodern world.* Sydney: Pluto Press.

Williams, R. (1988). *Keywords: A vocabulary of culture and society.* London: Fontana.

PART V

METHODOLOGICAL AND THEORETICAL DEVELOPMENTS

Chapter 14

SENSE OF COMMUNITY IN RURAL COMMUNITIES
A Mixed Methodological Approach

Brian J. Bishop
Curtin University

Sheridan J. Coakes
Coakes Consulting

Pamela N. D'Rozario[i]
Private Practice

INTRODUCTION

Psychological sense of community (SOC) was proposed to be the central aspect of community psychology by Sarason (1974). At the Society for Community Research and Action conference at Yale in 1999, Sarason was asked by Bob Newbrough why he had formulated the concept of SOC. He stated that as a child during the depression he experienced the terror of being at the point of having no physical and emotional support. Sustained experiences of this kind then form the basis of alienation that individuals and groups in our societies experience. Sarason argued that this was a profound experience and is a considerable risk factor for psychological and social problems. Understanding SOC, thus, is an essential aspect of community psychology.

SOC has been investigated in a variety of settings such as organisations (e.g., Pretty & McCarthy, 1991; Royal & Rossi, 1996), religious organizations (Pargament, 1983), universities and colleges Lounsbury & DeNeui, 1996). SOC has been assessed in a number of ways. Most quantitative research is based on Chavis and McMillan's (1986) model of SOC using the scale developed by Chavis, Hogge, McMillan, and

Wandersman (1986). While this scale has been found to have good reliability and validity (Chavis, et al., 1986), the subscales have not been demonstrated to be as reliable (Chipuer & Pretty, 1999). However, Kelly (1996) found that two communities of older persons had similar levels of SOC as measured by the Chavis, et al. (1986) scale, but that they were the same for different reasons. This suggests that maybe the scales may be tapping different aspects in different communities. Other measures of SOC have been developed (Bachrack & Zautra, 1985; Buckner, 1988; Davidson & Cotter, 1986; Doolittle & McDonald, 1978; Glynn, 1981).

Central to all of these scales is that SOC is an 'etic' construct. McMillan and Chavis (1996) asserted that the concept could be generalised to "...all types of communities" (p.19), even though some theories of community that suggest that communities can differ quite considerably in structure and function (Kirkpatrick, 1986; Newbrough, 1995; Tönnies, 1957). Why would it be assumed that the same dimensions of SOC prevail in many, if not all types of communities, even in what appears to be relatively homogeneous communities, such as rural communities?

We started thinking about these issues when they noted that their perceptions of a number of communities in the south west of Australia differed from community to community. The locals were well aware that they had different histories and that these differences were important to them. One community, for example, had been established for over 150 years and its social structures reflected the importance of two families that had been in the region since it was founded. This community was highly structured and firmly established (although it is undergoing quite considerable change now). Another community had been relatively recently established. It was developed as part of the 'soldier settlement' schemes just after the Second World War. The community was more egalitarian and less structured. This community was also more vulnerable as it was located on fairly marginal farming land.

The questions that arise when considering these communities are: do these communities differ in SOC, both quantitatively and qualitatively? Is the structure of these two communities SOC similar or are they different? Our aim was to examine the structures of SOC in different rural communities both qualitatively and quantitatively. This study is a re-analysis of previous work (see Coakes & Bishop, 1998), and is based on women's participation in, and perceptions of, their communities.

RESEARCH DESIGN

The research design employed was of a cross-sectional nature. In this design, a sample of the population is selected and information is collected from this sample at one time. The focus of a cross-sectional design is one of description, describing the characteristics of a population or the differences among two or more populations. Cross-sectional studies are also used to assess interrelationships among variables within a population. Therefore, the descriptive and predictive functions of this design were salient.

Furthermore, an attempt has been made to strengthen the study design through methodological triangulation, the combination of methodologies in the study of the same phenomena. As Denzin (1978) states "no single method ever adequately solves the problem of rival causal factors...Because each method reveals different aspects of empirical reality, multiple methods of observations must be employed" (p. 28). Survey and interview methods have been utilized in the present research.

The Communities

Six communities from the south west of Western Australia (WA) were selected because they vary on a number of dimensions such as population stability, size and period of settlement. Some of Shires were experiencing growth in the last two decades. Albany had increased by 162% and Esperance by 44%. Kent and Plantagenet were relatively stable, and Kojonup and Tambellup had declined by 15% and 28%, respectively. All of these communities are wheat-sheep farming communities, although timber production has become a major issue in one (Plantagenet). While the periods of settlement shown in Table 1 do not indicate vast differences, two of the shires have developed more recently. All regions have experienced changes in populations. For example, Kent was devastated by deaths of soldiers from the region in the World War I. The wars have affected the development of all shires, with soldier settlement schemes creating influxes of people after each world war. Albany's growth has been both rural and urban. Kent and Esperance have experienced considerable growth in their farming sectors since the World War II. As more remote communities, they can be characterized as frontier development, with newly cleared areas of land.

Participants and Sampling

In total 443 women participated in the study. They ranged in age from 18 to 87 years, with an average age of 43.7 years. In all, 388 women responded to a telephone survey, while 57 attended personal interviews in their local township. Table 1 indicates the percentage of the population sampled within each shire for both the telephone survey and the personal interview methods.

The sample of respondents within each of the six Shires was obtained through information provided in the South-Western and South-

Eastern telephone directories. This technique was adopted because an inability to obtain information from the telephone company in order to conduct a random digit dialing technique.

   Localities within each Shire were identified, and then through the use of a database program *Australia On Disk 5* listed telephone numbers for each locality were generated. A BASIC computer program was then used to randomly select numbers to ensure a uniform sampling of households throughout each Shire.

Table 1. Percentage of population (females) sampled across shires using statistics from the Australian Bureau of Statistics Census 1991.

Shire (Settlement Date)	Population	Number of Telephone Interviews	Number of Face-To-Face Interviews
Albany (1830s)	5,507	66	10
Plantagenet (1830s)	1,946	65	10
Kojonup (1837)	1,081	65	11
Tambellup (1872)	324	66	9
Esperance (1860s)	4,960	66	10
Kent (1910)	381	60	7
Total	14,199	388	57

Community Survey

   A survey was constructed to measure how rural women perceive their communities and the nature and extent of their participation within their communities. The survey consisted of items comprising four scales: the Moral Community Scale (Johnson & Mullins,1990); the Mass Society Scale (Johnson & Mullins), the Neighborhood Cohesion Instrument (Buckner, 1988), and the Core Social Network Inventory (Brims, 1974). The Buckner scale was preferred to Chavis, et al. (1986) as it was more amenable to aggregate scores. Other items were used to measure the participation of women in community networks, and demographic variables.

Procedure

   The initial stage of the research was to establish contact with the local Shire Office in each of the six Shires to request the use of their office facilities (office space and telephone) for a period of approximately one week. In accordance with the rural calendar, data was collected over a seven-month period ranging from March to September 1993.

Telephone Survey: A random sample of approximately 60-66 female participants, in each shire, were contacted by phone and asked to participate in a telephone survey. The interviewer used to contact women in each shire was extensively briefed on the content of the survey and the procedure in which the survey was to be administered. This interviewer was responsible for the administration of the telephone survey in all six shires in order to ensure consistency, and reduce the possibility of interviewer bias. The interviewer was required to identify themselves and inform the respondent of the intent of the survey. The respondent was then asked if they would like to participate in the survey, if they agreed the interview proceeded.

Per'sonal Open-ended Interviews: Approximately 7-10 women, in each shire, were randomly selected and asked if they would be prepared to attend a personal interview at the local Shire office in their area. One interviewer was responsible for conducting the personal interviews across all six shires. The data obtained from the interviews was used to validate the information obtained in the community telephone surveys and was related to the women's participation in personal and community social networks.

Interviewees were contacted by phone using the above sampling procedure one week before the research team arrived in each shire. This was to ensure that the required number of interviews was scheduled for the following week. A total of 57 interviews were conducted across all six shires. Unstructured interviews were conducted covering aspects of community and participation in community activities.

FINDINGS

Quantitative Findings

The following results are reported as theory generative, rather than theory testing. The use of statistics is descriptive, rather than inferential. This is done, firstly, because there is little theoretical basis for predicting outcomes. Secondly, we are attempting to investigate some issues that are speculative. Finally, it is acknowledged that inferential statistical testing is based on a set of assumptions that are unfounded. Lamiell (1995), and Girgerenzer, et al. (1989) have argued that the assumptions underlying inferential statistics are incoherent. Lamiell has shown that inferential statistics can be used in theory generation, and this approach is being adopted here. Statistics are used here in an exploratory manner (e.g., Bishop & Syme, 1995) and less conventional fashion than in typical experiments.

Buckner's Neighborhood Cohesion Index was summed across the items to give a sense of community (SOC) measure for each community. Overall, the mean for the six communities was 66.3 with a standard deviation of 9.2. When the communities were contrasted, there were slight differences, ranging from 68.9 to 63.8. The more remote communities scored lowest (Kent and Esperance, respectively), the highest was Kojonup, followed by Albany and Plantagenet. Planned contrasts showed small significant differences between Kent and Esperance and the other communities.

Mean differences are not the only way in which communities can differ. It is possible that the sense of community construct operates differently in different communities. One way to examine this is to look at the relationships between the sense of community scale and other variables. The social support scale and the other social factors (number of friends, frequency of contact, length of time having known friends) were all interrelated and a composite score was derived for each participant through the use of principal components analysis and the generation of factor scores. The PC analysis was done separately for each community. A single factor solution was needed for 5 of the 6 shires (variances accounted was 64% for Plantagenet and between 78% and 80% for the remainder). Albany's results were complex. The social factors were not all positively related; number of friends was negatively related to social support and the length of knowing friends. Frequency of contact was unrelated to the other variables. A two-factor solution was found accounting for 77% of the variance (51% and 26%).

In spite of the small sample sizes, structural equation modeling was conducted separately for each community. Schumacker and Lomax (1996) discussed sample sizes and indicate that the upper bounds of sample size is in the thousands and the lower bounds are at least 5 subjects per variable for normal or elliptical distributions when latent variables have multiple indicators, and at least 10 subjects per variable for other distributions. The current samples fit within this range. Again, the speculative nature of the analysis allows a less cautious approach. Amos (Arbuckle, 1997) was used to analyze the data. A basic solution was used to start each analysis and the models were modified until non-significant χ^2 was obtained. Selection of the model is very important. Moral community and Alienation can both be seen as structural properties of the community and are thus more likely to affect individual variables such as SOC, community participation and social factors. Thus the basic starting model had Alienation and Moral community as exogenous variables, and the others as endogenous.

As χ^2 (and other measures) is affected by sample size, it is recommended that other fit measures are also used (Schumacker & Lomax). Standardized residual mean squares (SRMR) were also used along with the comparative fit index (CFI) as recommended by Hu and Bentler (1999).

Modifications were made to increase the parsimony of the solution without reducing the fit measures greatly. All solutions had non-significant χ^2s, SRMR less than .080 and CFIs greater than 0.95. The solutions for the six shires are shown in Figures 1 to 6. Given the size of the path coefficients (standardized), the differences must be treated with some speculation.

A result common to all communities is the relationship of Alienation and SOC, and the relationship between Moral Community (MC) and the number of groups participated in. The relationship between Alienation and SOC is consistent with Pretty, Conroy, Dugay, Fowler and Williams (1996) and Chipuer (2001) who found loneliness correlated with SOC.

The relationship of MC and participation is understandable if the items that load most heavily on MC are examined (Coakes, 1995). These items were:

- The goals and objectives of my community group are very important to me.
- I feel that I am accepted and my values are shared by other people in the group.
- I believe it is important for those involved in the group to share (a) common vision.

These who see the importance of a strong local community are those who are most likely to participate in community groups. It is also interesting that MC and Alienation were not consistently negatively related. In the majority of analyses the relationship was non-existent, leading to the view that being alienated in a community is independent of the extent to which you value a strong community and community values.

The relationships between the social factors, SOC and participation is somewhat confused. More often, the social factors do not relate to SOC. A high loading for social support on the social factor was found for all communities (except Albany, see below). Given that the social factor is a social support component, the distinction between SOC and the social factor is consistent with other findings (Pretty, 1990; Pretty & McCarthy, 91; Pretty, et al., 1996). For example, Pretty, et al., found the correlations between the two measures of SOC they used with social support were 0.11 and 0.13.

One striking finding is the failure of participation to relate to SOC (except for Esperance). This is inconsistent with other findings (Brodsky, O'Campo, & Aronson, 1999; Chavis, & Wandersman, 1990; Davidson, & Cotter, 1989, 1993).

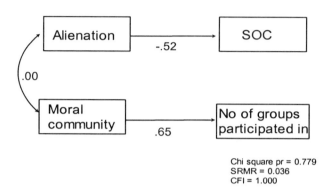

Figure 1. AMOS Model for Tambellup

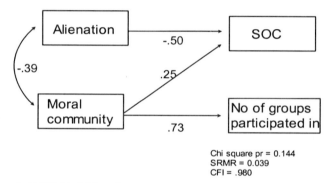

Figure 2. AMOS Model for Albany

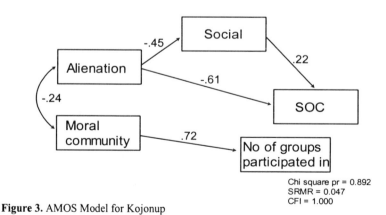

Figure 3. AMOS Model for Kojonup

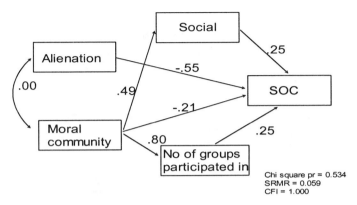

Figure 4. AMOS Model for Plantegenet

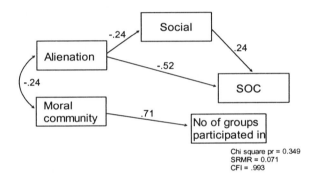

Figure 5. AMOS Model for Esperance

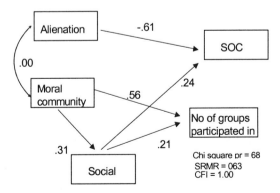

Figure 6. AMOS Model for Kent

There are differences between the communities. Each model is different enough not allow easy interpretation. Tambellup's model is the simplest with simple independent relationships between Alienation and SOC, and MC and participation. As Tambellup is a community in which the population has decreased, it is possible that the social aspects of community (Alienation and SOC) have been separated from the issues of working and valuing the community. SOC is thus only predicted by Alienation.

The solution for Albany looks similar, but the interpretation would be quite different. The social factors are not related to any of the variables. The factor patterns were unusual for Albany as there were negative correlations between some of the variables. Here, the picture is one of overlap between all the variables, except that Alienation does not predict participation. SOC is influenced by both Alienation and MC.

Kojonup and Plantagenet have similar outcomes. MC predicts participation, MC and Alienation are related. SOC is predicted by Alienation both directly and indirect through the social factor. Thus SOC in these communities are related to the extent to which you feel alienated from the community. and the depth of social contact and social support.

The models for Esperance and Kent are more complex. Alienation is not related to MC in either community. MC predicts participation. In Esperance SOC is predicted by Alienation, MC. MC predicts SOC both directly and indirectly. The indirect paths are through both the social factor and participation. SOC is then seen as being related to valuing the community and its values, social interactions and support, and participation. Kent is different again. Alienation independently predicts SOC, which is also predicted by the social factor. MC predicts participation both directly and indirectly through the social factor.

These results are speculative. The sample sizes do not warrant definite conclusions, but they do indicate that the nature of the relationships between SOC and the other variables is not consistent across communities. SOC can then be thought of as varying in its structure from community to community. In the next section we turn to the qualitative data to see if these speculative differences are reflected there.

Qualitative Findings

The interviews were transcribed, and theme analyses performed using NVivo (Richards, 2000). Themes were developed from the transcripts from the ethnographic data (Creswell, 1998; Miles & Huberman, 1994). Second order themes were also developed to attempt to understand the latent structure of the communities.

Rural communities differ from urban ones in that they are more likely to be geographically defined rather than being relational (Heller,

1989). The local boundaries of communities have changed over time. While the we have treated the shires as the communities, as they are the political and economic boundaries, many of the participants still refer to smaller units. Historically, the southwest was dotted with numerous communities. Tradition has it that travel defined communities and in the early days horse travel came to define communities. Small towns sprang up about a day's ride from each other. Modern transportation has changed this, but still many people use the original boundaries. McMillan and Chavis (1986) reflected upon the emergence of 'them and us' and while farming practices means relatively uniform distribution of people in a region (except for greater densities in the towns), people do still identify with a particular community. While this tends to be geographic, it is not always the case. One participant reported that, although her family lived in one shire, her community was the neighboring community, because she and her siblings went to school there and the family did its business there.

The six shires studied here have differences and similarities. Most participants were very positive about their communities. Many comments were told of the friendliness of the community. Typical example were:

> ... I felt at home straight away, it was wonderful, and everyone was very friendly, my next door neighbor came over the second day I was there and it's just, I don't know, everyone's so nice, they don't have all the hangups that people have in Perth

> [When we moved into the community]...the next door neighbor had come along and put the fire on so that it heated the water and his wife had baked a cake and it was sitting on the table, and somebody else had come along with a bunch of flowers and it was just there...

One gets a positive sense about people in these communities. The openness and willingness to help in this study is testament to this. There is a paradox in that people many commented that their community was the best they had been in, and we suspect this not to be simply a processing bias, but reflects some of the operations of community. Community membership requires allegiance and this could be reflected in their comments. It could also reflect people's inabilities to detect change in themselves and in the community around them (Sarason, 2000).

Other common comments were about the importance of institutions in the communities. The churches, sporting associations and schools are an essential part of rural community life. Many people mentioned their involvement in these institutions, as well as voluntary groups. For example, two women made the following comments:

> I played a lot of sport so I met a lot of people, if you play sport in the country you're right...

> I think sport is an enormous comfort to women in the country, as you can see our sporting groups are our main support systems...well it's a reason to go to something and an outlet and it takes your mind off your own problems...

Not only do these institutions have a central role in the life of the community, they provide a mechanism for new comers getting involved in the community. People commented that immigrants needed to show they were willing to work for the community and getting involved on the committee of a sporting body allowed entry to the community. A woman in another community stated that:

> You have to get involved (in sport). If you don't your dead. This is where you meet and become part of the community.

Another woman said:

> I thought of playing pennants that was good, because I'm a sporty sort of a person and that came quite easily .... it helps being good at sport anyway, sport has a major role in country communities as a socializing participation role ...

It could be speculated that sport and church participation for the new arrival not only offer access to socialize, they allow a gradual learning of local culture and social rules. Sport and religion have some basic rules and these provide the new arrivals with an access to the more complex culture. Also, sporting rivalries between neighboring communities is very strong and probably helps develop strong senses of in-group and out-group.

There is a sense that people are provided initial support, but are expected to learn the local social rules and fit in quickly. This is reflected in the following comment:

> I was so innocent to country towns I never expected much, and was glad to have people to talk to...it's not until later you realize the things that might have been said behind your back or the dynamics that were happening around me that I wasn't even aware of.

One issue that seemed to occur in most communities was that the women felt they could only develop a small range of friends. The following comment reflect this:

> I've found in a small community I have, in [a town], I have a lot of good friends and we get on very well, but I only have one very close friend and I think that's the key to survival and I think that's where a lot of people who have had nothing to do with a small community in the country, make the big mistake, they come in, they confide in too many and it doesn't work that way....

A key comment that is true of all communities is that there is considerable instrumental and social support. While social support is seen as a major aspect of Trade in McMillan's (1996) reformulation of SOC, instrumental help and collaboration seem to be more common. Some of this help is reflected in the following comments.

> ... especially this Iron Ore thing, they've all banded together, there's a few people, not for quite a while, have lost property and through a big house fire or something like that, that's sort of all banned and they help them ... and I mean, they're always running raffles and they always seem to have people to buy the tickets and things like that, but they raffle off mallee roots, they can always sort of depend on the public to support the what fund raising things.

> The community. You know that you are definitely not on your own. If something happens, there is always help ...

> ... and see that's another thing, mentioning neighbors, see if one of them is sick, if your husband gets sick during the seeding or whatever, in a small town the neighbors will get in there and seed for you, you're just there, you know you come home hospital from having a baby and you've got women driving down the drive with casseroles ...

Belonging to a rural community can have its costs. Privacy is one main issue. The following comments reflect some of the issues:

> ... well there is the aspect that everyone knows everyone so there's quite a bit of, a bit of gossip goes on.

> ... it's difficult to get the same depth of friendship here that you had elsewhere, and being in such a small community you have be very careful what you say...it's really nice to be able to go somewhere where you can simply talk to someone and be completely honest.

An important variation on this was the comment that:

> ...most friendships are really sincere, I think you know people say, oh country towns gossip and all this sort of thing, but, sure people talk, but it's not necessarily in a malicious way, it's more an interested way because they know all the people.

One frequently heard comment relates to the length of time required to become really accepted in the community. While there is a degree of acceptance when people first move into a community, full membership of the social structure does not come quickly. This is reflected in the following comments:

> I'm better off, because my husband's born and bred here, he, himself has noticed some distance, placed between people that aren't bred here so to speak, and who come in from the outside, they may have been here for 45 years, but there's still, oh you came from such and such, they don't forget

> When I said we'd been here 15 years, someone said oh your only a newcomer, I said sure they're joking, well it is, they see it as a joke, but...we weren't born here so I don't know if that makes us in or out

There were differences between the communities. The older, established communities responded differently from people coming into the community. For example:

> very friendly, very open, there were cliques of course, like there are in all communities, and they're still there but if you went to the right school you were immediately accepted, even if you were an outsider, you had to go to the right school.

> I suppose there's a pecking order and cliques, and the hierarchy you know, I mean there's Mrs CWA you might say here...but you know, she's sort of possessive about it and lets everybody know, makes sure they know...but obviously you know it's a town that's run by about four major families...it's very established.

> People have established roles already, maybe roles is too stronger word, but established identities ...

In the newer communities, there was a sense that the communities faced more adversity in the recent times. There was a sense that the communities formed to create mutual help in the face of very difficult farming conditions. Kent and Esperance had developed (or redeveloped) recently and the survival is an important aspect of their communities. This is reflected in their response to new community members. In older communities, immigrants have to fit into the existing communities. They have to play a subservient role until they are accepted. In some communities, there is a solid, if not rigid, structure. The previously mentioned comment about 'doing time' on committees came more from the established communities. Migrants to the new communities were seen more as 'joint venturers' in a new place. In the newer communities, people join in a developing community. This is reflected in the following story of an Esperance woman:

> Well we were the start of the community, it was good to come into a community that wasn't there, if you know what I mean...we had no phones or anything to start with...everyone was young, they were homesick and this is when Mrs M sort of decided all the ladies should get together and have one night a month where we could go out, leave the kids at home, and we were going to something to stimulate us, because when you're sort of out there and you've got little kids around you, you talk baby talk and your mind goes blank, like it tends to deteriorate and so we were going to have a stimulating night out, where everybody sort of sits around gets to know everybody and you have interesting things, like this was before TV and everybody had come from different states or different parts of WA into this new land area, and so we called ourselves 'Captive Wives' because we were actually captured and taken there by our husbands, I willingly went, but a lot of the others didn't, and it was a battle ... and it really did help a lot of the ladies keep their sanity.

In one of the newer communities, one woman reflected positively on the diversity in the community in terms of age and origin. This did not occur in the established communities. McMillan (1996) reconsidered the concept of diversity in community. He argued that his original view (McMillan & Chavis, 1986) was that communities could tolerate diversity. In the newer formulation, he saw similarity and the process of consensual validation as more important and rejected his previous contentions. It is interesting that diversity seemed to be respected in the newer communities and less so in the established ones. Some of the established communities had experienced population loss and, thus, may be less willing to tolerate diversity. Bishop and Syme (1996) found considerable tolerance of diversity in a neighboring community that was also increasing its population in size and mix.

McMillan (1996) implied that there are developmental stages in the development of Spirit, Trust, Trade, and Art. In these newer communities, it is Trade that appears to emerge first, and other aspects emerge later. The need for social and physical exchange is a major component of the developing community. While it is difficult to identify the staged development of SOC in the more established communities, it is possible to speculate that their development was not different from the emerging communities. The conservative approach seems to be based in a common historical understanding of conquering adversity and it could be speculated that their resistance to change reflects that collective sense of vulnerability. This vulnerability would be more keenly felt in those communities experiencing population decline.

Paradoxes

The above commentaries could be easily seen as reflecting poorly on some of the communities. Resistant to change, superficially social pleasantry, not sustaining of a breadth of friends are some of the aspects of these communities that could be seen negatively. This perspective does not take into account the historical difficulties and hardships faced by these communities and the costs associated with daily living in rural and remote communities. The development of communities was based on instrumental needs and much of the key component of SOC, Trade, was seen in instrumental terms. Within in these comments are paradoxes; the communities are reported to be very friendly and yet their stories relate to instrumental help, not social support. Again the communities are seen as being friendly, yet many people have commented on the need to have a small number of close friends (especially in the newer communities). A confound exists when talking of the newer and older communities. Farm size is also greater in the newer communities and the land has lower rainfall (and more land is needed to be viable). Thus, distances increase, and increasing distance increases the cost of social interaction.

The social structures of these communities reflect adaptation to the context. The older communities are established, but they were established in the face of adversity and this is reflected in their structures. When a community's survival is dependent on the efforts of the community, it will be conservative, as conservative practices are necessary to survive. Many of the original farm sizes were based on the area a person could clear in a lifetime, and as such viability was always an issue. The soldier settlement farms were also too small to be economically viable and as the world commodity prices have fallen over time, farmer failure has always been in the minds of the communities. The cost of interacting with others is greater in rural communities. Having a small number of friends means that the social costs of maintaining friendships is kept manageable. As one of the comments, above, indicated, trying maintain a wide range of friends is impossible. Friendships require constant maintenance and to do this in a rural community requires considerable time and effort.

The instrumental focus of help does not contradict McMillan's (1996) notion of social exchange as an important aspect of Trade. In these communities where there is a serious problem of lack of human resources (Coakes & Bishop, 1998) (what Barker, 1966, referred to as "undermanning") symbols of community achievements are required and physical symbols are more easily identified. There was a constant undertone of social support. Where emotional exchange is covert, overt symbols are required. This is reflected in a comment reiterated here:

> It's a shame, I think you lose a lot living in a city, it's not for everyone of course, living in the country, but for me, you don't realize how much you've lost the community spirit, except for when you come and actually live in a country town.

Concluding comments

Pepper (1942) argued that research based on different 'world theories' or epistemological bases could not be integrated. The modeling presented here and the qualitative analysis would seem to be a case in point. The two approaches do indicate that SOC varies across communities. The structures of the communities vary, and the relationship of SOC to other variables is not consistent. Beyond that, integrating the findings cannot be done.

The qualitative analysis addressed issues about the nature of community and community life. The quantitative approach was assessing something completely different. This later research model only allows us to look at how people differ within a community. The patterns of relationships can be compared across communities, but the cannot be easily related to the qualitative differences. The modeling is based on an individual differences approach and the qualitative research is based on similarities and regularities within the communities.

Sarason (1973) made a similar point when addressing assessment of the impacts of nature and nurture. The impacts of culture on people cannot be assessed using individual difference models, it simply does not make sense to consider some people being less socialized than others (as much as we would wish to do so). These models are providing different commentaries on the same communities. The patterns of relationships between the quantitative variables provide support for the concept of SOC being rethought. McMillan and Chavis (1986), and more obvious in McMillan (1996) developed models of SOC from a collective perspective. Spirit, Trust, Trade and Art are all features of a community and community development. To develop a scale out of this model to be used in individual differences models may be fraught with difficulties.

NOTES

[i] The authors wish to thank David MacMillan for his constructive comments on the draft of this chapter.

REFERENCES

Arbuckle, J. L. (1996). *Amos user's guide: Version 3.6.* Chicago: SmallWaters Corporation.
Bachrach, K. M., & Zautra, A. J. (1985). Coping with a community stressor: The threat of a hazardous waste facility. *Journal of Health and Social Behavior, 26,* 127-141.
Barker, R. (1968). *Ecological psychology.* Stanford, CA: Stanford University Press.
Brim, J. A. (1974). Social network correlates of avowed happiness. *Journal of Nervous and Mental Diseases, 158,* 432-439.
Bishop, B. J., & Syme, G. J. (1995). The Social costs and benefits of urban consolidation: A time budget/contingent valuation approach. *Journal of Economic Psychology, 16,* 223-245.
Bishop, B. J., & Syme, G. J. (1996). Social change in rural settings: Lessons for community change agents. In D. R. Thomas & A. Veno (Eds.), *Community Psychology and social change: Australian and New Zealand perspectives* (pp. 157-181). Palmerston North, NZ: Dunmore Press.
Brodsky, A. E., O'Campo, P. J., & Aronson, R. E. (1999). PSOC in community context: Multi-level correlates of a measure of psychological sense of community in low-income, urban neighborhoods. *Journal of Community Psychology, 27,* 659-679.
Buckner, J. C. (1988). The development of an instrument of measure neighborhood cohesion. *American Journal of Community Psychology, 16,* 771-791.
Chavis, D., Hogge, J., McMillan, D., & Wandersman, A. (1986). Sense of community through Brunswik's lens: A first look. *Journal of Community Psychology, 14,* 24-40.
Chavis, D. M., & Wandersman, A. (1990). Sense of community in the urban environment: A catalyst for participation and community development. *American Journal of Community Psychology, 18,* 55-81.
Chipuer, H. M. (2001). Dyadic attachments and community connectedness: Links with youth's loneliness experiences. *American Journal of Community Psychology, 29,* 429-446.
Chipuer, H. M., & Pretty, G. M. H. (1999). A review of the sense of community index: Current uses, factor structure, reliability, and further development. *Journal of Community Psychology, 27,* 643-658.
Coakes, S. J. (1995). *Participation of women in rural communities: The influence of social structural and contextual factors.* Unpublished doctoral thesis, Curtin University, Perth.
Coakes, S. J., & Bishop, B. J. (1998). Where do I fit in? Factors influencing women's participation in rural communities. *Community, Work & Family, 1,* 249-271.
Creswell, J. W. (1998). *Qualitative inquiry and the research design: Choosing among five traditions.* Thousand Oaks, CA: Sage.

Davidson, W. B., & Cotter, P. R. (1986). Measurement of sense of community within the sphere of city. *Journal of Applied Social Psychology, 16*, 608-619.

Davidson, W. B., & Cotter, P. R. (1989). Sense of community and political participation. *Journal of Community Psychology, 17*, 119-125.

Davidson, W. B., & Cotter, P. R. (1993). Psychological sense of community and support for public school taxes. *American Journal of Community Psychology, 21*, 59-66.

Denzin, N. K. (1978). *The research act: A theoretical introduction to sociological methods* (2nd ed.). New York: McGraw-Hill.

Doolittle, R. J., & MacDonald, D. (1978). Communication and a sense of community in a metropolitan neighborhood: A factor analytic examination. *Communication Quarterly, 26*, 2-7.

Girgerenzer, G., Swijtink, Z., Porter, T., Daston, L., Beaty, J., &, Kruger, L. (1989). *The empire of chance: How Probability Changed Science and Everyday Life*. Cambridge, UK: Cambridge University Press.

Glynn, T. J. (1986). Neighborhood and sense of community. *Journal of Community Psychology, 14*, 341-352.

Heller, K. (1989). The return to community. *American Journal of Community Psychology, 17*, 1-15.

Hu, L., & Bentler, P. M. (1999). Cutoff criteria for fit indexes in covariance structure analysis: Conventional criteria verses new alternatives. *Structural Equation Modeling, 6*, 1-55.

Kelly, G. (1996). *Sense of community in two communities of elderly people*. Unpublished thesis, Curtin University, Perth.

Johnson, M. A., & Mullins, P. (1990). Moral communities: Religious and secular. *Journal of Community Psychology, 18*, 153-166.

Kirkpatrick, F. G. (1986). *Community: A trinity of models*. Washington, DC: Georgetown University Press.

Lounsbury, J. W., & DeNeui (1996). Collegiate psychological sense of community in relation to size of college/university and extroversion. *Journal of Community Psychology, 24*, 381-394.

McMillan, D. W. (1996). Sense of community. *Journal of Community Psychology, 24*, 315-325.

McMillan, D. W., & Chavis, D. M. (1986). Sense of community: A definition and theory. *Journal of Community Psychology, 14*, 6-23.

Miles, M. B., & Huberman, A. M. (1994). *Qualitative data analysis: An expanded sourcebook* (2nd Edition). Thousand Oaks, CA: Sage.

Mitchell, C. M., & Beals, J. (1997). The structure and positive behavior among American adolescents: Gender and community differences. *American Journal of Community Psychology, 25*, 257-288.

Pepper S. C. (1942). *World hypotheses*. Berkeley, CA: University of California Press.

Newbrough, J. R. (1995). Toward community: A third position. *American Journal of Community Psychology, 23*, 9-37.

Pargament, K. I. (1983). The psychological climate of religious congregations. *American Journal of Community Psychology, 11*, 351-381.

Pretty, G. M. (1990). Relating psychological sense of community to social climate characteristics. *Journal of Community Psychology, 18*, 60-65.

Pretty, G. M. H. & McCarthy, M. (1991). Exploring psychological sense of community among women and men of the corporation. *Journal of Community Psychology, 19*, 351-361.

Pretty, G. M. H., Conroy, C. Dugay, J., Fowler, K. & Williams, D. (1996). Sense of community and its relevance to adolescents of all ages. *Journal of Community, 24*, 365-379.

Richards, L. (2000). *Using NVivo in qualitative research*. Bundoora, Vic.: QSR International.

Royal, M. A., & Rossi, R. J. (1996). Individual-level correlates of sense of community: Findings from workplace and school. *Journal of Community Psychology, 24,* 395-416.

Sarason, S. B. (1973). Jewishness, blackishness, and the nature-nurture controversy. *American Psychologist, 28,* 962-971.

Sarason, S. B. (1974). *The psychological sense of community: Prospects for a community psychology.* San Francisco: Jossey-Bass.

Sarason, S. B. (2000). Barometers of community change: Personal reflections. In J. Rappaport and E. Seidman (Eds.), *Handbook of community psychology.* New York: Kluwer Academic/Plenum.

Schumcker, R. E., & Lomax, R. G. (1996). *A beginner's guide to structural equation modeling.* Hillsdale, NJ: Lawrence Erlbaum.

Tönnies, F. (1957). *Community and society* (C. P. Loomis, Trans.). New York: Harper.

Chapter 15

NEIGHBORHOOD SENSE OF COMMUNITY AND SOCIAL CAPITAL
A Multi-Level Analysis[i]

Douglas D. Perkins and D. Adam Long
Vanderbilt University

INTRODUCTION

In many ways, social capital (SC) is to political science, sociology, applied economics, and community development what sense of community (SOC) and empowerment have been to community psychology. SC is the norms, networks, and mutual trust of "civil society" facilitating cooperative action among citizens and institutions (Coleman, 1988) and has had considerable influence on political thinking and action over the past decade. It is generally observed and analyzed as a characteristic (or lack) of communities or societies, rather than individuals.

By contrast, SOC has been conceived of and measured by most researchers as an individual-level construct. Some studies have examined it at the group or community level (Buckner, 1988; Fisher & Sonn, 1999; Kingston, Mitchell, Florin, & Stevenson, 1999; Perkins, Brown, & Taylor, 1996; Perkins, Florin, Rich, Wandersman, & Chavis, 1990; Sampson, 1991). A very few have used it in multi-level analyses (Brodsky, O'Campo, & Aronson, 1999; Hyde, 1998; Kingston, et al., 1999; Perkins & Long, 2001; Sampson, 1991). But we found no previous study that analyzed sense of community at multiple levels simultaneously to see whether it operates differently at each level.

We have four main goals for this chapter. One is to inform researchers and program planners in community development, urban policy, and social services that many concepts thoroughly studied by community psychologists (sense of community, collective efficacy/empowerment, citizen participation, neighboring) are part of SC. Our second goal is to introduce more community psychologists to SC. Third, to both audiences, we expect to show that residential neighborhood sense of community is at least as strongly related to other SC dimensions as are demographics and other widely studied community-focused cognitions (place attachment, community satisfaction, community confidence, and communitarianism -- or community values). In addition to those interdisciplinary aims, our fourth goal is to explore SOC and its relationships to SC using multi-level analysis. The relationship between SOC and SC -- whether they operate together, separately, or nested one within the other -- and on what level(s) they operate are critical to our understanding of both concepts.

Social Capital: Community-Focused Cognitions and Behaviors

In observing that Americans are generally now "bowling alone" rather than in the leagues so popular a generation ago, Putnam (2000) was less concerned with the disappearance of recreational clubs, *per se*, than what he saw as the loss of the glue that binds together the social fabric of our local communities and, ultimately, our society. His obituary for the American community may be exaggerated, but the importance of SC to the functioning and quality of community life seems indisputable.

The bipartisan and multidisciplinary popularity of SC has led to many different, and often vague, definitions. Until recently, psychologists have largely ignored SC despite, or perhaps because of, its being little more than a collection of more specific community-focused behaviors and cognitions long studied by community psychologists. We, therefore, may be skeptical of a term from outside the discipline which seems to cover ground we feel we already know well, and for which there appears to be no clear, precise, and agreed upon meaning. The only advantage we see in SC, as a construct, is that it speaks to economists and policy makers and draws their attention to non-economic assets (Kretzmann & McKnight, 1993). But that is also the danger in SC: as with empowerment (Perkins, 1995), anti-government neo-conservatives are co-opting SC to justify reducing public spending on critical social services under the misguided assumption that the overburdened private community service sector can suffice. As SC seems to have strong appeal and staying power, the challenge to researchers is to try to unpack the construct and make it as useful as possible while being fully aware of the political ramifications: that is, what issues can SC address directly and, where government intervention is required, how can SC be turned into political clout?

Given the expanse of theory and research on SOC over more than a quarter-century,[ii] it may provide the greatest contribution to understanding SC. Yet much of the usage of the term SOC is also vague and counterproductive. The original subtitle of this chapter was "All the things you are" to make the point that, similar to "community" and "empowerment" (Perkins, 1995), both SC and SOC have meant, if not all things to all people, then too much and too varied to too many.

While there is power in such ambiguity, SC would benefit conceptually, empirically, and practically from a more precise definition. In particular, it is important to measure and analyze the specific behavioral and intrapsychic dimensions of SC separately to gain a clearer understanding of what aspects of SC operate in what ways and under what conditions. There is a critical need to dissect, examine, and understand, not only the differences between various forms of SC, but also the many different factors and processes that make up, and are related to, each form. Only with careful attention to the construct and predictive validity of SC can we develop a more psychological and complex, yet clearly defined, conception of SC.

Dimensions of Social Capital

Saegert and Winkel (1998) were among the first psychologists to study SC, and found that it significantly predicted the successful revitalization and maintenance of distressed inner-city housing. They distinguish two measures of informal SC (neighboring and perceived pro-social norms) and two formal factors (leadership activity and basic voluntary participation). The emphasis on leadership is particularly important, especially for maintaining the momentum and effectiveness of voluntary organizations. Neighboring is the instrumental help we provide, or get from, other community members (e.g., watching after a neighbor's house or child; Perkins, et al., 1990; 1996; Unger & Wandersman, 1985). Ordinary social interaction with one's neighbors, especially as it encourages more community involvement, either formally or informally, may also be included as a form of neighboring.

We appreciate, and generally agree with, the utility of Saegert and Winkel's (1998) and Putnam's (2000) emphasis on behavioral definitions of SC; but as long as the dimensions are analyzed separately, there may be some added utility in considering possible intrapsychic dimensions or predictors. Community psychologists have researched many attitudes, emotions, and perceptions related to SC. The most exhaustive attention has been paid to two constructs: empowerment (Perkins, et al., 1996; Saegert & Winkel, 1996; Speer & Hughey, 1995) and SOC. Empowerment is about perceived control. A primary benefit of SOC is social support from one's community. (Briggs (1998) identified social leverage (information) and other forms of social support as key dimensions of SC. Thus, SC provides at least three forms of social support: communal (SOC), instrumental (neighboring), and informational. The fourth form of support, emotional, may also be involved, depending on the quality of one's relationships with community members.) Control and social support are two of the strongest and most consistent predictors of positive individual outcomes. The same may be true of community-level outcomes as well.

Thus, we define SC in terms of four distinct components: (1) trust in one's neighbors (SOC) and (2) in the efficacy of organized collective action (empowerment), (3) informal neighboring behavior, and (4) formal participation in community organizations (see Figure 1). This four-part definition adds the idea of formal and informal community "trust" to formal and informal pro-social community behaviors (cf. Saegert & Winkel, 1998). SOC and collective efficacy are the cognitive or intrapsychic components of SC. Citizen participation in grassroots community organizations and neighboring are the behavioral components of SC. Each dimension of SC is consistently related to the others.

	Cognition/Trust	Social Behavior
Informal	Sense of community	Neighboring
Formally Organized	Collective efficacy	Citizen participation

Figure 1. Four Dimensions Of Social Capital

Sense of community is a consistent and widely valued indicator of quality of community life and a catalyst for both behavioral dimensions of SC: organized participation and informal neighboring (Beckman, et al., 1998; Chavis & Wandersman, 1990; Hughey, Speer, & Peterson, 1999; Perkins, et al., 1996; Wandersman & Giamartino, 1980). The link between organized participation and SOC has been found at both the individual and community levels of analysis (Brodsky, et al., 1999; Perkins, et al., 1996). It makes sense that a group of residents must have at least some SOC to be interested in organizing an association and working together to solve common problems (Ahlbrandt, 1984). Chavis and Wandersman (1990) found that, over time, SOC leads to greater self- and collective-efficacy and neighboring, which all increase participation. Their results suggest that participation, in turn, enhances SOC. SOC has also been related to community satisfaction, collective efficacy, neighboring, communitarianism, and informal social control, less fear of crime, litter and graffiti (Perkins, et al., 1990) and better-maintained yards (Varady, 1986).

Interest in SOC has been international as have empirical findings on its psychometric properties (Chipuer & Pretty, 1999: Australia) and its relationship to participation and neighboring (Garcia, Giuliani, & Wiesenfeld, 1999: Venezuela; Itzhaky, & York, 2000: Israel; Prezza, Amici,

Roberti, & Tedeschi, 2001: Italy), type of common land (Li, 1998: Taiwan), investment in home and community building processes (Garcia, et al., 1999: Venezuela), community satisfaction and local friendships (Sampson, 1991: U.K.); life satisfaction and loneliness (Prezza, et al., 2001: Italy), minority community identity (Sonn & Fisher, 1998: Australia), and university residence social climate and well-being (Pretty, 1990; Pretty, Conroy, Dugay, Fowler, & Williams, 1996: Canada).

Collective efficacy, or trust in the effectiveness of organized community action, is closest to the concept of empowerment among all the social capital dimensions and their predictors. Some definitions of individual psychological empowerment are little different from traditional theories of self-efficacy or locus of control. In order to distinguish it from those concepts, we argue that a necessary component of empowerment, even at the individual level, should be its connection to collective action and organizational and community levels of empowerment. Empowerment is thought both to lead to participation in community organizations and to result from it. Perceived efficacy of collective action is important for maintaining participation in a community organization (Florin & Wandersman, 1984; Perkins, et al., 1990; 1996) and may be important for initiating it.

Note that our definition of collective efficacy differs importantly from that of Sampson, Raudenbush, and Earls (1997). They define it as "social cohesion among neighbors combined with their willingness to intervene on behalf of the common good" (p. 918) and operationalize it as a combination of SOC and informal social control (ISC).[iii] We do not adopt this definition because (1) we think it conceptually sound to separate the intrapsychic and more general SOC from the narrower, more behavioral ISC and (2) collective efficacy should be an appraisal of group behavior that is, as the term suggests, both collectively organized and efficacious. ISC is, by definition, unorganized and is undemocratic, unrelated to formal participation (Perkins, et al., 1990), and inconsistently effective in reducing crime (Perkins, Wandersman, Rich, & Taylor, 1993).

Neighboring behavior is informal mutual assistance and information sharing among neighbors. In a stress and coping framework, it can be considered a form of local "instrumental social support." Some researchers include non-instrumental social contact as neighboring (e.g., Brown & Perkins, 2001). All forms of neighboring allow residents to become better acquainted and discuss shared problems (Unger & Wandersman, 1985). Prezza, et al. (2001) found that women, long-term residents, those with more children, those living with a spouse, those with less education, and members of community groups had more neighboring relationships. Unger and Wandersman (1983), using a similar survey measure of neighboring to that used in the present study, found that greater neighboring prior to organizing a block may facilitate subsequent efforts towards forming a block association. In turn, they found that once a block organized, association members engaged in more social interaction, which may lead to more neighboring. Perkins, et al. (1996) found that neighboring was, generally, the strongest single predictor of participation in community organizations in three cities, cross-sectionally and one year later, at both the individual and block levels of analysis.

It is surprising that, despite the important role of neighboring to the quality of community life, so few studies have related neighboring to other community-focused behaviors and cognitions. Brown and Werner (1985) found neighboring to be related to community satisfaction. In Time-1 of the present data, controlling for demographics, block-level neighboring was related to participation, sense of community, communitarianism, block satisfaction, and informal social control (Perkins, et al., 1990).

Citizen participation in block, neighborhood, and building (tenant or co-op) associations, faith-based community service or advocacy committees and coalitions, school-based associations, and other grassroots community organizations are examples of formal social capital behavior. These organizations address a wide variety of local needs, from housing, planning and traffic issues to cleaning up residential property, vacant lots, and parks to youth and recreation programs and block parties to crime prevention.

Research on civic participation has been a staple of sociology and political science from their beginning (or even longer: Tocqueville, 1935/ 1969). But the emphasis in much of the research has been on demographic predictors. For example, replicating their own 1958 study, Hyman and Wright (1971) found that greater resources (income), investment in the community (home ownership, length of residence) and skills and knowledge (education) motivate or permit greater participation. More recently, poor and middle-class mothers' participation in block clubs, neighborhood or tenant groups, and other community organizations was associated with greater education and income, but not with age, employment, marital status, number of children, or tenure in neighborhood (Rankin & Quane, 2000).

The psychological research on participation generally controls for these demographic differences, but goes beyond them to find that participants, and their organizations and communities, have a greater sense of collective efficacy or empowerment (Florin & Wandersman, 1984; Perkins, et al., 1996; Saegert & Winkel, 1996; Speer & Hughey, 1995), SOC (Chavis & Wandersman, 1990; Perkins & Long, 2001), neighboring (Perkins, et al., 1996; Unger & Wandersman, 1985), community satisfaction (Perkins, et al., 1990), and other positive community attachments and organizational activities (Perkins, et al., 1996).

Psychological Predictors of Social Capital

Place attachment is an important construct in its relationship to SOC and SC, but one that is often overlooked by community psychologists. It refers to emotional bonding, developed over time from behavioral, affective, and cognitive ties to a particular socio-physical environment (Brown & Perkins, 1992). These bonds are integral to individual and community aspects of self-identity and provide a source of stability and change for individuals and communities alike. Place attachments are a resource that individuals (especially women, minorities, lower-income people, and elders) and communities can draw on to help revitalize all aspects of home and neighborhood environments (Brown & Perkins, 2001; Saegert, 1989).

Politically, place attachment may motivate residents to participate in community organizations (Saegert, 1989). Participation, at both the individual and community levels, also leads to greater community attachment (Zhao, 1996). Socially, place attachment can help bring residents together to address social problems as well as environmental threats (Brown & Perkins, 1992). Economically, where residents, through their history in, and attachments to, a place discover what is unique about their community, they can preserve or develop places and events that generate tourism and other business opportunities. Those who feel no particular attachment to the place they live invest little time, energy, or money in it and are more likely to move (Vinsel, Brown, Altman, & Foss, 1980).

Place attachment and SOC are closely related. The Sense of Community Index includes four items measuring attachment to place (one's block; in the present analyses, these items were removed to create a new place attachment scale). The two constructs were combined with block satisfaction and knowing one's neighbors in an analysis of participation in neighborhood improvement organizations (Perkins, et al., 1996). In all three cities studied, that combination was significantly correlated with participation at the individual and block levels, both cross-sectionally and over a one-year lag. In multivariate analyses, however, it was a significant predictor in two cities and only at the individual level.

Cuba and Hummon (1993) identify three loci of place identity -- home, community, and region -- and find that *formal* organizational participation, not sense of community, is key to community identity. Puddifoot (1996) argues that psychological theory supports the analysis of "community identity," based on a combination of place identity or attachment, SOC, and community satisfaction. Pretty (this volume) expands on that argument, suggesting that SOC and place attachment are part of the same overarching self-in-community psychological framework with emotional, cognitive, spiritual, and behavioral dimensions all contributing to the development of individuals' community identity.

Despite these connections, we view place attachment as distinct from SOC because the former is a spatially-oriented emotional construct (Brown & Perkins, 1992) and the latter is more of a socially-oriented cognitive construct. Furthermore, keeping the concepts separate allows us to consider how one may lead to the other or whether different community changes might affect place and social attachments differently. For example, there is intriguing evidence that SOC may be encouraged by "New Urbanist" planned communities that minimize the impact of automobile traffic and emphasize walkable, mixed residential/commercial space (Nasar & Julian, 1995; Plas & Lewis, 1996). But more research is needed to determine whether SOC gains are due to increased social interaction in private and public outdoor spaces, increased place attachment, both, or neither (people attracted to New Urbanist communities may be predisposed to more SOC).

Community Satisfaction is also related to place: Brown and Werner's (1985) research showing that block satisfaction and neighboring behaviors are related also found such community ties to be stronger on cul-de-sacs than through streets. Perkins, et al. (1990) found block satisfaction to be higher on blocks with more attached homes as well as SOC, collective efficacy, and neighboring and (surprisingly) *fewer* trees, gardens and shrubs as well as less criminal victimization, disorder, and fear. Block satisfaction was also the strongest predictor of block association (BA) participation in their multivariate analyses. It remains to be seen whether that relationship was as strong at Time 2 and in a multilevel analysis at both times.

Chavis and Wandersman (1990) also found block satisfaction to be associated with BA participation, neighboring, collective efficacy, and SOC. Using data from the same Nashville project, Florin and Wandersman (1984) found perceived community problems and community dissatisfaction to load as one factor and so combined them into "encoding strategies," which was modestly associated with individual BA participation. But satisfaction is very different than a lack of perceived problems. In fact, Perkins, et al. (1990) found that two of the strongest predictors of participation were community satisfaction and *more* perceived disorder (again, a physical environmental concern). Residents who are very attached to their community may have high satisfaction, but because they care about it so much, they are also the most critical of community problems.

Communitarianism is the value placed on one's community and on working collectively to improve it (Perkins, et al., 1990). This is the original meaning before Etzioni (1993) politicized the term as a compromise position among competing ideologies of autonomous individualism *vs.* communal socialism and Liberalism *vs.* Conservativism. If residents participate more in communities they value, a communitarian climate should encourage greater collective participation. Florin and Wandersman (1984) used the cognitive social learning concept of "subjective stimulus values" to encompass a variety of constructs, including communitarianism, self-efficacy, collective efficacy, and SOC. This composite predicted individual participation in BAs far better than any other variable they considered. At the block level of analysis, Perkins, et al. (1990) found communitarianism alone to be related to blocks with more minorities, less income, more home owners, neighboring, collective efficacy, and to various features of the block physical environment, but only marginally to SOC, and not significantly to participation in BAs.

Community Confidence is another vital cognition, especially in older neighborhoods that may be deteriorating and considered "transitional" due to changes in local businesses or residential demography (income, tenure, racial composition; Ahlbrandt 1984; Varady, 1986). As residents perceive their neighborhood declining, if they still have confidence in its future, they may stay and upgrade their own property and pressure neighbors and the city to do likewise. A lack of community confidence, however, may spell commercial and residential disinvestment and flight and may explain why many urban policies and revitalization projects have failed (Varady, 1986). As other, more objective, development indicators -- such as building permits, residential stability, higher owner occupancy and property values -- are slower to appear, confidence is considered by many to be a benchmark indicator of a community's capacity to revitalize.

Varady (1986) examined the impact of a major federal "urban homesteading" program on neighborhood confidence and property upgrading. Program spillover effects on neighbors' upgrading and confidence were negligible. Nor were home improvements related to confidence at the individual/household level, a result confirmed in a more recent study (Brown & Perkins, 2001). But neighborhoods in better physical condition had residents who were more confident about the future of the neighborhood (Varady, 1986). Confidence was also associated with neighboring, SOC, and resident decisions to move or stay.

MULTI-LEVEL ANALYSIS OF SENSE OF COMMUNITY

Almost all studies of SOC, other community cognitions, or social capital behaviors (as opposed to organizations), while targeting the block, neighborhood, or vaguely defined community level, have analyzed *individual level data*. There is no doubt that we need more and better data collected at the community level (Fisher & Sonn, 1999; Puddifoot, 1996; Shinn, 1990; Theodori, 2000). But another approach to more ecologically valid research is multi-level analysis. Social scientists have long aggregated individual perceptions to the group level to create contextual or social climate variables. With the advent of multi-level analytic statistical programs, this practice is becoming even more common. Yet psychologists' individualistic bias has made us slower to respond to these powerful new techniques. The criteria for validating aggregate individual perceptions as group climate variables are clear and simple, however (Shinn, 1990). Climate variables must (1) exhibit adequate inter-rater agreement among members of the same group, (2) show reliable differentiation, or variance, between groups, and (3) correlate significantly with other variables at the group or individual level.

There have been just a few recent multilevel studies of SOC. Brodsky, et al. (1999) used multilevel analysis to identify individual- and community-level predictors of *individual* SOC, but they only compared three communities and do not report the extent to which SOC varies at the community level. Kingston, et al. (1999) show that perceptions of neighborhood climate (SOC) vary at the community level. But possibly due to (a) low neighborhood-level variance, (b) low statistical power at that level, and (c) using dichotomous predictors, they fail to find a significant correlation between SOC and either neighborhood organization or the boundedness of the neighborhood by arterial streets. Their results show the importance of an adequate sample size at the group as well as individual level in multi-level analysis. Sampson (1991) used a British nation-wide sample in finding that neighborhood-level social cohesion increases individuals' community satisfaction (independent of personal characteristics).

A multi-level study by Hyde (1998) made, we believe, another important advance by analyzing SOC and place attachment separately. She found significant neighborhood-level variance in both. She also found that both resident perceptions of disorder and independently assessed disorder predicted SOC and place attachment, suggesting that physical and social conditions of place influence community attachments. Similarly, using the present data, Perkins and Long (2001) found that between 9% and 30% of variance in individual-level SOC was due to block-level differences and that SOC was predicted by place attachment and other community-focused cognitions and behaviors at both the block and individual levels.

None of the above, however, has considered SOC at multiple levels simultaneously. Multi-level analysis is critical to determine how, and how much, SC is manifested at the community level vs. the individual level. This could lead to better targeted interventions to encourage the right form of SC for a given community or a particular group of its individual members. In addition, it can identify differences in SC dimensions among individuals with different social attitudes and demographic profiles living in communities with different levels of social cohesion and place attachment. (For example, what does it mean to have a strong SOC in a community where that is not shared versus one where it is?) And it can address the critical question of whether, controlling for individual and/or community demographics, individuals engage in more or less formal SC in communities with more informal cohesion. That is, do communities with more SOC encourage, not only neighboring, but also more collective efficacy and voluntarism, or does it tend to replace and thus lessen the formal forms of SC?

We aim to unpack the broadly defined and loosely understood concept by examining the construct validity of the various dimensions of SC and other variables that are related to SOC and how they are inter-related. We will present a new analysis of one of the major studies of SOC, blocks, and block associations (Perkins, et al., 1990).

Community Cognitions and Social Capital: Reanalyzing the Block Booster Data

The present data were collected as part of the Block Booster Project, a two-year (1985-86), multimethod, action study of the social effects, organizational dynamics, and viability of urban residential BAs (Chavis, Florin, Rich, Wandersman, & Perkins, 1987). The purposes of the Project were to: (1) examine the role of BAs in community development and crime control and (2) develop an intervention process and set of training materials to help voluntary associations maintain and strengthen themselves. Clustered, resident survey data from 47 street blocks (the homes fronting on the same street between two cross streets or a cross street and dead end) in five neighborhoods in Brooklyn and Queens, New York, permit comparisons over two points in time (T1 n = 1,081, T2 n = 638, panel = 438) using multilevel analyses (HLM) of the constructs as both individual psychological and community climate phenomena. (For details of the site selection, sampling, and survey methods, see Perkins, et al., 1990.)

Measures

The following scales were confirmed in principal components analyses (PCA) as distinct and coherent constructs. All predictors were standardized. To reduce skewness, variables were transformed using either the square root (number of children, neighboring, participation) or the exponential method (length of residence, SOC, place attachment, communitarianism, collective efficacy). This was not done in previous publications of these data (Perkins, et al., 1990; 1993; 1996). All four SC dimension scales (Sense of Community, Collective Efficacy, Participation, and Neighboring), items, and reliabilities are displayed in Appendix A. Most items were dichotomous, which lowered the internal consistency of all scales, we recommend Likert response scales be used in future. (More information on the creation of scales and their descriptive statistics is available from the authors.)

Brief Sense of Community Index (BSCI) is a new eight-item scale adapted in part from the 12-item Sense of Community Index (SCI; Perkins, et al., 1990).[iv] PCAs confirmed SOC as distinct from neighboring behavior, informal social control, block satisfaction, and communitarianism. But a PCA of the SCI alone failed to confirm McMillan and Chavis' (1986) dimensions of emotional connection, group membership, needs fulfillment, and influence. One or two factors, which cut across their framework, is, we argue, a separate construct, that is, place attachment. After removing four place attachment items, we added three face-valid SOC items to a second PCA. Three of the original items failed to load cleanly on a single factor and were removed. The remaining eight items form the new BSCI and were included in a third PCA resulting in three subscales, confirmed across two surveys: social connections, mutual concern, and community values (Perkins & Long, 2001). Only the total scale was used here.

Place attachment (α (Time 1) = .65, n = 903; α (Time 2) = .63, n = 480) is the mean of four items removed from the SCI (true/false): I think my block is a good place for me to live; I feel at home on this block; it is very important to me to live on this particular block; I expect to live on this block for a long time.

Communitarianism (α = .56, n = 1,053; .62, n = 624) is the value placed on one's community and on working collectively to improve it. Unlike Perkins, et al. (1990), it was measured using the mean of just two items: the importance to the respondent of what their block is like and the importance of neighbors working together rather than alone to improve block conditions (not important, somewhat important, very important).

Community (block) satisfaction (α = .36, n = 946; .39, n = 613) was measured here using the mean of just two items: satisfaction with the block as a place to live (satisfied/dissatisfied) and, compared to adjacent blocks, whether the block is a better or worse place to live or about the same as other blocks in the area. Using the same data, the satisfaction scale by Perkins, et al. (1990) combined these items with the following two.

Block confidence (α = .62 n = 923; .63, n = 567) was measured using the mean of two items: "In the past two years, have the general conditions on your block gotten worse, stayed about the same, or improved" and "in the next two years, do you feel that general conditions on your block will get worse, stay about the same, or improve."

Demographic variables. The present analyses included the following control variables: sex, age, income level, education, race, length of residence, home ownership, and number of children in household.

In order to examine the relationship of SOC, relative to other community-focused cognitions and demographics, to SC, all the above were used to predict each of the other three dimensions of SC (see Appendix A):

Collective efficacy was measured here using the mean of six items: whether it is "not likely, somewhat likely, or very likely" the respondent's BA (or a hypothetical association on unorganized blocks) can accomplish improvement of physical conditions, the persuasion of city officials to provide better services, getting people on the block to help each other more, a reduction in crime, getting people to know each other better, and getting information to residents about where to go for needed services.

Participation in BA activities was a sum of eight items coded zero to one (all but one item were yes/no): membership and participation in a BA, whether the respondent had attended, spoken in, served as member or officer in a BA meeting, or done work for the organization outside a meeting in the past year, and monthly hours working for the BA outside of meetings.

Neighboring behavior was measured using the mean of five items indicating how many neighbors (none, one or two, or several) asked: to watch their home while they were away, to loan food or a tool, to help in an emergency, to offer advice on a personal problem, and to discuss a block problem. (This differs from the scale by Perkins, et al. (1990) who used block aggregates only, including neighboring received as well as given.)

Individual and Block-Level Bivariate Correlations

Table 1 presents individual and block mean level bivariate correlations at both time points for the four dimensions of SC (collective efficacy, participation, neighboring, SOC), the other four informal community cognitions (place attachment, communitarianism, block satisfaction, block confidence), and eight demographics (number of children, age, education, white ethnicity, income, sex, resident tenure, home ownership). Below the diagonal are individual-level coefficients, above the diagonal are block mean aggregated coefficients; these cells display cross-sectional coefficients at both time points as follows: T1/T2. On the diagonal are displayed the T1 by T2 correlations for the respective variables (for data available at both time points); each cell on the diagonal displays coefficients as follows: individual-level/block-level. Coefficients are displayed only if significant at $p < .05$ for individual-level correlations and $p < .10$ for block-level correlations. (It is common to relax the significance criterion when analyzing group data, which tend to be more stable than individual-level data (Kenny & LaVoie, 1985).

Interestingly, there is virtually no correlation between collective efficacy and neighboring. Otherwise, the correlations among the four dimensions of SC are significant, suggesting some internal consistency to the overarching construct. Participation in BAs (individual $r = .68$, block-level $r = .87$) and SOC (individual $r = .58$, block $r = .77$) were both highly correlated between T1 and T2. The correlations between T1 and T2 for the other SC scales (collective efficacy and neighboring) and other predictors were also significant, with block confidence being the least stable. The five substantive predictors (SOC, place attachment, communitarianism, block satisfaction, block confidence) also showed some intercorrelation. As expected, the relationship between SOC and place attachment was strongest (individual $r = .40$(T1), .51(T2); block $r = .73$(T1), .63(T2)). However, communitarianism was not significantly related to block satisfaction, confidence, or (at the block level) place attachment. SOC was the only predictor to correlate significantly with all the other community cognitions at both levels.

Table 1. Social Capital Variables and Predictors: Individual Correlations Below Diagonal/Block Above (Decimal points deleted)

	DEPENDENT VARIABLES			DEMOGRAPHICS						INDEPENDENT VARIABLES						
	1	2	3	4	5	6	7	8	9	10	11	12	13	14	15	16
1. Collective Efficacy	**27/28**	29/ns		38/ns		-36/ns	-31/ns					34/49	ns/55	52/38	ns/36	ns/26
2. Participation	19/25	**68/87**	39/59				ns/-25	ns/-23			ns/21	54/54	25/ns		ns/32	34/23
3. Neighboring	07/ns	32/37	**38/56**							36/38	38/34	47/63	39/39	29/ns		ns/35
4. Children	09/ns	07/ns	10/ns		-46		-44	-27	26	-44/-36			42/31		ns/-22	-28/ns
5. Age	ns/21	12/ns		-28		-23	40	26		50/50						
6. Education	-11/ns		06/ns		-22			36						-49/-28		
7. White Ethnicity	-13/ns	-07/-14		-24		10		36	-24				ns/36	-59/-39	26/ns	31/ns
8. Income		13/ns	15/ns			36	15		-24						28/ns	
9. Sex	ns/13					-06		-18								
10. Length-Residence		21/13	24/24	-12/-16	45/42	-10/ns	14/13	20/13		**83/68**	47/55	52/26	59/34	ns/29	ns/29	
11. Homeowner		26/24	30/25	09/ns	21/23		-13/ns			42/47	**83/85**	36/22		25/ns		
12. Sense-Community	26/42	36/33	42/37		13/17	-16/-12		08/ns		23/17		**58/77**	**73/63**	ns/29	37/49	29/28
13. Place Attachment	12/33	15/14	18/19	06/10	20/27	-12/-08	07/ns			19/16	40/51		**37/50**	17/23	31/65	43/47
14. Communitarian	30/37	14/19	16/20		13/15		-17/-14	-08/-10	ns/12	09/09		27/36		**33/50**		
15. Block Satisfaction	ns/14	ns/11	ns/11			07/ns			-06/ns			17/29	23/37		**23/45**	39/34
16. Block Confidence	16/28	17/14	09/13		09/ns	12/ns						27/24	27/31		31/28	**26/20**

The diagonal cells are Time-1 by Time-2 autocorrelations. Significant coefficients at p < .05 in bold. For most demographics, autocorrelations were not possible and intercorrelations are only at one point in time, as they were asked only at T1 or T2. For the off-diagonal cells, correlations are arranged as follows: Time-1 / Time-2. All coefficients printed are statistically significant at p < .05 or better at the individual level or p < .10 or better, block level; empty cells denote no significant correlation at T1 or T2.

Of all the predictors, none showed greater or more reliable (i.e., significant at both T1 and T2) correlations with all three dependent variables than did SOC (individual-level r = .26 to .42; block-level r = .34 to .63). Like SOC, place attachment, communitarianism, and block confidence showed significant and reliable correlations to all three dimensions of SC at the individual level. Due to the much smaller n of blocks than individuals, several of the corresponding block-level correlations, although larger, were nonsignificant at either T1 or T2. Curiously, block satisfaction correlated significantly with the three dimensions of SC at T2, but not at T1. This is particularly surprising given the finding by Perkins, et al. (1990) that block satisfaction was one of the strongest block-level predictors of participation at T1, albeit moreso in multivariate than bivariate analyses. Both variables were computed differently in the present analysis, however. (In Perkins, et al. (1990), participation included items from a BA member survey and satisfaction included block confidence items.)

Among demographics, home ownership and residential stability were the strongest correlates of SC -- both were significantly related to participation, neighboring, and SOC, but not to collective efficacy. Other demographic effects were less consistent. Nonwhite residents and blocks showed more collective efficacy at T1 (only), but more participation at T2. In contrast, individual older residents participated more at T1, but felt more collective efficacy at T2. Individuals and blocks with more children and (unexpectedly) less education felt *more* collective efficacy at T1.

Multilevel Models Predicting Social Capital Dimensions

In a series of HLMs, SOC and four other community-focused cognitions (place attachment, communitarianism, block satisfaction, and community confidence), at block and individual levels, and individual-level demographics were tested for their ability to predict collective efficacy, informal neighboring, and formally organized citizen participation. Each of the three dependent variables was predicted cross-sectionally at two points in time, about a year apart, see Table 2).[v]

Collective Efficacy Time 1. In the HLM predicting collective efficacy at T1, about six percent (p < .001) of the total variance in individuals' sense of the efficacy of BAs was due to block differences. The only significant block-level predictors were SOC and communitarianism. At the individual level, communitarianism, SOC, block confidence, block satisfaction, and education were significant. Surprisingly, block satisfaction and education were associated with *less* collective efficacy. The model explains approximately 50% of block differences in collective efficacy and 13% of individual variance. In testing for random effects among the individual-level substantive predictors, SOC was significant (p < .01), indicating that the slope of the relationship between efficacy and SOC varies across blocks. In an effort to explain that variation, we tested for significant cross-level interactions with SOC, but none were found.

Collective Efficacy Time 2. At T2, just over 7% (p < .01) of the total variance in individual collective efficacy occurred at the block level. SOC and communitarianism were again significant block-level predictors, but this time, so too is block confidence. At the individual level, SOC, communitarianism, block confidence, minority status, and length of residence were significant. Surprisingly, newer residents showed greater collective efficacy. The model explains 99% of block differences in efficacy and 25% of individual variance. There were no random effects.

Table 2. Block and individual-level sense of community and other predictors of three social capital factors at two points in time: Hierarchical linear models

	Collective Efficacy		Participation		Neighboring	
	Time 1	Time 2	Time 1	Time 2	Time 1	Time 2
Block Level: Approx. df	44	40	42	57	42	58
% total variance at block level	5.7***	7.3**	30.5***	40.0***	3.0**	7.2***
% block variance explained	49.4	99.0	40.0	45.4	82.0	95.0
Intercept	13.80***	12.81***	1.01***	0.77***	1.15***	1.12***
Sense of Community	1.23*	2.21**	1.36***	1.32***	0.17*	0.29***
Place Attachment			-0.96**	-0.93***		
Communitarianism	2.71***	1.98*			0.11#	
Block Satisfaction			-0.45#		-0.17*	
Block Confidence		2.62***	0.80**	0.56**	0.14*	0.14#
Individual level: Approx. df	1,022	303	996	555	1,060	625
% individual variance explained	13.0	25.2	20.6	16.4	20.9	15.9
Children			0.09***		0.05*	
Age			0.10**			-0.09***
Education	-0.31*		0.07*	0.09**	0.06***	
White Ethnicity		-0.53*				
Income			0.08*			
Length of Residence		-0.58*	0.12***		0.07**	0.10***
Home Owner			0.13***	0.18***	0.08***	0.08**
Sense of Community	0.87***	1.84***	0.24***	0.20***	0.22***	0.16***
Place Attachment						
Communitarianism	1.23***	1.14***	0.06*	0.12**		0.05*
Block Satisfaction	-0.46*				-0.04*	
Block Confidence	0.86***	0.83**				

Note: Fixed effects unstandardized coefficients. #$p<.10$, *$p\leq.05$, **$p\leq.01$, ***$p\leq.001$.

Participation Time 1. In the HLM predicting T1 participation, about 31% ($p < .001$) of the total variance in individuals' participation in BAs is due to block differences. Significant block-level predictors include SOC, place attachment, block satisfaction, and block confidence. Unlike the bivariate correlations, which were modestly positive or nonsignificant, in the HLM, block-level place attachment and satisfaction were associated with *less* participation. At the individual level, SOC, communitarianism, number of children, age, education, income, resident tenure, and home ownership were significant. The model explains 40% of block differences in participation and 21% of individual variance.

In testing for random effects, individual-level SOC was significant ($p < .01$), with four significant cross-level interactions emerging. On blocks with more children, more educated residents, more long-term residents, and low communitarianism, the positive relation between SOC and participation was stronger than elsewhere.

Participation Time 2. In the HLM predicting participation at T2, 40% ($p < .001$) of the total variance in individuals' participation in BAs was due to block differences. Significant block-level predictors again included SOC, place attachment, and block confidence, but block satisfaction was nonsignificant at T2. Block-level place attachment was again associated with *less* participation. At the individual level, SOC, communitarianism, education, and home ownership were significant. The model explains approximately 45% of block differences in participation and 16% of individual variance.

In testing for random effects, individual-level communitarianism emerged as significant ($p < .05$). Four significant cross-level interactions were identified to help explain the variation in slopes across blocks. Communitarianism and participation were virtually unrelated on most blocks (even marginally negatively related on some). However, on blocks with few children, blocks with younger residents, blocks with more ethnic minority residents, and those with more long-term residents, the relation between communitarianism and participation was positive and much stronger.

Neighboring Time 1. In the HLM predicting neighboring at T1, three percent ($p < .01$) of the total variance in individuals' neighboring behavior is due to block differences. Significant block-level predictors included SOC, communitarianism, block satisfaction and block confidence. Surprisingly, in the multivariate context, higher block-level satisfaction was associated with *less* neighboring. At the individual level, SOC, block satisfaction, number of children, education, resident tenure, and home ownership were significant. Like at the block level, block satisfaction was associated with less neighboring. The model explains 82% of block differences in neighboring and 21% of individual variance. None of the random effects were significant.

Neighboring Time 2. In the HLM predicting neighboring at T2, about seven percent ($p < .001$) of the total variance in individuals' informal neighboring behaviors is due to block differences. Significant block-level predictors included SOC and block confidence. At the individual level, SOC, communitarianism, age, length of residence, and home ownership were significant. Neighboring behaviors decrease with age. The model explains 95% of block differences in neighboring and 16% of individual variance. No random effects were significant.

CONCLUSIONS

This study represents a new, multi-level analysis of the original Sense of Community Index data (Chavis, et al., 1987; Perkins, et al., 1990). The BSCI used in the present analyses is shorter than previous scales and has adequate psychometric properties (Perkins & Long, 2001). The data and analyses we present meet the three criteria for validly deriving contextual or social climate variables from group-aggregated individual responses. Although, for all variables, block-level variances were less than individual-level variances, the significance of all six HLM unconditional models, and the many significant block-level predictors (between two and four out of five in each model), confirm the existence of: (1) substantial within-block agreement as to community-focused attitudes and behaviors, (2) significant block differentiation in those variables (and in half the models, significant block-level variation in slopes), and (3) predictable relations with other block-level constructs (above diagonal, Table 1), as well as predictable effects on individual-level SC outcomes in our HLM models. The variable showing the most block-level variance was participation, which is not surprising given that the sample included blocks with BAs of varying activity, and about a third of the blocks had no BA. What is more noteworthy is that at T2, SOC was as much a block level variable (30%; Perkins & Long, 2001) as participation was at T1.

Strong evidence was shown for our four-component definition of SC. Each dimension was significantly correlated with at least two other dimensions at the individual and block-aggregate levels. The only exception was the nonsignificant link between collective efficacy and neighboring. This is not surprising given that efficacy is the formal-intrapsychic dimension and neighboring is the informal-behavioral dimension. The fact that SOC (informal-intrapsychic) and participation (formal-behavioral) are so highly correlated, particularly at the block level, is perhaps more impressive. SOC emerged as the strongest and most consistent predictor (at both levels) of the other three dimensions of SC. In fact, it was the only individual-level predictor, including demographics, that was significant in all six models and the only block-level predictor that was significant in all six. Living on a block with higher mean SOC *and* (whether block SOC is high or low) having higher individual SOC relative to one's neighbors was related to more collective efficacy, more neighboring, and more participation in block organizations.

Our findings that SOC positively relates to neighboring and participation in grassroots community organizations corroborate numerous other studies (Beckman, et al., 1998; Brodsky, et al., 1999; Brown & Werner, 1985; Chavis & Wandersman, 1990; Hughey, et al., 1999; Itzhaky & York, 2000; Perkins, et al., 1996; Prezza, et al., 2001; Wandersman & Giamartino, 1980). What is new, in addition to finding the effects to be significant at both the individual and community levels simultaneously, are the cross-level interaction effects at T1: SOC and participation being most closely linked on blocks with more children, more educated residents, more long-term residents, and low communitarianism may help community organizers and leaders target their organizing strategies accordingly. (The T2 cross-level interaction, in which communitarianism and participation were slightly *negatively* related on blocks with more new residents but had a clearly positive slope on more residentially stable blocks, may be due to communitarians feeling alienated or frustrated on blocks with high turnover).

The link between SOC and collective efficacy (Perkins, et al., 1990) had not been well established. Thus, the significance of SOC at both levels and time points represents a major contribution to the literature. There are a number of publications that deal with SOC and empowerment. But with very few exceptions (e.g., Itzhaky & York, 2000; Speer, 2000), most of those are either non-empirical or use both constructs as either independent or dependent variables, rather than relating the two, which is surprising given the prominence of both empowerment and SOC in community psychology.

Several other reliable effects (i.e., present at T1 and T2) were noted, especially for community confidence, a construct that has been largely ignored by psychologists. Individual and block mean communitarianism and individual confidence in the block's future related positively to perceptions of collective efficacy. Individual resident tenure, home ownership, and a block climate of community confidence related to higher rates of neighboring. More confidence and *less* place attachment at the block level, as well as individual home ownership and more education, related to higher participation.

The negative coefficients for block-level place attachment should be discounted as suppression effects as the bivariate correlations were modest, but positive. Place attachment was strongly correlated with SOC at both levels. It likely would be less so if the measures did not derive from items taken from the same scale, as was necessary here. Place attachment is clearly an important construct independent of SOC (Brown & Perkins, 1992; Cuba & Hummon, 1993; Hyde, 1998; Li, 1998; Manzo & Perkins, 2001). Even discounting the negative suppression effects, however, one of our most surprising multivariate findings is that place attachment was largely unrelated to collective efficacy, participation, and neighboring at both the block and individual levels. It is not surprising that social attachments would be more closely related to SC than are place attachments. In light of all the evidence that place issues are critical to community participation and development (Manzo & Perkins, 2001), however, place attachment deserves further scrutiny in this context with a stronger measure than we had available to us.

The following effects were significant ($p < .01$), but were less reliable (i.e., appearing at just one time-point). Higher block-mean community confidence related to higher individual perceptions of collective efficacy. Greater resident tenure, more children in the home, and age were associated with higher rates of participation in organizations. Neighboring behaviors decreased with age, but increased with education. The correlations with race suggest the possibility that nonwhite residents and blocks felt more collective efficacy at T1, which may have resulted in higher participation at T2. But the racial difference in efficacy was no longer significant at T2, which may imply a degree of disappointment or frustration with their organizations.

Collective efficacy has been shown in past research to be related to organizational participation, both as an effect (Schultz, Israel, Zimmerman, & Checkoway, 1995) and as a cause (Perkins, et al., 1996). Thus, policies encouraging collective efficacy will have a positive impact on behavioral dimensions of SC. In this study, individual perceptions of communitarianism, SOC, and confidence in the future of the block were strongly associated with increased collective efficacy. Living on a block with high average SOC and communitarianism was related to higher individual perceptions of collective efficacy. Although less reliable findings, collective efficacy was also shown to increase with higher block mean confidence in the future of the block, but decrease with individual education, length of residence, and the proportion of white residents living on the block. This may be due to longer-term, white, and more educated residents having more personal ties to power and thus not needing as much formal collective efficacy.

Like Rankin and Quane (2000), we also found a positive association between greater education and participation in grassroots organizations. However, where Rankin and Quane found no relation between participation and number of children, age, employment status or tenure in the neighborhood, we found that participation was greater among older, better off (i.e., higher income), more tenured residents, and those with more children. Our finding for age and participation is supported in another recent study (Prezza, et al., 2001). Also like Prezza, et al., we found that neighboring behavior increased with education and number of children in the household. Unlike Prezza, et al., we found no relation between neighboring behavior and sex. Controlling for other predictors, younger residents engaged in more neighboring which, coupled with the above age-participation link, suggests a possible developmental strategy for community organizing: facilitate neighboring among young families (e.g., semi-formalized baby-sitting co-ops), and later, as residents grow older and have more time, they may participate in more formal organizations.

There are some constraints on the generalizability of the present findings. Comparisons between organized and non-organized blocks (not reported) suggest that there may be unique social processes occurring on the two types of blocks. The data are now 15 years old and social capital and political processes may have changed. There are some important cultural, political and economic differences between the neighborhoods selected for this study. It may be questionable, therefore, to draw conclusions about the entire sample (across all three neighborhoods) based on block and individual-level data. It would be even more questionable to infer anything about communities unlike those represented here. Some of the exceptional features of the sample include: (a) two out of three areas being low-income or working-class and minority yet with a large proportion of homeowners, (b) all neighborhoods experiencing increasing rates of reported crime while city-wide rates were holding steady or declining, and (c) a housing density and architectural style that is more crowded and "urban" than most suburban areas but less so than most of the rest of New York City or other large inner-city residential areas. The sample is not unique, however. Each of these characteristics describes the growing "inner ring" of poor and working-class neighborhoods that are surrounding the gentrifying city cores throughout the U.S. and other countries. The inhabitants of these ring neighborhoods have either moved up and out of poorer inner-city areas or have been forced out of neighborhoods with rapidly increasing housing costs.

Possibly the greatest concern with the present data is the relatively weak internal consistency of the predictor scales due to a combination of few items per scale and limited response options (dichotomous for many items). SOC's being most consistently related to the other SC dimensions may be partly due to its having the most items (thus more variance) and highest α. But given that its α is substantially higher than only block satisfaction, we doubt that is the only explanation. With better scales, the already impressive results would likely have been even stronger.

Puddifoot (1996) and others recommend the use of qualitative methods. Clearly, the ideal study combines both qualitative and quantitative methods. But as valuable as ethnographic data are, they have their own reliability and validity limitations, including the fact that they generally represent a small sample of individuals. New, truly community-level (not aggregated individual-level) measures of sense of community and other social capital constructs are needed (Shinn, 1990). They could be used in multilevel analyses and provide descriptive or comparative context in qualitative studies.

Our task was to search for more sharply defined and ecologically valid conceptual, psychometric, and analytical "needles" in the haystack of research and vague rhetoric on SC and SOC. We believe the dimensions and predictors, measures, and multi-level analyses used here, while not perfect, can only enhance the construct validity of SC and SOC. Both concepts clearly have individual and community-level (not to mention organizational) properties. Multi-level analysis gives us a sense of *how much* each concept operates at the community, as well as individual, level and how they operate at different levels simultaneously. The fact that SOC was such a strong and consistent predictor at both levels suggests, not only that people with SOC are more likely to help their neighbors, to join a BA, and to be empowered by it, but that *blocks* with more SOC enjoy those same results even for residents who may not share that SOC, but who get involved for more selfish reasons.   In future studies, we plan to use the other SC dimensions (collective efficacy, neighboring, and participation) and other community-focused cognitions, at the individual and block levels, to predict the BSCI and its subscales. We hope the needles we have identified will help researchers and community leaders and organizers knit tighter, more politically effective neighborhood social fabrics.

NOTES

[i] Collection of the data reported was funded by the Ford Foundation (Co-Principal Investigators: David Chavis, Paul Florin, Richard Rich, and Abe Wandersman). We thank Chavis, Adrian Fisher, David McMillan, and Chris Sonn for their comments on the study that developed the Brief Sense of Community Index (Perkins & Long, 2001) and Fisher and Jo Lippe for editorial assistance with this chapter.
[ii] A PsycINFO search of "sense of community" found 398 publications through November, 2001, starting with a 1930 article. Sarason's 1974 book was the 15th record and thus something of a watershed. The 398 do not include works referring to "social cohesion," "community spirit" or other near synonyms.
[iii] ISC is the degree to which residents spontaneously regulate everyday public behaviors and physical conditions within the bounds of their community. Although SOC and ISC are highly correlated at both the block ($r = .65$; Perkins, et al., 1990) and neighborhood ($r = .80$; Sampson et al., 1997) levels, other studies have generally treated them as separate constructs. There is also a methodological/conceptual problem with ISC in that it is often thought of as a behavior but typically measured as a cognition (e.g., prediction of how neighbors would act in hypothetical situations, e.g., youths painting graffiti). Clearly more work needs to be done measuring actual ISC behaviors and comparing them to perceived ISC. Given the high correlations between measures of SOC and ISC, Sampson may be justified in combining the two, but should perhaps add neighboring items and call it "informal collective efficacy."
[vi] The SCI is often incorrectly cited. It was developed in 1985 by Chavis and colleagues for use with the present dataset and published in the appendix of Perkins, et al. (1990). Although it was ostensibly based on McMillan and Chavis' (1986) theory, their four dimensions have not been found in the SCI factor structure in these and other data. Furthermore, McMillan had nothing to do with creating the SCI and has challenged its validity. Chavis, Hogge, McMillan, and Wandersman (1986) used a 46-item scale (including component scale items) called the Sense of Community Profile, which is much broader than the SCI and includes many other constructs, such as participation and neighboring behaviors, collective efficacy, community satisfaction, perceived block conditions, and even demographics, such as home ownership and length of residence.
[v] Each procedure began with an "unconditional" model indicating the amount of variance in the dependent variable due to differences in groups (blocks). In step two, demographic control variables (income, age, race, sex, education, children, home ownership, length of residence) were added at the individual level. (Sex was not a significant predictor in any model.) In step three, all nonsignificant demographics were removed and the five cognitive predictors were added at both the block and individual (block-mean centered) levels. (Cognitive predictors at the individual level are each deviations from the mean of one's block so as to be independent

of their block-level counterparts.) In multi-level analysis, degrees of freedom are more limited both within groups and across groups. Therefore, in step four, all remaining nonsignificant (block-level $p > .10$; individual-level $p > .05$) predictors were trimmed to produce the most parsimonious model (Bryk & Raudenbush, 1992). As this increases the risk of Type-I errors, each step-four model was compared with the corresponding step-three model and the correlations in Table 1. In step five, each remaining individual-level cognitive predictor was tested, one-by-one, for a significant random effect, which would indicate a cross-level interaction. First, block-level demographic variables were modeled in interaction with the significant random individual-level predictor. Second, all nonsignificant (at $p < .10$) interactional demographics were trimmed before modeling the five block-level cognitive predictors. Third, any nonsignificant block-level interactional predictors were trimmed from the model. Interpretation of cross-level interactions used a strategy exemplified by Watson, Chemers, and Preiser (2001) in which the relation between the individual-level interactional predictor and the outcome variable was compared differentially between high and low (one SD above and below the mean) status on the block-level interactional predictor.

REFERENCES

Ahlbrandt, R. S. (1984). *Neighborhoods, people and community*. New York: Plenum.

Beckman, P. J., Barnwell, D., Horn, E., Hanson, M. J., Gutierrez, S., & Lieber, J. (1998). Communities, families, and inclusion. *Early Childhood Research Quarterly, 13,* 125-150.

Briggs, X. S. (1998). Brown kids in white suburbs: Housing mobility and the many faces of social capital. *Housing Policy Debate, 9,* 177-221.

Brodsky, A. E., O'Campo, P. J., & Aronson, R. E. (1999). PSOC in community context: Multi-Level correlates of a measure of psychological sense of community in low-income, urban neighborhoods. *Journal of Community Psychology, 27,* 659-679.

Brown, B. B., & Perkins, D. D. (1992). Disruptions in place attachment. In I. Altman and S. Low (Eds.), *Place attachment* (pp. 279-304). New York: Plenum.

Brown, B. B., & Perkins, D. D. (2001). *Neighborhood revitalization and disorder: An intervention evaluation*. Final Report to the National Institute of Justice. Salt Lake City: University of Utah.

Brown, B. B., & Werner, C. M. (1985). Social cohesiveness, territoriality, and holiday decorations: The influence of cul-de-sacs. *Environment and Behavior, 17,* 539-565.

Bryk, A. S., & Raudenbusch, S. W. (1992). *Hierarchical linear models: Applications and data analysis methods*. Newbury Park, CA: Sage.

Buckner, J. C. (1988). The development of an instrument to measure neighborhood cohesion. *American Journal of Community Psychology, 16,* 771-791.

Chavis, D. M., Florin, P., Rich, R. C., Wandersman, A., & Perkins, D. D. (1987). *The role of block associations in crime control and community development: The Block Booster Project*. (Final Report to Ford Foundation). New York: Citizens Committee for New York City.

Chavis, D. M., Hogge, J., McMillan, D., & Wandersman, A. (1986). Sense of community through Brunswik's Lens. *Journal of Community Psychology, 14,* 24-40.

Chavis, D. M., & Wandersman, A. (1990). Sense of community in the urban environment: A catalyst for participation and community development. *American Journal of Community Psychology, 18,* 55-82.

Chipuer, H. M., & Pretty, G. M. H. (1999). A review of the sense of community index: Current uses, factor structure, reliability, and further development. *Journal of Community Psychology, 27,* 643-658.

Coleman, J. S. (1988). Social capital in the creation of human capital. *American Journal of Sociology, 94,* S95-S120.

Cuba, L., & Hummon, D. M. (1993). A place to call home: Identification with dwelling, community, and region. *Sociological Quarterly, 34,* 111-131.

Etzioni, A. (1993). *Spirit of community: Rights, responsibilities, and the communitarian agenda.* New York: Crown.

Fisher, A. T., & Sonn, C. C. (1999). Aspiration to community: Community responses to rejection. *Journal of Community Psychology, 27,* 715-725.

Florin, P., & Wandersman, A. (1984). Cognitive social learning and participation in community development. *American Journal of Community Psychology, 12,* 689-708.

Garcia, I., Giuliani, F., & Wiesenfeld, E. (1999). Community and sense of community: The case of an urban barrio in Caracas. *Journal of Community Psychology, 27,* 727-740.

Hughey, J., Speer, P. W., & Peterson, N. A. (1999). Sense of community in community organizations: Structure and evidence of validity. *Journal of Community Psychology, 27,* 97-113.

Hyde, M. M. (1998). *Local sentiments in urban neighborhoods: Multilevel models of sense of community and attachment to place.* Unpublished Doctoral Dissertation. University of Maryland-Baltimore County.

Hyman, H., & Wright, C. (1971). Trends in voluntary association memberships of American adults: Replication based on secondary analysis of national sample surveys. *American Sociological Review, 36,* 191-206.

Itzhaky, H., & York, A. S. (2000). Sociopolitical control and empowerment: An extended replication. *Journal of Community Psychology, 28,* 407-415.

Kenny, D. A., & Lavoie, L. (1985). Separating individual and group effects. *Journal of Personality and Social Psychology, 48,* 339-348.

Kingston, S., Mitchell, R., Florin, P., & Stevenson, J. (1999). Sense of community in neighborhoods as a multi-level construct. *Journal of Community Psychology, 27,* 681-694.

Kretzmann, J. P., & McKnight, J. L. (1993). *Building communities from the inside out: A path toward finding and mobilizing a community's assets.* Chicago: ACTA.

Li, C. (1998). The contribution of common land to sense of community. In J. Sanford & B. R. Connell (Eds.), *People, places and public policy.* (pp. 57-70). Edmond, OK: Environmental Design Research Association.

Manzo, L. C., & Perkins, D. D. (2001, July). *Neighborhoods as common ground: The importance of place attachment to community participation and development.* Paper presented to the Environmental Design Research Association, Edinburgh, Scotland.

McMillan, D. W., & Chavis, D. M. (1986). Sense of community: A definition and theory. *Journal of Community Psychology, 14,* 6-23.

Nasar, J. L. & Julian, D. A. (1995). The psychological sense of community in the neighborhood. *Journal of the American Planning Association, 61,* 178-184.

Perkins, D. D. (1995). Speaking truth to power: Empowerment ideology as social intervention and policy. *American Journal of Community Psychology, 23,* 765-794.

Perkins, D. D., Brown, B. B., & Taylor, R. B. (1996). The ecology of empowerment: Predicting participation in community organizations. *Journal of Social Issues, 52,* 85-110.

Perkins, D. D., Florin, P., Rich, R. C., Wandersman, A., & Chavis, D. M. (1990). Participation and the social and physical environment of residential blocks: Crime and community context. *American Journal of Community Psychology, 18,* 83-115.

Perkins, D. D. & Long, D. A. (2001). *Neighborhood sense of community and social capital: "All the things you are."* Paper presented at the Biennial Conference on Community Research & Action, Atlanta, June.

Perkins, D. D., Wandersman, A., Rich, R. C., & Taylor, R. B. (1993). The physical environment of street crime: Defensible space, territoriality and incivilities. *Journal of Environmental Psychology, 13,* 29-49.

Plas, J. M., & Lewis, S. E. (1996). Environmental factors and sense of community in a planned town. *American Journal of Community Psychology, 24,* 109-143.

Podolefsky, A. (1983). *Case studies in community crime prevention.* Springfield, IL: Thomas.

Pretty, G. (1990). Relating psychological sense of community to social climate characteristics. *Journal of Community Psychology, 18,* 16-65.

Pretty, G. M. H., Conroy, C., Dugay, J., Fowler, K., & Williams, D. (1996). Sense of community and its relevance to adolescents of all ages. *Journal of Community Psychology, 24,* 365-379.

Prezza, M., Amici, M., Roberti, T., & Tedeschi, G. (2001). Sense of community referred to the whole town: Its relations with neighboring, loneliness, life satisfaction, and area of residence. *Journal of Community Psychology, 29,* 29-52.

Puddifoot, J.E. (1996). Some initial considerations in the measurement of community identity. *Journal of Community Psychology, 24,* 327-336

Putnam, R.D. (2000). *Bowling alone: The collapse and revival of American community.* New York: Simon & Schuster.

Rankin, B. H., & Quane, J. M. (2000). Neighborhood poverty and the social isolation of inner-city African American families. *Social Forces, 79,* 139-164.

Saegert, S. (1989). Unlikely leaders, extreme circumstances: Older Black women building community households. *American Journal of Community Psychology, 17,* 295-316.

Saegert, S., & Winkel, G. (1996). Paths to community empowerment: Organizing at home. *American Journal of Community Psychology, 24,* 517-550.

Saegert, S., & Winkel, G. (1998). Social capital and the revitalization of New York City's distressed inner city housing. *Housing Policy Debate, 9,* 17-60.

Sampson, R.J. (1991). Linking the micro- and macrolevel dimensions of community social organization. *Social Forces, 70,* 43-64.

Sampson, R. J., Raudenbush, S. W., & Earls, F. (1997). Neighborhoods and violent crime: A multilevel study of collective efficacy. *Science, 277,* 918-926.

Sarason, S. B. (1974). *The psychological sense of community: Prospects for a community psychology.* San Francisco: Jossey-Bass.

Schultz, A. J., Israel, B. A., Zimmerman, M. A., & Checkoway, B. N. (1995). Empowerment as a multi-level construct: Perceived control at the individual, organizational and community levels. *Health Education Research: Theory & Practice, 10,* 309-327.

Shinn, M. (1990). Mixing and matching: Levels of conceptualization, measurement, and statistical analysis in community research. In P. Tolan, C. Keys, F. Chertok, & L. Jason (Eds.), *Researching community psychology: Integrating theories and methods* (pp. 111-126). Washington, DC: American Psychological Association.

Sonn, C. C., & Fisher, A. T. (1998). Sense of community: Community resilient responses to oppression and change. *Journal of Community Psychology, 26,* 457-472.

Speer, P. W. (2000). Intrapersonal and interactional empowerment: Implications for theory. *Journal of Community Psychology, 28,* 51-61.

Speer, P. W., & Hughey, J. (1995). Community organizing: An ecological route to empowerment and power. *American Journal of Community Psychology, 23,* 729-748.

Theodori, G. L. (2000). Levels of analysis and conceptual clarification in community attachment and satisfaction research: Connections to community development. *Journal of the Community Development Society, 31,* 35-58.

Tocqueville, A. de (1935/1969). *Democracy in America.* (G. Lawrence, Trans.; J.P. Mayer, Ed.). New York: Doubleday.

Unger, D. G., & Wandersman, A. (1983). Neighboring and its role in block organizations. *American Journal of Community Psychology, 11,* 291-300.

Unger, D. G., & Wandersman, A. (1985). The importance of neighbors: The social, cognitive, and affective components of neighboring. *American Journal of Community Psychology, 13,* 139-170.

Varady, D. P. (1986). Neighborhood confidence: A critical factor in neighborhood revitalization? *Environment and Behavior, 18,* 480-501.

Vinsel, A., Brown, B. B., Altman, I., & Foss, C. (1980). Privacy regulation, territorial displays, and the effectiveness of individual functioning. *Journal of Personality and Social Psychology, 39,* 1104-1115.

Wandersman, A., & Giamartino, G. A. (1980). Community and individual difference characteristics as influences on initial participation. *American Journal of Community Psychology, 8,* 217-228.

Watson, C. B., Chemers, M. M., & Preiser, N. (2001). Collective efficacy: A multilevel analysis. *Personality and Social Psychology Bulletin, 27,* 1057-1068.

Zhao, L. (1996). *Community attachment in rural Iowa: Multilevel test of a theoretical model with intervening variables.* Unpublished doctoral dissertation, Iowa State University.

APPENDIX A: Social Capital Survey Scales

Brief Sense of Community Index (overall scale α Time 1 (T1) = .65, n = 713; α Time 2 (T2) = .74, n = 422):
Social Connections Subscale (α = .55 (T1), .50 (T2)):
Instructions for items 1-5: "I am going to read some things that people might say about their block. For each one, please indicate whether it is mostly true or mostly false about your block" (coded 1 = "false", 2 = "true"; Note: Likert scale recommended for future research).

    1. Very few of my neighbors know me. (Reverse)
    2. I have almost no influence over what this block is like. (Reverse)
    3. I can recognize most of the people who live on my block.
Mutual Concern Subscale (α = .50 (T1), .64 (T2)):
    4. My neighbors and I want the same things from the block.
    5. If there is a problem on this block people who live here can get it solved.
    6. In general, would you say that people on your block watch after each other and help out when they can, or do they pretty much go their own way? (coded 1 = "go own way", 2 = "a little of both", 3 = "watch after")
Community Values Subscale (Face-valid SOC; α = .51 (T1), .61 (T2):
    7. Would you say that it is very important, somewhat important or not important to you to feel a sense of community with the people on your block? (coded 1= "not", 2= "somewhat ", 3= "very")
    8. Some people say they feel like they have a sense of community with the people on their block; others don't feel that way. How about you; would you say that you feel a strong sense of community with others on your block, very little sense of community or something in between? (coded 1 = "very little", 2 = "in between", 3 = "strong")

Collective Efficacy Scale (α (T1) = .82, n = 918; α (T2) = .82, n = 270):
    "The following are things a block association might try to do. For each one, indicate whether you think it is very likely, somewhat likely, or not likely that the association on your block can accomplish that goal" (coded 1 = "not likely" to 3 = "very likely").
    1. Improve physical conditions on the block like cleanliness or housing upkeep.
    2. Persuade the city to provide better services to people on the block.
    3. Get people on the block to help each other more.
    4. Reduce crime on the block.
    5. Get people who live on the block to know each other better.
    6. Get information to residents about where to go for services they need.

Citizen Participation Scale (α (T1) = .78, n = 384; α (T2) = .80, n = 184):
    1. Are you currently a member of the block association?

2. Have you ever taken part in an activity sponsored by the block association?

3. Thinking about work you might do for the block association outside of meetings, how many hours would you say you give to the association each month, if any?

"We would like to know what kinds of things people have done in the association. In the past year have you:"

4. Attended a meeting,

5. Spoken up during a meeting,

6. Done work for the organization outside of meetings,

7. Served as a member of a committee,

8. Served as an officer or as a committee chair?

Note: Each item was coded 1 for participation and 0 for no participation (#3 was recoded to match this scale, from 0 = "none" to 1 = "8 or more hours").

Neighboring Behavior Scale (α (T1) = .78, n = 1,037; α (T2) = .77, n = 615):

"The following is a short list of things neighbors might do for each other. Please indicate how many times in the past year, you have been asked to do each one for a neighbor on this block" (coded 0 = "none", 1-7 = "exact number", and 8 = "eight or more").

1. Watch a neighbor's home while they were away.

2. Loan a neighbor some food or a tool.

3. Help a neighbor in an emergency.

4. Offer a neighbor advice on a personal problem.

5. Discuss a problem on the block with a neighbor.

Chapter 16

EXPANDING THE CONCEPTUALIZATION OF PSOC

Anne E. Brodsky
University of Maryland Baltimore County

Colleen Loomis
Veterans Affairs Palo Alto Health Care System; Stanford University School of Medicine

Christine M. Marx
Johns Hopkins Bloomberg School of Public Health

INTRODUCTION

The chapters of this book are but a small example of the continually growing body of evidence showing that psychological sense of community (PSOC) is a meaningful construct across a range of types of communities, as well as being a construct that is significantly related to individual and community outcomes. These findings appear to be the case whether community is defined as a geographic territory (e.g., Brodsky, O'Campo & Aronson, 1999; Davidson & Cotter, 1986; García, Giuliani, & Wiesenfeld, 1999), a physical setting (e.g., Battistich, Solomon, Watson, & Schaps, 1997; Brodsky & Marx, 2001; Pretty, Andrewes, & Collett, 1994), a relational community (e.g., Brodsky & Marx, 2001; Compas, 1981), or an identity group (e.g., Catano, Pretty, Southwell, & Cole, 1993; Sonn, 1996; Sonn & Fisher, 1996). The outcomes associated with PSOC range from positive individual mental health (McCarthy, Pretty, & Catano, 1990; Pretty, Conroy, Dugay, Fowler, & Williams, 1996), physical health (Ahern, Hendryx, & Siddharthan, 1996), community involvement (Chavis & Wandersman, 1990; Kingston, Mitchell, Florin, & Stevenson, 1999), political participation (Davidson & Cotter, 1989), job-related behaviors such as interacting with others, support, and appreciation (Lambert & Hopkins, 1995), and positive community indicators such as safety (Levine, 1986; Perkins, Florin, Rich, & Wandersman, 1990), resources (Chavis, Florin, Rich, & Wandersman, 1987), satisfaction with public services (Sagy, Stern, & Krakover, 1996), and social control and empowerment (Levine, 1986).

In most of this work, PSOC is conceptualized as a unipolar factor that denotes the feelings of an individual for a single target community. While all of this work on PSOC shows great promise for better understanding the relationship between an individual and a particular community, in this chapter we suggest that an expansion of the common conceptualization and measurement of PSOC is necessary to better comprehend the multidimensional space in which individuals and communities exist. We maintain that in order to explore this multidimensional space, PSOC must also be thought of as a much more complex concept, one that captures gradients of PSOC across multiple simultaneously assessed community settings. This expansion of PSOC allows for the exploration of the larger context of individuals and communities and leads to a number of heretofore unexamined but important interactional issues and questions. This, in turn, has direct implication for increasing our knowledge about the impact of PSOC on outcomes for individuals and communities and informing the design of interventions aimed at enhancing individual and community lives (Dalton, Elias, & Wandersman, 2001).

In this chapter we consider a two dimensional expansion of PSOC. The first is the extension of PSOC from a unipolar, dummy coded variable (present vs. absent) to a continuous, bipolar construct in which PSOC ranges from positive, through neutral and negative (Brodsky, 1996). The second dimension expands the number of communities explored, from one to many, reflecting the fact that individuals are simultaneous members of multiple communities including both *distinct* territorial and relational communities and *nested* macro and subcommunities (Brodsky & Marx, 2001). That is, one may live in a particular geographic neighborhood, work in a setting which is located in another geographic community, attend school in a yet another distinct community and have community allegiances to any number of relational communities which may or may not share a geographic locale with each other.

One way to visualize the expansion along these two dimensions is with a graph where the extension of PSOC occurs vertically along the y-axis and the addition of multiple communities is graphed horizontally along the x-axis (see Figure 1). Thus, looking at the y-axis, individuals' psychological sense of community can be positive, negative or neutral for each of the multiple communities (represented along the x-axis) in which they simultaneously interact. We argue that these multiple psychological *senses* of community (M-PSOC) do not operate independently of each other, but that there is an interactional effect between the M-PSOC experienced by any one individual. Further we suggest that this two dimensional expansion of PSOC also might be useful in explaining individual and community outcomes over and above that explained by a unipolar PSOC experienced in one community.

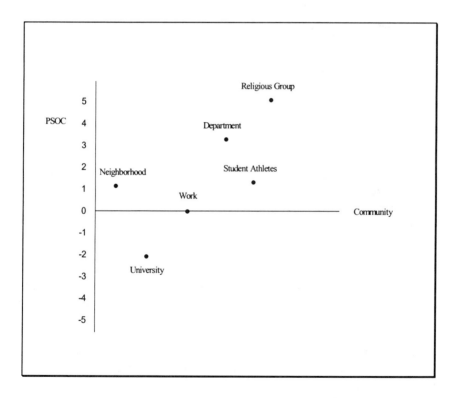

Figure 1. A Two-Dimensional Expansion of PSOC

PSOC and the Vertical Expansion

Although traditionally expressed as a unipolar dummy variable, present or absent, PSOC is actually treated solely as a positive factor in most research. That is, the presence of a positive psychological sense of community is associated with positive individual and community level outcomes (e.g., Brodsky, et al., 1999; Chavis & Wandersman, 1990; Davidson & Cotter; 1991; McCarthy, et al., 1990). Our prior and current work, in contrast, suggests PSOC exists on a continuum passing through three possible conditions -- positive, neutral and negative (Brodsky, 1996; Brodsky & Marx, 2001; Loomis, 2001; Marx, 2000). Generally speaking, it is not difficult to envision how an individual might perceive a positive feeling of membership, mutual influence, integration and fulfillment of needs, and shared emotional connection with a given community (McMillan & Chavis, 1986). Nor is it difficult to theoretically comprehend how an individual might report the reverse of this: an active lack of feelings of membership, influence, fulfillment of needs, and shared emotional connection. A third position is also possible in which PSOC is neutral, with no active positive or negative feelings. This third scenario might be reflected in a response of "don't agree or disagree" on a Sense of Community Index (SCI) item such as "I think my community is a good place for me to live" (Chavis, et al., 1987), showing a passive lack of feeling. There has been very little work done on this idea of neutral PSOC. On the one hand, one could imagine that this neutral feeling could exist for a setting that is not deemed important by the individual. On the other hand, a neutral PSOC could be a step in the development of a more active negative or positive PSOC in a community that does have some importance. Clearly, more work needs to be done in exploring the meaning and impact of neutral PSOC.

This expansion of PSOC was first described, and the negative and positive conditions explored, in a qualitative study of resilient single mothers raising daughters in a risky urban neighborhood in an eastern U.S. city (Brodsky, 1996). In this study, resilience was found to be, in part, a product of a negative PSOC. Living in risky, resource poor communities, the women participants described active efforts to resist membership and shared emotional connections with the neighborhoods in which they lived, as well as a profound lack of mutual influence and integration and fulfillment of needs. They did not view their communities as competent (Iscoe, 1974) to offer the resources, influence, and values they needed for success and thus maintained a purposeful distance from their community as a necessity to keep their children safe and headed in what they saw as the right direction. Thus, they actively cultivated this negative PSOC in both themselves and their families. As one of the participants explained:

> I don't go out here. I don't start things with people. I don't bother people. I go home, I close my door, I lock my door, I stay in my

house. Don't bother me and I won't bother you. Don't bother my kids, I won't bother you.

While prior research has associated a positive PSOC with positive outcomes, this study showed that in communities that are not able to provide necessary resources, values, connections, and need fulfillment, a negative PSOC may be associated with positive outcomes such as resilience in the face of community risk.

In another example of the operation of negative PSOC, Marx (2000) found that women from low income communities, attending a holistic educational and job training center in the hopes of obtaining living wage jobs, used both physical and emotional distance from their neighborhoods as an essential part of their own success and personal fulfillment. Participants described their neighborhoods as inhabited by people who did not have the same values as they did, people who did not want to "do something" with their lives. The following quote illustrates one participant's description of negative PSOC- she feels like she does not "belong," has no impact on, and eventually actively avoids connection with others in her neighborhood:

> ...you see them just sitting there just doing nothing with theirselves. It makes you want to do better. You see their little kids outside just running around looking all raggedy. And you want to do better. You want to help them too but you keep telling them 'come on let's go'and they don't want to go. That's putting you down too. So, I just don't say nothing ... I just hate the same people that even though you know they could do better, they just want to sit around and just, um, have a beer in their hand all day. I can't live like that.

In this example, the neighborhood, vis a vis its residents, is viewed as unfulfilling, resource-poor, and a source of frustration. Indeed, a majority of participants in this job training setting described a desire to move out of their neighborhoods as an important step in "doing something" with their lives. Thus, negative PSOC can operate as a constructive motivating force.

In a third example, Loomis (2001) has found that individuals can rate their PSOC specifically as negative, neutral, and positive when explicitly asked. Respondents (n=231) attending an urban, historically black college were asked to rate their sense of community with their university campus community using the following response set: very negative, moderately negative, neutral (neither negative nor positive), moderately positive, and very positive. Results showed that 12.3% expressed a negative sense of community, 43.1% reported neither a positive nor negative sense of community, and 33.5% had a positive sense of community. In the same study respondents also were asked to rate their sense of community with their neighborhood, using the same response set. Findings show a variation across all three types of sense of community, 7.3%, 33.8% and 47.3% negative, neutral, and positive, respectively. Further, respondents' qualitative rating of their sense of community, from very negative to very positive, was positively and significantly ($p < .01$) correlated to their quantitative PSOC scores.

All three of these examples show that an expansion of PSOC, from a perception that is merely present or absent to one that has various gradients, has benefits for capturing some of the complexity of feelings that exist between an individual and a community, and for furthering our understanding of the effects of one on the other.

Multiple Communities and the Horizontal Expansion

Most prior literature has limited the conceptualization of the community to one, usually researcher-selected, setting. Attending to only one community restricts the assessment and conceptualization of PSOC in several ways. Selecting a single community within which to assess PSOC limits our measurements to a single behavior setting (Barker, 1978), while people exist in multiple, independent, and nested behavior settings. Thus, this single appraisal of a single PSOC does not consider the full context of an individual's life. In addition, because the target, researcher-selected community is seldom if ever compared to other participant settings, it is unknown how the chosen community compares (in PSOC, importance, salience, value, etc.) to other communities that make up the context of participants' lives. Including multiple communities and providing for research-participants' input on choice of communities to be studied, therefore, is necessary to reflect the real world.

In addition to expanding the conceptualization of PSOC from one to multiple communities, there is also a need to expand the definition of "community" as it relates to PSOC. All of us live in multiple communities simultaneously, some of these communities are independent non-overlapping and others are nested. Non-overlapping communities may be territorial, physical, or relational; we may work in one setting, live in another, go to school in a third, feel belonging with a separate ethnic, professional, religious, or identity community, etc.

The other type of multiple communities in which people operate are the nested subcommunities that exist in any larger community; what Hunter and Riger (1986) refer to as a "hierarchy of symbolic communities" (Hunter, 1974 in Hunter and Riger, 1986, p. 65). Wiesenfeld (1996) conceptualized community belonging as being made up of "macrobelonging" which incorporates all into the larger community and "microbelongings" that are made up of "the multiple collective identities" of the sub-communities (p. 341-342). For instance, a school setting may engender a global sense of community that is shared by all who identify as members of that school community, but also microbelongings with separate sub-communities such as students, faculty, staff, athletes, Muslim students, employees, etc.

Prior to our own work (Brodsky & Marx, 2001) there had been only a few studies exploring PSOC and individuals' as they exist in multiple communities, both independent and nested. Pretty, et al. (1994), for example, compared students' PSOC in two nonoverlapping territorial communities, their home neighborhoods and their schools, finding that neighborhood and school PSOC were correlated. Royal and Rossi (1996) explored nested communities, looking at the PSOC of four groups of students in one school setting. The groups were divided in two, based on their membership (or not) in a smaller specialized learning community, and divided again by researcher instructions to answer a PSOC survey in reference to a sub-community (microbelonging) or to the school setting as a whole (macrobelonging). Each student however only answered the PSOC questionnaire for one of the four target communities. While Royal and Rossi found that students who were members of the small, specialized sub-community had (positive) PSOC for both the sub-community and for the setting as a whole, this research did not measure the same student's PSOC at both the sub-community and macro-community level.

Our work has built on these prior studies. Working with women participants of the job training and educational center mentioned above, we asked participants to simultaneously report PSOC for three different communities (Brodsky & Marx, 2001). In this mixed-method (qualitative and quantitative) study, women living in low-income communities reported significantly different quantitative PSOC for their home neighborhoods, the center as a whole, and the sub-community of center students. Thus, participants were able to differentiate M-PSOC operating concurrently in both distinct territorial communities of the Center and their neighborhoods as well as in nested sub and macrocommunities with the Center.

In another study in the same setting, Marx (2000) further explored the meaning of the differences in PSOC in two territorial communities. The first community was defined as other women in the student's home neighborhoods and the second defined as the women student members of the center. After completing a PSOC measure for both communities, nine women were purposely chosen to be interviewed based on their responses -- six of whom reported high (positive) PSOC for the center and low (negative) PSOC[1] for their neighborhoods, and three who reported positive PSOC for both settings. Participants described how their lives were simultaneously impacted by a positive PSOC at center and negative PSOC in their home neighborhoods. They felt, for example that the center and its attendees had common goals, and that the center provided for the fulfillment of material and social needs. In contrast, eight of the nine interviewees described a low (perhaps even negative) PSOC for their neighborhoods. (In fact, two of the three interviewees who were chosen because they had quantitatively reported positive PSOC for neighborhood, in fact qualitatively described negative PSOC for their neighborhoods.) Participants discussed having very different goals and values than their neighbors, and how their neighborhoods do not have much to offer that meets their needs. It is clear from this example that M-PSOC are operating simultaneously and having distinct impacts on the women who experience both of these settings.

In the examples above, different communities were found to have different PSOC. It is also important to note, however, that, as is seen in Figure 1, multiple communities may also have the same PSOC score and that these PSOC may be negative, neutral or positive. This does not mean that M-PSOC do not exist or that the communities with the same PSOC score operate in the same manner. The same PSOC score may have different meaning in relation to different community contexts and distinct individual-community interactions (to be discussed further, below).

PSOC by Community Interaction: A 2 x 2 Example

Having described an expansion of the *range of sense of community* one can experience (from present or absent to negative, neutral, and positive) and an expansion of *number of communities* as well as the types of communities with which one may simultaneously experience PSOC, the next step for this chapter will be to explore what happens when these two conceptual expansions are combined. It is clear that not only is any given PSOC a result of an interaction between an individual and a community, but looking at Figure 1, one can also see that the various M-PSOC may result from an interaction among the multiple communities in which an individual interacts. Further, it appears probable that this interaction has implications for the operation, meaning, and impact of various M-PSOC on both individual and community outcomes. This impact includes behavioral, cognitive, and emotional consequences for the individual as well as social consequences for relevant, multiple communities. Thus, we hypothesize that the interaction effect that operates when an individual belongs to multiple communities impacts the PSOC felt in each community as well as impacting various outcomes associated with PSOC.

The various hypothetical effects of this interaction can be most easily seen in an example of a two by two interaction, where PSOC is

limited to positive and negative, and the number of communities is limited
to two as well (see Figure 2). For simplicity sake in this example we will
also initially assume that both communities are competent in terms of
power, knowledge, and self esteem (Iscoe, 1974). In this two by two
example, there are three possible conditions that an individual might feel: 1)
positive PSOC in both communities (quadrant I); 2) positive PSOC in one
community and negative PSOC in the other (quadrants II & IV); or 3)
negative PSOC in both communities (quadrant III).

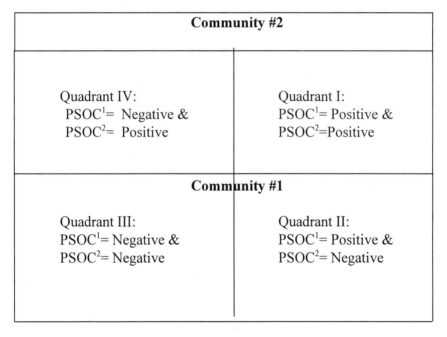

Community #2	
Quadrant IV: $PSOC^1$= Negative & $PSOC^2$= Positive	Quadrant I: $PSOC^1$= Positive & $PSOC^2$=Positive
Community #1	
Quadrant III: $PSOC^1$= Negative & $PSOC^2$= Negative	Quadrant II: $PSOC^1$= Positive & $PSOC^2$= Negative

Figure 2. M-PSOC Two by Two Example

There are a number of potential impacts of this vertical and
horizontal expansion of PSOC. For instance, let's take the example of an
individual who has a positive PSOC in both communities (see quadrant I). In
this case, one might expect there to be two community pathways to positive
outcome, including a dual set of community resources in the form of sense
of belonging, fulfillment of needs, mutual influence, as well as the other
community resources that generally flow from a positive connection. The
individual may also be expected to commit energies to both communities.
But this circumstance raises a question as to whether the energy and time

available to each community would be less than that of an individual who only feels positive PSOC with one community (quadrant II & IV)? That is, would the total energy, time and commitment to the communities be split in half in the quadrant I case?

Another scenario suggested by this two by two example would be the person who has a positive PSOC in one community and a negative PSOC in another (quadrants II & IV). Predictions for individual and community outcome in this case would be confusing if based on the extant literature alone. Much of the prior literature suggests that a single positive PSOC is related to positive outcomes (Davidson & Cotter, 1991; Levine, 1986), while work on negative PSOC shows some association to positive outcomes in some circumstances (Brodsky, 1996). Thus, outcomes in this hypothetical case, in which an individual has both a positive and a negative PSOC to different communities, are not easily predicted. There are several possible outcomes for this scenario. Assuming both communities are competent, the individual may gain resources and benefits from the positive PSOC community while avoiding the community in which s/he has negative PSOC. If the benefits of the one positive-PSOC community are enough, then, the outcome may be positive. If, however, the individual misses out on crucial resources that could have been obtained from the other negative-PSOC community, then having an M-PSOC comprised of one negative and one positive PSOC community might lead to less positive outcomes than in the case of quadrant I. In terms of energy to commit to a setting, the second scenario (Quadrants II & IV) raises the question of whether an individual would have more time and energy to commit to the single community with which s/he feels a positive PSOC than an individual in quadrant I who might need to divide time and energy. On the other hand, might the sense of a negative PSOC with one community somehow sap energy or positive outcome? Or would the person in this scenario have even greater appreciation for and commitment to the positive PSOC setting, having the example of the negative PSOC setting as a comparison point?

Another important interaction effect involves the impact of the PSOC of one community on the PSOC of the other community. Belonging to some communities can negatively impact the possibility of belonging to another community. A child who feels a positive PSOC for their after-school athletic team, for example, may be less likely to develop a positive PSOC for the neighborhood clique that hangs out at the 7-11. The interaction of these two communities may be a result of lack of time to be a full-fledged member and participant of both groups, it may result from a lack of need on the part of the child to be part of another after-school group, it may be because membership as an athlete leads to lack of acceptance by the neighborhood clique. Of course this difference in PSOC also has implications for the outcomes that might be more likely through membership in one group versus the other, in this case an athletic scholarship versus a police citation for loitering.

The interaction between two communities becomes more complex if one or both of these communities is not a competent community. The competence of the positive PSOC community may be particularly important. Having a positive PSOC with a competent community and a negative PSOC with a less competent community might be doubly protective.

The third scenario, illustrated in quadrant III, is the case in which PSOC for both communities is negative. In this case, given the majority of the literature on PSOC, we might hypothesize a negative outcome for the individual. Of course if neither community is competent, this negative response might be protective and individual outcomes might be positive.

Findings from several of our previous studies shed light on the interaction suggested above. In qualitative interviews with women attending the job training and education center, discussed above, positive PSOC within the Center had different meaning and potential impact on outcome if a participant had a negative PSOC with her home neighborhood (Marx, 2000). This interaction effect might be particularly salient because the two communities are highly different in terms of values, goals and resources. For example, as one woman stated:

> I don't go outside 'cause...there is so much trouble nowadays, you don't know where to go and be safe. So, I don't have a lot of friends. And when I come here it's like a relief. Like, you know, you know you're safe and no drugs, no nothing. I like it here. I recommend this place to, you know, I recommend a lot of people to come here.

The women establish emotional and physical boundaries to protect themselves and maintain distance from their neighborhoods, for which they reported having negative PSOC. This separation initially carries over to the relationships among the women at the Center, so as not to let anything distract from their programmatic goals. While the women at the Center are initially resistant to developing connections, reportedly because of this prior experience of negative PSOC for their neighborhoods and for other settings in their lives, at the Center needs are met, values are shared, and the women develop emotional connections with each other and to the Center.

> We talk about ourselves -- what our goals are, what we want to accomplish, that sort of thing. And we introduce ourself, we tell -- anything about ourselves. What we have been through. Where we

are and where we hope to be. And talking ... realizing that, 'Oh I have looked at her in a different light, 'cause she had been through the same thing that I been through.' And that creates a bond (I: mm-hmm). You know (I: yes). They'll come to you, and you'll go to them, and you'll talk, and say well, you know, I'm so glad that I'm not alone. You were or you are at the same position that I was in, so -- we're family.

The Center not only provides a positive PSOC and positive relationships, but also fills the psychological, emotional, and material needs that are not met in neighborhoods in which the participants live. This interaction intensifies the importance of positive PSOC at the Center for these women, and could potentially act to make the women's allegiance to the Center stronger, which could in turn make it easier and more important for the women to complete their job training and education goals. As another participant described new arrivals to the Center:

They don't know what to expect. You know, they don't know the unknown.... And that makes them apprehensive.... And then when they found out that it's altogether different, then, you know, minds have been changed. Um, attitudes have changed. Positive goals takes place, you know, and it's, it's -- to watch the change, it's, it amazes you. And I like to see that in people. That something is being done for them.

In a quantitative analysis in this setting we looked specifically for the impact of this interaction effect on student outcome, hypothesizing that women's PSOC with their neighborhood would interact with their PSOC with the Center and effect program successes. Although not significant, findings suggested a trend in the predicted direction. As PSOC with the Center increased so did successes in Center related outcomes such as job attainment and as PSOC with the neighborhood decreased successes increased. The interactional impact of these two PSOC on success, however, was not statistically significant. More research is needed to improve our assessments of M-PSOC.

Salience and Meaning: Further Expansions of the Conceptualization of PSOC

Adding to the complexity of these scenarios are issues of community salience and meaning. These issues are related to Fisher and Sonn's (1999) concern about the role of the "primary community." As we described above, a neutral PSOC may be related to a community lacking salience or importance for an individual. That is, one doesn't have an active psychological feeling for a particular community because that community is not important in one's life. An alternative interpretation is that a neutral PSOC could be a developmental step in forming a more active PSOC for a community that is important. This latter possibility of neutral PSOC as a stage in a developmental process raises a question regarding the relative importance of communities and how the degree of importance may affect the meaning of having a positive or negative PSOC. Further, adding these dimensions of salience and importance to researchers' conceptualization of PSOC raises the issue of who is the proper judge of these qualities.

For example, take the case of an adolescent with a negative PSOC for school and a positive PSOC for his family. The adolescent also believes that his family is more important than his school. He learns a great deal from parents, cousins, aunt and uncles and grandparents; he expects to go into the family business and live in a setting surrounded by family. Contrast this with another adolescent with a positive PSOC for her family but a negative PSOC for her school. In this case, however, the school is seen as more important than the family. That is, this adolescent is in a developmental stage in which peers and peer settings are more salient than family and further she hopes that the educational and social opportunities will allow her to leave a family she does not see as competent to aid her transition to economic independence and adulthood, even though she feels strong membership, influence, etc. with her family. This is a child who wants to belong at school with her peers, wants to feel that she can influence the setting, and wants the school to meet her educational needs and desires for shared emotional connections. And yet she has a negative PSOC because these needs and desires are not met.

These two hypothetical cases illustrate how the lack of a positive PSOC to a community which is less salient may not be as related to negative outcomes as the lack of a positive PSOC to a more salient community. Further, however, we need to ask if either of these adolescents might be better off for having at least one positive PSOC than if they only had multiple negative PSOC? It seems clear that our understanding of the meaning one's PSOC for a given community is contingent upon knowing about context that includes the PSOC with the other communities in one's life? In other words, in order to understand an individual's PSOC with one community we need to understand an individual's M-PSOC. We need to clearly identify the multiple communities of an individual's life, the PSOC with every community identified (e.g., positive, negative, or neutral), and the salience and importance for those communities.

The other way to think about this interactional effect (on the individual) is to pay more specific attention to the concept of a primary community, a setting that is central to an individual's identity and feeling of belonging (Sonn & Fisher, 1998). It seems clear that a positive PSOC to a primary community might be more important for outcomes than a positive PSOC to a nonprimary community. And a negative PSOC to a competent primary community might result in a more negative outcome. Similarly, a negative PSOC for a primary community from which one wishes to escape, say a primary identity as a gang member, may result in a positive outcome (e.g., eventually terminating gang membership). Further having a positive PSOC to a non-primary community while simultaneously having a negative PSOC to a primary community may indicate that primary community allegiance is in transition.

Another issue raised by this complexity is that when a researcher predetermines the PSOC target community, it is unclear if that community has the same salience and/or importance to all research participants. Thus the aggregate community measure may be more meaningful as an indicator of individuals' commitments to the community, but be less useful as an indicator of individual outcome. The context for M-PSOC thus includes competency, salience, importance, as well as other individual and community factors.

DIRECTIONS FOR FUTURE RESEARCH

Expanding the conceptualization of PSOC is, we think, important in order to refine our understanding of the role of context, individual, and community interaction in outcomes. In order to fully explore this new concept of M-PSOC, a set of variables that spans positive, neutral and negative feelings for multiple simultaneously experience communities we see the need for future research in, at least, six specific areas, which we will discuss briefly below: (1) assessment of continuous PSOC; (2) assessment of M-PSOC; (3) PSOC studies which leave the selection of multiple communities to research participants; (4) assessment of the salience and importance for selected communities; (5) attending to the type of communities involved; and (6) investigating aspirational PSOC and perceived PSOC. This line of future research will begin to provide a more refined and complete picture of PSOC and its associated outcomes, informing and strengthening our interventions designed to contribute to healthier, happier individuals, communities, societies, and the world.

Future research of PSOC and M-PSOC should consider alternative ways of assessing positive, neutral, and negative feelings for multiple simultaneously experienced communities. To assess continuous M-PSOC we will need to employ various research methods such as scale development or modification and new interview protocols. Qualitative and quantitative work is also necessary to better understand these interactional processes operating in an individual's perception and meaning making regarding their M-PSOC in multiple, concurrent, independent and nested communities of various salience and primacy.

In order to more fully include research participants' real-world context, future research designs need to consider ways for research participants to be involved in selecting which communities will be the reference communities when assessing PSOC. Related to assessing an individuals' M-PSOC, future research needs to consider how to determine the salience of each community for an individual as well as whether community salience is related to PSOC and associated outcomes.

Other research questions are made increasingly pertinent and salient by the M-PSOC concept. For example, how many communities are enough for positive outcomes? Can there be too many communities toward which one feels PSOC. Can there be too much of a good thing, stretching an individual in too many community directions? Is there a point where a community suffers from individual's splintered allegiances, even if the individual doesn't? Another such question involves whether M-PSOC has an aggregate effect. That is, is there a global PSOC that is the average (or sum) of all M-PSOC across all experienced communities or can a single community predict global PSOC, based on its salience, primacy, etc. And does this salience have to do with identity alone, or is it impacted by the level of met needs, time spent, demands, and resources? Relatedly, can an aggregate M-PSOC predict a global outcome or does PSOC with a particular setting predict outcome better? Does each community's PSOC best predict outcome in that particular setting?

Research is also necessary to explore the differences in the meaning, operation, and interactional-outcome of place-based versus relationship-based communities. Another issue that is pertinent regardless of PSOC conceptualization, but whose salience is more obvious in thinking about M-PSOC is whether the salience of the setting and the PSOC reported is impacted by the physical setting in which the participant is located when they participate in the research. That is, does our current context impact our perception of salience and PSOC?

Another important area of future research is to explore the differences and interactions among aspirational, perceived, and real PSOC. That is, does desire for sense of community impact reported (perceived) PSOC? Further, what is the impact of differences between our perceptions (i.e., self-report) of PSOC and the realities of one's influence, need fulfillment, etc. (i.e., actual/real PSOC)? Future research in this area might be informed by the research on attitudinal and behavioral differences as well as attending to such issues of an individual's role in the community and the reporting source (e.g., self-report, peer- report, observation). Relatedly, if PSOC is associated with an interaction of perception, expectation and interaction among other contexts, future research is needed to continue to explore the meaning and operation of community level PSOC? (Brodsky, et al., 1999). Specifically, one might ask if M-PSOC can it exist at the macro level, or if its measurement would mask the more important individual interactional meaning for each individual?

Further exploration of this expansion of the theoretical conceptualization of PSOC, which includes negative, neutral and positive M-PSOC experienced across multiple contexts, will hopefully lead to a better understanding of the ways in which the interaction of individuals and communities impact outcomes in the real world.

NOTES

[i] In this study positive and negative PSOC were established based on a mean split of the SCI scores (Chavis, Florin, & Rich (1987). The fact that low scores were negative rather than neutral was further collaborated by the qualitative data. There are some measurement dilemmas in this quantitative definition of positive and negative however. It is our opinion that a revised measure of quantitative PSOC would be necessary to best capture the meaning and operation of positive, negative and neutral PSOC.

REFERENCES

Ahern, M. M., Hendryx, M. S., & Siddharthan, K. (1996). The importance of sense of community on people's perceptions of their health-care experiences. *Medical Care, 34*, 911-923.

Barker, R. (1978). Behavior settings. In R. Barker & Associates, *Habitats, environments, and human behavior* (pp. 29-35). San Francisco: Jossey-Bass.

Battistich, V., Solomon, D., Watson, M., and Schaps, E. (1997). Caring school communities. *Educational Psychologist, 32*, 137-151.

Brodsky, A. E. (1996). Resilient single mothers in risky neighborhoods: Negative psychological sense of community. *Journal of Community Psychology, 24*, 347-363.

Brodsky, A. E. & Marx, C. M. (2001). Layers of identity: Multiple psychological senses of community within a community setting. *Journal of Community Psychology, 29*, 1-18.

Brodsky, A. E., O'Campo, P. J., & Aronson, R. E. (1999). PSOC in community context: Multi-level correlates of a measure of psychological sense of community in low-income, urban, neighborhoods. *Journal of Community Psychology, 27*, 659-679.

Catano, V. M., Pretty, G. M. H., Southwell, R. R., & Cole, G. K. (1993). Sense of community and union participation. *Psychological Reports, 72,* 333-334.

Chavis, D. M., & Wandersman, A. (1990). Sense of community in the urban environment: A catalysts for participation and community development. *American Journal of Community Psychology, 18,* 55-81.

Chavis, D., Florin, P., Rich, R., & Wandersman, A. (1987). The role of block associations in crime control and community development: The Block Booster Project. Final Report to the Ford Foundation, New York, NY.

Compas, B. E. (1981). Psychological sense of community among treatment analogue group members. *Journal of Applied Social Psychology, 11,* 151-165.

Dalton, J. H., Elias, M. J., Wandersman, A. (2001*). Community psychology: Linking individuals and communities.* Belmont, CA: Wadsworth/Thomson Learning.

Davidson, W. B., & Cotter, P. R. (1986). Measurement of sense of community within the sphere of city. *Journal of Applied Social Psychology, 16,* 608-619.

Davidson, W. B., & Cotter, P. R. (1989). Sense of community and political participation. *Journal of Community Psychology, 17,* 119-125.

Davidson, W. B., & Cotter, P. R. (1991). The relationship between sense of community and subjective well-being: A first look. *Journal of Community Psychology, 19,* 246-253.

Fisher, A. T., & Sonn, C. C. (1999). Aspiration to community: Community responses to rejection. *Journal of Community Psychology, 27,* 715-725.

García, I., Giuliani, F., & Wiesenfeld, E. (1999). Community and sense of community: The case of an urban barrio in Caracas. *Journal of Community Psychology, 27,* 727-740.

Hunter, A., & Riger, S. (1986). The meaning of community in community mental health. *Journal of Community Psychology, 14,* 55-71.

Iscoe, I. (1974). Community psychology and the competent community. *American Psychologist, 29,* 607-613.

Kingston, S., Mitchell, R., Florin, P., & Stevenson, J. (1999). Sense of community in neighborhoods as a multi-level construct. *Journal of Community Psychology, 27,* 681-694.

Lambert, S. J., & Hopkins, K. (1995). Occupational conditions and workers' sense of community: Variations by gender and race. *American Journal of Community Psychology, 23,* 151-179.

Levine, M. D. (1986). Working it out: A community re-creation approach to crime prevention. *Journal of Community Psychology, 14,* 378-390.

Loomis, C. (2001). *Psychological sense of community and participation in an urban university: Predictions, trends, and multiple communities.* Unpublished doctoral dissertation, University of Maryland Baltimore County, Baltimore, Maryland USA.

Marx, C. M. (2000). *Exploring women's psychological sense of community in two relational communities.* Unpublished senior honors thesis, University of Maryland Baltimore County, Baltimore, Maryland, USA.

McCarthy, M. E., Pretty, G. M. H., & Catano, V. (1990). *Psychological sense of community and student burnout. Journal of College Student Development, 31,* 211-216.

McMillan, D. W., & Chavis, D. M. (1986). Sense of community a definition and theory. *Journal of Community Psychology, 14,* 6-23.

Perkins, D., Florin, P., Rich, R., & Wandersman, A. (1990). Participation and the social and physical environment of residential blocks: Crime and community context. *American Journal of Community Psychology, 18,* 83-115.

Pretty, G. M. H., Andrewes, L., & Collett, C. (1994). Exploring adolescents' sense of community and its relationship to loneliness. *Journal of Community Psychology, 22,* 346-358.

Pretty, G. M. H., Conroy, C., Dugay, J. Fowler, K., & Williams, D. (1996). Sense of community and its relevance to adolescents of all ages. *Journal of Community Psychology, 24*, 365-379.

Royal, M. A., & Rossi, R. J. (1996). Individual-level correlates of sense of community: Findings from workplace and school. *Journal of Community Psychology, 24*, 395-416.

Sagy, S., Stern, E., & Krakover, S. (1996). Macro- and microlevel factors related to sense of community: The case of temporary neighborhoods in Israel. *American Journal of Community Psychology, 24*, 657-676.

Sonn, C. C.(1996). *The role of psychological sense of community in the adjustment of 'coloured' South African immigrants.* Unpublished doctoral dissertation. Victoria University of Technology, Melbourne, Australia.

Sonn, C. C., & Fisher, A. T. (1996). Psychological sense of community in a politically constructed group. *Journal of Community Psychology, 26*, 417-430.

Sonn, C. C., & Fisher, A. T. (1998). Sense of community: Community resilient responses to oppression and change. *Journal of Community Psychology, 26*, 457-472.

Wiesenfeld, E. (1996). The concept of "we": A community social psychology myth? *Journal of Community Psychology, 24*, 337-346.

INDEX